MW01038655

THE
EARLY SESSIONS
Book 8 of The Seth Material
Sessions 334-421
4/12/67–7/8/68

THE EARLY SESSIONS

The Early Sessions consist of the first 510 sessions dictated by Seth through Jane Roberts. There are 9 books in *The Early Session* series.

THE PERSONAL SESSIONS

The Personal Sessions, often referred to as "the deleted sessions", are Seth sessions that Jane Roberts and Rob Butts considered to be of a highly personal nature and were therefore kept in separate notebooks from the main body of the Seth material. *The Personal Sessions* are expected to be published in 6 to 9 volumes.

"The great value I see now in the many deleted or private sessions is that they have the potential to help others, just as they helped Jane and me over the years. I feel that it's very important to have these sessions added to Jane's fine creative body of work for all to see." –Rob Butts

THE SETH AUDIO COLLECTION

Rare recordings of Seth speaking through Jane Roberts are available on audiocassette and CD. For a complete description of The Seth Audio Collection, request our free catalogue.. (Further information is supplied at the back of this book.)

For information on expected publication dates and how to order, write to New Awareness Network at the following address and request the latest catalogue. Also, please visit us on the internet at www.sethcenter.com

New Awareness Network Inc.
P.O. BOX 192
Manhasset, N.Y. 11030
www.sethcenter.com

THE
EARLY SESSIONS
Book 8 of The Seth Material
Sessions 334-421
4/12/67–7/8/68

© 2000 by Robert Butts

Published by New Awareness Network Inc.

New Awareness Network Inc.
P.O. Box 192
Manhasset, New York 11030

Opinions and statements on health and medical matters expressed in this book are those of the author and are not necessarily those of or endorsed by the publisher. Those opinions and statements should not be taken as a substitute for consultation with a duly licensed physician.

Cover Design: Michael Goode
Photography: Cover photos by Rich Conz and Robert F. Butts, Sr.
Editorial: Rick Stack
Typography: Raymond Todd, Joan Thomas, Michael Goode

All rights reserved. This book may not be reproduced in whole or in part, without written permission from the publisher, except by a reviewer who may quote brief passages in a review; nor may any part of this book be reproduced, stored in a retrieval system, or transmitted in any form or by any means electronic, mechanical, photocopying, recording, or other, without written permission from the publisher.

Library of Congress Cataloging-in-Publication Data

Seth (Spirit)
  The early sessions: volume 8 of the seth material / [channeled] by Jane
Roberts ; notes by Robert F. Butts.
  p. cm.–(A Seth book)
  ISBN 0-9652855-8-8
      1. Spirit writings. 2. Self–Miscellanea
  I. Roberts, Jane 1929–1984. II. Butts, Robert F.   III. Title
  IV. Series: Seth (Spirit), 1929–1984 Seth book.
  Library of Congress Catalog Number: 96-69349

ISBN 0-9652855-8-8
Printed in U.S.A. on acid-free paper

I dedicate **The Early Sessions**
to my wife, Jane Roberts,
who lived her 55 years
with the greatest creativity
and the most valiant courage.
-Rob

FORWARD BY ROB BUTTS
CONCERNING THE PRIVATE OR "DELETED" SESSIONS

July 6, 2000. It's with much feeling indeed that I try to write briefly about the 16 private or "deleted" Seth sessions, ranging from numbers 367 to 387, that aren't included in this Volume 8 of *The Early Sessions*. This is the first group of full-length sessions to be omitted in all of the volumes of *The Early Sessions* so far. Jane held only five "regular" or public sessions while delivering this large group, and those five are presented in Volume 8.

For the most part over the six years and 510 sessions covered in *The Early Sessions*, from December 2, 1963 to January 19, 1970, Jane spoke for Seth in her own creative yet also objective manner. A way that, although still very emotional at times, allowed us the freedom to encompass this most unusual and continuing adventure in as easy and conventional a manner as possible. Unusual? Yes. Surely her intuitively-chosen manner helped us acclimate to the highly original and creative fact that Jane was learning to speak in a dissociated (or trance) state for Seth, a disembodied worthy who called himself an "energy personality essence." (I'll bet that he still does, 16 of our time-bound years after Jane's death!) Jane's method was her very individualistic way of developing her great, yet consciously unsuspected powers.

My wife died in September 1984, and given her reincarnational relationship with Seth, as described by him, I strongly suspect that the two of them are together now. In what kind of a relationship? I have no idea: I can only speculate that many kinds are possible—while keeping in mind that yes, they may have chosen to go their separate psychic and psychological ways.

In 10 of the sessions between the numbers 314 and 325 in Volume 7 we see how, with Jane's need and consent, Seth was reaching into deeper, more penetrating material involving her conscious and unconscious lives. And mine, too! (I'm correcting the page proofs for Volume 7 now.) We had never called those sessions in Volume 7 deleted, though, and I'm happy now to trust that they may help readers gain insight into some of their own challenges. We deeply appreciated Seth's insights and suggestions about Jane's and my visible and invisible psyches, the challenges we had chosen to create for ourselves in our present lifetimes. With the publication of Volumes 7 and 8 I'd like to hear from readers about benefits they may have derived from experimenting with Seth's ideas. The two volumes are to be published at the same time in 2001 by Rick Stack, the proprietor of New Awareness Network, Inc. Rick has of course published the first six volumes of *The Early Sessions*.

Not that those personal sessions in Volume 7 represent the beginnings of Seth's efforts—always with Jane's and my permission, indeed encourage-ment—to offer his understandings of our challenges. Such material began to come through the Ouija board as mostly reincarnational data way back in the second session, for December 4, 1963. See Volume I of *The Early Sessions.* (Only then a personality fragment of Seth's, named Frank Watts, was speaking to us. Seth himself didn't announce his presence to us most definitely until December 8, in the fourth session. I deleted some of his early information for us from Volume I.)

Seth's personal material was startling in its unexpected clarity, although always quite brief. We didn't push for details. How could we? We didn't know enough to do so, for in ordinary terms we had no way to anticipate the breadth, the depth, of the material Jane and Seth were to produce. Sometimes in those early sessions Seth would mention a current relative or friend of one or the other of us—or both of us—as being involved in our personal material. Sometimes he mentioned reincarnational relationships or heritages—again, briefly.

As the personal material began to unfold we started calling it the "delet-ed" material because we kept it separate from the more general "regular" or pub-lic sessions. After all, in the conventional sense what was one to do with personal material from whatever source but keep it personal? As the years passed after 1963 we acquired two sets of Seth material, then, one public, one private. It wasn't until after Jane's death in 1984 that I took the "time" to understand that Jane's Seth material—her great passionate body of work—really didn't need to be categorized as public or private—that all of it was simply one multifaceted creative entity.

"Now," I mentally said to my departed loved one in all sincerity, "if we had the chance to do it all over again, I'd suggest that we dispense with all divi-sions—that we regard the Seth material as a great whole, any part of which, pub-lic or private or in between, has the creative power to help not only us but many others. Let all of it be available to all." I think that my wife would agree—after first disagreeing!

Anyhow, the deleted material from the very beginning is now due to be published. As soon as Rick Stack finishes publishing *The Early Sessions* (proba-bly with Volume 9, it seems at this time), we plan to launch the Personal Sessions series. Actual title and number of volumes unknown at present. I'm proud to be involved in this work with Rick and his wife, Anne Marie O'Farrell, who is my literary agent. Their long-term commitment is all important.

For some years Jane and I devoted much work to learning the process-es detailed in all of those early unpublished sessions, which were followed by her series of published books like *The Seth Material, Seth Speaks, The Nature of*

Personal Reality, and so on. My wife's later deleted material even contains a complete and unpublished book that she delivered just for me, about the artist Rembrandt van Rijn. Page by page, Jane presented her gift to me during the last year of her life, when she was hospitalized. I'm going to be most interested in the responses of others to Seth's book about that highly creative and world-famous individual. I already know that it's good!

And so the unification of more facets of the Seth material continues. I trust that I'm offering enough intriguing hints in this essay to keep readers interested in pursuing Jane's and Seth's and my loving work. Apropos of that statement, what's left after publishing the deleted sessions? Well, how about the transcripts in book form of the ESP classes Jane conducted from 1967 to 1978? Rick Stack was one of her students, with friends often making the weekly 400-mile-plus round trip from New York City to our apartment in upstate Elmira, NY. (And the members of that group had to be back in the city to go to work the next day! Jane and I used to marvel at their endurance.) Rick recorded and has produced many audio tapes of Jane and Seth speaking in those classes; at this time he's also producing an additional group of tapes. Then there's Jane's business and personal correspondence; much of her poetry; her journals; her unfinished autobiography; several novels she wrote before publishing the three *Oversoul Seven* books; the later essays she dictated to me, while in the hospital, about Seven's childhood; her family history as far back as it can be researched; an objective biography of her physical and creative lives including her two marriages, and Jane's and my struggles to survive before the advent of the Seth material. And there could be more; there always seems to be more, I'm glad to note.

How long would it take to publish all of those categories? I don't know who would have the patience to read them, but I'd really like to see all of them out there, on the record. Part of the Collection, as I call it, is already available at the Yale University Library, but how many have the time to visit there? Of course, I can always indulge my secret desire and write my own book about Jane and me. All I'd need is the "time" to do that while overseeing the projects already listed. The book would include Jane's simplistically beautiful and brilliantly colored art; also my own quite different art—especially those drawings and paintings of and from my dreams that began to blossom as Seth discussed his dream material. Some of his work is presented in *The Early Sessions*. In all modesty, I think that my art and its subject matter are unique; that for each one of us dreams are an original and unending source of inspiration and knowledge.

But also, in my own book I'd want to write about my second marriage. Laurel Lee Davies, a native of Iowa, wrote to me from California after Jane's death in September 1984, She was 29, I was 65. After months of letters and telephone calls we met in Elmira, and kept on developing the intuitive and loving relationship we had already begun. With our strong beliefs in the Seth material our ages and temperamental differences don't seem to matter all that much. Laurel has been a marvelous help to me for all of the years we've been together, just as I've tried to help her. I've often thought, and hesitantly told her, that I think she saved me after Jane's passing. And I add that Laurel and I were married at our home on Pinnacle Road in Elmira at 9:30 PM on December 31, 1999 - just in time for the new millennium.

In the meantime, I thank each reader for caring. Now if only I can catch up, once again, on answering the fan mail! I'm most fortunate that people continue to write, for it shows that Jane's work still lives. I welcome each letter and package, just as I know Jane does, and I save them all. Oh-oh: Now there's another idea for a book—one built around the fan mail, with permissions, of course. Hmmm...

Sayre, a community of about 7500, only 20 miles from Elmira and just across the Pennsylvania border, is my hometown. It's loaded with memories for me. Jane and I also spent the first four years of our marriage here, before moving to Elmira in 1960. Laurel and I bought the house in Sayre, just around the corner from the house I grew up in, to get more living and working room. Now each time we make the beautiful drive to Elmira, it's like moving back in time—just like it used to be when we traveled from Elmira to Sayre. And I speculate that Jane and Seth watch Laurel and me with much amusement now as we manipulate that quality called "time" on our journeys back and forth between the two houses...

Most sincerely,

Rob

SESSION 334
APRIL 12, 1967 9 PM WEDNESDAY

Good evening.

("Good evening, Seth.")

Now. If you paint a picture, its overall quality comes from the inner atmosphere of your being.

In the same manner, you create your physical image and your world. If anything in that physical image or world needs changing, the change must first be made in the atmosphere of the inner self.

For this projection of inner into outer is automatic. Understanding the processes involved is of great benefit. The physical self <u>seems</u> (underlined) to react to physical stimuli. Actually, of course, it is reacting to its own reality, projected outward.

The objects in the physical universe are but symbols to express other realities existing within private realms. The inner will always be projected outward within your system. If, for example, a letter comes to you bearing good news, and you react to the letter with high spirits, then you should understand that the high spirits existed first, and created the materialization of the letter within the physical systems, through the multilayered and complicated reactions that bind together the physical system.

If an annoying letter arrives and you react to it negatively, the negative quality preceded the letter and caused it to materialize in your system. Now you do not force someone to write such a letter, you see. You broadcast the negative feelings, which were then picked up by whomever was ready to receive them, for their own purposes.

I cannot emphasize too strongly that this is automatic. I do not want to put it in such a way that it is oversimplified. Neither do I want it to get too involved in too many complications.

The intensity of the inner feeling is the dominating factor here. A sudden but intense feeling of hatred or resentment or fear may cause tragic physical circumstances, for example. A sudden and intense exaltation, however, will have the same immediate and literally astounding but opposite physical effect. That is, pure joy, even of brief duration, can literally change the direction of a life.

Between these extremes lie all the other colors and hues of inner feeling. A variety of poor or negative feelings, however, of fairly low intensity, can add up to a general negative emotional climate, which projects itself outward into physical reality.

These negative feelings will be translated in physical terms. It does you little good to know that physical symptoms or inadequate physical surroundings are symbolic unless you realize that the inner situation can be changed.

Now it <u>appears</u> to you that a difference is worked when you exchange a poor physical symbol for a constructive one. The change of course comes before this in the inner self. The physical being simply uses the physical system as a checking board.

It must be realized that the physical conditions are <u>not</u> (underlined) permanent, but everchanging. To imagine otherwise is to become hypnotized by the physical symbols. Each day should be considered a new day. Ruburt should not think for example: "I have had these symptoms for such and such a time." This reinforces the idea of permanency. The day should be considered as a psychic rebirth.

You may take a break and we shall continue.

(9:25. Jane's pace had picked up a little speed; her eyes had opened at times, her voice had been average.

(It was now time for the data on the Gallaghers, who are vacationing this week in New York City.

(9:36.)

Give us a moment please. These will be impressions concerning our traveling friends.

A row of apartment houses. It is dark so I presume it is nighttime. A visit to a third or second floor. A church, this is separate, with decorations that seem spider shaped. A vestibule in red. An underground place where they eat or drink, with shutters and an atmosphere depicting an era, 1871.

Separate now, something to do with <u>mines</u>, navy and a war. A gray-haired man telling a story, with a red sweater or shirt, speaking to the Jesuit. About 61 years old.

Separate: A fine-arts academy in an area of churches, with a large federal building nearby, and a bus stop or terminal. A book or movie about spies. Something loaned to or by our friends.

A fragment of paper that seems important. Something to do with fish, and another journey. I do not know here: A mine tapping, or mine trapping incident, and an embargo. A hat is nearly lost. Tea time, in a place that sounds like Abercrombie. A room four stories high, where they stay.

You may take a break.

(9:50 to 9:58.)

A group encounter and a specialist. This to go with the Gallagher material. This will be a brief session. There is a possibility of another later in the week.

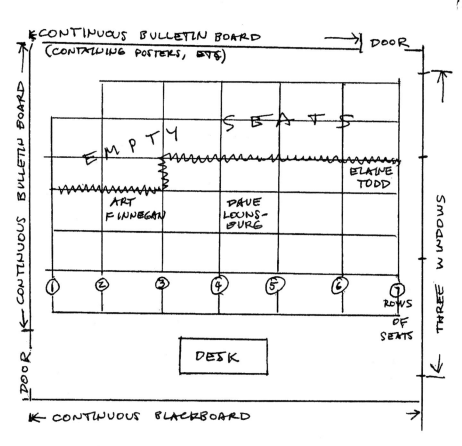

DIAGRAM of PAT NORELLI'S BOSTON HONORS
CLASSROOM, after drawing by Pat.

("How did the tape of the 329th session for go over for Pat Norelli's class in Boston?"

(Pat is due to visit us briefly on her way to her home in Pittsburgh, PA, on Saturday, April 15. On March 25th, she recorded the 329th session, with the intent of playing the tape for her honors class in high school. She has written us since then that the tape has been played. Seth had delivered an excellent lecture to the class, in two parts. See Volume 7.)

Very well indeed, as I intended that it would. It impressed several youngsters in a particular manner. A boy in a third seat in a near-center row. A girl in a fourth seat in one of the rows far right.

(It is Sunday, April 16, as I type this. Pat did visit us on the 15th, and confirmed much of Seth's data given here. See my copy of the map she drew yesterday of her classroom. The boy in the third seat near a center row is, according to Pat, named Dave Lounsburg. The girl in a fourth seat in a far right row is Elaine Todd.

(Seth also correctly picked out the seat of Art Finnegan, to whom he referred in the 329th session. "There is a boy in a third or fourth seat, back from the front, in the left row toward the wall. He is on the last reincarnation within this system.")

Someone with a name like Davis, or with Davis in it; that is in the whole name.

(This would be Dave Lounsburg.)

Do you have any other questions?

("Did anybody else at the school hear the tape beside the students? Any adults?")

Others have heard it.

("At school?")

It was not played at the school for these people, I believe two men and a woman. H B may be pertinent in this material.

(Pat could offer no confirmation concerning H B. Pat also said that two women were in her honors class when she played the tape; one of these being a Radcliffe student teacher. Pat also played the tape for a girl friend of hers outside of school: Ellen Tabb, and Ellen's friend, Adrian, a male. This makes a total of three women and one male who have heard the tapes besides Pat, whereas Seth names two men and a woman.

(Nor, evidently, is Seth referring to the two adults sitting in on the class the day the tape was played. Although he states that "Others have heard it," my interpretation is that this reference is to Ellen Tabb and Adrian. This interpretation results in one man and one woman hearing the tape, versus Seth's mentioning of two men and a woman.)

If you have further questions, I will answer them, or you may end the session.

("What's Jane's next book going to be about, after the dream book?")
The next book will be my book.
("Is she going to change it from the way she has it begun?")
Indeed.
("Can you say in what way?")
There is no need now. A changed format in the main.
("Okay. I guess that's it.")
My heartiest wishes to you both, and a most fond good evening.
("Good night, Seth.")
(10:05.)

SETH'S IMPRESSIONS CONCERNING THE GALLAGHER'S TRIP TO NEW YORK. IMPRESSIONS GIVEN IN SESSION 333 ON APRIL 10, 1967.

(Following the impressions are the Gallagher's notes and comments. We went over the material on their return, but some time has passed now before they found time to go over it in detail. Both Gallaghers agreed on answers.)

These impressions will apply to our friends, the Jesuit and the cat lover.

The room: A green modernistic plastic chair with wooden legs. Dark green. A spread with upraised pattern in hobnail fashion. An appliance into which one places coins.

([The Gallaghers:] "There was a green modernistic chair with wooden legs in our room. It was light green. There was also a hobnail-type spread on the bed. No coin appliance.")

The number 202, perhaps an address or room number.

([The Gallaghers:] "Not that we recall. Hotel room number was 916.")

A combo, South American. Conchita.

([The Gallaghers:] "Several combos, but none South American.")

A scroll, which I do not understand.

([The Gallaghers:] "No.")

A meeting with an acquaintance.

([The Gallaghers:] "Yes. Bill met Mrs. Ed Lagonegro on Eighth Avenue.")

The number 12, 14 steps and a circular clock, very large, above a stairway, with spokes out from it in gold, of wood, of nautical design.

([The Gallaghers:] "The number 12 may be significant in that one night Bill spoke very loudly in his sleep, saying we had to make our way to 12th Street. Neither of us remembers being on 12th Street, though we were in the area.")

Three friends and a story of disaster, though not that strong.

([The Gallaghers:] "No.")

Something cracked in the room in which they stay, a glass perhaps or mirror. A small insignificant accident. A finger cut slightly.

([The Gallaghers:] "Both of us noticed that the toilet was cracked, the enamel part.")

An antique they prize.

([The Gallaghers:] "In one antique shop, I [Peg] pointed out two antique crocks which were very much like two we have and like.")

A miscellany of objects arranged in pyramid form.

([The Gallaghers:] "Nothing significant that I remember... could be anything in a bookstore, fruit stand or any number of shops we visited.")

And people dressed as constables who are not constables.

([The Gallaghers:] "One of the most interesting shops we stopped in was an Army-Navy type store in Greenwich Village. This shop specialized in unusual military type uniforms... jackets that buttoned up the side of the type that possibly an early western constable might wear. Young people were trying them on in the store." [Note: The Gallaghers also told us that the rage in the village is to wear such uniforms.])

They went to their room shortly after seven and leave it again. They eat at a place that begins with a D. This is not it: it sounds like Den-I-ah however.

([The Gallaghers:] "No.")

Their dinner comes to $7.95. Their menu has pictures of mermaids or Hawaiian dancers on it.

([The Gallaghers:] "No.")

There is a long dark bar, a long narrow establishments, tables to the left, and too many people to be served, they must wait.

([The Gallaghers:] "In the East Village we stopped at a very interesting long narrow establishment with a long bar up the right side of the rooms and tables all along on the left. However, very few people were there.")

A stop at 74th street, and a 82nd street address.

([Jane added:] Peg in this exact neighborhood for specific reason. She walked on Madison Ave. from 86th to 74th Street to visit particular shops—one on 74th—one may have been on 82nd—one on 86th.)

FROM SESSION 334   APRIL 12, 1967

A row of apartment houses. It is dark so I presume it is nighttime. A visit to a third or second floor.

([The Gallaghers:] "No.")

A church, this is separate. With decorations that seem spider shaped.

([The Gallaghers:] "No. Although we passed St. Patrick's Cathedral.")

A vestibule in red. An underground place where they eat or drink with shutters and an atmosphere depicting an era, 1871.

([The Gallaghers:] "A number of places might fit that description.")

Separate now: Something to do with mines, navy, and a war.

([The Gallaghers:] "Yes. We visited the Seamen's Institute [Museum].")

A gray-haired man telling a story. With red sweater or shirt, speaking to the Jesuit *(Bill)* about 61 years old.

([The Gallaghers:] "No.")

Separate: A fine-arts academy in an area of churches, with a large federal building nearby and a bus stop or terminal.

([The Gallaghers:] "The Metropolitan, we visited it. There is a bus stop in front, and churches in the neighborhood. Can't recall a Federal building though.")

A book about spies.

([The Gallaghers:] "Bill looked at several spy books in various bookstores.")

Something loaned to or by our friends. A fragment of paper that seems important.

([The Gallaghers:] "No.")

Something to do with fish and another journey.

([The Gallaghers:] "We passed and noticed several fish markets.")

A mine tapping or mine trapping incident and an embargo.

([The Gallaghers:] "No.")

A hat was nearly lost... Tea time in a place that sounds like Abercrombie. A room four stories high where they stay.

([The Gallaghers:] "No to all of these.")

A group encounter and a specialist.

([Jane added:] Yes. At Metropolitan, alone, Bill met a group being lectured on medieval warfare.)

SESSION 335
APRIL 17, 1967 9 PM MONDAY

(By 9 PM it was dark. There was a rather unusual rain and lightning storm of a mild nature, which kept up through the session. The lightning flashed silently followed several seconds later by distant rolling thunder, Seemingly coming from beyond the surrounding mountains.

(We were having trouble with our car, and at suppertime I had been voicing fears that it might be finished.)

Good evening.

("Good evening, Seth.")

Now. You must watch your expectations, Joseph.

I am speaking in highly practical terms. Your expectations literally create your life as you know it. Your attitude toward transportation needs adjustment. As long as you believe firmly that you cannot afford the kind of automobile that you want, this will be literally true.

Your expectations alone will change your material circumstances. The belief that you can afford the kind of car you require will in itself form the circumstances that will make such an automobile literally possible.

Your belief otherwise automatically shuts you off so that the necessary climate, the psychic climate, is a barrier to what you want. The belief will cause attractions, in which physical circumstances will change. It is highly impractical to believe as you do, regarding your automobile or prospects, for another.

There are many distortions in the universal mind book that Ruburt reads, and yet overall the ideas presented are highly advantageous. I cannot put this emphatically enough: your beliefs form a psychic climate that in itself attracts and forms the materialization of those beliefs.

They are made material through quite automatic processes. Change your beliefs and you change your material circumstances. Your beliefs now concerning finances and the automobile are actually keeping you from bettering your financial situation. This is directly caused by the fact that you suspect such ideas as these, beneficial on theoretical grounds, but quite impractical in your actuality.

On the contrary, an understanding of the rule of expectation is the one truly practical step you can take whenever any change in physical circumstances is desired. You must replace the negative images you have with positive ones. The negative ones are being faithfully reproduced in physical terms, and this is hardly to your advantage.

There is a resistance here on your part, a resistance to the kind of material that I am giving you this evening. A rather stubborn resistance that has its roots in your childhood in this life. The resistance is allowing you to cheat yourself in more areas than one. While you are somewhat better about this, there has been no profound change in your attitudes in this one particular area.

In other respects of course there have been profound changes. By your attitude you are effectively forming a barrier against any financial betterment of any significant kind. You repulse the circumstances in which such betterment could take place automatically, because of the effect of your expectations.

It goes without saying that a full-time job would better the financial situation, but this is not the sort of thing to which I am referring. Your situation could be bettered financially while you retain basically the same schedule you now enjoy, if—and a very large if—if changed expectations were creating the psychic climate in which supply would flow. Doors would open that you do not know existed.

You may take now break and I shall continue.

(9:25. Jane's pace was average, her eyes open at times, her voice better than usual, yet not loud. Lightning still flashed.

(9:31.)

You are caught between two attitudes that battle each other. A desire for austerity and a desire for physical materials.

The two of you, working together, could change your material circumstances in truly astounding ways. I wanted to speak to you about this, since the matter came up this evening.

Our own physical climate is a poor one for a session, however. The electrical currents are not working to our advantage; this being a peculiar circumstance, incidentally, having to do with a changed ionization of the surface of the ground, that sometimes occurs about this season. This in connection with the high electrical content of the near atmosphere.

Instead of a steady flow of electromagnetic current, generally speaking, there is a rather erratic bombardment that affects such psychic affairs as ours. Under different conditions, an electric storm can be beneficial to our purposes. It is the altered ground ionization, somewhat peculiar to this season, that causes the difficulty.

If it is somewhat bothersome to me, it is of great benefit to growing things however, and quickens the chemical responses of plant life. This, in combination with the rain, you see.

I am going to end the session directly for this reason. We will hold our normal session Wednesday. If <u>you</u> feel cheated, my friends, then you may if you <u>wish</u> hold a brief session tomorrow. This is up to you.

The particular circumstances involved are interesting however, and I will explain them more clearly at our next session. They also have an effect upon projections and dreams, incidentally, and they affect the habits of birds.

My best wishes to you both. I would continue the session, but though Ruburt feels no difficulty at <u>his</u> end, I am involved at my end. Again, a fond good evening.

("Good night, Seth."

(9:43. Jane said she felt no trouble. In fact, she thought Seth was coming

through very well, particularly when he started explaining why he was having trou-
ble. She noticed no unusual pauses within, in the flow of the material, etc.

(After the session, Jane said she felt that Seth was still around, which was
unusual. She felt that Seth was "localized" right beside her as she sat on the divan;
that is, that he was standing just beside and in front of her. But neither of us saw
anything unusual.

(As far as we recall offhand, this is the first time Seth has held a short session
for the above mentioned reasons.)

SESSION 336
APRIL 19, 1967 9 PM WEDNESDAY

(Bill and Peggy Gallagher were witnesses to the session.

(Jane began speaking in a good voice, more emphatic than usual; her eyes
opened at times, her pace was average.)

Good evening.

("Good evening, Seth.")

Good evening to our friends.

([Bill:] "Good evening, Seth.")

It is some time indeed since I have had the pleasure of their company,
although I have looked in on them.

([Bill:] "We appreciate it.")

I found New York a dizzy encounter indeed, and I wish that in the future
you would seek more quiet environments. Now. Give me a brief moment here,
and let us see what we can do for our so-fatigued friend. *(Pause.)*

(Here Seth refers to Bill, who leaves for Syracuse tomorrow on a business trip
for the Elmira newspaper.)

The tangle in Syracuse will not be quite as tangled as he imagines. Two
men will be fairly reasonable. These are impressions. A stout man who either
wears glasses, or has worn them, with pale eyes; or the lenses of his glasses are
extremely pale. *(Pause.)*

The number 12; whether or not this is a street I do not know. Two men,
somewhat younger than the stout man. Now by stout I do not mean monstrous,
but overweight. Some connection with an account that has Midwest connotations, or is connected with the Midwest.

I am not sure of Ruburt's physical interpretation here of my meaning. You
will have to let the Midwest stand as is. It could however refer to something as
simple as riding; but in connection with the account I do not mean the obvious

trip, of course.

An incapable gentleman with a crew cut, brownish hair, precisely in the middle of his organization. JC and a back page. An attempted filibuster, though not in political terms. Rather amusing. An attempt to minimize or steer away from a main issue here, on the part of two gentlemen, who seem to offer instead a grab bag of tricks. The term "formica" (*my phonetic interpretation*). I do not know to what it refers. An engagement that is not scheduled will be important, and the crux of the matter.

Madison Avenue and tactics and a tall, fairly well-proportioned gentleman with a striped tie. An initial encounter here. Perhaps our friend meets him for the first time, or sees him clearly for the first time.

Toomey or Tomey (*my phonetic interpretation*) and 95601. (*Pause.*) The Midwest connection again, though at this time I cannot be more specific. A mill or mileogram (*my interpretation*), Seven, perhaps seventh floor.

You may take a break and we shall continue.

(*9:15. Bill could not say much about Seth's data. He said that Seth had correctly described the stout man with glasses, though the description was so general it could apply to many.*

(*9:15. Break.*

(*9:25. Resume session.*)

Now. Our Jesuit finds spontaneous projections most beneficial on a subconscious level, to relieve pressure. Quite literally he does indeed step out of himself. This happens much more frequently than he realizes. He has not utilized suggestion, however, to any significant degree as an aid in controlling his symptoms.

I told you, Joseph, that I would discuss the magnetic alterations that caused me to call a quick ending to our last session. Now as a rule these conditions occur only during this particular season. All living things exist, as you know, in other than material form. Every living thing has what you would term an astral form or vehicle. This consists of electromagnetic realities operating within specific frequencies.

In this particular season, the electrical potentials are highly charged. The thrust and potential of growing things creates an overexuberance, you might say, saturating your atmosphere and changing the ionic charges both of the ground itself and the atmosphere extending upward.

There is a preponderance of negative ions followed by an opposite effect that occurs with great rapidity immediately following sunset. On occasion there is an oversaturation that amounts to an extra envelope of atmospheric vibrations. This can persist on occasion until the following dawn.

Physically, you have storm conditions, but for our session purposes the atmosphere is highly unstable and not reliable. It places me, though not Ruburt, under additional pressure. Such circumstances occur infrequently. They can cause accidents, within your system, sudden and not always advantageous. Sometimes mass alterations of mood and the exhaustion of energies.

They can be disastrous in a projecting personality, incidentally.

You may take a break and we shall continue.

(*9:40 break. At rest, Peg said that the above ideas fit into a pet theory of her own. Recently she conducted a small informal survey to discover the effect of weather upon human activities. Both Peg and Bill mentioned a chaotic state existing at the newspaper office where they work, though Bill said this was merely the result of a natural evolution of policies perhaps. Peg felt the situation was building up to some kind of climax; she spoke of small matters like limits being placed on personal phone calls, etc; various economies being instituted; the dissatisfaction of employees.*

(*9:55. Resume.*)

Now I found intermission highly amusing. The conditions of which I have been speaking are one thing. As far as the effect of weather upon the moods of individuals, we do have something else. For the weather is created by you, on a subconscious level. The weather, at any given time, is a direct physical interpretation of the inner mass mind. You do indeed react, but you have already created the conditions, you see, and you then react to these in both psychic and physical ways.

The inner state of each individual mind is projected outward. The inner state causes chemical changes in the physical body. Chemicals are thrown outward into the atmosphere. Hormones are released of particular varieties. Very definite and unique electrical changes occur in the skin, which change on a mass level the atmosphere at any given unit.

All of these conditions merge to create the peculiar weather with its innumerable and constant changes. These exterior conditions then affect the individual physical structures and individuals react to the peculiar conditions which they have themselves created.

The process is constant. The weather causes psychic activities, to some extent assassinations and accidents. On the other hand, the atmosphere was originally mental and the weather originates from this mental level.

Now. Give us a moment.

This has to do with the question of the pussycat lover.

(*Peg Gallagher at break had wondered if Seth would tell what might happen at the paper.*

(*Jane's eyes closed. Her voice became slower. She had been holding a glass par-*

tially filled. Now it began to slip from her hand. Bill Gallagher took it out of her hand. Obviously she was going into a deeper trance and continued to do so as this material was delivered.)

February and a change of leadership. An affair will come to light that will shock many. An unfortunate affair indeed, and a breakdown. A man relieved of duties because of a severe health situation. And then after the health situation *(gesture)* policies or events from the past will make sense, but there will be a shocking element involved.

There will be other people who leave in the meantime, and autocratic behavior. You had better stay clear of involvement. The full extent of these policies in their underline form is not realized by the man's superiors. The man thinks he is acting in response to demands put upon him by his superiors.

(Here Jane's voice grew uneven and quiet at times. I felt some alarm.)

He is behaving in a compulsive manner. *(Jane's head drooped)* His activities will cause a near-(underlined) crisis situation at the paper. He is squeezing the life from it symbolically and he senses the emotional *(Jane's voice sounded almost drugged here)* crisis toward which he is propelled. There will be repercussions at his home first, and signs appearing there first.

You had better take a break.

(10:17 break. Jane had a time coming out of the trance. Her eyes wouldn't open, etc. Peg said that the atmosphere bit fits perfectly and that she and Bill had suspected a couple of the points already. Peg says that H [the man] does believe he is acting in response to his superiors. Jane agreed with my idea that Seth put her into deeper trance in order to allow the material to come through [since it is emotional, related to friends and so forth. After five or ten minutes Jane felt better, and had a cigarette.]

(10:31 resume. Jane's eyes closed, head down voice slow with pauses. She goes into deep trance now, at once.)

We will shortly end the session. There will be a hint first in the home situation, with which our friends may (underlined) be acquainted, though it will not be generally known, involving a child. Female. Approximately two months before the main crisis.

There have been others, kept secret.

(Jane's head fell at an odd angle, her voice became lower.)

Some drug situation, not necessarily of the highly illegal nature, however. A doctor and a man are forcibly restrained.

(Now Jane seemed to be whispering to herself and then mouthing the words just a bit louder, but so low I had to lean close.)

The breakdown will be emotional but it will show a physical nature affecting circulatory (*hesitated on word*) symptoms and the heart, but this will be secondary.

The situation will appear sudden. I do not believe death is involved. However: a breakup. Then the superiors who will have already suspected the man's compulsive behavior, will see the true situation. There will be a scandal. The word may not be the best one, but a shocking occurrence.

(All through here, Jane mouths the words, and repeats them a bit louder than a whisper.)

We had better end the session. The shocking nature mainly appearing in the home. However some observable psychotic reactions will be apparent at the (*barely whispering now*) business place, involving temper tantrums of growing infantile nature.

The session is closed.

("Good night Seth."

(10:42. Session over.

(In this last segment of the session, Jane's voice was extremely low, and dwindled almost into nothing as the last words were spoken. I was very near interrupting the session. It was strange to see her whispering the words to herself then trying to make them audible to us. Many were repeated in this way. Jane didn't feel particularly well before the session. After finally coming out of the trance—this took awhile —she felt good. She knew the glass was going to fall dimly, but after that she lost contact. She felt that her face was different in a strange manner, that muscles were relaxing into different forms but no one noticed any change. I rather think that Seth put her in a deep trance for this highly charged material to protect her from the sort of thing she went through with Barbara when he wasn't around.)

RESULTS OF BILL GALLAGHER'S TRIP TO SYRACUSE.
HIS IMPRESSIONS GIVEN, ON MAY 5, 1967.

The trip will not be as tangled as he imagines.
([Bill Gallagher:] "It wasn't as bad as I thought it would be.")
The number 12.
([Bill Gallagher:] "My room number 552 adds up to 12.")
Midwest connections with account.
([Bill Gallagher:] "None that I know of.")
Incapable gentleman with a crew cut.
([Bill Gallagher:] "No.")
Attempted filibuster.
([Bill Gallagher:] "No.")

An engagement that is not scheduled will be important, and the crux of the matter.

([Bill Gallagher:] "An unscheduled meeting was held the evening Bill arrived. The agency representative with whom he makes arrangements asked to see him.")

Madison Avenue. Tactics and a gentleman Bill sees clearly for the first time.

([Bill Gallagher:] "No.")

Formica.

([Bill Gallagher:] "No")

SESSION 337
APRIL 26, 1967 9 PM WEDNESDAY

(The session regularly scheduled for Monday, April 24, was not held. Jane felt out of sorts tonight and had been tired Monday.)

Good evening.

("Good evening, Seth.")

Now, our friend seldom attempts to block during a session as he did in the past. After a session in which he has been in a deep trance, a portion of him becomes leery, however. This is why we did not have our last session. (*Pause.*)

The data that I gave that evening was indeed legitimate. It seems that two other men will become involved as a result of the occurrences that I mentioned. A reshuffling and changes of personnel will result. There will be some changes in the business department and, I believe, in advertising. Also one particular change in the editorial department. There will be changes in the meantime that will affect correspondents writing for the paper in nearby areas, and directives. Give us a moment on something else.

It is possible (*pause, long*) that the changes of which Philip has been told will not occur and were furthermore not intended to occur: that he has been told so for other reasons.

(John Bradley is called Philip by Seth. Recently he told us that his territory might be changed, effectively cutting out Elmira and including instead an area of small towns in Pennsylvania. Since Seth goes into something else shortly, I will note here that John Bradley and Bill Gallagher engaged in lively argument here the evening before this session, on the subject of war.)

A man with balding, very dark hair and dark brows who did have or has a mustache, belongs to Pat Norelli's family. (*Pause.*)

Now we can do no more with our friend this evening. It is all right. He is all right. One small note. The episode last evening was aggressively disrupting to some extent. Mainly because of the inner attitudes of those involved. Symbolically, you see, and beneath it all, both men showed characteristics that under different circumstances could have led them into violence for the sake of their beliefs.

A belief must not possess. They were psychically adding to the unfortunate circumstances over which they argued, and both equally were at fault for this reason. A battle recreated in the mind reinforces the original psychic explosion and contemplation of war helps project that disaster into the future. To argue aggressively that war is wrong is ironic stupidity, for such an individual already displays those characteristics that lead to war.

It is wrong to think that restraint under such circumstances or discussions is cowardly, though of course, it <u>may</u> be. To refrain from argument while simultaneously and deliberately forcing thoughts or pictures of peace, represents a positive action. The intensity of the peaceful images or thoughts unfortunately rarely match the intensity of the bitterness, you see. Thoughts of reconciliation or peace actually and practically do their bit to destroy the causes of war. Since Ruburt has somewhat come around, you may take a break and I shall continue.

(9:28 Break. Pace picked up as delivery progressed.

(9:37. Resume session.)

Now, H at the paper is not doing all of this on his own entirely. Through poor habits he attracts negative influences from others, and actually amplifies them, projecting them outward in a highly magnified manner. This takes much of his energy.

There is a connection here between last night's episode, and the emotionally charged psychological climate behind the overt behavior itself: the behavior for example was not violent in any way.

("Yes.")

There are deeply hidden areas of human behavior far below the surface of actions, and these cause the actions. They are psychic exchanges. Before the beginning of any war, subconsciously each individual knows not only that a war will occur, but its precise outcome. Battles like other physical acts exist first in the mental realm. When this realm is peaceful there are no wars. All of your physical activities, from the political to the economic and to the most insignificant individual concerns have their origin in mental existence, and their outcome is known.

To create a harmonious inner existence is a positive act with far-reaching effects, and not an act of isolation. To desire peace strongly is to help achieve it. To accept war helps prolong its physical existence. These are not idle words nor are they meant symbolically.

Wars are not only disruptive within your system, but cause some severe repercussions for individuals who die while in battle. The seemingly small episode of last evening presented in miniature the basic attitudes that are behind aggressive acts.

There is a short-circuiting process in which even good intentions are distorted and turned to other purposes. That which is feared is feared so strongly and concentrated upon so intensely that it is attracted rather than repelled. The approach should not be fear of war but love of peace; not fear of poor health but concentration upon the enjoyment of good health; not fear of poverty, but concentration upon the unlimited supplies available on your earth.

Desire attracts but fear also attracts. Severe fear is highly dangerous in this respect and in this context.

You may take a brief break and we shall continue.

(9:55 break. Jane's pace was faster during this delivery, and her eyes were often open.

(10:04. Resume session.)

Our friend is finally learning to take his concentration away from his symptoms, and he is losing them. Attention prolongs them. Intense concentration even upon an object is useful whenever he is bothered. Concentration, an imagined journey, any exercise that is intense and diverting is beneficial. Now, to show our friend that I can also make concessions, we will close the session.

("Good night, Seth."

(10:08. End of session.)

SESSION 338
MAY 1, 1967 9 PM MONDAY

(Jane began speaking with many pauses, some of them quite long.)
Good evening.
("Good evening, Seth.")

Now. The physical universe as you see it represents in all of its complicated patterns, the far more vast, unbelievably more complicated inner workings that are not physical.

The immediate physical environment of your own apartment, for example, is the result of continual inner processes with which you are not acquainted. The existence, maintenance, and appearance of that environment depends upon inner manipulations and automatic transfers that are as natural and as necessary to your existence physically, as breath.

Each minute variation of physical matter that you perceive is caused by inner minute variations that you do not perceive. Each insignificant shading of color, change in texture, in degree or kind, are directly caused by corresponding inner differences.

In many respects the physical body itself aids in these transformations, through chemical interactions, changes in delicate electromagnetic balances, temperature variations, and through other methods that will be discussed shortly.

The physical with its multitudinous and astonishing complexity, merely hints at the full nature of inner reality however, for all of inner reality cannot be translated in physical terms. Your own physical environment is constantly <u>tended</u> by you automatically. It constantly reflects in its own way the nature of your inner environment. Again, this is far from symbolic. Every least alteration of psychic and emotional existence immediately alters the nature of the physical environment through instant interaction.

If, for example, at two o'clock your apartment appears comfortable, cozy and peaceful and twenty minutes later it suddenly seems crowded, uncomfortable and cluttered, then you see this is not imagination. You have changed the relationships existing within the immediate physical environment, and you perceive the change physically.

The change itself is the direct reflection of inner psychic and psychological alterations; but you have actually altered the nature of the physical environment and the quality that pervades it. The influence of others is also involved.

You understand now what space is, or is not, in physical terms. In psychic terms also there is something that can be loosely explained in terms of spatial relationships, but having to do with intensities. A strong intensity of a particular nature can give you the feeling of clutter or lack of space. This is the nearest I can come at this moment in telling you how <u>this</u> particular sort of transformation can occur.

There is obviously a cooperative element here, for each living consciousness has its part to play in maintaining the environment, which in turn gives its nourishment.

You may take a brief break and we shall continue.

(9:27. Jane's pace had remained quite slow with many pauses. Her eyes opened occasionally. Her voice was average. Resume in the same manner at 9:35.)

Thoughts and emotions directly activate the mechanics of physical matter, alter and transform it, maintain it, and also destroy it.

The beginning of your physical universe occurred when conscious energy directed enough of its attention *(long pause)* in what was generalized dimension, to spark the formation of physical properties. The creation was just that. The first explosion of psychic energy in an ungeneralized dimension sparked the birth of specifics.

Before this the generalized dimension was simply nonexistent, a vacuum, which consciousness had not yet filled. Since consciousness or action can never fully materialize itself, there are literally infinities of such nonexistent areas from which new dimensions can spring.

Consciousness or action forms all realities. What is not simply represents a possibility which consciousness may bring to life. *(Long pause.)* Consciousness then formed out of itself a new dimension which was the physical one. The formation, the <u>explosion</u>, of energy, shattered consciousness into an infinity of parts, each with all the abilities in here within consciousness itself.

From itself, therefore, and of itself, consciousness gave birth to its new dimension of experience, and then experienced what it had created, further extending itself and in turn bringing forth further possibilities of development.

Consciousness therefore continually creates and maintains itself, and this includes the physical materialization, the properties of the dimension, and yet basically there is no difference between the creator in these terms and the created. Nor between inner reality, which forms physical matter, and physical objects themselves, for the atoms which are manipulated to form objects are themselves a portion of consciousness, and alive in those terms. They respond to emotional and psychic directives as the physical body responds to light.

You may take your break and we shall continue.

(9:54. Jane's pace had picked up a bit by break, but was still slow. Resume at 10:02.)

All of this talk about consciousness and action does not mean that consciousness is without identity.

You could not appreciate nor understand, nor can I, the nature of identity as it is known in the overall. What we know of identity represents fragments and splinters that we call ourselves. These are part however of the prime identity. The splinters are possessed of individuality, and such units will never be dissolved.

They are still but a portion of prime identity, and without them, prime identity could not know itself nor act upon itself nor develop its own abilities or potentials.

Now in the same way that consciousness originated the physical dimension, you as portions of consciousness continue to maintain and create it anew. Your source of energy is that first creation, in which consciousness focused, where before it had not. You also then know and develop yourselves through your own creations, and you automatically create and maintain your physical environment in the same manner that you breathe. Your physical image and your physical environment are both materialized extensions of your inner selves.

The physical body itself however has much more to do with the maintenance of environment than is realized, for you use it so that your environment becomes almost like a second body, extending outward from the first, through which you express your inclinations and characteristics. There are intricate complications that arise as environmental elements merge and mix with those of others. You can see here the formation of nationalistic characteristics on a mass level.

This is constant creation. The initial creation provided the energy, the dimension, of possibility itself, but every particle of consciousness will always attempt to express itself within as many possibilities as possible. The inner self therefore creates the physical body and the land upon which it moves.

We will end the session but continue this material on Wednesday. My heartiest wishes to you both. Bear in mind also that as individuals, you are creating new dimensions through which consciousness can know itself, both in physical experience and within other systems. As a part of consciousness other systems are not closed to you, but as physical organisms other systems are closed to you.

("Good night, Seth."
(10:27)

SESSION 339
MAY 3, 1967 9:45 PM WEDNESDAY

(Bill and Peg Gallagher attended the session.)
Good evening.
("Good evening, Seth.")
And good evening to our friends.
([Bill:] "Hum de do.")
Our best, as always, to the jovial Jesuit.
([Bill:] "Thank you and the same to you, Seth.")
Now we find an old man with failing eyesight and partial cataract in the left eye, a hint of partial paralysis on the left side. A tremor from an old disorder, affecting the nervous system. The man from whom Ruburt received the letter. A marginal motor disturbance. A disordered personality, quite legitimate

psychic abilities, however, fairly well developed. A missionary fervor, a congregation or student body of approximately 200, but in name only—the center, however, of about 26 participants. Indeed, a many-talented gentleman. A well-educated but misunderstood man, whose childlike tendencies are now in prominence. He can barely see out of one eye.

(Seth is discussing the Gonzolus letter from Indianapolis, Indiana, that we received this week. The old man and the school of spiritualism. Letter on school notepaper—palsied and hard to read. Simple sentence structure—childlike. Mailed from New York City.)

There is a woman close to him with whom he has a brotherly relationship, and who helps tend to his wants. He is about 54, and up and about, and still at work in his way, however. A Bombay connection and an involvement with some brilliant work as a young man. Now, give us a moment.

In connection with the brothers and the other letter. *(Pause.)* Entirely different temperaments, but very close. Some years difference in their ages. 54 and 36, or that number of difference in their ages. *(Pause. Eighteen years, then.)*

Scrub. One perhaps extremely fastidious. Restrained. Not the one who wrote the letter. The one who wrote the letter is usually the less dominant of the two. *(Pause.)* A father, a very old man, still living in a place that is foreign or far distant from the brothers. *(In Australia, we learned later.)*

You may take a break and we shall continue.

(9:59 PM.

(10:17. Resume.)

Give us a moment please. I believe the mother of the family is no longer living in your terms. There seems to be a disastrous event connected with the family's past, and having to do with death. Perhaps in the 1930's; and a relationship with an aunt. The event happening in an unfamiliar location, unfamiliar that is to the victim or perhaps victims, at the time. Something to do with a priest or monk, something of that order: a member of the family or confidant.

Ferd, in France, very approximately 1831, Versailles. He knows of me, he is not aware of all the levels of his own identity or personality. A trip in the French life to China.

(Long pause.) A small yard with lemons for the brothers. A pink stucco house, two bedrooms in the rear, not a new house. A peculiarity on the left side of the house. A flight of stairs inside, though it does not seem to be a two-family home. *(Pause.)* They used the board in the kitchen. There is some space between the house and the next structure on the right. Perhaps a lot. They are near the corner to the right, but not at the corner.

The building to the left is closer. It appears to be a garage, a private garage, but I do not believe that it is. It has a large square design at the front like a garage or large barn door or even a firehouse. They are not far from water. There are not many structures between them and the water. High grass for awhile, and some wooden posts and wire.

("Are you at the location now?")

To some degree. Sand dunes of a sort. There, I have changed position. Now I am facing the house. Directly behind it, it seems clear of structures. It seems clear of structures to the water. But now to the right: the directions have changed now due to my position. The garage structure is now to my right, and behind it there are other structures leading down toward the water. And beyond, some dune area, a beach, the tide is in.

("What time of day is it?")

It is early evening. There are these fairly thin wooden posts, but not round (frown, gestures) rectangular at the top, you see. Perhaps hip level, to the left from my same position. The coastline is not straight here. Some sort of a bay effect, to the left. (Gesture right hand.) The land is like this, you see, not straight. The land curves and juts out again.

("Is your vantage point now from above?")

For the coastline information, though you can see this from the beach. You may take a break and we shall continue.

(10:40 PM.

(This proved to be the end of the session. My questions hadn't bothered Jane. Up until I asked if Seth was at the location, she saw what she described, but not clearly [or Seth did]. After, however, she felt bodiless, changed position to answer my questions more clearly and get a larger view. She had no awareness of the room in which she sat giving the session, yet of course she did [or Seth did] hear my questions and answer them. She felt that a partial projection took place, not a full one since only vision operated in the other location, rather than, say, all the senses. She felt suspended in air, but capable of movement.

(We had not checked any maps, etc., for the location of Chula Vista, California [where the brothers live], before the session of course. Before finishing these notes, however, we did check to find that Chula Vista is indeed near a bay; that the coast is not straight there.)

SESSION 340
MAY 10, 1967 9 PM WEDNESDAY

(The session scheduled for Monday, May 8, was not held. May 8 was Jane's *birthday and we celebrated at the Gallaghers' home.*

(Barbara Ingold, who lives across the hall from us, attended this session.)

Good evening

("Good evening, Seth."

([Barbara:] "Good evening, Seth.")

Good evening to our friend. Now, to our fine young lady: you must watch the pictures that you paint with your imagination, for you allow your imagination too full a reign. If you read our early material, you will see that your environment and the conditions of your life at any given time are the direct result of your own expectations. You form physical materializations of these realities within your own mind.

If you imagine dire circumstances, ill health or desperate loneliness, these will be automatically materialized, for these thoughts themselves bring forth the conditions that will give them reality in physical terms. If you would have good health, if you would have good health for the child, then you must imagine this as vividly as, in fear, you imagine the opposite.

You create many of your own difficulties, if not all of them. This is true for all individuals. The inner psychological state is projected outward, gaining physical reality. This holds true regardless of the nature of that inner psychological state. The way that this is done has been discussed often and is on record in the material. I suggest you read it. The rules apply to everyone. You can use this for your own benefit and change your conditions, once you realize what the rules are.

You cannot escape your own attitudes, for they will form the nature of what you see. Quite literally, you see what you want to see, and you see your own thoughts, your own emotional attitudes, materialized in physical form. If changes are to occur, they must be physical and psychic changes. These will be reflected in your physical environment. Negative, distrustful, fearful, or degrading attitudes toward anyone work against the self and against the individuals involved. Now if you would change an individual, change your thoughts toward him, and changes will appear in the sense data world.

You may take a break and we shall continue.

(9:15 break.

(9:21 resume.)

Now: you must understand, for one thing, that telepathy operates constantly at a subconscious level. If you continually expect any individual to behave in a particular manner, then you are constantly sending him telepathic suggestions that he will do so. Every individual reacts to suggestion. According then to the specific conditions existing at the time, such an individual will to some extent or another act according the mass suggestions he has received.

These mass suggestions include not only those given to him by others, both verbally and telepathically, but also those suggestions that he has given to himself while in the waking or dream states. If individual A is in a period of despondency, then this is because he has already become prey to negative suggestions of his own and others. If now you see him and think that he looks miserable—or that he is an incurable drunk—then indeed these suggestions are picked up by him subconsciously though you have not spoken a word, and in his already weakened condition, they will be accepted and acted upon.

If, on the other hand, thinking of him under the same conditions, you stop yourself and say gently to yourself: he will begin to feel better now—or his drinking is temporary—and there is indeed hope here, then you have given him aid, for the suggestions will at least represent some small telepathic ammunition to fight off the war of despondency.

There are obviously ways in which you can mold your own conditions, protect yourself from your own negative suggestions and those given to you by others. You must immediately erase a negative thought or picture by replacing it with its opposite.

If you think, "I have a headache," and if you do not replace this suggestion by a positive one, then you are automatically suggesting that the body set up those conditions that will result in the continuation of the malady. You may take a break and we shall continue shortly. I will give you a commercial that is better than your Excedrin, you see. The short headache. We shall tell you how to have none at all.

(9:35 break. Jane's eyes were open at times, her pace good.
(9:45 resume.)

Now: You are not listening to what your own inner voice says. You are listening to what your ego says, and this I speaks through your mouth and then you hear this I's words. But these are not the words of the whole self. These are merely the words of the one part of the self with which you are most acquainted.

You are not speaking of basic issues. You are flying paper dragons to be punctured, but these are not the real dragons. You must learn to listen to the voice of your inner self, for if you know the use you are to this man, you do not recognize the nature of his use to you.

You have built defenses so strongly that you have not heard the voice of the inner self. The inner self is hardly to be feared. You have allowed the ego to become a counterfeit self, and you take its word because you will not hear the muffled voice that is within you speak.

You have been examining others, rather than examining the self. What you see of others is the materialization of what you <u>think</u>, subconsciously, that you are: not necessarily what you are. For example: if others <u>seem</u> deceitful to you it is because you deceive yourself and then project this outward onto others.

These are simply examples now. If an individual sees only evil and desolation in the physical world, it is because he is obsessed with evil and desolation and projects them outward and closes his eyes to all else. If you want to know what you think of yourself, then ask yourself what you think of others, and you will find your answer.

This is, of course, on a subconscious basis. Another example only: a very industrious individual thinks the majority of mankind are lazy and good for nothing. No one would ever think of calling him lazy or good for nothing, yet this may be precisely his own subconscious picture of himself, against which he drives himself incessantly, all in an effort to prove that his erroneous self-image is, indeed, wrong. And all without realizing his basic concept of himself and without recognizing the fact that he projects it outward onto others.

True self-knowledge is indispensable for health or vitality, and this means in every instance. The recognition of the truth about the self means that you must first discover what you think about yourself subconsciously. If this is a good image, build upon it. If it is a poor one, recognize it as simply the opinion of the subconscious and not as a definite truth.

The subconscious has its opinions as the ego does.

You may take a break and we shall continue. Aside here: (*Jane's eyes closed*) Pat Norelli. These are impressions, and I will give them as they come. N-A-R. You had better separate those with dashes. A recorder or record player: in particular, three women and a man. Or one may be present, I do not know. A rug long and narrow, a front entry. An unbelievable story told. Patterns on a wall. Something to do with a Greek chorus, a missionary encounter, that is, having to do with a fervency, you see. M I C H. Down in the valley. Take your break.

(*10:07 break. Jane "not there" during this last data.*

(*10:15 resume.*)

Now. This will be a relatively brief session and we shall end shortly. I will here repeat my earlier suggestion that our friend read my earlier material. It is important that you all realize the ways in which your attitudes and feelings affect others through telepathic workings, and the ways in which the smallest thought affects your own emotions, and the physical condition of your image.

For our guest: you should tell yourself frequently, "I will only react to constructive suggestions," for this gives you some protection against your own negative thoughts and those of others. You can observe these laws in operation where you work and also, privately, when you are alone. A negative thought, if it is not erased, will almost certainly result in a negative situation, a momentary despondency, a headache, according to the original intensity of the thought.

Now: if you find yourself saying to yourself: "I have a headache," you must immediately say "That is in the past. Now in this new moment, this new present, I am already feeling better." Then immediately turn your attention away from your physical condition entirely. Concentrate upon something pleasant, or begin another task.

In this way you are no longer suggesting to the body that it reproduce headache conditions. The exercise may be repeated. This is basic, though the pendulum exercises, Joseph, are of great benefit particularly when added to this prescription.

I am now going to end our session. My heartiest wishes to you all.

("Good night, Seth.")

([Barbara:] "Good night, Seth.")

(10:28. End of session.

(Note: May 22, 1966. In a letter received today, Pat Norelli had this to say pertaining to the material given by Seth concerning her in this session:

("The information Seth had concerning me is very interesting. It could have meaning, especially since I'm dating a Greek boy, and Seth mentions a Greek chorus. I'll have to ask my date if the information means anything to him. The description of the long rug in a narrow front entry fits his apartment. It should be fascinating.")

SESSION 341
MAY 15, 1967 9 PM MONDAY

Good evening.

("Good evening, Seth.")

Now. Since we are alone, I would like to discuss some material mentioned in another recent session.

Creation is constant. Due to the nature of action creation cannot be anything but simultaneous. Each act of creation brings forth another, and opens up further dimensions of activity. Within your own system, thought becomes materialized, and there is literally no end to the activity of thoughts. Thoughts however are connected with language and with highly organized ego development. They are translations and symbols for inner activity. As a rule they are highly physically oriented, their function being to acquaint the physically adapted ego with some inner data.

The thoughts may rather faithfully, though never completely, translate such data, or they may considerably distort it. Behind thoughts are images, which are more basic but still physically oriented. Because they are more basic, they have a stronger effect. They are more emotionally charged, more concise than thoughts, and they are directly connected with the mechanics involved in translating inner data to physical reality.

Behind these, so to speak, exist what you may term temperature pictures, in which delicate gradations of heat form ever-shifting emotional patterns that do have a semiphysical outline. From these, you see, normal images are built up, and from the images thoughts are formed.

Consciousness itself perceives directly, and these various methods of perception have been adopted to meet varying physical circumstances. Such thermal pictures are found in what is called the old brain, and to these, the body responds with changes of temperature that sparks various chemical reactions.

In for example the worm, the process ends here. In so-called higher forms, the chemical process itself allows for the creation of an ordinary image. This brings about further thermal responses and chemical alterations, that allow the thought processes to proceed.

All of these procedures are unnecessary to consciousness itself, however. They are necessary to develop communication between nonphysical consciousness and the physical form which it has adopted. Consciousness, in forming an image, or creating it, then responds to it creatively, setting up frameworks for further creative actions. Consciousness experiences reality directly, but having formed physical matter into a personal image, it must then creatively translate data to that physical brain. It must keep it informed.

The brain looks out upon the physical universe, and consciousness then reacts, again creatively, to that environment. Information is now carried in reverse fashion back to the inner self, in an instantaneous and automatic procedure. Thus thought becomes an inner image which is translated into a thermal image, and then into intuitional form, into highly condensed and codified data, and then into a pure and direct sort of experience which you cannot understand as physical creatures.

All of the information of the inner self is highly condensed and codified, and exists in electromagnetic purity.

You may take your break and we shall continue.

(9:27. Jane's voice had been stronger than usual. She had used frequent short pauses and her eyes had been closed most of the time.

(Resume at 9:40.)

This automatic procedure works both ways, then, constantly. Various portions of the self retain memory of the information, still in the form in which they have interpreted it. The thoughts and images, while being condensed, are nevertheless then retained in their particular levels of the personality in their own form.

Now, the process does not cease at the physical boundaries of the self however. The data thus far has been seen as traveling from the inner self outward, as being translated from pure knowledge into thermal pictures, inner images and thoughts. Obviously words and action follow.

The actions result in concrete physical materializations. These are all highly colored and charged, however, and the stuff of physical materialization is in itself conscious and alive. There are hidden but very definite connections between the self and the objects of which it has created in its environment. The environment is simply an extension of the self, and those objects within it are a part of the physical or the physically materialized personality. Hence your ideas of ownership.

Objects carry a strong emotional and psychic charge. The personality exists inward in ways that are not at once apparent, but it also exists outward in ways that you do not see. There are, of course, mergings where selves quite literally merge with other selves, forming a corporate self. But the unit selves retain their identity, as in a nation the citizens retain theirs, even though the nation at times may act as a unit, and share particular mass characteristic drives and desires, and work toward various goals.

All it involves constant creativity, not only maintenance but entirely original and new creation.

I have been speaking of your present system only, yet there is always progression to other systems. The growth of each (underlined) seed requires a separate act of creation. There is no mass creative act, for all portions of consciousness have their part to play in creativity. This is the meaning of action, of consciousness, and of individuality: the freedom to create.

Without this there would be only a sham creativity, without involvement and without the involvement of action. Every dream is a creative act, that could be initiated in no other way, highly individual.

You may take your break and we shall continue.

(9:59—10:10.)

Now, you arbitrarily decide on the personal physical image as the exterior boundary of the self. As you know, in actuality, no such physical boundary exists. It is the result of your perception. Even physically, you see, no such boundary exists. You can see this for example in epidemics.

The physical self extends outward, literally, to the ends of your universe, but the physical brain could not handle this amount of manipulation, and it has become subconscious. Early man recognized his relationships more clearly. Specialized man, physically, cannot afford to.

Physically you are a part of your environment, and you form it as you form your image. There is much more to be said here, and we shall go into it more deeply soon. For this is not a symbolic relationship but a practical one.

Jung was correct in postulating a collective unconscious. But with his limited knowledge he did not see that this unconscious would exist outside of your three-dimensional system entirely, holding future as well as past, nor that it has such a cohesive effect upon humanity as a whole. It is the one self with its <u>origins</u> within your system, but its existence outside.

The collective unconscious is not static however, and itself interacts and constantly changes. These are all phases of constant creativity within your system. You constantly add to the collective unconscious, and constantly receive from it. You change what you receive, however. Each physical object has a psychic effect on all other objects, and a psychic existence that is independent of its physical existence.

There is constant interaction between all objects, and several will create a pervading psychic climate that affects those who come in contact with it.

Now. Separately, the letters, in capitals: S, and A, and G or C or Z. In connection with a letter to Ruburt, and also perhaps with a letter written by the same individual to someone else.

We will close our session. My heartiest wishes to you both.

("Good night, Seth."

(10:25. Jane's pace had been faster, her eyes open often, her voice average. She said that Seth "didn't leave fast, after he said good night." She thought he was going to say something else.

(Jane was on Edna Bartlett's program over WELM on Monday, May 15, 1967, in Elmira.

(A letter Jane received Tuesday, May 16, may or may not be referred to in the above last session paragraph. The letter is from her correspondent in West Brookfield, Massachusetts, the Reverend James C. Crosson. Reverend Crosson did not refer to the WELM program, of course, but in his letter offers Jane an opportunity to lecture to a group on ESP in Massachusetts, which is the same type of activity. It develops he also writes book reviews for the Garrett publication, Parapsychology, *which recently carried a review of Jane's book. Jane feels Crosson would have given the book a better review, and an entirely legitimate one, than it did receive. Then she added:*

(Much later, November 1968—Crosson without my knowledge writes to an editor at Doubleday telling them about my book, Dreams, Astral Projection & ESP

and suggests they take a look. I did not learn this till January when Crosson told me in a letter. Crosson—the C, of course, and the two S's give a Z sound.)

SESSION 342
MAY 17, 1967 9 PM WEDNESDAY

Good evening.

("Good evening, Seth.")

Now: All creation is constant, and physical reality is formed and maintained in mental realms, sparked by psychic (*pause*) experiences. These inner events are the results of action's own characteristics. Action continually working upon itself creates more action.

Initially this is mental action, an action-event. This action-event will then affect all other events, spiral inward and outward in all possible dimensions, and may be perceived in these dimensions in quite a different form from its original nature. In each system it can only be perceived according to the camouflage patterns inherent there.

This physical room and this particular moment within this room all exist simultaneously in other systems, though they may or may not appear in the same form. The energy generated in sparking a given action-event is never lost. Some is retained by the initial materialization, and by the succeeding ones. The term succeeding is used as a matter of simplicity. You know what is meant.

All of these forms, however, are you understand spontaneous and instantaneous. In the same way that an idea may appear within your system as a thought, a mental image, a dream picture or as a physical object, so does any action-event appear in many forms.

Your psychological life is dependent upon your ability to perceive and react to such action-events. Your reaction, of course, creates new ones. Your identity, your inner self, is a main action-event, forming other such events that are the various portions of your personality.

There are both private and mass action-events, all of these being physically materialized within your system. Creation, then, continues constantly and each consciousness has its part to play. The interwoven working of telepathic communications lends itself to mass patterns. Many individuals reacting to a given event may do so by combining their energy to produce <u>one</u> major action-event in response.

Such mass materializations gain tremendous emotional force, and seemingly sweep aside any conflicting actions. Great movements in history are an example here. Certain ideas also are agreed upon and held so intensely that they mold much of physical activity simply because of the strong mental and psychic energy they engender.

This does not mean that such ideas are necessarily valid, you see, but in your system they certainly appear as such, due to the intensity with which they are held. This intensity brings forth the corresponding physical materialization which the senses then perceive, and the circle becomes complete.

The materialization is dependent upon the thought intensity behind it. If wars are considered inevitable, you see, there will be wars. If death is considered the end of all, then for all practical purposes individuals in physical life will behave as if this were indeed the case.

You may take a break and we shall continue.

(9:26 break.

(9:35 resume.)

Now: conversely, if you do not accept the idea of reincarnation, this does not mean that reincarnation is not a fact. It does mean that this insufficient energy will keep this reality at such a low ebb that it will not sufficiently materialize as an event within your system. For the egotistical self it will be a nonfact and the physical senses will of course find no sense data to confirm reincarnation.

I mentioned long past that creativity continued to operate in a work of art long after its physical completion. The intensity that first generated, say, a painting, continues to operate and there is new creation sparked in the interchange between such a painting and each observer of it.

The resulting thoughts and images in turn are expressed and affect others, and not only symbolically. As you should know, mental acts have an electromagnetic reality which directly affects the inner self, which directly _forms_ the constantly changing nature of the inner self. For the inner self is, after all, composed of mental actions, and the entity itself is everchanging.

Never think of it as static. There is constant give and take between all portions of the self, and the entity changes as it interacts with other levels of the personality. Any given thought experienced by you is experienced by all possible you-selves, though in various forms.

A thought experienced by you is also experienced by your probable selves, you see, in one way or another. They will react in their characteristic way, and experience the thought in their own manner, which may be quite different than your own.

The thought may be rejected, but there will be something to reject. The thought may be relatively meaningless to any given probable self and it may be very fleeting. The probable selves in one way or another will react, forming other action-events. Constant creativity applies to every system, then, and what you create in one system has its effects in other systems also.

Your physical image and your environment are exterior materializations that represent your interior action-events at any given time. These are observed by the physical senses of yourself and others. You can therefore check your inner status by observing your outer status. Such checking always involves action, however, that already changes that which is perceived. All of these seeming separate actions belong together, you see, and occur at once. (*Pause, long.*)

I am trying here to get a rather complicated idea through to you, but we have not sufficiently broken it down yet. Take a break and we shall see what we can do. I will try to break it down while his mind is momentarily otherwise engaged.

(*Break 9:55. Jane said Seth was thinking of something having to do with moment points; she had some images, "like star shapes, only layered thick.."*

(*Resume 10:05.*)

We will, instead, begin our next session with this material and for now I have a few comments to make. When you rubbed our friend's (*Jane's*) back the other evening, you did indeed improve his condition. This was not basically because of the physical action involved, though in this case the physical actions were necessary for your own expression.

You sent vital healing energy and resolution to his physical body, and the heat he felt was the result of this energy. The feeling had built up in you to help him. The rubbing expressed this feeling from you, and then acted directly on a sense-data level which both of you needed at the time to confirm what was an inner experience.

Much of man's creativity is expressed directly through his hands, and for this reason they are often used in healing experiences. They have a significance intuitively felt by the inner self.

When Ruburt is involved in activity and his mind directed elsewhere, away from his symptoms, then his symptoms are greatly minimized, and at times disappear. This represents a good amount of development on his part, since earlier he found it difficult to address himself to activity.

When he ceases activity however, he has a tendency to activate the symptoms rather than direct his attention elsewhere. The letup of physical activity is not the issue, though he thinks it is at the end of the day. An exciting conversation, an exciting inner mental activity serves well to divert him. A series of such lapses accentuate the condition of course. Then he uses his book and suggestion to clear the air and begins again anew.

The overall improvement is definite.

We will end our session. My heartiest wishes to you both. One small word: your hands the other evening served, of course, as a bridge of understanding and constructive understanding, correctly applied: that is, a constructive help not an over-anxious sympathy nor implied accusation. And now again, good evening.

("Good night, Seth."

(10:18. End of session.

(We received a letter from Pat Norelli today in which she substantiates some clairvoyant material concerning her, given by Seth in Session 340. Notes are included in that session.)

SESSION 343
MAY 22, 1967 9 PM MONDAY

Good evening.

("Good evening, Seth.")

Now. Moment points are indeed composed of action, action experiencing itself. What you see and experience physically represents but a small portion, a mere fraction of what reality is. There are universes within universes. Action is, and yet forms its own experience. Thoughts take electromagnetic patterns that have their own materializations as universal systems. Your physical body is a series of actions, though the word series is being used for simplicity's sake only.

The nature of action causes depths in terms of intensities that you do not understand, but these intensities build up to the appearance of physical matter within your system.

You will never find a first action, and only within your system does such a search have any meaning. You form the reality, the shape, of thoughts, for they have shape, in much the same way that you breathe; and you have as little control of them, once you have created them, as you have of your breath.

Complications are far too intricate to explain to you. You form your image and the physical matter of your environment, and these, being action, are perceived as reality in other systems. They may not be perceived as physical objects, but as reality that conforms to the particular camouflage structure within.

Thoughts have what you may term color and shape, as well as electromagnetic structure and intensity. These combining together form your physical image, in your terms. Action can never be broken down to a prime or original unit, for it automatically builds upon itself, and can never be, therefore, subtracted from. Nor can it be isolated. It is within all things that you see, and invisible because it makes up the <u>appearance</u> of any physical construction.

It isn't what you see, and yet what you see is it. Sight itself is it, the thing seen and the perceiver. You cannot stop action even in your mind, for the attempt to stop action is in itself an action. What you term death is an action. It is not the end of acts. The self at death is indeed more active as a rule than before, and the resources of the self are used to greater advantage.

The self goes on. Even the stuff of the physical body however continues to act. Action divides itself into various selves, and then explores the moment points of experience, for each new self is indeed a new action, an original act.

There are births that have nothing to do with physical birth, and offspring quite as real. Physical offspring are originally projections, but these originate new acts despite the original idea behind them. That is, the parents wish to project themselves, you see, but instead are the participators of a new personality.

Thoughts as offspring have a strong effect in all systems, and directly change the camouflage material of any system.

You may take a break and we shall continue.

(9:25. Jane's eyes had been closed most of the time. Her voice was average, with pauses. Resume at 9:31.)

Now. I am trying to make this clear. Moment points have a structure, electromagnetically.

The structure has nothing to do with the intensity however. Now, very slowly: your entire physical universe represents one moment point in a whole overall design. Yet the design itself is ever-changing, and there is no beginning or end to it in your terms.

In studying your physical universe, the distances seem great only because of your own point of reference within. The electromagnetic structure of your universe, in a basic manner, is divorced from its physical structure, though part of it can be deduced through a study of the physical structure.

Your physical universe represents one thought in changing aspects of becoming, with all possibilities inherent within the thought unfolding into existence. The thought also exists in other systems, being materialized according to other camouflage patterns, and entirely different possibilities arising because of the differences.

Again, this is not symbolic. Only by the use of the inner senses can you obtain a viewpoint that is to some extent free of your own system. The inner self realizes the nature of its own reality, is sure of its identity and well aware of its power in the creation of actions which it projects outward from itself.

The inner senses allow you to follow some of these actions into other realities. The moment point on the one hand is of course a minute division of action. On the other hand it is an entrance into unknown possibilities and new dimensions. As you probe into any given moment point, <u>you</u> automatically become a part of it and change it accordingly as it makes its impressions upon you. These interchangings occur on many levels: psychologically, chemically, electromagnetically, psychically. There are subtle variations, as you know, in your known self from one instant to another as you affect your physical environment and form it, and as it in turn forms you. And this is just on the physical level.

The psychological alterations are miraculous, and so swift that you could not follow them. The smallest thought alters chemical and electromagnetic changes in the body that directly affect the structure of the immediate physical universe. In the dream state the alterations are even stronger.

You may take your break and we shall continue.

(9:50. Jane said she couldn't remember much of the material. Resume at 10:00.)

Now. It is possible for an individual to experience a portion of one moment point in such a way that it <u>seems</u> (underlined) there is no end to it.

He may, for example, continue within it for several reincarnations. Reincarnated selves are no more than probable selves, choosing to experience various forms. In such circumstances, the personality does not leave your system, in your terms, for some time, though this is all subjective. Experience is the only reality, you see.

Now some comments on another subject.

You are of great benefit when you help Ruburt with the pendulum sessions. There is an implied statement of purpose then, in which you both work together toward the complete restoration of his image. Without this he tends to stray.

There is also the psychic advantage in that the desire for help is doubly intensified. And when you both are present, I am present also, and can help you.

("I'm probably not correct on all the conclusions I make during the pendulum sessions, though.")

You have been doing rather well. The encouragement of your presence is of psychic benefit to Ruburt, and the exercise in working with the personal subconscious is of help to him also. He is also used to working with you in our sessions, you see.

I told him some time ago, before sleep, to see himself in highly flexible forms of activity, running, jumping or dancing, and I repeat this now. He should also begin again to suggest that his own subconscious will help him in the dream state, for the <u>images</u> he encounters there can be most beneficial.

There is no doubt he prefers the door open, but he does understand the reasons for the doors closed. He finally realizes the advantage in walking home. This will be a definite help. There should be no discussion of this with the Gallaghers. You should both go out dancing now.

These suggestions should suffice if followed. By all means, as you suggested, a complete honesty of feelings should be admitted. The swearing when he drinks is a direct result of the fact that he tries to deny aggressive feelings otherwise. The garden should be begun as an outlet, and a creative one, for aggressive feelings.

We will now end our session. My heartiest wishes to you both.

("Good night, Seth."

(10:15. Jane reported that she was "pretty far under.")

SESSION 344
JUNE 7, 1967 9:10 PM WEDNESDAY

(Tonight after supper I took Jane to the chiropractor for treatment of her stiff neck. Before the session I spoke aloud to Seth, asking him for straight answers to my questions about Jane's symptoms lately. On June 5 I held a two-hour pendulum session of my own, concerning Jane's symptoms, and received some revealing answers about the role I have played in them. This is written down, and may still be added to.

(Practically as soon as I finished speaking to Seth, Jane's eyes closed. We were sitting at the living room table. She began to speak in an average voice, with pauses, eyes mostly closed.)

Now. The personality has felt as if it were held in bounds, tied, lacking the opportunity for action.

Ruburt's statements a few moments earlier, regarding his feelings, concerning his future, were and are important. What he accepted as a temporary condition he fears to be a permanent one—that is, the temporary positions. He expected more. Unfortunately he then projected a present situation into the future, which to some extent, resulted in a lack of mobility; the present conditions then seen as continuing indefinitely.

(Jane had voiced these thoughts while getting supper this evening; it was the first time I had heard her speak this way. Perhaps my pendulum session recently helped her become aware of her own feelings in this way.

("Well, certainly my own rigid attitudes contributed to her lack of mobility.")

He, as I explained earlier, has a strong spontaneous self, which he had been taught to fear. It was because of distrust of this spontaneous self that he accepted your suggestions so readily and without argument. This did indeed result in further lack of mobility, with strong emotional blockages because of his feeling for you. This explains some of the difficulties incidentally in your intimate life together.

("Are we going about dispelling these restraints in the right way now?")

Remove as many limitations as possible. The spontaneous self is remarkably resilient, and bounces back from its own errors when it makes any.

A vacation <u>will</u> be of great benefit, because of the physical mobility in space, you see. As many small trips beside this as possible will help.

("Has Jane got arthritis?")

There is no arthritis here. There is a severe panic reaction against restrictions, both from within and without, the immobility of fright. He who does not move can make no errors; and he felt he had made a severe error in allowing Fell to publish the book. Your own feelings toward Fell had strong emotional power.

("I believe that now.")

And Ruburt was frightened. He would have, I believe, otherwise gone to New York and charmed his way into at least more specific results.

("Did Jane block this material from you earlier?")

She closed off the material from me, which is something different.

("Do you think it was wise for us to go to the chiropractor tonight?")

The treatments should be of benefit.

("We're very concerned about when these symptoms will let up, of course.")

Give us a moment. (*Pause, eyes closed.*)

You understand I cannot tell you <u>when</u>, categorically, because of possibilities. If sufficient restrictions are lifted, so that Ruburt feels he has your blessing, and not just mute acceptance, for example, to try various possibilities; if you take a good vacation out of your immediate environment; if Ruburt feels he can foresee freedom to some extent of activity, in which to manipulate next year—

("He can have all the freedom he wants.")

—then you should see some fairly immediate improvement when he realizes these steps will be taken. He has frozen up out of fear. The actions that he has taken he has not approved of. Those he wanted to take seemed, for inner or outer reasons, forbidden, and in frustration he adopted the symptoms.

Much of this because he projected this uncomfortable present into the future, you see. This was all he had to look forward to. That was his inner thought, and this was interpreted literally.

("From now one he can have all the freedom he wants.")

You must understand that he will need your help now in order to use it. This is rather important. He will be afraid of making errors; and fears that you may blame him for them.

("Not me. I mean it. What I want to know is whether you can help impress my own changed attitude upon Jane so that it helps her in daily life? The idea being that she has freedom, and so forth.")

I will endeavor to do so, and believe I can to some extent. The adoption of the arthritis symptoms did have some mother identification, but also they were adopted simply because they were symptoms with which Ruburt was familiar. (Eyes open, emphatic.)

The annoying or frightening symptoms began when Ruburt began his search for work, unknown to him consciously. His attitudes had by now changed. In the past he did think of work as temporary. Now it meant failure.

He felt particularly sensitive looking for a job precisely when his book had arrived in the bookstores. This seemed the one time when he should not have to look, you see.

The hand symptoms also have to do with a feeling that he has not come to grips with reality. He wants the chance to do so in his own way, although he realizes his way may not, you see, pan out financially. He wants to try.

("I want him to try too.")

He is frightened because if this does not work he will have to face the other situation again. Your illness was a shock to him, and he has been afraid of doing anything that would make you feel insecure.

("I think I feel more secure than I ever have before.")

Your personality has indeed grown and matured in most respects since our sessions. Ruburt's fear, once set off, unfortunately serves to release unreasoning childhood fears that then trigger these sensitivities.

His mother was immobile, and yet as a child he had to rely on her. It is his fear that sensitized him again to old issues.

You may take a break.

(9:40. Jane said that before the session she told Seth to blot her out, so that we would get undistorted material. She was aware of what she said as she said it. Resume in the same manner at 9:50.)

The dreams with the various apartments were a release, for here at least he could move in new situations, where he felt he was caught now in stationary ones.

If I speak slowly it is simply because I am casting about in his mind for what I can find of help.

("Is he open to you now?")

Fairly, yes.

("Do you think he's blocking anything?")

I do not believe he is blocking. There are still some closed doors, however.

("In what way?")

Doors automatically closed.

("Do you think it's anything we should know in dealing with this problem?")

Give us a moment. *(Pause, hand to closed eyes.)*

You understand that because of both his father and his grandfather, <u>par-ticularly</u> his grandfather, he grew up believing it a weakness to work for others, because of the immobility involved. His grandfather as a salesman walked about freely, and his grandfather feared working for others. This aside from the writing.

("Yes." Today, also, Jane received a letter from her father, who lives in Florida. Enclosed was some belated birthday money.)

He did wait long before looking for work, and fought every step of the way, until he feared you would simply become furious. But he became more immobile, you see.

("Did the nursery school job contribute to the symptoms?")

Not the job as such.

("That's what I meant.")

It was the only kind of job he could have taken and kept for any time, outside of the Avon job. If he can realize that working out may only be temporary, he could continue doing so with no difficulty.

For a long-term arrangement, private classes, if they work financially, would be more beneficial.

("Has he suffered any physical damage from the symptoms?")

He has not so far. The chiropractic treatments should help in releasing the arms physically, and in keeping the structure in balance, since he has been unable to do so on his own. This should quiet nervous reactions, and give him time to recover.

("How about the cod liver oil suggestion?" [by the chiropractor.])

The cod liver oil is now safe enough. In the past, however, it tended to aggravate his condition because the word arthritis alone carried such emotional force. This force has now become weaker.

("Yes, but you'd never know it, watching him.")

The symptoms became aggravated again after he signed up for next year's work schedule at nursery school. Consciously he was pleased. Unconsciously, this verified his fear, that next year also he would make no money writing. He was pleased with the raise on a conscious level, but felt it blood money.

(Jane's signing a "contract" to work next winter was a point that completely

escaped both of us when her symptoms became aggravated. I also missed it in my pendulum session. It is actually merely a piece of paper, and the agreement it contains can be terminated at any time by either Jane or her employer.

("Should he consider going back to nursery school next year?")

If he is going to have an outside job it is as good as any, and after the summer should not bother him. It fills certain spontaneous needs. If however effort is to be made to find another solution—

("I thought Jane had that in mind.")

—the very fact of seeking another solution will be of great benefit, in itself, and leaves open several possibilities. The job could be kept for a semester. It could be dropped entirely, or it could be kept while trying the experiment. The fact of trying the other experiment is really important in his present state of mind particularly. It offers him an alternative beside a regular outside job, to supplement the writing income.

He has a need for mobility. What you call a normal job is confining to him because of his background, and stops up energy.

("Well, I would like to say here that I am perfectly willing to give Jane all the help she needs to attain the necessary mobility. I do understand her needs in this respect. I'd also like to say that in the future I wish she wouldn't take my word for things concerning her own feelings and affairs so literally—that she be much more independent in this respect.")

("I also ask you to help Jane understand this.")

I will help him to understand this.

Give us time for a moment. (*Pause.*) If, and whenever possible, a New York trip would benefit both of you, incidentally. He has felt held in for some time. He was also frightened because of your illness, and literally afraid to make a move. He shut off usual methods of expression, trying to be a good example to others. But this fit in beautifully with earlier conditioning.

("Yes.")

Have him buy what he likes to eat, particularly for a while, for he will eat better then. Encourage this.

("Is there anything he shouldn't eat?")

The order to eat, he interprets as an order, you see. The encouragement to eat is different. Now wait. (*Pause, eyes closed.*) Again, fried foods should be avoided. He has been right, avoiding tomato juice in the morning, instinctively. He does not need that acidity then. It is aggravating to him. The apricot you see is soothing. He has avoided fresh salads however, and you both need them. Eggplant is good. Too much whole milk is bad. In his coffee is sufficient.

Take a break and rest your hand.

(10:15-10:28)

He has felt hampered down to the most minute circumstances of his daily life. Some of this, of course, projections. You hit upon several important items in your own pendulum sessions. Hearing them voiced helped Ruburt temporarily, and then the old fear clamped down.

Your are not to blame yourself here, Joseph. This is <u>vitally</u> important, you see—

("Yes")

—and underline vitally. You did not like the radio station that he played, particularly because it was so unrestrained and noisy and blatant, and this he interpreted as a further restraint. He enjoyed Voice of the People simply because gripes were so emotionally and freely given.

It <u>may</u> be advantageous, though this is a small point, to change the living room furniture to a position that it has not been in since his illness, you see. The bed should definitely be north and south, now. That bathroom barrier should be pulled in half.

Do you have questions?

("We'd like to know how to keep those old fears from clamping down again, once they've been released.")

As a climate of permissiveness and encouragement is maintained, the symptoms will quickly vanish. You are not responsible for all of these restraints, you understand. He did not feel he had to run to move, because of the reasons given. In ordinary circumstances frequent small trips are of benefit in maintaining his overall health and efficiency level.

In times of stress this is all the more important. He had no change of environment as a child, you see. The automobile to him means freedom, and is a symbol of release.

("Is it okay to let the nursery school job for next fall, and the contract, ride for now?")

You may let it ride for now, and there is some blockage here on this particular question alone, caused by fear. Nor is it wise to overlook the fear, you see.

Summertime may or may not be a good time to begin private classes. He may be frightened to give up the job ahead of time. Any move in writing will serve him well.

(At break I asked that Seth say what he think of our recent idea that Jane show some book ideas to Don Wollheim, at Ace, as a means of mobility in her writing.)

He has been afraid to try anything new for fear of failure. Not through fear that a book would not be published necessarily, but through fear that the, publication would mean nothing. This is why the dream book is not finished.

Because of your attitude toward Fell, he did not believe you were pleased with him or the ESP book. He did not believe you considered it the achievement that he considered it. He expected you to throw a party for him.

("I did, and do, consider it an excellent achievement, and always have. But I can see how he felt the way he did, in the light of my expressed opinions about Fell. Was it a poor idea of mine to insist that Jane finish the dream book before sending it out again?" [After it was twice rejected.])

Unfortunately it was, and yet he needed to do much work on it, and in the overall you will gain. Had it been accepted, sent out and accepted later, but before this present date, the symptoms would have vanished.

He is extremely strong, open, and giving and spontaneous when he is functioning well. Any strong impediments cause him to retreat however, though for a while a smiling surface personality hides this fact.

Do you have questions? The symptoms will vanish as quickly as he <u>feels</u> restraints lifted. But he will need your encouragement, for he is himself afraid of lifting them, you see.

("Yes, but now that he understands more, his fear should fade away.")

One of the symptoms, you understand, is a fear of his own spontaneity.

("Which one?")

And therefore a fear or distrust of what may be said in these sessions. It is for this reason that I have given him evidential material, you see, in other respects, so that he could see for himself.

("Which symptom is related to a fear of his own spontaneity?")

This has been rather explained earlier this evening, and in previous sessions: Previous conditioning, and we explained why he became sensitized to this. The fear of spontaneity is what made him so passive in following suggestions of yours, to which he did not agree.

Do you have other questions?

("I guess we can call it a night.")

Then I do think I have been of help. I will endeavor to contact Ruburt as you suggest.

("One question: How about my hypnotizing him?")

There will be no danger there, and it should be of benefit.

(10:50. Jane now reported that for the last couple of deliveries she had been far-out, and remembered little of the material.)

SESSION 345
JUNE 12, 1967 9 PM MONDAY

(I spent the afternoon using the pendulum and compiling a list of foods Jane shouldn't eat, according to my own subconscious ideas. The idea was to see how accurate my delineations had been. Jane and I discussed the list before the session. A copy of the list will be found at the end of the session.

(Jane sat at the living room table with me and began speaking with her eyes closed, in a normal voice and at a good pace.)

Good evening.

("Good evening, Seth.")

Now. We have made several important breakthroughs here.

A major one completed since our last session. This happened this morning when Ruburt allowed his true feelings toward the work situation to emerge on a conscious level. (*Re Jane's own use of the pendulum after breakfast.*)

The feelings were responsible for the blocking mentioned in our last session, and represent the plucking of the sorest thorn from his flesh, symbolically. Without the emergence into consciousness, the difficulties would have continued to some degree.

There would have been no overwhelming conflict for him, hence no such physical symptoms as he has encountered, if he was content, you see, basically to let you carry the financial ball—in other words, if he were truly a dependent personality.

In that case, the symptoms, whatever they were, would most likely have been yours.

The conflict has never been that he resented having to make extra money outside of writing. The conflict—when it was touched off you see by the need to make more money again—the conflict resulted from what would <u>appear</u> to be two methods of making money. One method he felt was highly favored by you, and by far it seemed the most dependable, and he chose it.

In the past, it had been at least acceptable to him, because he felt it a temporary means. His own overexpectations, or rather unrealistic expectations concerning his book, and the mistakes he felt were connected with it, sensitized him, until he felt that outside money would be a permanent part of his life.

The method, a job, now became unacceptable. But only the method. The signs were obvious. Whenever he fights what you want, or believe necessary, there is a very strong reason, and you had both better inquire into it, for he does not cross you lightly. And when he does, he does so in such a manner as to shield himself from the knowledge, you see.

The symptoms then began as he began to think in terms of job hunting. Your remarks concerning the benefits of a regular job would bring the symptoms to a pitch, and did so as recently as a week or so ago.

("How about Sunday, on the way home? [The 11th; yesterday.])

Ruburt was quite too psychically upset to get clear access to me. Not a case of blocking necessarily here. A case of tumultuous activity that automatically clogged our communication, on quite key matters.

This is a rather natural result of Ruburt's brief experience. As our sessions continue, I will be able to help you more and more, you see.

The nursery school was at the time the only move he felt really open to him. He was afraid he would not manage a steady income with the Avon, and already frightened of the mobility it demanded. Nursery school seemed to offer a compromise between your idea of a regular job, and his own dislike of one. He felt guilty at turning down the yoga classes, yet he felt that to match your performance he was expected to work five afternoons. His symptoms were aggravated again on the signing of the contract, and highly again when he refused the summer position.

For various reasons, the men in his family, his grandfather on his father's side, whom he did not know, his maternal grandfather and <u>his</u> father, were highly independent, insisting upon working for themselves. Ruburt picked up this <u>Indian</u> trait from the maternal grandfather.

<u>His</u> father, in his old age, did have a job for others, as did Joe in <u>his</u> late years. In both cases, the jobs were considered marks of degradation. From the Irish side, a woman who worked for others, you see, was a domestic. There was, in the family history, always a struggle to work for oneself, this being a matter of class pride and independence.

All of these issues bear on Ruburt's idea of a job. His money potential will be strengthened if these matters are highly considered. It is not a question of fearing to face reality financially. There is an effective and efficient way for him to do so, and he has been too frightened and panic-stricken to try it.

He is for that matter still frightened, and will need your support. If this were not the case he would have given notice for next year now. All of these have been involved with his writing, obviously. When he was enthused about its future, the secondary aspects of making additional cash did not critically concern him.

He was bothered particularly, you see, because his own mother's position makes him terrified of being financially dependent, yet the way he chose to make, money at this particular point was precisely the wrong way for him at this time.

The thought—do you want to rest?

("Yes.")

You may take a break.

(9:32. Jane said she was far-out. She was not aware of outside noise, etc, and spoke fast, eyes open often as the delivery progressed.

(Resume at 9:45.)

The need for money, and the fear of being dependent then, led him to seek money through a method which, once acceptable, was now highly and critically unacceptable for the reasons given.

He felt his own respect and yours, he must take a job, and a regular one—and for the reasons given this had highly unpleasant repercussions that led to symptoms of immobility. These symptoms further aggravated his fears of dependence, and in his worse moments he feared that he would become a cripple and you would leave him. This was when the mother identification was at its peak—now long past.

The result, of course, was a complete stoppage of writing for a time. We managed to get some signs through to you in our sessions, and he would have been in worse condition had they been cut out.

Had the same time and effort been given then to the kind of endeavors he is now planning, as was given to the selection of a job, there would have been no further difficulty.

Now, unless you have further questions on this specific material, we will discuss the foods.

("Okay.")

Give us a moment here. *(Pause, eyes closed.)*

Were it not for the close connection between you, you would not have been able to receive the material that you did through the pendulum.

It was correct, even to the percentage. This is not unusual however, but happens often. When the whole personality is in a high period of stress, and unbalanced, it works against itself even chemically. Various foods are then used in a destructive way, representing the emotional conflicting forces.

In periods of health this is greatly minimized. Cutting out the foods however will not cure a condition alone. The inner problems must be recognized and solved. Then the foods will no longer be a grave matter of concern.

Avoiding the foods during periods of stress is indeed a benefit however. The whole problem, discussed this evening and in the last session, is indeed the major thorn behind the difficulties, and all symptoms, and caused the food reactions you see.

The problems were related to Ruburt's own writing, as you see. This last

Saratoga episode was highly beneficial, even though it frightened Ruburt because he was afraid to use the freedom offered to him. There was great emotional charge behind the whole reunion question, and the "shall I go—shall I not go"—questioning discharged long withheld energy. Symbolically Ruburt came to grips with the whole Saratoga problem with his mother and the past.

(Last Saturday morning, June 10, I offered to take Jane to the 20th reunion of her high school class in Saratoga. A week before that date, I wouldn't have considered making such an offer. At the last moment Jane decided not to go, and I did not insist, hoping she had still benefited from the thought of going, at least.)

Even though he did not make the trip he came out on top. He was afraid to go in the last analysis, but he was not afraid to go for the old reasons.

Now. There is no distortion or blockage here. There has been a great clearing, and there are massive improvements and openings psychically and emotionally, that are resulting in a resumption of health.

A large percentage of this improvement is based upon the fact that Ruburt is anticipating a future joyfully again, in the contemplation of classes, privately given. (*In ESP.*) This sort of endeavor cannot be stressed too highly as an antidote to all symptoms. (*Pause.*)

The endeavor should be begun realistically. There is a difference between excellent expectations thoroughly believed in which are beneficial, and superficially adopted overexpectations that are not basically believed.

Ruburt should expect to do well, and he shall. Patience and stubbornness can also be used here in this endeavor, as he used them to poor advantage to a job. Do you see my point here?

("Yes.")

At the first sign of failure last autumn with the ESP column, he pulled out entirely, while he applied for job after job.

You may rest or end the session as you prefer.

("We'll rest.")

(10:10—10:20.)

There is literally tremendous energy that can be used and tapped for your benefit, and for the benefit of others in connection with Ruburt's idea for classes.

Considerable thought and contemplation should be used here, and as much energy devoted as would be given in the search for a job, for the potentials are far greater. Let Ruburt's determination be applied here and it will meet with constructive benefits. It will solve a long-standing problem that otherwise will always be of some concern.

It is a central material problem in your lives, and you have the equipment to solve it, and the opportunity. You, Joseph, will also be benefited here, and in ways you cannot now see. The matter should be given primary energy, concern and interest. I do not mean <u>above</u> Ruburt's work, for example, but it will blend with it.

Do avoid the foods for now. Except for a barrier, yes, Ruburt may do what he wishes with his furniture. The desire to do so represents the fact that he is beginning to realize his freedoms.

I will end our session. However we shall hold our regular Wednesday session to these same matters. For Ruburt's benefit: He is being forced to solve his problem now, to find the solution for <u>him</u>. Had he been alone he would simply have been forced to solve it earlier.

My heartiest wishes to you both; and again to Joseph, there is no <u>blame</u> here, you see, for you. These are challenges set, and you are both facing them.

(*"Good night, Seth."*

(*End at 10:30.*

(*Below is a copy of the question-and-answer session I held with myself and the pendulum on the afternoon of June 12, 1967, today, in an effort to see what subconscious knowledge I might have that would benefit Jane.*

(*It will be remembered that Seth has mentioned allergies re Jane and food on occasion in a mild way. I thought a detailed report of what foods Jane should avoid would help alleviate her symptoms, if there was any relationship. My pendulum said there was. The answers I obtained did not vary and the pendulum gave definite yes-and-no answers, without quibbling. To me this meant there was legitimate data there.*

(*The list is a summary of three other pages of detailed notes, which are on file. To my surprise, when Jane checked the list with her own pendulum at about 8PM, before the session, she received definite answers that agreed with each item on my list. A qualification appeared only under the chocolate headings where Jane's pendulum said she could use the dry malt mixes now in stores, as opposed to the regular old-time cocoa used in baking, hot chocolate, etc. I definitely did not expect such complete agreement on Jane's part with my list.*)

COPY

(*June 12, 1967. Summary of my pendulum question-and-answer session about Jane's food allergies. According to the pendulum the answers obtained are not projections of my own problems.*

(*Jane should not eat:*

1) <u>Any</u> fried foods, no matter what cooked in, even their own juices. This *includes meats, vegetables, pancakes, French toast, potatoes [and chips], doughnuts, any pastries, etc.*

2) Lemons or extracts.

3) Mushrooms and mushroom soup. [All other soups okay, store and home-made.]

4) Olives.

5) Beer.

6) Ice cream.

7) Chocolate in any form: Cake, ice cream, donuts, pie, candy, cookies, drinks or malts, puddings and sherbets, etc.

(Here, Jane's pendulum said it was okay for her to use the dry malt mixes recently introduced in food stores, because these contained no emotional charge for her. But her pendulum stressed also that all other chocolate and products should be avoided.

1) Margarine, with corn oil. [Okay to use margarine without corn content.]

2) Corn—either fresh or canned, any kind, including corn oil in margarine.

3) Corn oil in cooking.

4) Garlic and garlic salts.

5) Tomatoes, including fresh or any kind of canned. No canned beans in tomato sauce, or salad dressings with tomato ingredients. No sauce with tomatoes on spaghetti and meat balls. [Strangely, can eat tomatoes on pizza; and chili; the only two exceptions according to my pendulum.]

6) Canned tomato juice.

7) Canned grapefruit juice.

8) Jane shouldn't use skimmed milk in coffee or on cereal. Can drink it.

9) Jane shouldn't drink whole milk. Can use it in coffee or on cereal.

(At the moment, 7:30 PM on Monday, June 12, pendulum tells me the above list is complete and correct. Ordinarily these foods responsible for about 15 percent of any physical symptoms Jane may have, including sinus. Now when she is sensitized, they account for about 80 percent of physical symptoms. Energy is at present being diverted from the sinus condition to other physical symptoms. It is okay for Jane to take Rexall Plenamins [vitamins].)

SESSION 346
JUNE 14, 1967 9 PM WEDNESDAY

(Once again Jane sat at the table with me as I took notes.)
Now. Give us a moment, please. *(Pause.)*

Ruburt's habit is to direct his energies unstintingly focused in a more or less single direction. When he feels desolate, therefore, the desolation you see is almost complete to him.

He is as stubborn in it as he is in preserving his joy when he is joyful. Compromise is very difficult for him. In periods of spontaneity therefore he will sometimes be overly spontaneous, and in a times of rigidity will be overly rigid.

He was beginning to learn a beneficial balance when this trouble began. His loyalty to you is unswerving, as unfortunately many of his bitter attitudes toward those in his past are unswerving.

He tempers the bitterness with understanding more than he realizes however, and because of his particular sense of right and wrong, he overly blames himself for what bitterness he has. He is learning now, finally, to be more flexible. The stubborn qualities will later serve us well. The release and self-knowledge gained is this last painful episode will allow him to bring more freedom to our sessions.

This will result in complete belief on his part, and this belief will enable us to achieve results denied us in the past. He will fight <u>for</u> us, you see. He is now completely determined upon health, and the recovery will be remarkably fast, now that it has truly begun, simply because his released energies will now work at it with their accustomed vigor—only now for his benefit.

The releases in his personality could have been achieved in other, easier methods. Nevertheless without these alterations our work could not be fulfilled in all the ways possible. His rigidity of attitude resulted in a trend for self-destruction, tempered it is true, but dangerous. There was a resultant manufacture of various chemicals within his system that tended to reproduce and perpetuate the depressed state of mind. An overproduction of adrenaline that kept him stirred up, but also an overproduction of certain chemicals that physically slowed him down.

He felt danger strongly but could not run, you see. The resultant heaviness of limb, the swelling of various portions of the body having to do with an overproduction of a chemical, I believe, called pectorin, or something very similar.

These conditions are already being reversed due to the change of mental climate. The alarms are off. The treatments being taken did indeed physically relieve nerve pressures and rigidity, but would not have done so had the mental condition not already been relieved.

There is far less danger when his spontaneity overerupts. The ensuing difficulties, if any, are those he dealt when as an adolescent. <u>Then</u> they were heightened by lack of experience, you see. He feared them, adopting instead now the opposite tendency.

Give us another moment. (*Pause, hand to closed eyes.*)

The symptoms occurring much less frequently now in the middle of the night refer back to preadolescent fears of immobility because of the parent. Helplessness when laying flat, you see, unconscious and in bed. They can be minimized in three fashions, in any of three fashions.

Your suggestion that he arise at once is an excellent one, intuitively received. This of course presupposes the fact that the symptoms are present to alarm him. If the alarm is set at four-hour intervals, this can eliminate the onset of symptoms, but in each case he would then rise and move about some. This does not seem necessary since the symptoms are now minimized, but I believe the step would prevent them entirely.

He may, on the other hand, tell himself that I am there, watching out for him, and I shall be glad to do so as I have on many an occasion. Often I could not get through to him, but now I will tell him that I will be present.

If he had awakened you, or if he would, the comfort of your presence would largely dissipate the symptoms, for it is the fear of being alone and immobile, you see, that is to him at such times, because of the parent, terrifying. This condition is temporary and already disappearing, as you know.

It was difficult in very early years for his mother to get about in the morning. Later he learned that his aunt was a slow riser, feeling sickly in the mornings. These two suggestions had much to do with the early morning symptoms, and these also, you see, are now vanishing.

You may take a break.

(9:30—9:40.)

Now. This oversubmissiveness was caused by fear, and masqueraded as a quite legitimate loyalty. The loyalty was always there.

When he felt he could not act following his uncompromising nature, he attempted to submit, you see. The resulting resentment was the true basis for all symptoms, and attracted the other sensitivities that nourished them.

For your vacation, choose definitely a place with water, a large body, for it is healing. Drive if possible along a seashore for your route. (*Pause.*)

I am casting about to see what I have missed of importance. (*Pause.*) A bedroom with two windows would be of help but is not feasible now. A pale yellow on the walls rather than the white would be of benefit, in that room, you see. It is imperative that Ruburt throw considerable energy into his idea for classes; whether in writing or in psychic matters, that all available, practically available time and effort be given here to such an endeavor; that it not be adopted half-heartedly.

The dream book should be concentrated upon, and the other ideas he has in mind worked up. He will quite possibly end up finally with other quarters for classes.

The predictions concerning money were made before Ruburt's energies were so misdirected, <u>thrown</u> so suddenly against himself, that even I was appalled. They were based as you know on probabilities, and this tumultuous reaction, while a probability, was not a strong one. All these energies were suddenly swept in the wrong direction. They are now swinging to his aid, and you can now at least be thankful for their amazing nature, for the healthful turn will be ever more evident.

Give us a moment. (*Pause.*) The thyroid, strangely enough, was depressed in activity because he feared you see his previous history. The nervous energy however grew by leaps and bounds despite this fact, and the body did not properly use the foods that were consumed.

This condition has vanished. The weight will now show gains, and the thyroid is operating at normal rates. The resentments are largely being nullified. They are not completely gone, or no symptoms would remain.

Your attitude has much to do with his improvement. He felt alone, this his fault, surely as much as yours, though no fault in those terms is meant. At his worse moments, he thought that he could not love a cripple, since he did not love his mother, so how could you.

He will most likely still need help in embarking on your vacation, although his progress is improving. There may be mail from Wisconsin that will have a bearing on some future plans. A male involved in connection with the psychic matters. He has not purchased shifts because of the old picture of his mother in the sun, wearing a dress you see. The loss of weight was partially a defense mechanism, for his mother grew stout. He did not feel it safe, you see.

Now. Buy some peanut oil indeed, and rub it on the elbows and shoulders and knees for three days. Wait three days and renew the treatment.

("*How many times a day?*")

Once. This will also benefit the back and neck region if used there. This may be washed off after three hours.

("*Why will this be of benefit?*")

There is a quality in the oil, an extract from the peanuts, that is immediately dissolved through the skin, that lubricates and eases both the joints and muscles. Peanut butter is also beneficial, and peanuts eaten raw. These are merely aids.

("*Why aren't his arms straight?*")

Give us a moment with this. Not in order necessarily here; at one time he feared a wheelchair, and has a long-forgotten image of his mother in one, with bent arms. He felt helpless to push away his difficulties, and unable to <u>support</u> himself.

The arm crookedness developed shortly after he turned down the summer position, though by stages, and is related to the fact that the dream book, a possible means of support, is not ready to be sent out. Work on the dream book will help relieve the arm symptoms. Indeed his fingers released when he began to type again on that book.

("What happened to him in the middle of last night?")

His pendulum answered correctly. However the reasons I have given for evening symptoms entered in here. The night sensitivity, you see, vanished when our sessions began, and returned masked with symptoms when his difficulties began. Speaking his name will also help here. Such instances will become further separated however, and finally disappear.

You may take your break. He felt incapable of motion, you see, and interpreted this physically. Now the symptoms vanish because he realizes he does have mobility and freedom. He did not dare look to the left, nor the right.

(10:09—10:22.)

We will shortly end our session.

This evening's present symptoms are the result of the fact that Friday is already thought of as a school day. These can be dissipated if Ruburt reminds himself before sleeping of his intent to work on the dream book <u>tomorrow</u> and Friday morning.

The plain apricot juice is best for breakfast, rather than the orange combination, which is acid. The orange apricot juice is all right with eggs and toast, but not with milk and cereal.

("How about canned peaches?")

Very good. Or grape or banana. (*Long pause.*) The concentration upon the dream book, along with other writing ideas and the classes, will insure the rapid recovery. The vacation will break up any lingering patterns of habit, and serve to disconnect him from negative elements of the past. The water and the sun will have an overall curative effect, and your continuing overall support will add the necessary and quite vital reassurance.

Your suggestion of time in the sun daily is excellent. An evening walk is also advantageous. He will literally soak up affection now as he soaks up the sun, and it will have equal healing effect. The resulting exuberance and strength will be solidly based, and add to your overall happiness as well as Ruburt's. All of these help him release his energy and focus it in the proper directions. This energy, used to solve your financial problem, or Ruburt's financial problem, will yield rich benefits. Now to Ruburt: I am with you this evening, and to you both my heartiest wishes.

("Got time for a question?")

Indeed.

("Why doesn't Jane like to iron?")

An old response, caused by the necessity to iron on occasion as a child on demand, and her mother's unreasoning fastidiousness, as the <u>child</u> saw it. Here a mark, one of the few small marks, of rebellion he allotted himself. You had another question in mind.

("Yes.")

His mother often demanded the bedpan just before meals, and he thought this was to annoy him. He did it to annoy you, and show resentment. Also to deny himself, since the food would be cold.

Do you have any other questions?

("No.")

We will then end our session. The peanut oil can be applied before sunning, or before sleep.

("Good night, Seth.")

(10:38.)

SESSION 347
JUNE 19, 1967 9 PM MONDAY

Good evening

("Good evening, Seth.")

Now. The change of schedule is a good idea this week, because it will get Ruburt used to the idea of using freedom again, before your vacation starts, and will therefore offset <u>possible</u> symptoms. Do you see?

(Yes.")

The breaking up of patterns is also beneficial, and is of course one of the reasons I suggest your vacation.

("Is it okay for us to go to Saratoga?")

This should be perfectly all right. Ruburt should not visit his mother however, nor waste any time wondering about the matter.

The vacation falling between and breaking up, you see, the nursery school pattern and the remainder of the summer, will be most beneficial. Much better than a later vacation—more useful.

The breaking up of patterns in this respect is most important. It is a sort of shock therapy. There should indeed be fairly frequent weekend trips, perhaps camping if you prefer, during the entire summer.

Now the benefits of such activities, and hear me now, cannot be over-emphasized. They will aid you both. and they are great preventive measures, for precisely the sort of difficulties you have both in the past been heir to. They force a stir of thought and psychic activity. They automatically interact against any kind of rigidity.

This is most important for this summer. The same sort of activity last summer could have broken Ruburt's pattern sufficiently enough to prevent the severity of the past difficulties. You cannot afford not to take these steps. Not only this year but as a matter of course. While we are here, let me add that some sort of away-environment should be kept up as long as weather permits. This does not necessarily mean long trips.

The anticipated change of schedule now will help Ruburt conquer problems that otherwise could be bothersome this week, and will head off any difficulties. The next week, the vacation week, will see a remarkable change for the better. The result of the breakup of pattern giving him time to rest and utilize, through constructive habit, what he has learned.

The change of schedule will help break up the symptoms, old C U E (*spelled*) points being scattered. The mental and psychic state is indeed radically improved. There is some lapse here for physical expression. While it is completely possible for the mental state to express itself at once, nevertheless within your system, under most circumstances, there is a lapse, as the symptoms themselves did not immediately appear, although the mental state was in dire circumstance.

The lag is partially the result of cues to action. These gradually lose their strength and as the personality, in a better state of mind, is no longer as sensitive to those cues. For a while it is still somewhat more sensitive, for example, to moods or depressions that it would ordinarily sail through. The overall condition has indeed remarkably improved, as I told you, and there is no distortion here.

The physical results are now showing in greater daytime freedoms, and will continue to improve. The definite steps you plan will quicken the results so that they become more apparent to you physically. Ruburt's mental energies, as I told you, are now accumulating and working to recovery.

In the beginning of this recovery they were used to maintain the status quo, and prevent any further worsening of symptoms. This meant that a complete stop was made in all destructive issues. Such an action requires enormous energy alone, for it is the stoppage of a process which is in itself action.

This state was maintained steadily, and held, and then the recovery process begun. In this case this represented an entire, almost complete, transformation of the circulating system, and a change of chemical interactions. The mental condition you see has not deteriorated since its improvement. The whole outlook of the psychic self has changed for the better.

Energy was released. Much of this was used in immediate repair, and in a complete reversal of the illness-health cycle; that is, the symptoms were not allowed to worsen. When this condition again was held, recovery began.

The cue points began to break up of themselves, and your anticipated activities will further aid in their deterioration. The offending foods were cue points, you see. Once the reversal process has begun and the personality swung back toward health, then the process shows what seems to be remarkable recovery.

The main and indispensable job that makes recovery possible, the all-important reversal process, has already occurred, however. Your treatments from the chiropractor for example are of benefit now, but would not have been earlier. They are a physical aid now to a process already begun.

The morning symptoms here represented in concentrated form the vanishing power of the illness that swept him through, the vanishing force of what was an all-day condition at one time. Do you understand me here?

("Yes.")

They are the ghost, you see. Perhaps I did not put myself clearly. (*In the last session.*) They are vanishing, in that they no longer have the power to frighten him in the same way that his physical symptoms had in the past. He can see, even in them, his way out of them. Physically speaking in your terms, they will be largely, and I mean largely, minimized as these actions of yours break up the cues. This week and next, in other words, if you follow your plans.

They are being squeezed into a smaller and smaller portion of his life. Do you see?

("Yes.")

A certain plateau seems to have been reached, after at first more noticeable improvement, after our session. (*The 344th session, June 7, 1967.*)

("Yes.")

The personality holds its own after each improvement, you see, and then makes further ones. This does not mean the process could not be quicker. There has been an improvement today in the left arm. This represented a mental decision, finally made, to use this week to work on his book.

The left arm is in the position of having held its own now, and now starting toward physical improvement. Barriers are now falling away. The rubble is being cleared, you see. This week could have been a bad one. Ruburt learned however from his experience and has taken steps so that it will now add to his recovery. This represents a considerable step forward.

He is making an endeavor to speak to you, not only in the resentments, but wishes. There was therefore interaction last evening when he felt resentful on a sensitive matter. He already felt he had reached a victory in approaching you after arguing with himself. He will not always be so sensitive to rebuff, you see.

("Yes.")

In the matter of weight also there was first a point where weight process was reversed, where the weight was held steady before a gain could be made. There should be no difficulty here now. The poor lunches on nursery school days were the result of resentment because of the school hours.

Often he wanted you to approach him in intimate terms, but felt unworthy because of his condition, and because he <u>felt</u> that you found it distasteful, and even degrading. This set up conflict on going to bed, you see.

("I found his condition inhibiting, but only at times. And there wasn't any thought of degradation.")

He knew this, this being fairly natural, but he exaggerated your feeling, you see, because of his mental attitude, and felt he would be asking for alms.

You may take a break and we shall continue briefly.

(9:50. Jane's delivery had been a long and active one, her eyes open often as she spoke forcefully, and there had been no hint of the usual break at about 9:30. Resume at 10:06.)

Reasonable daily exposure to the sun is physically beneficial to him, and symbolically beneficial, in the sense that the sun is light.

By all means, you should go to the seashore for some part of your vacation. The sea is especially healing. The arthritis symptoms as such have largely vanished. What you have now is a stiff condition, you see, and all arthritis symptoms have been cut off from any actual development, in your terms. There was <u>never</u> any arthritis, but now those adopted symptoms are disappearing.

("What's the swelling actually due to?")

The swelling has to do with a chemical that encouraged in certain parts of the body only a retention of fluid, and this was aggravated by beer consumption, and also by the drinking of whole milk.

("Can you name the chemical, approximately?")

(Pause.) PEC... P E C... I believe, (shakes head) Pectorillin... (My phonetic interpretation). I am no medical man... Because of the psychological condition he extracted, or he used this in both whole milk and beer, in such a way that it left residues near certain joints, blocking passageways and allowing fluids to accumulate. These are now working outward normally through the system as the circulatory system becomes normally activated. There may have been a connection with salt here also, but this is past.

(See pages 47-48, for the list of foods I learned that Jane should avoid through my own pendulum. Beer and whole milk are contained in the list. My pendulum said salt was okay for Jane. I believe the chemical Seth may have been groping for is purine. I knew this word but Jane did not; nor did she understand the formation of crystals near joints because of this chemical, which could then cause swelling. The chiropractor verified this data the day after this session was held.)

The arms are responding, and as they do so then the fingers will resume their normal condition. Some yoga exercises, <u>gently</u> done, will now be of benefit. The peanut oil will also help the arms and loosen the neck and shoulder areas. The oil should not be kept in the refrigerator, but should be fairly warm.

Do you have any further questions?

("I guess not.")

The oil will also benefit the knees.

("How about if he uses some of it tonight, if he stays up to write as he plans?")

He may use it any time it is convenient. I do not know whether it stains, for example. It would be particularly beneficial before sleeping, massaged in or before swimming. We will then end our session. My heartiest wishes to you both.

("Good night, Seth.")

(End at 10:26.)

SESSION 348
JUNE 21, 1967 9 PM WEDNESDAY

Good evening.

("Good evening, Seth.")

Now. For your vacation there should be a balance of rest and activity, dancing for example, and an interchange with others.

There should be sunbathing, but also activity, you see.

Psychic interchanges with others will be beneficial. Ruburt has indeed done well this week, the symptom storms becoming less and less frequent, and much briefer in duration as well as weaker in overall intensity. The old patterns are breaking down.

A truly enjoyable vacation is indeed the best medicine now for reasons given. This and your encouragement, by all means stay away as long as possible, and keep in mind my advice pertaining to the rest of the summer. I gave you this advice some time ago and it was not heeded.

You are also in need of a change of environment *(pointing to me)* and you will receive insights concerning your work as a result. This will be a brief session, as I believe I have covered all the pertinent material concerning Ruburt's state at this time.

If you have questions, however, I shall answer them.

("Want to say a few words about the group in California?")

Give us a moment. (*Pause.*

(My question came because we had just received a long emotional letter from Julie Murtough in Chula Vista.)

The girl will not be involved in an airplane accident. The boy is using day-dreams concerning Australia to avoid facing present problems. There will be a return to Australia, but not for some time. (*Long pause.*) Ruburt is bothered by traffic this evening, and it interferes. I do not want to attempt information on the friends in California until conditions are better. There is however uneasiness, as you know, in the family, and the boy operates in such a manner that he picks up the inner feelings of the others, and is left to handle them as best he can. The mother is more important in the family group than our friends realize.

In a strange manner she holds the family together, simply because they unite so strongly against her. Without this they would be less united. A rather delicate psychological gestalt operates with the family as a whole. The father actually is not the uniting principle here, but the feeling against the mother, at this time.

There are reasons for this of course that can be discussed if our friends request it or desire it at another time.

Do you have other questions? Ruburt, incidentally, because of his blessed literal nature, will not feel fully released from his job until the last day is over.

("Is the contract he signed going to bother him?")

When it begins to bother him he will break it. There will be no difficulty with the organization.

I believe that his (*ESP*) class will work up to seven by the end of spring, or very early fall, stay at that level, and then be joined by others. This, in line with the probabilities now acting.

Put down here, F A M. These may be considered separately... I do not know. Also perhaps a private student.

I will here end the session unless you have further questions. I will be available whenever you may want to speak to me, if you do, during your absence from here.

> ("Good night, Seth.")
> (9:19.)

SESSION 349
JUNE 28, 1967 APPROXIMATELY 11 PM WEDNESDAY

(A short unscheduled session was held on this date, with Bill Macdonnel and his friend Joanie Gilbert as witnesses. The session resulted after the stage had been set earlier in the evening, through Jane's playing the tape recently received from the Murtough family in Chula Vista, CA; and, afterward, her playing part of the tape made some time ago for Dr. Instream.

(Jane spoke actively, her eyes open much of the time. Bill began scribbling notes after the session began; I was not taking any, and hadn't planned to. Jane spoke rather rapidly and Bill couldn't keep up verbatim-wise, but did get down most of the gist of what Seth was saying.

(The following is taken from Bill's notes. I tried not to add to these unwittingly in order to make the content better, but did attempt to make them a little more readable.)

...Instream is due to join me soon, February at the latest. He will then speak to you, but not as he would like to speak... He is now living in a town beginning with the letter A.

(Jane now placed her right hand over her heart, and repeated herself several times, eyes closed.)

...An excitement of the heart... Dr. Instream will die of an excitement of the heart... 5 2 7 levels... Doctor Brownallen... Brownline... Allen Brown, the doctor. The write-up will be in the *International Journal of Parapsychology*.

(Bill did not indicate any month, and I do not recall if a month was mentioned for the death notice.)

The Wisconsin material will develop shortly... Involve Ruburt's work...

(Jane pointed to Joanie.) Our friend here should stay away from lettuce... *(I asked why.)* There is oversimulation, reacting upon her system... that does not enable her to correctly perceive the nature of her own experiences... Too much stimulation without understanding.

(Seth here refers to the psychic experiences Joanie had been describing to us, and doesn't go into any detail re the lettuce.

(We took a break. During it Joanie enthusiastically verified that she has the odd habit of eating lettuce, a head at a time, as another person might eat candy or

pretzels. She will do this with her mother, for instance, while they watch a late movie on TV, etc. She has had the habit since childhood, she told us.

(Jane and I have met Joanie a few times before, without any knowledge of her lettuce-eating habit, and can attest that Seth's data here was as much a surprise to us as to Joanie or Bill. We regard this one line of data as a direct hit on Seth's part.

(After break I took verbatim notes for the rest of the session.)

Now my dear friend, I will leave you. My heartiest wishes to you all. Look after Ruburt.

([Bill:] "Seth...")

And indeed, yes.

([Bill:] "What about your visit to me?")

All right. Here we have a legitimate occasion, in which Ruburt projected to your room, and I acted as his guide. You saw me and you did not see Ruburt. We were both there.

([Bill:] "What about the cigarette?" Bill saw a cigarette in Seth's hand.)

The cigarette was your own construction, representing your inner realization that the cigarette-smoking Ruburt was there but not present. I smoked cigars. You constructed the idea of the cigarette you see. Now give us a moment. *(Pause.)*

There is an S A G. If you meet someone with these letters significantly in their name, avoid them. *(Bill is about to embark on a tour of the country.)*

Ruburt is finished, and I shall, of necessity, say good evening.

("Good night, Seth."

(End at 12:12 AM. Joanie Gilbert reiterated that she eats a head of lettuce at a time, and has done so since she was a little girl.)

SESSION 350
JULY 6, 1967 9 PM THURSDAY

(On July 3 and July 5th, I held long pendulum sessions, trying to learn what subconscious role I have been playing in Jane's symptoms. I obtained much valid information. Jane at first did not agree with my findings, but her own pendulum verified my results.

(We were most anxious to have a session Wednesday, as scheduled, to check the findings. We had company however at the last minute, so put off the session for a day.)

Now, good evening.

("Good evening, Seth.")

We have come to our moment of truth, I see.

I knew it was approaching, and I gave you all the hints that I could in the past. I was not allowed to speak but in the most opaque of terms.

Your combined emotional state amounts to an atmosphere, highly charged, through which I must penetrate. I have done my best, and yet I highly regret I could do so little. The blockage was not only Ruburt's, but your own. It was an emotional shield, and I gave you all the hints I could.

Now, my dear Joseph... You have also been jealous of Ruburt's part in our sessions, and at times highly resentful, particularly of the attention he received when others were present. In the overall however while you were delighted on the one hand to have the sessions, you were jealous of the part Ruburt played.

Ruburt therefore, sensing this, and abnormally sensitive to your wishes at this time, would not let the sessions be used to wound you, and bent his efforts to block such material. You also put up resistance because of your jealousy. The combined efforts held any help I could give to a minimum.

This contest between you had much to do with Ruburt's fear in obtaining reincarnational material that could perhaps be checked. He felt you did not want him to succeed here, and that despite what you <u>said</u>, for you always verbally encouraged him, you did not want him to receive clairvoyant checkable material. You were jealous of his rather limited projection attempts, and he stopped them for this reason.

As far as the sessions were concerned, he felt for some time that you demanded them, and on the other hand resented his part in them. You were also pleased with the sessions on quite another level, and on this level honestly accepted Ruburt's part in them, although you still wished this part were played by yourself.

You knew that the sessions were highly beneficial, and you were convinced of my own legitimacy. It was indeed because you were so convinced that you envied Ruburt's part. While you asked Ruburt to let me give you help for Ruburt's condition, for some time the symptoms' continuation was important to you for the reasons you now understand.

The climate has cleared enough so that I can give you this material now. Consciously Ruburt did not even suspect it. There are many matters to discuss here, you see, and reasons for your own behavior, which should be understood.

Now Ruburt has said, and I have said, do not blame yourself, and this is valid in those terms. It is much more important that you understand the mesh-works that exist, and the importance of integrity in dealings with the self.

Denied feelings gather emotional impetus, and form emotional storms. There are ways to prevent such buildups. I strongly suggested a vacation, and it is because prior conditions were still operating that the two of you did not overcome your obstacles and leave.

Your friend's invitation was a direct answer to your need, which was telepathically received. The way, in other words, was provided. Such a change, drastic and complete, would have resulted in a shock to your own psychic system as well as Ruburt's.

(On July 4, Pat Norelli telephoned us from Boston inviting us up for as long as we wanted to stay at her apartment.)

You had also been operating on inner cues which would have been broken, and in these lapses buried intuitions would have leaped up, bringing these truths in their wake. Frequent changes, as I told you, are beneficial <u>for that reason</u>.

Objects and conditions within the habitual environment become changed with various emotions, to which you can then rather automatically react, without questioning their validity. Free from these charged objects and conditions, the same response you see may suddenly strike you with surprise, and you will question it. This is highly simplified, but very valid indeed.

Some of your feelings of jealousy, <u>some</u> (underlined) come from your knowledge of your mother's feelings. Once the jealousy became charged enough then you became sensitive to these telepathically received feelings of hers, and they nourished your own.

Ruburt indeed felt attacked, but he would not fight against you, you see. He fought, but without ever daring face what it was he was fighting. Conditions in his own past prepared him for this docility, for which indeed his mother ridiculed him frequently; and yet the symptoms themselves, you see, were a way to fight you. For if he suffered because of them, he knew that you would also suffer, until finally you would have to admit the truths that could set you both free.

He knew that he would never do this. There is a strange, indeed rock-bottom refusal here, on his part to hurt anyone deeply, for whatever reason. It is impossible for his personality therefore to do anything <u>he feels</u> (underlined) would hurt the one person in the world with whom he feels close.

This is the result of his intimate knowledge of what it is to be so hurt, connected with the mother experience. Therefore in this situation he would fight back but he could not hurt you. This did not leave him with much room. You did leave him with some however, for the symptoms themselves were the means that would bring you to these realizations. And he knew underneath that it would only go so far before you would realize what was happening. He did not know where the point was however.

Do you want a rest?

("I think so."

(Break at 9:40. Jane's pace had been a bit fast, the voice stronger, eyes open often, many gestures, etc. Resume at 10:50.)

Now. The duality in your own psychic condition, Joseph, would have eventually destroyed your capacity to work.

This would have operated as a self-punishment for the symptoms inflicted upon Ruburt, had they continued throughout any period of years. Such duality cannot exist for long without destroying creative aspects of the personality.

Ruburt would have continued to work, though physically quite incapacitated. These conditions however would not likely have resulted. You both had something very strong working for you, still strong enough to help, and that was the creative intuitive nature, which would have in one way or another made the facts plain.

The time element however could have been lengthened. Both of you actually decided that the situation had gone too far, and had telepathically communicated. The strength of Ruburt's telepathic communication terrified you because you then felt the terrific burden that had been upon you, and this set you to work with the pendulum.

You had made your peace, both of you, at another level, but the two personalities as you know them still had to come to terms in <u>your</u> normal reality. Ruburt has an unfortunate sense of unworthiness, without which the situation could not have developed.

He did not work on his book, incidentally, because he felt you did not want him to. *(Long pause.)* You resented it when he began typing some of the sessions. *(I thought this was my idea: RFB.)* You felt he was trying to deprive you further of your part. He felt particularly poor at your parents because there he felt under combined attack. He does have a natural aggressiveness also however, and a rebellious nature.

He has been afraid of directing either outward for fear of hurting others. *(Long pause.)* He must learn to handle normal aggressions, and yet when he is operating spontaneously his natural exuberance is a mechanism for such release. *(Long pause.)* He was aware of your feelings. He felt that any success of his was a threat to you. *(Long pause.)*

There will be much to say concerning Ruburt's part in the whole situation, and we will try to lead the way so that your characteristics and needs help each other. What has happened here happens frequently, as you have guessed.

There are also quite beneficial forces in your personalities that uphold you both, and of which you are unaware.

("Are you going to be given more freedom to speak in the future?")

Indeed, I hope so. *(Seth amused.*

("Me too.")

I expect fully that I shall.

The painting of the apartment is beneficial, in its symbolic representation, and for what it means to you both on other levels. Now give us a moment. *(Long pause.)* Incidentally, you also wanted Ruburt thin, you see. You did not want to nourish his success.

Do as you wish concerning the boy. You can help him very much, and <u>will</u> in any case. You will also meet in any case.

(Young Peter Murtough, from Chula Vista, CA, wants to visit us.)

Ruburt's morning symptoms were also connected with you. You did not like to face morning at the Artistic Card Company, but Ruburt had the symptoms, you see. Other reasons also operated here, from his own background.

("Why has he been so hungry lately?")

He felt that you begrudged him the food he ate, hence the shopping symptoms. As your attitude changed these symptoms began to vanish. And as your attitude has further changed he has begun to eat more. Now his own background, with its self-denial and early religious esthetic training, also played its part, you see.

You may take a break or end the session as you prefer.

("We'll take a break."

(10:20—10:35.)

Several things here that have come to mind.

Dating back, Ruburt's barriers about the work area were also barriers against you. At times <u>before</u> he buried the feeling, he resented it when you sat at <u>his</u> (underlined) table. Do you recall?

("Yes.")

This was the beginning of your jealousy, and he picked it up.

The bookcase did represent a changed attitude on your part, for the better, and he also knew this.

Now, one brief explanation here, for this sort of thing operates in good as well as poor circumstances. Ruburt's morning symptoms, for example. I told you why he had them this evening, but then they become associated with certain objects and surroundings, which serve as an automatic perpetuation, you see, in varying degrees.

Simple alterations in the objects can therefore result in a quite real change of pattern, psychic pattern, to disrupt the association. Painting is a wholesale change, for example. In other words, the ghosts of these things can linger. A

<u>complete</u> (underlined) house cleaning, a change of details within the environment, these are all practically beneficial, and of great benefit in relieving <u>lingering</u> symptoms.

The change of bedroom color is highly important, and this is why I suggested it. Remove the rug. It should not be used again. Rearrange the paintings in the bedroom. You may... Let your friend in....

(There was an interruption while I let Catherine in; he had been scratching at the door. Yes, Catherine is a male cat.)

These are important details however. The chests in the bathroom should be painted. The bookcase there *(just moved in)* breaks up old conditions, and is good. The chests should be covered as soon as possible to break up associations. Ruburt should change the arrangement of his clothes in those chests. The shoes should be kept in another place than the accustomed one.

These measures will all help in disrupting any lingering ghost patterns you see. I <u>would</u> (underlined) suggest a change in the kitchen if any were remotely possible. If no major rearrangement is possible, minor changes should be made.

I cannot emphasize too strongly the breakup of associations that will result. This will aid in the complete disappearance of symptoms. Otherwise you could have lingering, though far minor ones, while these habitual objects lost their associative powers, you see.

The associative conditions are not Ruburt's alone. Once projected upon the objects, they become part of the objects until some alteration is made. The alteration actually changes atomic alignments, and shakes off such influences that have been soaked up.

Ruburt's arms, now—he wanted to rock himself in comfort. *(Jane cradled her arms in this characteristic gesture.)* The elbows then bent, straining toward this position, representing a need for comfort, and the attempt to comfort himself. The fingers, connected with his work... Here he refused to budge. They could have been so bad he could not type, and this he did not allow. They still represented his feeling that his writing was a threat to you, and were a reminder of the whole situation. They were also fat however, for he still considered them powerful in regards to his work.

I suggest we end the session. You would do well to paint your entire room. *(The studio.)* It will clear your mind and help your work. I will speak briefly about this if you are not tired.

("Okay.")

Give us a moment. *(Pause, eyes closed.)*

You have rationalized your window arrangement. You have the windows covered *(with the plastic winter weatherproofing material)* as a self-punishment.

It prevents you from seeing clearly a view that you deeply love. The rug should be removed. You do not like it.

The difficulty with your work indeed involved the situation we have been discussing. I may speak quickly here.

You felt oils murky, representing the subconscious hidden fears and desires of which you were frightened. You considered them threatening, too easy, oils. Explosive, you see. *(Pause.)* The temperas meant discipline, but every tempera you did contained an oil within it.

(Excellent data from Seth; this is exactly how I felt about the problem and I had never mentioned this to Jane.)

Symbolically now, you transformed the subconscious feelings into the sparkling temperas. Working with the meticulous temperas, you actually worked out inner problems in a way that was not frightening, and gave you a sense of challenge and accomplishment.

There is a darkness in the oils however which you find frightening, and a heaviness, you see. You were afraid of letting go with oils, for fear of facing the subconscious forces they represented. *(Again, excellent data.)* The color of your studio is a good one.

This will do for this evening. My heartiest wishes to you both, and welcome to the light again, the two of you.

One note: Ruburt felt guilty over your second cat *(Catherine)* initially, feeling you did not want him. As you grew affectionate to the cat, Ruburt's feeling vanished.

("Good night, Seth."
(11 PM.)

SESSION 351
JULY 10, 1967 9 PM MONDAY

Now. Good evening.

("Good evening, Seth.")

The tree, or trees, Ruburt had painted on the kitchen wall, were not beneficial symbols. They were winter trees, you see, done in black. If he intends decorating there, sun symbols would help.

The blandness, comparatively speaking, in previous paintings of your apartment did not overall reflect Ruburt's personality, which is given to contrasts. He is correct. The bathroom should be redone, and gaily. For too long it has represented the place where he faced the results of conflict—his symptoms.

When it is possible, the shoes should be replaced, pair by pair. Whatever stockings or winter legwear he has should be discarded. The black boots should not be worn next year. The bathroom area is a sensitive one for the reasons given.

The cupboards there should particularly be repainted; the ceiling is not important, do as you wish. This room collected about it the atmosphere of Ruburt's desperation. The soap dish in the shower should be replaced. The bathmat should be put away for some time. It may be used later in the future.

A complete change of color is strongly recommended. A gay contrasting color. These measures will dissipate lingering ghost images and associations. The new bath towels, incidentally, these are an excellent idea. Ruburt was strongly attracted to your new rug because of the contrast, this in itself allows steady and harmonious expression of his own personality.

I still tell you to paint your own room, though the same color is fine. The things that you think you save by not painting, hide associations—old patterns that you still are partial to, to some extent. You yourself also need this change in immediate environment. Inner knowledge is reflected in new physical ways. The very resistance you feel, you see, here in this case is significant.

Ruburt's classes will do well *(very true, July 1971)*, and will serve as a natural spontaneous and <u>beneficial</u> outlet for his aggressions. These have built up for some time; will now be released beneficially, for all concerned, in springs of enthusiasm and energy directed outward through the teaching encounter.

For the first time, you will soon be in a position where Ruburt's energy will be correctly utilized for your psychic, spiritual and financial benefit. All energy should be directed on his part into making the classes a success.

His book will do very well now—the dream book. *(No, July 1971.)*

I recommend that he serve his notice to his Mr. Miller, though he on his own does not feel quite ready to do so. There should be full steam ahead in the proper direction. However a touch of this docility operates in that he fears saying no to the nursery school proposition.

Your own work will improve as you make the changes in your room I have advised.

As to my being your child *(amused)*, I am somewhat reluctant to say mama or da-da. However later in our session I will discuss this, as it does contain some validity in theory.

(Here Seth refers to my own pendulum session of July 10, which is on file.)

A small remark here. Ruburt is still slightly distrustful of the new conditions, asking will they last. This results in the lingering strong sensitivities, which will vanish as he becomes reassured. He was literally terrified. I cannot stress this too strongly. It is taking him a while to realize that he is free. But he is doing so, and energy is being released and is available to him, that was not available earlier.

Soon the old native exuberance will completely return, and now there will be a direction for it. A very small point here for you. You resented your mother's frequent house cleaning for several reasons. First of all you deeply feared that in rearranging her house she was merely playing with surface arrangements, and would not touch the deeper dilemmas of the family.

But you also feared the opposite, that she would disrupt a status quo that was highly delicate. Unpleasant but bearable, and that the resulting situation would be pure chaos and disruption. You have feared disruption, not realizing that it results in creation, and yes, in birth.

You may take your break.

(9:30. Jane reported she had been "pretty well out of it" while speaking. Her pace had been fast, eyes open often, voice about average.

(Resume at 9:40.)

I will indeed be freer to speak, Joseph.

You did not want children, physically speaking. You wanted to reach out in the way that people do when they have children. You wanted a fulfillment indeed, that would of course have physical repercussions in three-dimensional terms, but that was not primarily physical.

You wanted something that your work provides, but in a different fashion. Do not mistake me here. This is a general statement, subject to some specific alterations. However, generally speaking, those completely focused in physical reality will look for their prime fulfillment within it. They will also have children.

Those who are not completely focused in physical reality will look for other ways of fulfilling their needs. As a rule with other issues taken into consideration, they will not have children. They will be left with the need for fulfillment however. This was your case and Ruburt's.

I am hardly a child substitute, you see. Conversely, if you had a child it would have been much more difficult for you to make communication with me, because of the direction of your own energy and focus. Because of the physical connotations Ruburt's age was a fairly significant circumstance as far as the beginning (underlined) of his development was concerned. He finally knew that it would not be in usual physical terms.

He was intellectually certain of this in the past, but not emotionally certain. The same can be said in your case. Now you amplify our communications in a very highly charged manner. This is why your relationship with Ruburt, you see, is so important in the sessions. When he is confident of you, he is free in the sessions.

The birth principle is also here on your parts, not mine, in that the sessions involve a projection into a reality that is largely new, and a birth on your parts, you see. Out of the womb of earth into a new dimension. There is some sexual basis in the hidden man-woman symbolism in this respect, this being on a psychic level.

All of these issues prepared you psychically and psychologically to make this kind of contact. The balance between aggressiveness and passivity on Ruburt's part also forms a highly charged medium that allows him to act in his present capacity in the sessions. Any exploration into other realities involves an aggressive thrust on the one hand toward fulfillment, with hope of freedom you see. This has its psychological connotations within your system.

The desire to father or mother a child is a materialization of the desire for fulfillment—one of many that happens to be predominant within physical reality. If you consider what I am saying, along with some of our early material, you will see what I mean here.

You may take a break and we shall continue.

(9:58. Jane again was "out of it". Resume at 10:10.)

We will shortly end the session.

I am thinking of practical suggestions to give you. Yellows and blues are good. Ruburt need not go to the chiropractor for a while. Somewhat later a few adjustments may be of help, simply as a physical measure of correcting any misalignments that have not been corrected otherwise. Though this may be unnecessary. Tell him to use peanut oil in his salads. Continue with the cod liver oil for now.

("How about rubbing the peanut oil into parts of his anatomy that bother him?")

This is always beneficial for him, particularly on a troublesome area of the body. The time in the sun is also important. The classes represent an encounter on his part, with the rest of the world on his terms. A very healthy sign, and a sign that after some years you two are solving a long-standing problem concerning Ruburt's contribution.

("Why is he benefited when he gets up at night to write?")

There are many reasons. Shall I go into them?

("It can wait 'til next time if it's complicated to explain.")

It will take some while. I am perfectly willing to discuss them now, or you may wait until our next session.

("I guess we'll wait then.")

You are not avoiding problems by dealing with temperas, incidentally. You are merely solving them on a different level.

("I used to wonder.")

From the chaos of which you are frightened, you make your order in temperas. You could however do some excellent in oils if you could rid yourself of the fear that they represent. There is no need to force this. I believe you will automatically work out of these fears, and find yourself free to choose either medium.

(Yes—by 1969 at least, possibly earlier. Do only oils by 1970: RFB.)

We will now end the session unless you have any questions.

("What will Peter [Murtough] think when he gets Jane's letter?")

He had hoped for a longer stay, and will feel some dash of cold water, from which he will quickly recover. He may hope to find a stronger job in Elmira, and a room you see, so he could stay longer.

I will then end our session. Good evening to you both.

("Good night, Seth."

(10:24.)

SESSION 352
JULY 12, 1967 9:15 PM WEDNESDAY

Good evening.

("Good evening, Seth.")

Now. The suggested vacation would have broken up the last of Ruburt's symptoms more quickly than your present course.

This course however will work, and is working. Thus far you have been struggling against an environment in which many items have been charged, and now you are endeavoring to change this charge.

The charge alone you see is not sufficient enough to initiate such symptoms, but it is strong enough to feed a steadily diminishing continuance of them unless changes are made, and you are making them. The vacation would have automatically given you freedom from these daily charged items of environment, allowing the symptoms to break up completely without the added resistance.

As energy and strength grew while you were away, susceptibility to the environment would have largely diminished. This way is somewhat more difficult but will prove effective. Working with the charged environment in this manner can cause various flare-ups, which however disappear immediately as the changes continue.

(And which Jane is well aware of.)

When Ruburt's work is done in the bathroom and bedroom there will be another marked improvement, and a new plateau of recovery, from which he will climb still further. He has more energy now you see, though you may not realize it—energy to think of classes, and energy for enthusiasm.

There are no other reasons than those given but these are longstanding and deep-seated.

("He's not covering up anything else?"

(Before tonight's session I had emphasized to Jane that I was very much interested to learn whether we had uncovered all the reasons for her symptoms through the various means we have tried—our pendulums, dreams, these sessions, etc. I asked her to let Seth speak freely.)

There is nothing to my knowledge of a new nature. He is in need of your emotional support, and active proclamations of love and affection. More than ordinarily, in need of your reassurances emotionally.

("Well, lately I've been making a great effort to improve my attitudes.")

You have indeed. Active emotional warmth and its manifestations on your part will now hasten complete recovery immeasurably. Such measures alone can make up for any mistakes you see that might be made. Without them no other correct measures are enough. He does not need, nor want, to smother you emotionally. He fears that you fear this.

He fears that you will feel forced to give him more love than you want to. This is partially a leftover from his realization of your feelings of jealousy, you see. All of this material is very important.

As he becomes reassured again you see he will not require as many proclamations. The rejection he felt however was quite real, and you did feel it—the jealousy—for whatever reason, was felt as valid. Therefore, the necessity for the reassurances.

("Last night my pendulum told me my hand developed a tremor as a result of this jealousy."

(I had not told Jane this.)

The tremor in your hand began when the jealousy began to take hold. You felt you had a shaky hold then, and that the foundations of your work and married life were shaky.

The classes will be like psychic fresh air in your environment. The visits from your friends will also be of benefit. You may take a break and we shall continue.

(9:35—9:45.)

Ruburt must make an attempt, and a good one, to express his feelings, positive and negative.

Your intimate lives, your intimate experiences, suffered. Ruburt, sensing your jealousy, ran away and would not be deeply touched. This was to some extent in retaliation. Also however he had shut down so many spontaneous feelings toward you, because he feared them, that it was difficult to be spontaneous when he wanted to be.

He has ways of escaping that are devious, for they are not obvious, and they are to some extent automatic responses adopted in childhood. He will not hurt you if you hurt him to retaliate, but he will escape, close himself off from further hurt, leaving a shell behind, an animated but empty one.

This is a last-ditch escape so to speak, but dangerous because its signs are not obvious. "Well, all right, I will close you out then." This is the emotional feeling behind it. Such a recourse, again, is only a desperate final one, but with his stubbornness it would be very final, and a means of self-defense.

His symptoms were adopted in place of such a move. This is a highly significant piece of material.

("Yes.")

He literally thought too much of you to do the other.

Now. For some belated notes on your wife's personality. They *(smile)* may be beneficial at this late date even. His loyalty is indeed deep and unswerving. It has been yours for several existences. It is given, his loyalty, to very few, even throughout various lives.

It demands little in physical terms. However he thrives and literally demands a luxurious sense of inner love, an abundance of warmth and affection. Given this, his energy on your behalf and in your behalf knows no bounds within the potentials of his personality.

If he feels this is withdrawn his secure confidence is shattered and his energy dwindles. In his case however there is no danger that you would be emotionally smothered, for he has also this love of work and isolation, and feeling for his and your independence.

("Have I been concerned about this emotional smothering bit?")

He has been afraid that you felt this way, and has perhaps exaggerated this. But it is a point with you also. This is a result of the connection between emotionalism and your mother. *(One minute pause.)*

We are working through some material here. Give us a moment. *(Pause.)* He will give you immeasurable freedom when these requirements are met. I say give you, since these are freedoms an individual could not obtain alone. His literally tremendous energy, given spontaneity through his confidence in you, is to some degree then turned over to you, and can be used in your work.

This is difficult to explain. *(Long pause.)* You both use energy in different ways. He suddenly began to withdraw his energy in fear, and created what you could think of as an implosive hole that had begun to drain your existences.

This was largely caused by his realization of your jealousy, and his reaction. He must learn to express fearful or negative thought, as they occur, so that they do not build up this charge again. Simply because his energy is so concentrated it resulted, misdirected, in such severe symptoms.

This session should lead to a very important understanding on both of your parts. *(Long pause.)* I believe the small bed pillow used by Ruburt has a connection with your mother, and should not be used.

("A small red pillow?"

(I wasn't sure whether Seth had said a red, or bed, pillow.)

The small pillow he uses beneath his regular bed pillow.

Now, you are doing well and progressing. This session contains material that is highly significant. It should be read and reread, and the advice followed.

Unless you have questions we will end now.

("I can't help wondering what I have been offering him lately, other than negative and jealous thoughts, and so forth.")

Do you mean recently?

("Well, during the course of the symptoms. Or haven't I offered much?")

You have always offered a deep love. You have always offered a spiritual rapport and support. These were however undermined.

Now. For your personalities in this existence, you both made the ideal choices. You had been waiting for each other. The possibilities of your relationship had the power to bring about the fullest possible developments of your personalities. Ruburt's energy has an explosive nature. Your more regulated pattern adds sustenance to his own, and sustains him when his energy output is low momentarily.

His explosive energy adds vitality and variety to your more evenly regulated pattern. You have often kept him from being hurt by overinvolvement. But then this was carried to a fault, you see, in the stress period.

Without each other, your possibilities for fulfillment would have been far less. He knew you were less emotionally demonstrative than he, and more or less accepted this, knowing that underneath was a foundation upon which he could rely. It was this foundation he lost faith in, that so frightened him.

In one sense, a limited sense, you could say that he acquiesced, feeling that his symptoms would break through the barrier. But he resented having to be ill in order to reach you. In a way, it was a plea for help, and he resented the need to plead for help.

There is an intuitive bond between you however, very deep. His poetry to you is good evidence of this. You do inspire him. He senses and reacts to parts of you with which neither of you are consciously familiar. He speaks out your sense of wonder and fantasy, that was squelched when you were a child, but finds release in your work.

He cannot love without this unswerving loyalty. It is a part of him. You bring it out, and if you did not do so a very vital part of him would remain unexpressed. The other face of this loyalty is the complete closing out that I mentioned earlier. A partial loyalty of this nature is not a part of his makeup. Do you have questions?

("No.")

Did I answer your last question sufficiently?

("Yes, very well.")

You, incidentally, can use this sense of loyalty, for you did not receive it in the past in this existence. It brings out the best in you and in your work, and represents a rich emotional loam that you need to draw out certain elements of your own personality. On Ruburt's part it is the main tie with the physical universe. A strong statement. But secure in it, you both are free to reach into other existences. Without it you would not be tied securely enough to this earth. There is an interaction, naturally. The loyalty is there but you bring it out and it serves you both therefore. Without you, literally, Ruburt in this physical life would not be able to express nor free it. Do you have questions?

("No.")

Then I shall end the session. My heartiest wishes once more, and mark this session well.

("Good night, Seth.")

(End at 10:34.)

SESSION 353
JULY 17, 1967 9 PM MONDAY

Good evening.

("Good evening, Seth.")

Now. Ruburt did indeed hear me today.

(While walking downtown this afternoon Jane received several messages from Seth.)

The first time in some while that he has been open enough, and a sign of improvement. I told you that some, though not serious, symptom flare-up could occur during the painting process. It is of less intensity than could have been possible, and is keyed off by particular objects. The whole bathroom you see is highly significant, as explained earlier.

The complete change of cupboard color is definitely advantageous. The last significant ghost images are being met head-on, symbolically, and conquered; this being given reinforcement in the physical universe because of the very physical work involved.

Now. *(Smile, eyes open.)* Some beneficial projection is going on here also for a change, as Ruburt psychically projects outward the last of important inner disturbances onto the ghost images, which are then completely, altered into constructive and healthy images.

(Another smile.) This is something like the fox he read of, who to get rid of fleas carries something like a ball of wool in his mouth and walks into the water, forcing the lice out further and further. In this case your full cupboard of dirty clothes has somewhat served. When the bathroom is entirely completed with the exception of the ceiling perhaps, then the clothing should be washed, and preferably, this time at a different laundromat.

Now these changes: let us speak of them. I have told you the very practical and symbolic meaning behind the painting and alteration of your physical environment. There is also more involved. As you know, your dwelling has always represented a temple to Ruburt, and the relationship between you. Therefore the alteration for the better represents his realization of a more beneficial relationship, and gives him a hand in it—represents his willingness to make necessary inner alterations also.

The contrasting color arrangement is a most healthy acceptance on his part of the spontaneous portion of his own personality. In a large manner in the past, he went along with your ideas involving the <u>overall</u> atmosphere—underline overall—of the apartment, feeling you would find contrasting elements irritants. The spontaneity is finding beneficial release. He is not so afraid now of making mistakes, or of trusting his own judgment, though he thinks it might conflict with your ideas in any given case. Hence his painting the cupboards blue.

He is still highly cautious at invoking your displeasure but he is not terrified, as at the wrath of some overbearing god. *(Jane, her eyes wide and very dark, leaned forward in amusement.)* This does indeed represent an improvement.

Now these changes have taken work, energy and time. Precisely because they <u>have</u>, they have validity in physical terms, and show the psychic impetus behind them. Do you want a break?

("No."
(9:24.)

In like manner, the visit of your young friend will also be beneficial *(Peter Murtough, from Chula Vista, CA)* and the visit of your Boston friend *(Pat Norelli)*. These will bring a breakup, again of pattern, and <u>prevent</u> effectively a falling back. They will carry you safely through in other words, or carry Ruburt.

Now, you both had much to do with bringing these events about. Neither of you said no to your Peter, and more important you did not say no to Ruburt. His somewhat induced invitation represented a new use of freedom. On both of your parts, the boy's visit will show that you have once again enough energy to use elsewhere.

The painting and the two visits, taken together, will be as effective as the lost vacation. You are, I believe *(meaning me)* about ready for a new breakthrough in your own work, and the boy's visit may bring this about more quickly.

You may take your break and we shall continue.

(Break 9:30—9:45.)

You will indeed have the opportunity to help this Peter at a very important time in his life, and his meeting with you will change the direction of his life; both inspire him and set him firmly and safely on his feet.

The healthy exuberant feelings of all your anticipated guests will also benefit you both, and you will be able to help them. There will be mutual benefits. Ruburt should definitely now concentrate on his book during the night hours, perhaps thinking of poetry toward dawn.

Now, he thought as a child that every night was literally a death, and every dawn literally a rebirth. He was terrified that his mother had died during the night when he was very young, and could not help him. She could not, you see, climb the stairs at his call. Later he felt that she would either commit suicide or kill them both while he slept, and he feared the night. *(Pause.)* In times of stress the old stay-awake-at-night fearful pattern reoccurs. In the deepest trouble he doubted your feeling for him also, and in exaggerated panic felt that you would feel released if he died, as he felt that he would feel released as an adolescent if his mother died. For in those hours he saw himself crippled as she was, and a stone about your neck.

This frightening identification has lost just about all of its strength. No significant vitality is now tied up there. The writing at night provides constructive outlet, you see, for any lingering conflicts of this nature, and is his way of triumphing over them in work.

He rarely slept for more than three hours at a time for years, without interruption, and the old remembered biological pattern returns. Some guilt here, since in the past if he slept four hours he would have known that he slept through his mother's call. Mainly however the three-hour biological pattern simply returns.

There was too the need to be alert and awake to protect himself. Through the writing at night, these issues are turned into constructive endeavors. As he becomes reassured again, the patterns will fade away. The biological pattern is not necessarily detrimental, however, and can be used to his advantage when he wishes.

Basically however you see he has lived through the night; the feared death was powerless against him. This in itself reassures him.

Now, I suggest he take vitamins. Before, his system would not utilize them regardless. For several months they will be of help on the physical level, showing his intent you see, carried out in <u>physical</u> terms.

The classes *(ESP)* will be of immediate benefit, and will represent a strong bridge toward an effective and satisfactory meeting of psychic and physical dimensions. Their success will serve his self-confidence. Their financial success will go a long way toward the start of a new phase of your relationship.

Do you have any questions?

(I thought Jane tired, perhaps wanting to end a little early.

("Nothing immediate, I guess.")

He should give notice to his Mr. Miller by August first, at the latest, if not earlier. He should expect to make his financial contribution through his classes, and to throw his energy into them, and be patient as he would if he had an outside job.

There is too much at stake to backtrack, and the nursery school position has unpleasant associations, unfortunately. He could try both for a while, but this would be by far the most difficult of choices, and I do not recommend it.

("What's that about the Wisconsin deal?"

(Several times in recent sessions Seth has told us that Jane is to hear from someone in Wisconsin, relative to a publishing venture and/or her ESP book, but nothing has developed yet.)

There is a connection that will materialize. A man with light brown hair, medium height. Some connection with teaching but not in public schools. A connection with the psychic work.

("Has he read the ESP book?")

He has, or will. *(Pause.)*

Your own attitude has helped greatly, and has helped you also, Joseph, and will be reflected in your work.

If you have no further questions, we will end the session.

("Okay.")
My heartiest wishes to you both, and good evening.
("Good evening, Seth."
(10:12. Jane's pace had been average, her eyes open often, manner active, voice average, etc.)

SESSION 354
JULY 19, 1967 9:30 PM WEDNESDAY

(Both of us felt a very pleasant tiredness this evening, and the session was late getting started. Jane felt very well indeed, the best she has been in many months. In view of this, we thought it better to have a brief session, at least, though ordinarily we might have passed it up.)
Good evening.
("Good evening, Seth.")
Now. We will keep it fairly brief.
The symptoms are released in blocks, as blocks of inner associations, negative associations, drop away and are cleared, you see. My instructions have been followed for a change, and you are seeing good results.
Ruburt's Mr. Miller should definitely be contacted.
Now I told you a new plateau would be reached, and he has reached it; and, incidentally, with your help. Your taking a hand at the painting, in the bathroom particularly you see, turned the tide more quickly than otherwise.
The beginning of his classes was another important element.
(Jane held her first ESP class last night.)
Symptoms, then, disappear in blocks and groups, for they represent inner groupings of negative associations. The so-sought-after weight gain can be expected shortly also. There is a releasing process unique with each individual that governs these matters. The body has been holding its own, weight-wise, as I told you.
Rather involved mechanisms had been altered however, so that proper chemical utilization was not made of the food eaten. The energy instead had fed the nervous symptoms, to such an extent that the body was starved, comparatively speaking. This energy has been largely released and the process reversed.
Nevertheless there is a lag, now nearly over here, however, before the organism recoups its losses and then begins to rebuild and gain weight. I recommended vitamins for the reasons given.
Your many notes *(to Jane)* have been a delight to him and your changed

attitude is being received by him with the most beneficial results, and this is beginning to add to your own health and energy. Blue, incidentally, is a healing color, which is why Ruburt craves it. The deep color, however, of the blue reflecting his own desire for contrast.

Do you have questions?

The weight gain, incidentally, should begin when the bathroom painting is completed. The color blue should be added to the kitchen, by the way.

("What did you think of the class last night?")

(This refers to Jane's first class in psychic development which she is teaching.)

It was amusing to watch our friend Ruburt. He did correctly hear me today. He cannot expect no problems with his classes; I hardly promised that. He can expect an overall successful class arrangement, however, over a sustained period, successful in all main aspects. He will have to work for success, but this is the kind of success he is personally equipped to work for and achieve.

This is an excellent way for him to handle many issues which in the past have caused problems, such as the financial aspect. I will indeed help him. I know that he will not misuse the privilege. He can allow himself more freedom in his classes, and he will, for he has learned much. There is no need to fear his own spontaneity now.

A good core group will be gathered. They will be drawn here. Rest assured of this, and let him do his best.

Do you have other questions?

("We can wait tonight.")

This plateau of his is not permanent, in that his condition will further improve. It does represent a new point from which he will not slip back for any amount of time, you see. Do you follow me?

("Yes.")

Any momentary slippages *(laugh)* will be of much less duration than any slippages from his past high plateaus, you see.

("In view of your past statements about old patterns being set, is it possible for these symptoms to return sometime, say, in the distant future?")

Anything is possible. This particular issue is being and has been faced squarely and seen through—a very difficult procedure indeed—but better now than later. Therefore, since the issues have been faced, there should be no such future repercussions.

("Could we be surprised? That is, could the symptoms creep up on us unawares, before we realized it?")

You will never be surprised in the same way again. As long as your channels of communication remain open as they are, or more, and not just artificially open. My instructions should be followed as Ruburt improves, until his condition is completely normal.

Do not stop your efforts, you see, until complete health has returned, for only then will the problems be completely conquered, and this complete conquest is your best insurance against any reoccurrence. A lingering group of minor symptoms over a period of years would represent instances that could cause difficulty, given the proper circumstances, or rather, the improper circumstances. Do you see?

("Yes.")

Your intimate life will also reflect Ruburt's complete recovery. Do not give up your efforts too soon. He is well on the road to complete recovery. There is an acceleration process here that will work to your advantage as larger and larger blocks of symptoms disappear. For with each day, he has greater vitality, you see, that he did not have earlier, that works for him and for complete recovery with ever-growing strength.

It will take, perhaps, some work to maintain your relationship at this necessary level, but for your own health and Ruburt's, such effort is more than worthwhile.

Do you have other questions?

("No.")

Then we shall end our session. My heartiest wishes to you both.

("Good night, Seth.")

(End of session. 10 PM.)

SESSION 355
JULY 26, 1967 9 PM WEDNESDAY

(Witnesses were Peter Murtough, who arrived Monday, July 24, from Chula Vista, CA, and Bill and Peggy Gallagher. No session was held Monday evening.

(Tonight's session was recorded. Just as she went into trance, Jane leaned forward to switch on the recorder, and had a little difficulty.)

I am not equipped to deal physically with your gadgets.

("Why not?")

Before Ruburt had the opportunity to turn your machine on, I was here and it was left to me to flip the switch.

My heartiest welcome to our young friend, and to our late-coming Jesuit *(Bill Gallagher, who arrived just as the session began)*, and of course, our cat lover *(Peg)*.

Now. Our young gentleman friend has come a long way to visit me, but then I also came a long way, you see, to visit you.

(*Seth, much amused, leaned toward Pete. Jane's eyes opened often; her voice was a bit stronger than average.*)

I know that you have many questions, but we shall have to take these slowly, so that the answers are as plain as possible.

Now. You have indeed many abilities to be developed, and you need to work in order to develop them fully. In later years if you continue, then you will find a considerable change in the Ferd (*trance*) personality. He is himself in a period of transition, and there are several difficulties that are operating.

On the one hand he cannot communicate with you clearly because of his own condition at this time. On the other hand you cannot receive him clearly enough because your own abilities have not yet been sufficiently developed.

In this respect you and Ferd are both involved in a mutual learning process and development of abilities. Continued endeavor will result in benefits for you both. He has recently left our area of existence for another, and he has not yet sufficiently learned to operate within the new set of conditions. This is a fairly normal state of affairs.

It is because of this that he speaks through you, because of your youth, and because your condition in this system or life somewhat approximates his own situation within another system. The difficulties will be ironed out as you work together. There is much that you can do, and indeed that you must do if you wish the situation to continue and improve.

My friend Ruburt has told you that you must read everything that you can, and so you should. There must be a sense of almost severe integrity on your part at all times in connection with your abilities. You must have patience while these abilities develop, while Ferd learns to perfect his own communication process, and while you learn to perfect your receptive abilities.

We will have a brief break and then continue.

I have a fine joke, for the Jesuit. My friend Ruburt has asked me to awaken you some morning at approximately three AM.

(*[Bill:] "I await with pleasure, my dear Seth."*)

I shall expect you then, dear Jesuit, down on your knees to pray.

(*[Bill:] "On whose behalf, Seth?"*)

Yours or mine. Now, we have somewhat balanced the atmosphere of the session. I am not always as serious, young man, as I intend to be with you.

(*Break at 9:18. The exchange between Seth and Bill Gallagher developed because last week, one evening, Jane succeeded in waking both Bill and Peg between 3 and 4 AM.*)

(Seth's manner in speaking to Pete was, on the overall, quite restrained and serious, and the difference from his usual manner was quite obvious to the Gallaghers and myself. Jane resumed in the same manner at 9:24.)

Now. Perhaps it is unfortunate, and perhaps it is not, but if you are to become involved to any important degree in this particular kind of endeavor, then you must be willing to devote time, energy and concentration to that work.

The validity and quality of any communications will rest primarily with the energy with which you are willing to develop your abilities. Halfway measures will not give you clear reception, nor reliable material. The systems with which we deal are too delicate, too finely balanced, to operate with any efficiency unless there is constant study, application, and devotion to the attempt. I tell you this because you are young, and must make your own decision. Halfway measures are not beneficial to the overall personality. They can lead to difficulties.

A steady and dedicated responsibility will best allow you to develop your ability and insure the validity of your communications. I tell you, young man, honestly, that halfway measures are worse than none. The personality with halfway measures is constantly in a state of stress and confusion. Halfway measures therefore are the pitfall.

Now. If you decide to devote this time, energy and concentration to these endeavors consistently, then you should indeed meet with success. Time is necessary, for certain portions of your personality must be given the opportunity to catch up with other portions. You have been doing very well. The breather and the change of environment is good for you just now. This is a rather a weighty endeavor, therefore you should indeed realize what it requires of you. If you are willing then you shall do well, for the abilities are indeed there, and you can learn to use them.

Now, give us a moment please. *(Long pause, eyes closed.)*

1571. A dancer, female, in Spain. A town by a river. Eventually four children, two of these now known to our friend as other personalities in this life.

(A puzzled gesture.) There is something connected with the town that has to do with the word west. Perhaps the Spanish word meaning west was in the town's name. I do not know, but the connection is there. *(Pause, eyes closed.)*

The first name... Aledona. *(My phonetic interpretation.*

("Do you want to spell that out?")

I do not believe I can get the name any clearer. Al E Donna.

(Pause; groping; phonetic.) The last name, Mess-Peralla. *(Again phonetic. Jane, or Seth, made another attempt at the last name that I could not interpret sufficiently to get on paper.)* Death at 56.

Now, a connection with a church. In English, the name would be Madonna of the White Waters.

You may take a brief break and we shall then continue. You were a lovely young woman.

([Pete:] "Thank you."

(9:40. Bill Gallagher said the Spanish word for west is occidente; and the Spanish Madonna of the White Waters would be Madonna de Blanca Agua.

(Seth's manner had continued on the serious side. Resume at 9:50.)

Now. We are not going to give you all this in one loving spoonful.

You will be here a while, and we shall take things step by step. I want you to realize first of all that such endeavors involve steady application over a period of years, for you should decide whether or not you are willing to devote such energy. An intensification of concentration will be required of you that is somewhat difficult to achieve.

The same care and attention must be given as would be given to any vocation, and this is no light matter. The fact that such communications began, and at your age, speaks well for your own abilities, but now you must be prepared to back these abilities with additional knowledge and application.

I am not sugar-coating the process for you, for this would not be to your advantage. Nor will I understate the advantages that can be yours if you do so continue, for there are many. There will be direct experience of inner reality that is encountered most infrequently, and expansion of consciousness and a resulting fulfillment of your own personality.

You shall know the answers to many questions, though others may only guess at them. But this is not a matter that you should go halfheartedly into. It should be studied with determination and dedication. Anything less will add little to your overall knowledge, simply suppositions and imaginative dallyings.

Those who search for truths must search wholeheartedly, or they find only half-truths, and some half-truths are as dangerous as lies. There is opportunity for you here, if you are willing to do the work involved, and a satisfaction that can be found in no other way.

Joseph, you may take a break or we will end the session, as you prefer.

(10:01-10:10)

Now. I did not tell you that Ferd was a figment of your imagination, for he is not.

I did not tell you that Ferd was merely a fabrication of the subconscious, for he is not. I have told you that you are a novice in an exciting and exacting program and I have asked you to ponder the implications of this situation.

Your material has not been coming through clearly for the reasons given.

This does not mean that it will not improve, for it will if you persist. The important element is your own intent. You do not have to set about converting others for example, but you do need to devote some large measure of mental and emotional intensity inward. You will have your material on past lives before you leave here.

(Amused:) I am concerned with how you live this one, you see.

Now, there were abilities shown on your part in Poland, in the 1200s. We will fill this in later. *(Pause.)* Then, you did not use your abilities properly and as a result they have only now reappeared. One of your children in the life given earlier is now your mother.

Another is a more distant relative in another country, and I believe a male. We shall go into these relationships at our next session. They will perhaps explain some current events.

(Bill Gallagher had scribbled a note to me and passed it along as Seth spoke: What country? City? Or territory?

("What country is the relative in?" This was my own question, unrelated to Bill's, however.)

The other relative is in Australia. Give us a moment please. *(Pause.)* There was a relationship existing between our young friend and the personality known as Ferd back in the Polish existence. They were then contemporaries.

Ferd was a soldier, I believe. An involvement in a Balkan military affair that was not a full-scale war. A military engagement.

(Again Bill was passing a note to me: What city? Who was leader of army? As far as I can recall, he has never passed such notes before during a session.

("Can you give us the leader of the military force?")

We shall see. *(Pause.)* Death in a mine explosion. Our young friend, in many of his lives, has been involved in traveling, living in a country in which he was not originally a native.

("What city or territory in Australia is the relative located in?"

(This question was inspired by Bill's note re city, country, territory, etc. I was somewhat reluctant to ask it. The first question on this theme, in which Seth answered Australia, was my own idea.)

We shall fill in this material as we can, and when we can. We are dealing with general overall impressions now. Any specific details that we can give will be given. At this point, however, interruptions can break up the general overall impressions.

Now. There was a large family from which this relative came. I believe he was the third born to the family. A connection here with the letter J, with a 1936 date, and something which I do not understand—a connection with an upside-down umbrella, that may represent a symbol, a coat of arms, a sign on a shop door, I have no idea.

You may now take a break and we shall continue.

(10:30. Peter Murtough told us that he has an Uncle John in Australia who is about 40, lives in Canberra and has two young children.

(At break, the Gallaghers left. Jane told us that my questions had irritated her greatly. They had interrupted her train of impressions, in which she was casting about freely, and she had felt she was on the verge of a projection that could have been most instructive. The questions re details snapped her back unpleasantly, she said, and were very irritating. The feeling of projection flew away at once.

(We, of course, knew of Peter's connections with Australia. Resume at 10:50.)

You should learn from Ruburt's experience you see, this evening and benefit from it in your own endeavors.

We were indeed about to embark upon a projection state, and the impetus had already been given. The questions, incidentally, were the result of subconscious aggression on our friend's part, our Jesuit; quite natural, over the condition of his father. *(Who is very ill in the hospital.)* We will go into your questions at tomorrow's session. *(To Pete.)*

The entity name here, Joseph, is an odd one: M-I-N-K-E *(spelled out.).*

Now. If I sound severe with you *(to Pete)* it is only because I want you prepared for these endeavors if you choose to go on with them. You have done very well, particularly in regard to your youth, and you have my congratulations indeed. But not much has been demanded of you thus far, you see, and you must prepare to work if you want to develop your own abilities.

Perhaps we can begin tomorrow's session at eight, Joseph—

("Yes.")

—so more time will be available. This has been enough for our first meeting. I wish you a hearty good evening and best wishes to you all.

("Good night, Seth.")

([Pete:] "Good night, Seth.")

(11 PM.

(The recording of the session was very successful.)

SESSION 356
JULY 27, 1967 9 PM THURSDAY

(Peter Murtough a witness. Session recorded for Pete.)

Now, my dear young man. You may indeed sit there and observe me. But

I also sit here and observe you, whether or not Ruburt's eyes are opened or closed.

Our session last evening was a rather serious one, for I believe it necessary that the terms of these endeavors be stated at once, and as clearly as possible. I do not want to burst any bubbles, nor did I want to encourage you along these lines unless you were willing to devote considerable energy in these directions. We can now to some degree relax and enjoy a quiet evening. I am aware of your considerable list of formidable questions. We shall get to these in good time.

The session last evening was to some extent inhibited because of the emotional climate that affected our good Jesuit *(Bill Gallagher)*. He was not at his best. We shall not encounter that difficulty this evening. This does not mean however that we shall necessarily put on any circus displays.

These can be enjoyable at times however. Now. Give us a moment.

(Pause.) Do not ask any questions here. These are merely loose impressions. A bad stumble. Difficulty with a third vertebra *(pause)*, leading to unequal nerve pressures. The condition originating in one incident some time ago, and further aggravated by a second incident in more recent times. *(Pause.)*

Two particular yoga exercises will be of benefit here. They must be done very slowly however. Only one of them a day to begin with for a two-week period, and then the two of them may be done each day. The one where the individual lies frontward down on the floor, and lifts up from the arms, Joseph, you know this one.

("Yes." The cobra.)

The other, the sitting forward stretch. *(Pause.)* Give us time here. *(Long pause.)* The condition leads at times to a bunching of muscles in the side of the neck in precisely this area *(Jane touched the right side of her neck)* that can occasionally appear almost as a hardish lump. Simply knotted muscles caused by strain. The same exercises will help here. *(Pause, head down.)*

Now. On the diet of your Stephen. *(Pete's brother.)* We find a confusion in body chemistry, caused either by the diet itself at present, or alternating changes of diet. *(Pause.)* Some actual, though not drastic, starvation of tissues from the same causes. Each individual utilizes carbohydrates and protein in a slightly different manner and what is good for one is not necessarily for another.

There is an overemphasis here on the one hand, and a lack on the other. *(Pause.)* There is not sufficient fat of the kind that the body derives through carbohydrates, that are sustaining. What is needed is a balanced diet, a normally balanced diet. If weight loss is desired then less should be eaten. No whole body of foods such as carbohydrates should be drastically reduced. This puts the body chemistry in an unbalanced condition.

Now give us more time. *(Pause.)* Incidentally, I suggest some peanut butter, as it contains some nutrients that are needed. There should be, again, no overreliance on any particular group of foods.

Now. *(Eyes closed, smiling, Jane leaned toward Pete.)* Now, my dear young man, quite innocently, you have made an early and understandable error. *(Smile.)* You will forgive me, for my slight amusement is also tinged with rather compassionate understanding. In the attempt to use your ability, to probe into the future, you allowed yourself to take more upon yourself than you should have.

There is nothing wrong in trying to perceive tomorrow. *(Pause.)* It is risky however to live today in such a manner. There are too many errors that can be made when dealing with precognitive elements. You are dealing with a world of probabilities. Now Ferd looked into a possible future, and this was quite legitimate—as a probable future. There is much concerning time that you do not yet understand, and I cannot explain it to you, unfortunately, in an evening. This may sound contradictory, but it is not. It is possible to perceive the future as it will be; on the other hand the future itself is always changing, for you change it in the present. *(Pause.)* In the precise moment in which you spoke the words, there was a probability, and a good one, that the event would occur as stated.

(This material concerns a certain horse race in late August; Ferd had predicted Steve would win a bet on this race.)

Two days later, the conditions had completely changed. This is too complicated, and you do not have the background now. However, the future event predicted was bound up with a series of events that would have had to occur within that two-day period. Some of these events would have been trivial, but all would have led him toward that predicted big win. There are two men in particular he would have met. These events did not occur, and another group of probabilities now exist.

Had your abilities been developed sufficiently, you could have seen through these probable futures into the actual physical future event that would come to pass. Now there is no great loss here, and take me seriously. Both you and Stephen shall have gained, and better now than later: for you cannot live your physical life in such a fashion. The development of your character and of Stephen's would be drastically reduced.

There was a hope on Stephen's part, and you responded to it. Not by any subconscious fakery, far from it. But you perceived the probable future that did exist as such; and I do not mean it only existed symbolically. Your desire to help him led to that perception. You would be the worse off, and your brother, if this were not so. You cannot use your ability in this fashion—purposely, you see.

Your ability will help you in your dealings with physical reality, in very definite ways. But not necessarily in the ways that you would consciously choose.

Are you tired, Joseph?

("Well, we can take a break.")

We will then indeed.

(9:37. Jane's delivery had been active, fast at times, with her eyes usually closed. Voice a bit stronger than usual. Pete said the back condition mentioned could apply to either his father or brother. Jane, of course, was aware of this. Resume at 9:45.)

Now again, give us a moment, please.

I am going to speak freely and again no questions now. We will clear up what we can when we can; but allow the impressions uninterrupted flow.

An R, the letter R, J, or an R and a J, being the initials of one name, or the first initial of two first names. *(Pause.)* In an Australian connection. A room *(pause)* that appears bare, though it is not necessarily, giving the impression of more size than it possesses. This is an Australian residence.

(Pause.) Now, by itself, ostriches. A connection here. A particular chest that has been in the family for some generations, or that is highly treasured. Among other things containing ribboned letters from a foreign land. *(Pause.)* It may be a handwrought chest.

Now give us time. *(Pause.)* It is connected to a woman. Approximately five foot five, though somewhat shortened now, as with age. Simply the word <u>Osburn</u> connected here. *(My phonetic interpretation.)* Perhaps letters from an Osburn at one time. This in the past, with the Osburn connection.

It seems she wears something that resembles an earring about her neck *(Jane gestured, as though describing something that hung about her neck and dangled to her waist)*, but I do not believe it is an earring.

The hair at one time a rather odd gray—a strange darkish gray. I <u>believe</u> a mole here *(Jane touched her right cheek)*; though it may not be a mole but some facial characteristic here, you see. *(Touch again.)* A voice with a clicking sound. I believe these impressions referring to the grandmother.

The impression of an extra back room, not used for daily living—for storage perhaps or mementos, and so forth. Perhaps it has some old rather elaborate furniture in it, stored, that had been used before by the family. Some fairly valuable objects.

Now. A man, sometimes mustached, brown hair and mustache, in the prime of life. Two front teeth more yellowed than the others. Likes to walk on Saturdays or Sundays, a walking man in any case. A nasal voice, he used frequent extra breaths between words or sentences and many ahs between words, you see, or syllables, as: well—ah—.

Some strange connection with him and geese. I do not know here. Perhaps he had a pet goose. I would not want a pet goose. We are speaking of the woman's husband, or father here. We shall try to clear it as we progress. I do not know if this is our young friend's grandfather, or the grandfather's father, you see.

There is a storm in the past, a physical storm, in which this man loses some animals. There is a connection with barns here.

("Can we have a break, Seth? Tape's running out.")

You may indeed.

(10:02. The last of the tape was used up, and the recorder turned off. Jane was a long time, comparatively, coming out of trance. She had been "way out", she said, and felt there had been no blocking on her part at all. She felt very good about this.

(While speaking for Seth, she had a mental image of a back room, and an "impression" of a storm. She also felt she had looked at a photograph, but could not say whether of a man or a woman; perhaps an old-fashioned photo. Jane said she feels it is "her end of the deal" not to block the material.

(Pete couldn't say anything about the accuracy of the Australian data.

(Resume at 10:15.)

Again these are impressions.

A pearl. Either a pearl, or Pearl, a woman's name. A connection with a woman distant, that is, a half relative. For example, a half sister or a half aunt. In the family history...

(Jane's words were slurred a bit, and I thought she was again in a deep trance. She was using pauses however, whereas before break she had been speaking rather rapidly.)

With the father, our friend's father, a connection with motors. Either a latent ability to handle them and work with them well, or some episodes connected with motors on his part. Also a filmed episode.

Give us a moment. The mother feels the family lined up against her. The same sort of a situation existed basically in her own family, though in a somewhat different manner. But the pattern was there.

Three children in a kitchen, sitting in a row, in her past, and she is one of them. She is six. *(Pause.)* There is an argument among adults, and a door slams. The location was near water, or the street had water in it, or there was a connection with swans—all of this applying to that episode.

A small cat, either involved in the argument, or caused the argument, or present during the argument. Her own sympathies were with the male. The woman, her mother, shows it, and she often puts herself in this woman's place, demanding the attention she does not <u>feel</u> she can otherwise obtain.

For all of this, a basic fierce loyalty to the family. She has particular disturbances in April and November. These following the patterns set early in her psychological heritage. Iron would be helpful in her diet. *(Long pause.)*

There is some resentment here, a smoldering one. She would have preferred to have been born a male. This is her first existence as a woman. An episode occurring when she was approximately in a sixth grade *(pause)* added to an already existing sense of insecurity. *(Pause.)* There are also other-life connections that enter in here. The family also uses the mother as a way of testing its own strength and unity, and as a method of channeling aggression. Often she picks up the aggression of the family, and then reacts for you all. You can then blame her without facing the fact of the underlying aggression.

She is one pole of the family, and you are the other *(to Pete)*. You have the loyalty and unswerving support of the others, partially simply because their aggressions are channeled in an opposite direction and toward another family member. *(Long pause.)*

All of this exists within the gestalt of the family. The mother has set up patterns of behavior that allow her to use aggressions in this way, and to dissipate the aggressions of others to a large degree. Within your family, no others save perhaps Stephen, could handle aggressions in this manner—that is, dissipate them. Although his way would be different from the mother's.

There is a balance within the family. Love is expressed to you on occasions when it could not be expressed to other members of the family; but still stays within the family, you see. The family, therefore, has its strengths and its safety valves. Australia serves as a uniting theme of common background, for all save your mother. It also serves as a uniting promise for the future, and gives you common dreams.

You may take your break.

(10:43. Jane was again far-out, she said. Her eyes were mostly closed, her pace fairly rapid. Resume at 10:55.)

Now. This evening's session will not run too much longer, though we may perhaps speak again.

I was in touch with your Ferd, briefly. He is not yet aware of many aspects of his new condition *(Jane's voice was becoming somewhat deeper and faster)*, and is now learning to manipulate within it. Therefore even for us, communication was somewhat difficult, distorted and restrained. We are on different levels. We exist within the same system but within different levels of it. His periods of communication are necessarily brief, simply because he is unable at this time to utilize his energy to that direction with any effectiveness.

This is simply a matter of time and development. You will learn together. *(Pause.)* You are both emotionally-based individuals, and you will be open to each other's communications, which is all to the good. Your material will come in a slightly different manner, and the psychological framework that develops about you will be of a somewhat different nature than that which exists between Ruburt and myself.

Your own talents will take a somewhat different direction as your abilities and Ferd's abilities join together in a workable arrangement. *(Voice stronger again.)*

There will be a great emphasis upon certain emotionally charged impressions. This means that you will perceive certain impressions that have a particular emotionally-charged origin, more easily than you will perceive others. This is because both you and Ferd have had similar events occur in various lives, and your subjective association patterns are similar also.

This gives you a workable framework within which you can operate. Generally speaking it means that the same symbols will have similar meanings to you both. The same of course applies to Ruburt and myself. I have tried to answer some of your questions in my own way.

(Jane's voice fairly good.) We shall not try to shatter the windows, with the volume *(deeper)* of our voice. Nevertheless you will know that I can indeed speak rather clearly and quite loudly when the occasion does arrive. My friends are understandably worried concerning the convenience and opinion of their neighbors, and therefore I shall not carry this insignificant display any further than I have at this point.

(Jane's voice, while fairly strong, didn't approach the volume and power she has displayed upon occasion.)

I give you all that I can, my blessing and good wishes. You may now end the session if you prefer, or, Joseph, continue for a while as you decide.

("We'll take a very short break."

(11:05. Jane was again far-out, she said, and as break came she was still aware of the surging power that lay behind such voice effects. It took her longer than usual to open her eyes, etc. At break we discussed more of Pete's questions. Resume at 11:20.)

Now. These tingles of which our friend speaks, these are simply his own way of letting himself know that he is dealing with other than usual physical reality. We will have more to say of this at another time.

We will also then give further information that should serve to identify the gentleman with the back difficulty. Ruburt has done well in this session, and is now exhausted. My heartiest wishes to you all.

Good evening.

([Pete and I:] "Good night, Seth."

(Long pause.) Ruburt may finish his glass of beer, and then return to the recommendation made earlier.

(11:24.)

SESSION 357
JULY 31, 1967 9 PM MONDAY

(Venice McCullough and Peter Murtough were witnesses. Jane began speaking for Seth in a voice somewhat stronger than usual, and with her eyes closed.)

Now good evening—

("Good evening, Seth.")

—and our greetings to our new friend.

Our young friend here has many questions. His mind is buzzing with them. He is so impatient. There is one question however that I will indeed answer now, and it has to do with the delight with which he views fire.

The light of fire has a soothing effect upon his nervous system, a relaxing effect. Not only fire is involved here, however. There is a tendency for spontaneous dissociation that has always been characteristic, and this tendency is simply given freedom when he stares into flames.

If I may borrow a quote from another elderly gentleman: that is elementary, Watson. He has simply discovered that fire affected him in this manner. But any warmth or flickering light will do the same.

Now there is a tendency here emphasized because of youth. This tendency actually involves a lack of focus, or a lack in the direction of focus. Our young friend shifts the focus of his awareness from inner to outer realities very often, and without realizing that he does so.

As he matures and learns, and studies and works, he will then be able to do this when he wishes to do so. There are no significant unhealthy elements connected in this rather innocent regard for fire. Now. The shift of his consciousness is unsteady. He has no discipline over it, and is sometimes in a state of consciousness that is between. Training will allow a strong disciplined focus within either reality.

Now, one other point. The man to whom I referred as having difficulties in the third vertebra is the younger man of the two in question.

Now if you please, give me a moment, and I shall use it well. *(Pause, eyes closed.)* These are simply impressions. I shall make no attempt to unscramble them at this point. They will have to do with our new friend. *(Venice.)*

The first is reincarnational data.

Amsterdam, 1631 to 1658, a shopkeeper and a male. The last name Brunswick *(my phonetic interpretation).* The shop seems to have had some relation to leather. A member of an organization, a group of males, a guild.

A guild or a group of artisans. A father of three children, one of whom later becomes a member of a parliament. *(Pause.)* One of whom joins a profession that had to do with keeping records of water levels or consumption, *(Jane shakes head)* this being a civil employment.

We are getting something here that is not clear: a small instrument used that seems to be the size of a thimble, but with *(pause)* something that resembles a slide rule on the top. This was the method of obtaining the data from which the water records came.

The wife dies young. She was of foreign descent, I believe French. Her people were destroyed in a plague. Her family name *(pause)* ... I hear it, you see, but I do not <u>see</u> it *(pause)*... You will have to work phonetically: V I S W A *(repeated),* from some place near Bordeaux in France.

Now. Our friend was a collector of dues within the organization to which he belonged. The name was on many records, but you would not find them now. There was a life in Arabia, a poor and humble one, and one much more recently in the Midwest of this country; as a woman.

(Pause. Jane paused often while giving this material.) We will try here... Joseph... The name of the town was either S A C O *(spelled),* or this formed the main body of the name, you see.

("Yes.")

I said Midwest, and yet it was further west, I believe. The population seems to have been no more than 13,000 at the time, at a peak period, and yet for a long time the population was but 3,000. Married to a man who dealt with cloth stuffs, and with some material that was made into large bags or sacks.

The owner of his own business. *(Pause.)* The town situated between one mountain range and a smaller plateau, rather midway between the north and south portions of the country. In the second group of states now, or from the West Coast... But more to the eastern section of this second group, you see, to the inside.

Are your suffering fingers tired?

("No.")

Now then. A Saint Cecelia Church here. The name Mathiatus *(phonetic)* I believe was shortened to another version, perhaps Methus. *(Phonetic. Pause.)*

Your first name, then, was Grace. *(Long pause.)* There were five children who lived and two who did not. Here we find you very ambitious.

You may take your break now and we shall continue... Our fire-loving young friend here can watch Ruburt light his match.

(9:31. Jane said she was pretty well dissociated. Her voice had been good throughout, her eyes closed. A general discussion between the four of us took place at break concerning Seth, origins, etc. Resume at 9:43.)

Now. I shall indeed answer some of your questions myself. *(To Venice McCullough.)*

First of all, though you did not ask, I am not the subconscious of our friend Ruburt, or as you call him, Jane.

There are automatic adjustments that are made, and nervous pathways that have been opened, pathways that become more useful as they are used. For habit enters in here, as in all endeavors.

In the beginning of our relationship our communication was somewhat less smooth. Ruburt was aware of uneven moments as certain transitions took place. He kindly allows me to use, or rather operate his vocal cords. And yet even this involves automatic translations of which he is not consciously aware.

For much of my communication is not initially verbal. The original perceptions are at a different level entirely. He receives them through several of the inner senses. Ruburt or Joseph will explain the term to you. These impressions must then be translated into terms that can become physical.

In our case the impressions emerge as verbal. They are translated and interpreted so that the end result is a verbal rendition. I am, as I have often told our friends, an educator. Ruburt, and Joseph also, have known me in past lives, and our overall psychological structures have very significant similarities that make our communications possible.

I am again, as I have said often, an energy personality essence, which means quite simply that I am a personality who does not now operate within the physical reality. I can at times impress your physical reality, but the focus of my existence no longer involves a three-dimensional psychological structure. *(Pause.)*

I have lived in physical terms within your three-dimensional universe, and I am aware of that universe. My main existence however is in a dimension of which your third-dimensional reality is only a part. I can therefore perceive, for example, portions of your future, simply because the future is only an illusion that exists in three-dimensional reality. *(Pause.)*

(To Venice:) Does that answer your question?

([Venice:] "Yes".)

That was a small yes indeed. *(Amused, eyes closed, Jane leaned forward.)* Now let us see. Ruburt and I engage in a cooperative venture, truly a psychological gestalt, in which our personalities meet, rather in a dimension that is neither here nor there. Together we form a sort of psychological bridge between dimensions, for I cannot completely exist within your three-dimensional system now, and he cannot completely enter the dimension in which I do have my primary existence.

So there is a projection of consciousness on both of our parts to some degree. Now, I like the type of questions that you ask *(to Venice)*, and I enjoy an inquiring mind. Do you have any other questions? *(Pause; voice good, eyes closed.)*

If you prefer you may voice them at break, and then I will answer them. I am having a most enjoyable evening, my friend Joseph.

("Are you?")

I am indeed.

("Do you want to tackle one of Pete's questions?")

(I had beside me a list of questions Pete had written out.)

Now give us a moment. *(Pause.)* We will see what we can do with our spiritual firebug here.

(To Pete:) You did not know Ruburt nor Joseph in a past life. That was one of your questions, I know. There was a distant connection however on the part of one of your relatives. He was on a journey from England to Boston, and stopped briefly at a Boston church where Joseph was then a minister. Merely a chance acquaintance. The man, I believe, was your father.

(According to Seth I have lived a life in Boston, and it ended probably just before the Civil War.)

He sailed on a ship, certainly with a strange name, for it was called G R I P P E, *(spelled)* I believe. With a Captain Stoner.

("Did I by any chance speak to him?")

You did indeed. There was no friendship developing however, nor any time for one. The mere meeting however provided contacts that will be worked out.

("Pete wants to know if he's sensed your presence since he's been here.")

I am afraid we should have to ask Pete. I have indeed been here, as Ruburt well knows. Ruburt however has been concerned, and quite properly, in keeping the atmosphere as uncomplicated as possible. I did not however address you, young man.

("Can we take a break?")

You may indeed, if it does not hurt you. *(To Venice:)* our new friend reminds me of the Jesuit when he first came to our sessions *(Bill*

Gallagher)—watching, when break came, to see when Ruburt and I should fall apart from each other. I hope no crack is expected.

(10:07. Jane was again well dissociated, her eyes remaining closed. Another discussion between the four of us followed. Resume at 10:22.)

Now. Think in terms of energy being action.

Energy is action. It must act and move. It constantly seeks to know itself, and to expand. It cannot remain static. Its survival is dependent upon change. Its very permanency is determined by its nature, and its nature demands constant change.

Energy or action is composed of an infinity of itself, and yet, forever acting upon itself, it forms forever new portions of itself. Each action causes another. Now until we have done more talking you will simply have to take my word, for the sake of our discussion—our one-way discussion—that any action or energy possesses consciousness seeking to know itself, therefore; and acting within itself it forms new consciousnesses that are individual and independent, and yet connected to every other consciousness.

The purpose is the expansion of consciousness itself, and this automatically leads to the knowledge that every consciousness is connected to every other, and that any harm to one is harm to all. Time simply does not exist as a series of moments. This is three-dimensional illusion. Therefore in actuality no one life is lived before nor after another.

Action acts spontaneously. In three-dimensional existence you must speak of reincarnation in terms of continuous lives, for it seems to you as if there is indeed a past, present and future. Imagine then action or energy which is conscious, exploding into bloom like some gigantic cosmic flower, spontaneously, instantaneously, and intuitively.

You however would view this in slow motion, so that eons of time would seem to have passed. And yet energy or action, which is consciousness, is always changing, and the shape of the flower and the blossom would constantly change. Energy can never be lost but only change its form.

The consciousness therefore would never be destroyed in reality. The most minute blossom within it would experience only an almost instantaneous change of form, and all of this would transpire in the breath of an instant. The individual petals would merely change, as the personalities of men change in what seems like a series of before and after reincarnations.

And no memory, you see, would ever be lost, and nor is any memory lost. The personality that you have now is simply the flower of the moment, not realizing that it has the knowledge of its own past histories; and all of this would be but one cosmic flower. Energy constantly renews itself. The various flowers could then be compared to the various dimensions through which action and consciousness know their own reality. The expansion of consciousness automatically leads you to understanding and compassion.

Now I will answer any questions that you have. Perhaps I should ask if my friends hands are tired.

("Let's take a short break.")

We shall then indeed.

(10:37. Jane had again been well dissociated, her eyes closed, her pace quite fast. Resume in the same manner at 10:45.)

Now. We will shortly close our session. However to the question about Spain, the answer is yes.

(Pete wanted to know if his love of anything to do with Spain was the result of a life lived there.)

(To Venice:) I enjoy our new friend's questions, and I enjoy answering them. *(Smile. To Pete:)* As to our young friend's question about his Lear Jet, I presume that is a snickering jet, we shall see.

(Pete wanted to know if a chance he had to fly home on a Lear Jet, without charge, would work out.)

You want the answers to the wrong questions. You want me to deprive you of experience that you need, and in the reality in which you now exist, and in which you are learning very well to manipulate. You shall not get in the habit of having me tell you what will happen. I say this in all good humor and with due affection. *(Pause, smile.)* Do you understand?

([Pete:] "Yes Seth.")

Very well then, we are still friends.

([Pete:] "Of course.")

Within your reality there are procedures with which you must deal. There are many occasions when a glimpse into your own future will be of benefit, and then you shall have them. *(Pause.)* Questions as to the nature of reality and of existence—these will serve you better, and I believe that you know this already. You are learning very quickly, for that matter.

Now, are there any outstanding questions on any matters that you wish that I discuss, Joseph?

(I read one of Pete's questions aloud: "I typed some very deep emotional, almost poetical words one afternoon and felt Ferd was expressing himself in this branch of automatic writing. Was this indeed legitimate?")

Indeed. This was an attempt on his part to reach certain levels of intuition that had not yet taken conscious form. On this particular occasion Ferd was not involved. Our young friend was developing his own intuitive abilities.

This was not, strictly speaking, automatic writing, however.

He was dissociated enough to allow knowledge to come through that he did not realize he possessed. *(Pause.)* There is a rhythm-making talent here to some extent. Also I believe an unrecognized ability to work with numbers.

("Can I change the subject?")

You may indeed.

("Why don't you give us the entity name for Venice?")

Give us a moment here. Saricke.

("Do you want to spell it?")

S A R I C K E. Do you have other questions?

(I could see Jane was quite tired. "No.")

We will therefore bid you all a fond good evening. My heartiest regards, and we shall now end our session.

("Good night, Seth."

(11 PM.)

SESSION 358
AUGUST 2, 1967 9 PM WEDNESDAY

(Marilyn Wilbur and Peter Murtough were witnesses.)

(Very recently, while falling off to sleep—in the hypnogogic state—Peter Murtough had a vision of his sister Julie falling. She fell rather heavily, he told us, and could have struck her head. He could not tell whether or not she hurt herself, but the vision has been on his mind since its occurrence. He wanted to know if Seth could help out here.)

Good evening.

([RFB & Pete:] "Good evening, Seth."

([Marilyn:] "Hello.")

Now. My regards to our friend, and please give us a moment. *(Pause.)* Now as to your picture of your sister, a period approximately six months distant and the <u>probability</u> of a bathroom tumble, that can be averted if no small rugs are used on the floor. This includes rubber-backed rugs.

There was some distortion in your picture. The tumble will not occur if no rugs are used. For safety's sake I would suggest an eight-month period. No <u>severe</u> (underlined) difficulty would result in any case, but an ugly bruise *(pause)*, I believe by the right ear, and some twisting of a foot.

I believe the purchase of a new rug for the room would be involved, and she would slip upon it. Now this probability can be averted in the ways given.

Leave the floor there uncluttered. There seems to be a possibility that I do not understand, where for one reason or another underline{newspapers} might be laid upon the floor, in that room. Perhaps beneath dripping clothes.

This should also be avoided. *(Pause, gesture to Pete.)* In this way, you switch from one set of probabilities to another, and in this case to your advantage.

Now a moment please. The other situation, regarding your Boston friend.

(Recently our friend in Boston, Pat Norelli, had visited a female medium who told her that she was under the influence of an evil eye, and would never have a happy day as long as she lived. This alarmed Pat so that she phoned Jane long distance, asking for some information from Seth.)

The so-called medium is a severely-damaged personality. She herself projects highly negative feelings outward underline{onto} her sitters, and then picks these up again on a subconscious level, and reacts to them. She tends to condemn her sitters because she is frightened of condemning herself.

She is sincere, and sincerely deluded, a psychopathic personality who delights in arousing fear in others. *(Pause.)* And for our romantic Boston friend *(smile)*, the following: at this time you are *(smile)* not wasting your time with your fine gentleman friend. No more should be read into that last sentence than I have given you, however, for I will not predict for you the outcome of the relationship.

For my so-industrious Ruburt, the writers conference should work out well, and I shall surprise you and say that I recommend it.

(The conference to take place on Star Island, off Portsmouth, NH, on Saturday, August 12, 1967; in the company of Pat Norelli and Dick Reed.)

I may in advance tell you something about your journey, since you have been so ambitious of late.

You may now take your break and we shall indeed then continue.

(9:16. Jane's eyes had remained closed. Her voice had been a little better than average, her pace good. Resume at 9:30.)

Now. There are times when underline{all} probabilities point in one direction, and I believe there is a mathematical theorem, a theoretical one, that defines such occurrences. In which case, the future is indeed locked.

This is not the case as far as your sister in concerned. Therefore changes in the probabilities alter that particular future, and the change that I suggested completely wipes out the prior, probable accident. Do you see? *(Facing Pete.)*

([Pete:]"Yes.")

Then if the advice is followed there is no danger.

Again, a moment please. *(Pause.)* An F S A *(spelled)* concerning the Boston affair. An afternoon gathering of 14 people, and a return engagement. A meeting on Ruburt's part with an old forgotten acquaintance. The possibility of <u>an unusual</u> Seth session.

(See the notes following the 360th session re the above data.)

For our long-haired blonde friend, *(Marilyn Wilbur)*, shortly a new element, another person who will play a significant part in her life, for either a long or brief period. The person either connected to her, or to her friend—a new personality element. Certainly in the long run beneficial. *(Pause.)* I <u>believe</u> but am not certain, that the individual will not be originally from this area, or, if so, will be connected with another area. *(Pause.)*

(At break Marilyn told us that she does react to people in the fashion Seth describes—either on a long-term or short-term basis. Jane told me later that she felt the new influence mentioned would be a male.)

Joseph, have you any questions?

("Not particularly.")

I hesitate to ask our young friend.

("Do you have a question, Pete?"

([Pete:] "My mind's a blank... My sister was thinking of a possible trip to Australia for Christmas.")

A possibility always exists. There is here however a fairly strong <u>possibility</u> (underlined), in connection with someone else she may meet—a male who wears glasses in his leisure hours. Brown hair, A L somehow connected with him. *(Pause.)* And with a distant Detroit connection. <u>Or</u> a connection, a strong one, with the individual and cars.

If the meeting takes place, and it is a probability, then he will be instrumental in arranging such a trip. The meeting, if it takes place, will occur between the first and fifth days of October or November. The man will have a connection with two children.

If you have no more questions than we shall end our session, as I know too well how many sessions are not yet typed.

("Do you want to say a few words about the dream the dentist's nurse told me about today?")

A moment, please. *(Long pause, eyes closed.)*

I do not like to go into this particular data. *(Pause.)* Quite frankly, it is none of your business.

("Oh." To my knowledge, this is the first time in all the sessions that Seth has given such an answer. My question was not meant to pry into a personal life, merely to obtain what I thought would be interesting information about a certain dream related to me by Dr. Colucci's nurse, voluntarily.)

The affair is highly personal. The events may or may not occur, and I do not want to add to their probability, you see, by any statement.

(This would make the dream precognitive.

("How's Wisconsin making out?"

(Several times recently Seth has told us we are going to get ESP news or corre-spondence, having to do with business, from someone, a male, in Wisconsin.)

The data is legitimate.

(I read from Pete's list of questions: "Could you tell me something about the time I had the feeling of Ferd entering my body while I was lying on my side in bed?")

You are becoming aware of higher levels of your own personality and you are trying to interpret them. The sensation was your own reaction to the psychological presence of your friend Ferd. He did not cause the sensations. But in another way he was their cause, since you interpreted his existence in that particular manner. Because of your own personality makeup you will lean to physical interpretations, and physical sensations in an attempt to understand nonphysical impressions.

If you have questions we shall answer them, and if not we shall close.

("I have no more."

([Pete:] "I have one.")

Go ahead.

([Pete:] "Well Seth, I was extremely bothered by my brother's reaction to what you said about the August 20th five and ten race—you told Steve not to bet on it. Any chance of this still working out, at all?")

Any chance whatsoever covers much territory, young man. At one time many probabilities pointed in that direction. At this time less than half of those chances remain, and even in your terms the odds are very much against it. *(Pause.)*

What is unfortunate, however, is something else. High expectations are good, but they must not be used as a crutch. You are too unacquainted with your own abilities to attempt to use them in the way that you did.

Your brother Stephen must have faith in his own abilities, for these represent <u>his</u> *(underlined)* freedom and eventual success.

(Pause.) Did you have a question, Joseph?

("No.")

We will then wish you all a most hearty good evening.

("Good night, Seth."

([Pete:] "Good night, Seth. See you Monday.")

Julie lived where there were few flowers—that is why she is so fond of them now. I will have some words for Julie and Stephen at our next session.

([Pete:] "Thank you, Seth.")

There are difficulties for Ruburt's associate of last year at the center. (*Nursery school. Long pause.*) For Boston, a dinner for five, and a package will arrive.

(*It is August 21 as I type these notes. As far as we can remember, no dinner for five worked out re the Boston trip. A package did arrive for Pat Norelli, containing her new glasses, however. Pat was most anxious to get these, and found them waiting at her Boston apartment upon our arrival there. Her first question of her roommate, after showing Jane and me our room, concerned the arrival of the glasses. The data are very general however.*)

(*To Pete:*) this Mary Ann of yours lived once close to mountains. Three children and a fourth who is somehow different. Perhaps a stepchild. Either this or she had a half-sister or brother. L A R, and someone with gray curly, very curly, hair. (*Pause.*)

An <u>angled</u> arm. (*Jane shakes head, pauses.*) Drinking is a turnabout in her case. These are simply impressions. We will make them clearer when we can. A very stormy 20 to 27-year-old period. Perhaps a Mexican connection. (*Long pause; very long, eyes closed.*)

We have the story behind your stout friend's dream.

(*"I thought you didn't want to discuss it."*)

The dream of Ruburt's student. The stout one.

(*"Oh." Seth meant Venice McCullough, I realized. At first I had thought he referred to Dr. Colucci's dental nurse. Venice's dream, a recurring one, was related to her efforts to reduce, and had troubled her a good deal, she told us before the last session.*)

We will not give the data this evening. It is too long and complicated. But she is not to worry. And now, good evening to you all.

(*[From all present:] "Good night, Seth."*)

(*10:10. Jane said that she had been far-out toward the end of the session, and felt that her consciousness had been "roaming around" without alighting upon anything definite.*)

SESSION 359
AUGUST 7, 1967 9:30 PM MONDAY

(*Peter Murtough was a witness for the last time. The session was recorded. Jane's eyes were mostly closed, her pace good.*

(*[Pete:] "Hi, Seth."*)

Good evening.

("Good evening, Seth.")

Now, good evening to you all. To our friend Pete, and to Stephen and Julie.

You are a very closely knit family, and there are advantages and disadvantages in being so emotionally involved. Give us a moment please.

There is much that you do not know regarding this kind of session, and the means to which it may be put. Ruburt has endeavored to speak to Pete and explain to him how his ability should be used and should not be used.

He understands what Ruburt has told him, and I am certain that he will explain it well to you. Briefly however, psychic development should lead to overall personality development. It should not be used in order to make things easier in physical terms, though I understand indeed that this is a temptation, and an understandable one. Nevertheless, the fact remains that psychic development results in something else entirely. The person involved must then demand more of himself...

(Here I lost a few words because of the rapid pace. Since the session was being recorded I didn't ask Seth to slow down.)

...It occurs to me that much of this may be new to you. Nevertheless, any physical benefits, any predictions that do occur in such sessions, come as a result of initial spiritual and psychic development. To expect the physical benefits first can indeed close off the very spiritual and psychic development.

Now, the love that binds you all is a close, sometimes open... *(words missed again)*...that which is too much for him at this time... *(and again.)*... This sort of session is not primarily to tell you what you should do, Stephen. It is not a means of helping you avoid decision, my good friend. The purpose of such a session is instead to help you develop, to grow in self-confidence and strength through making your own decisions.

Now, the following is to Stephen. You are highly impetuous, and this can be to your advantage, and, also, as you must know, to your disadvantage. You have not asked me, Stephen, the right questions for you. It is not to your overall benefit that you continue as you have in many ways.

Give us a moment.

<u>Your</u> particular personality is not helped if I should tell you what to do in the specific incidents that are requested. For <u>you</u> would not be strengthened, but you would be relying upon me; and any errors, dear friend, would also be laid to me.

You have been afraid, you see, for accepting the responsibility for your own decisions and actions, and I cannot help you continue in this direction. I say this in all good feeling. There are some points that I shall mention however.

As to the balanced diet, I will say this: you are not eating evenly. There is at some times an overreliance upon one type of food, and then another. It is not good for you to lose so much weight, and many of your symptoms are directly connected with various deficiencies brought about through your diet. There should be a daily balance of nutrients.

A balanced daily consumption of protein and carbohydrates, of meats and vegetables. 138 to 140 is the lowest you should go as far as your weight is concerned. Now, you may or may not take my advice as you prefer. In any case I have given it to you.

Now, let us see further.

Stephen, you should try relaxation techniques. You are overly nervous, partially as a result of your dietary deficiencies, and also by certain temperamental tendencies. You have fine qualities. You are not, however, using them to capacity now.

You will grow as you make your own decisions. You must simply take my word for it, that it would be highly disadvantageous to your development if I told you what you should do now, and what steps you should take.

We will have more to say to you shortly. I suggest now that we take a brief break. And Julie, I will have a few words to say to you also.

(*9:41. Jane said she had been well dissociated. She felt good about this, for it meant she had no worries about distorting the material, etc. Resume at 9:50.*)

Now, again to Stephen. Many of the things you want can indeed be obtained by you. If they are attained they will be attained through your own development and through the use of your own abilities.

Give us a moment. You must not scatter your energies. If you dislike your present job, then it is up to you to find another. Do you see?

Any true success must come through your own efforts, for no other success has any meaning at all. When you have achieved reachable goals then you will have the strength and freedom to follow through, and ability to achieve goals that are more difficult. There is a dangerous tendency here that should be mentioned, and it is this: you must not blame others when you do not achieve your goals.

You must remember it is easy, and, again, quite understandable, that oftentimes others seem to be the source of defeats. But these defeats are always caused by inner spiritual or psychic problems that have not been faced or solved.

Lose any bitterness that you may have toward others, for this bitterness is holding you back. The impetuous part of your nature can lead you to joy, and to spontaneous and intuitive understanding. There is a tendency, again, to lash out at others, and this should be restrained. Live every day to its fullest, and do not be a slave to your hopes for the future. If you do not learn to enjoy today you will not enjoy the future no matter what it may bring.

You have perseverance and strength, and these are good qualities and should serve you well. The return to Australia is a family lullaby, a family hope, a family dream. If you are to return to Australia it will be through your own individual efforts, and not through a windfall nor a gift from heaven.

Gifts from heaven are the results of individual spiritual developments, and if they are not then they only appear to be gifts. The fine qualities that you do possess should be used to aid you in making your own way. This is not unusual with you. This is the usual road for young men, and I have followed it myself many times.

My dear friend Stephen, there is no easy way, and often the way that seems easiest is the hardest way of all.

(The tape ran out on the recorder.

("Can we have a break, Seth?")

You may indeed.

(10:01. Jane was again well dissociated. Her eyes had remained closed. Resume at 10:10.)

Now. It is not easy, dear Stephen, at your age, nor indeed at any age, to hear words that you do not particularly want to hear.

You have the intelligence and the intuition to realize that what I am telling you is for your own good. I could instead have told you what you wanted to hear. Had I done so I would have done you a grave disservice.

You are misusing your body, for you are depriving it of necessary nutrients. You are not giving it what it needs. You are driving it too hard, and it is trying to tell you so. You must listen to its voice and return to your normal weight.

The eye symptoms are connected with the weight deficiencies. The tingling symptoms are also. You are not giving your body a steady daily balance of nutrients. For this reason it is misbehaving. You must straighten this out, for you are not able to make any clear decisions unless you feel well.

I have explained to your brother the reasons behind the Ferd prediction, and he will explain them to you. Ferd is not to be the family fortune teller, you see, and as my dear friends Ruburt and Joseph will tell you, I am hardly the grand chief fortune teller for them.

Fortune telling is not the reason for my presence here, you see.

Now give us a moment, please. You do have an ability with animals, and you will do well working with them. Now I will tell you something, dear friend, and I hope sincerely that in later years you thank me, though I do not believe you will thank me now.

You want to be a jockey because it seems so difficult for you to become one, and because so many barriers lie in your path.

For many reasons this is not best for you, nor is it what you really want. But in working toward a goal that is very distant, a goal that will be extremely difficult for you to achieve, you feel subconsciously that you will be excused from failure; if you fail you can then say that it was because so many obstacles were in your way.

You are very afraid of failure—hardly any crime—many are afraid of failure. But this causes you to avoid goals that you have a good possibility of achieving. If a goal is attainable and you fail to attain it, you see, then you feel you would have to blame yourself—and again, you do not want to accept the consequences of your own action.

I hope I have made this clear, for it is important that you understand me. In the general field, working with animals, however, you have admirable qualities that can be utilized if you use them toward a practical goal. Subconsciously you do not want to be a jockey.

You have chosen that goal because it does seem so difficult, and if you fail then you can blame circumstances rather than yourself.

Now. You need not be afraid of failure, and this is your main difficulty. You have strength and ability that you do not realize you possess, and it will withstand you. You do not have to be afraid of testing yourself against attainable goals. You do not have to look for windfalls.

You have your own abilities, and properly used they will lead to your own development and happiness. Remember, no one owes you anything, but you owe everything to yourself. Now if I sound like the old man from the mountain, so must it be. My heartiest good wishes to you however.

Now I suggest a brief break and I shall speak to Julie.

(10:25 to 10:35.)

Now. This is to our high-apple-pie-in-the-sky girl.

She is doing very well. I did not intend to be hard on Stephen, dear Julie, but it is very important that he understand what I say. Important to his health and future well-being.

Now you have been doing very well, and with attainable goals. Give us a moment, please. I believe there may be a change in the future for you, involving your area of employment. *(Pause.)* Perhaps within an eight-month period, though I am not certain here of the time element. There _may_ be a Denver connection.

Now this is only an impression. We will perhaps pursue it in a moment—a Denver connection, or a man's name... Dan, or the man will have a connection with Denver. This is a probability and not a frozen future, however. Now give is a moment. *(Pause.)*

Yours is an open, affectionate nature, but you are sometimes impatient. Learn to look still further beneath appearances and surface reasons, particularly for your own behavior, for the practice will serve you well.

Yours can be a nourishing element within the family, when you do not allow impatience to upset you. You are right in shielding your younger brother. But do not shield him too well. There will be time needed if his abilities are to mature. You two work well together. Do not accept without some critical analysis however, though I do not believe that you will. Nevertheless help <u>temper</u> Pete's natural enthusiasm with good common sense.

Julie, Steve, and Pete—You should all read any books you can find concerning parapsychology and psychic phenomena. The more you read the more you will understand of Pete's ability, and the more indeed that you can develop your own abilities. For each individual has inner senses, whether or not he knows that he does, and these should be developed.

There is in the world of probabilities a good chance that you will very seriously consider marriage toward the end of a two-year period. A quite serious romance in any case, that may or may not develop into marriage. Again, this is in the probability range.

I have explained how at certain times a definite future may be seen, and how at other times a probable future. On some occasions the totality of probabilities all point in one main direction. These tend to form a more or less definite future, all psychic forces rushing toward it. Even this however can be altered.

At other times the probabilities point in many or several directions.

Now give us a moment. We have enjoyed the presence of your brother very much, and we return him to you the better, we hope, for the experience.

Stephen—

(The tape, which had been flopped, now finished its run, shortly before the session ended.)

—there is now hope for your success, for you can now take the necessary steps to achieve it.

We will take a break or end the session, Joseph, at your preference and discretion.

("We'll see what the score is at break."

(10:50. Jane was by now beginning to look quite tired, but we could tell the session wasn't over yet. Resume at 11:05.)

Now. Here we are, young man. I hope that we have been able to be of some help to your brother, for it is time for him to change some of his ways.

You may speak to me freely.

([Pete:] "Right now?")

Right now indeed.

([Pete:] "Okay. I really have enjoyed hearing you, Seth, I think you are a real cool head.")

I am indeed pleased to hear that I am a cool head.

([Pete:] "Do you know any more about Ferd? Have you been in contact with him?")

I have not been in contact with him. We are on different levels, you see. You must have faith in your own abilities, but do not push them. If you read the material carefully that I have already given you, you will see that I have answered more questions concerning Ferd than you have asked me.

([Pete:]"That's right. Perhaps one of these days we can get together again—hold a joint Seth and Ferd session.")

I think there will be some time for such a joint session. However during our sessions I will look in on you from time to time, though I do not believe you will be aware of it.

([Pete:] "Unless my body warns me by tingles or something.")

I do not believe so, in my case. I do not want you to develop a habit of looking for me, you see—

([Pete:] "Oh no.")

—and I shall take pains therefore to effectively shield the circumstances. This does not mean that I shall spy, you see.

([Pete:] "The Red Baron and Snoopy... I think it's been great talking to you.")

I have enjoyed you very much. Do not expect too much too soon.

([Pete:] "I won't.")

This is your greatest assurance of fully developing your abilities. Do you see?

([Pete:] "Yes, I do.")

I give you then my very best wishes *(pause)*, and my warm affection. Joseph, I believe we shall now close for the evening.

("All right.")

([Pete:] "My best regards to you, Seth, and good night and good bye.")

("Good night, Seth."

(11:12. Jane was again well dissociated, although she said she started to "come out" toward the very end of the session.)

SESSION 360
AUGUST 16, 1967 11 AM WEDNESDAY

(The brief session was held in the office of Jane's publisher, Frederick Fell, in New York City. On August 15, Jane had declined to appear on the Alan Burke TV show, WNEW-TV.

(This session was not planned. See the notes at the end of the session for material related to this. Jane spoke for Seth while facing Frederick Fell across his desk, but her eyes remained closed. Her voice was a bit stronger than usual, without reaching anything like the volume it is capable of; her pace a little faster, her manner active.)

Good day. Now. It has taken me some while before I could manage to get our friend Ruburt *(Jane)* here.

I am very pleased that we did not appear on the TV program, but I <u>knew</u>, you see, that we would not do so.

I am, and have indeed always been, an educator. However there are some circumstances where education becomes difficult, and the circumstances were not those of our choosing or of our liking.

I am very pleased to meet you *(to F. Fell)*, and since you are the one who published Ruburt's book, I thank you. I do suggest, Joseph—

("Yes.")

—that in the future I help our friend arrange his business matters. Now, if you have any questions that you would like to ask me concerning my relationship with Ruburt, or myself, feel free to ask them.

(Seth spoke to F. Fell, who then asked Seth a question concerning his daughter's safety on an upcoming trip to Europe.)

Give us a moment, please. *(Brief pause.)* These are impressions, Joseph... There seems to be a trip with a stopover, a place stopped at for a short time before another destination is reached. I believe this to be a voluntary stopover, but a brief one. In any case before the final destination there is another place that will be visited.

(Pause.) There is safety for the daughter.

Give us a moment. These are impressions. Gray. This on the part of a name or perhaps place. *(Pause.)* Someone aged 14. A connection with someone aged 24 or 23. A J and a C. A linen shop on a cobblestone street, with the numbers 2 1 5; or separately 1 2 and then 215 connected. Run by a white or gray-haired thin person. Something wrong with the left wrist.

A W L connection—now this is separate. *(Pause.)* Give us a moment. A connection with a woman with reddish hair. A gift purchased that seems to resemble an object made of very small matchstick-size pieces of material, not necessarily of wood. *(Jane gestured.)*

You may take a break or end the session at your discretion. I am, myself, delighted to be here.

("We'll take a break, Seth."

(11:12. I thought F. Fell would be too busy to continue with a session much longer, but called for a break in case Seth had a few parting words.

(Jane said she was fairly well "out." F. Fell asked for clarification concerning Seth's remark about helping "our friend arrange his business matters." I said I thought Seth referred to Jane here.

(Resume at 11:20.)

I was not presuming to offer you my assistance on such a short acquaintance. Nevertheless if ever you should desire it, I should certainly be more than willing to comply.

(11:21. An exchange followed between Jane, F. Fell, and myself. F. Fell asked Jane if she would be willing to speak as Seth at, say, Town Hall, if he rented it. Jane said yes. She then resumed as Seth.)

We will now end the session. I am a cagey old gentleman...

(I missed a few words here, but did not interrupt. RFB.) ...I will at all times —and this is for your benefit, Joseph—I will protect your Ruburt, as I saw to it that he did not appear on the program. However, I will cooperate under more beneficial conditions.

(To F. Fell:) I tell you again, that I am most pleased to speak with you. And now we shall all take our leave. My heartiest wishes to you.

("So long, Seth."

(11:26. Jane was again well "out." F. Fell called the session "remarkable," etc., and noted the charge in voice, personality, expression, etc., that took place in Jane when she spoke as Seth.

(Much more, of course, was said at the meeting between Jane, F. Fell and me, than is noted here. The meeting was cordial and the conditions right for Seth to come through. Jane said she doubted that any such contact with Seth could have been established on the Burke TV show.

(F. Fell told us that his wife has red hair, in line with Seth's data on the previous page: "A connection with a woman with reddish hair." We herewith ask F. Fell to check the rest of the data given in the session whenever possible. If some of it is precognitive this will take a while.

(Here are some notes concerning how precognitive material can be distorted, yet still bear a good resemblance in physical life to the original data. In the 358th session for August 2, 1967, Seth stated, after mentioning Jane's speaking engagement at Star Island, off Portsmouth, NH, scheduled for Saturday, August 12: "A meeting

on Ruburt's part with an old forgotten acquaintance;" and "The possibility of an
unusual Seth session."

(Jane met no old acquaintances at Star Island or in Boston, nor was any
unusual session held. On August 9, Wednesday, Jane was invited by telephone to
appear on the Burke TV show in New York City. On the evening of August 15,
Tuesday, Jane and I were having supper at an outdoor restaurant, The Californian,
at 7th Avenue and Broadway in New York City. At 7:30 PM, we were approached
by Merle Cratsley of Odessa, New York, an old friend.

(Merle did not know we were eating there, but did know we were in New York
City, having been so informed by phone by his wife, with whom I work in Elmira.
He had planned to be in the audience at the Alan Burke TV show August 16. Merle
and his wife used to live in the apartment house we occupy in Elmira. They moved
perhaps a year and a half ago, and Jane has seen him perhaps once since then. He is
hardly forgotten however.

(At the time of the 358th session we did not know Merle was scheduled by his
company to be in New York City; nor could he have known where we would be eating supper at that particular time. He had not been to our hotel on 46th Street, since
when we met at the restaurant he asked us where we were staying. We believe, however, that he may have had a general idea that we would be staying in the Times
Square area.

(The second part of the data concerning an unusual session, can be interpreted as applying to this session, the 360th, which took place in F. Fell's office in New
York City on August 16, the day after the Cratsley meeting. However, the next session, the 361st, was also quite unusual, and took place in the coffee shop of our hotel,
the Paramount, at 235 West 46th Street. It was a different type of session, unique in
Jane's experience and was witnessed by myself and Raymond Van Over of the
Parapsychology Foundation. See the accompanying notes for that session. It took place
later the same day, August 16, as this session, the 360th.

(The above notes will show how complicated a task it sometimes is to interpret
data. In capsule form: The data given in connection with a Boston trip, with New
York City not heard from yet by us; yet events during the New York City trip, a couple of days after the Boston trip, bear a close resemblance to the data. We have
learned that data should be considered sentence by sentence, without considering the
whole body of material as necessarily related. Again and again it has been demon-
strated to us that two succeeding bits of material, seemingly related, can refer to
entirely different matters, separated in time and space.

(Two other pieces of data given in the 358th session have not been checked out
by us, and may never be by their very nature. One pertains to a return engagement
and could take months to work out.)

SESSION 361
AUGUST 16, 1967 3:45 PM WEDNESDAY

(This session was held later the same day as the 360th session, and again was not planned. It is typed up from notes I made during and immediately after it, but is by no means complete. Memory, which Jane and I treat cautiously, also enters into it, but the hard facts are noted where we are sure.

(This is the first time Jane held two sessions in one day, even though both were relatively brief. This second session is also unique in her experience, and promises well for the future. The witness other than myself was Mr. Raymond Van Over, associate editor of the Parapsychology Foundation of 29 West 57th Street, New York, NY 10019.

(Jane and I left F. Fell's office, where the 360th session had been held, at about 11:45 AM, with an appointment to meet Mr. Van Over at about noon. He had a very few minutes for us before leaving his own office to keep an appointment. At his office Jane was informed that a phone call awaited her from the Alan Burke TV show; a Mr. Shapiro was on the line at that moment. Jane spent some fifteen minutes explaining to him why she did not want to be on the Burke show.

(Mr. Van Over appeared to be interested in Jane's abilities, although he hadn't read her ESP book. He briefly outlined a business venture he was launching himself in the fall, if possible, and asked if we could meet him in the lobby of our hotel, the Paramount, at 3 PM. This session, the 361st, took place during our meeting in the coffee shop, called Rudd's, of the Paramount.

(There are no verbatim quotes here from Seth, since Jane obtained her information from him in a different way. The session began after we had had some time for an informative, get-acquainted talk, on parapsychology in general, methods of conducting tests, personalities, Seth's particular philosophy, etc. Mr. Van Over had much interesting information to impart; and also, much of what he had to say about the way mediums operate struck responsive notes within us, since we had seen the same things transpiring within, and in connection with, Jane.

(As in Frederick Fell's office that morning, Jane now announced that Seth was about and that she was capable of holding a session. But we sat in a public place and she did not want a display. We discussed going to our hotel room. Jane then said she thought she might be able to give Seth's data in a different way than she usually did. She felt Seth's presence "just below consciousness", she said, and thought she might be able to speak for him in a natural manner without attracting the attention of others. There was a constant stream of people passing our table in the coffee shop, but no one paid us any attention.

(Jane was also encouraged when Ray Van Over told her that many mediums

operated in the fashion she contemplated. This new departure was not particularly easy for Jane, and none of us wanted her to overdo it, but it was quite successful. Note also that Seth didn't make his presence felt, nor was he asked to, until a convivial atmosphere had been established between the three of us present. The same kind of atmosphere had been set that morning at F. Fell's office.

(Ray Van Over is leaving the Parapsychology Foundation sometime soon to launch his own business, which involves publishing. He was naturally concerned about the success of this venture, in which he was involved with others. Seth told Jane to tell him that the venture should be a successful one. There was some related data here that I did not make notes on. Then Jane, speaking for Seth, gave the initials W C, as those of a person very involved in Ray Van Over's publishing venture.

(Ray Van Over said that this data was "quite correct", the initials belonging to a person he proceeded to name. I did not write down the full name at the time, and so lost it. Seth also mentioned other initials: a J and a letter toward the end of the alphabet; this was not definite enough.

(Jane said later that Mr. Van Over's comments concerning W C during the session were distracting; she has made this remark before after sessions; it seems the mere sound of another voice can disrupt the flow of data, unless she has specifically asked for comment from witnesses.

(During this time I was watching Jane in an attempt to determine whether we should call a halt to the session. It was apparent that her control with this new method was somewhat unsure; she paused often while speaking, and appeared to have to make quite an effort to maintain just the right balance between being herself while allowing Seth to hover just below, or within her range of consciousness, so that she could pass along his data. Her eyes blinked often. I thought she could slip into a deep trance from this state, and she later agreed. She did not want to, however, in our location, and just as I was on the point of suggesting that she end the session, she called a halt to it herself. In a few moments she was out of the trance.

(This had indeed been a new experience for Jane, and she called it a new state of consciousness for her. She said that she had felt sensations of "freezing cold" at her forehead and a few other parts of her body. She also felt an internal "buzzing" which wasn't physical, and a sudden desire for urination at the end of the session. She was left with a general feeling of being shaky inside, and this lasted for a while. Jane said she could very easily have gone into a deep trance, and had to work to keep everything in balance—herself, Seth, etc. If memory serves me correctly Ray Van Over said some of the effects she described were effects experienced by other mediums also.

(Jane was pleased at the correct information she had given; though much of it was precognitive, and will have to await the passage of time in order to be checked out.

(Ray Van Over described in some detail certain experiments he was organizing in which astral travel would be predominant. He also asked Jane if she would be willing to participate in tests, and she said yes. Our meeting ended on this general note of promised further communication.

(After reading these notes Jane reminded me that during the session Seth also told R. Van Over that one of the sponsors or members of his new research society would pull out—that this person was somewhat of a disrupting influence, etc. When Jane mentioned this I too recalled it.

(R. Van Over also told us that Elaine Garrett wrote the review of Jane's ESP book, which appeared under a pseudonym in The Journal of Parapsychology.*)*

SESSION 362
SEPTEMBER 11, 1967 9 PM MONDAY

(The 303rd session was held on November 26, 1966 with Eugene and Sarah Bernard as witnesses. Recently Sarah telephoned Jane from Chapel Hill, NC, and asked for this session—the first held since August 16, 1967. Jane had needed a rest for some time, after the long grind of sessions from late 1963.

(John Bradley was a witness to tonight's session. He has witnessed many sessions, usually stopping in on his trips into Elmira as a drug salesman. He is from Williamsport, PA. Interestingly, John began to ask us questions about the Indian teacher, Baba, who was discussed by Seth and Gene Bernard in the 303rd session. John has never mentioned Baba before, nor had he read the 303rd session.

(On September 12, the day after this session was held, Jane bought the October issue of Fate Magazine. *Curtis Fuller's column deals in part with Gene Bernard, although the material therein was evidently taken from the wire stories concerning Gene last year.*

(Jane has also recently received a phone call from a young husband in Franklin, LA, asking Seth's help for his wife, who is very ill. We did not know who Seth would speak about first tonight, but surmised it would be Gene Bernard.

(Jane sat rather tensely in her chair as she began speaking for Seth. Her voice was quieter than usual, her eyes closed.)

Now, good evening.

([John and I:] "Good evening, Seth.")

Good evening to you all.

Joseph, give us a moment if you please. We are going to speak first concerning your Bernard. Will you close the window?

(John Bradley closed the window to reduce traffic noise.)

Thank you... There is a vitamin <u>D</u> deficiency here with our Bernard. Therefore a rather large dose of vitamin D is recommended daily, in any acceptable form.

There is a difficulty, a symptom, dryness of the skin, and some flaking. And I believe there is or can be, trouble—hair will fall out, or begin to fall. The diet is very deficient *(pause)* generally speaking, and is robbing the tissues.

(Jane was speaking with many pauses.)

The diet is more important here than it would seem. Certain types of protein are also not being taken in anything like sufficient quantities. The body itself is not equipped to fight its battle.

Before we discuss other more significant aspects of our friend's condition, these physical matters should be taken care of, for the physical and mental are so dependent one upon the other. Plain water should be taken often, a glass three to five times daily. *(Pause.)* Give us a moment...

He has literally frightened himself away. He has disrupted the part of the self that usually deals with physical reality, and its manipulation. He tried to dispense with this physically-oriented ego, using shortcut methods.

He had not found a strongly centralized inner self as yet, that could take over the organization of the entire psychological structure. He toppled his monarch, had no replacement, and opened his kingdom to ruin.

Now the question is: what can be done, and how can the battered sections of the self best be put together?

The physical matters mentioned should be taken care of immediately. That will be a start. Now, he does not entirely recognize his position. *(Long pause.)* He has temporarily abdicated, but there is no basic reason to believe that this will be permanent. The danger does exist. However, I told you the ego was set aside, and fear was at the root.

He intended a strong inner self to take over control of the entire personality. The ego however was terrified at the thought. Long after he wished the ego to return, the ego hid. He battered down his own doors. He is seeking enlightenment, but he was not strong enough to contain it.

There is a possible new beginning for him, however, and it will be a new reorganization of tendencies that results in the formation of a <u>new</u> ego, born out of the old. *(Long pause.)* It must be formed slowly, as the child's ego is. He wanted to cut out too many steps, you see, hence his difficulty.

This new ego that he must form will come slowly. It may be scarred, but it will be fairly dependable. He must face his responsibilities. It does him no good to let him avoid them, and it may do him severe harm.

He will emerge. The drugs allowed him to permit himself a luxury that he could ill afford. There are those who are so tightly meshed within physical reality that the soul is squeezed dry. They are tight, sore, and chafing beneath too-severe habits and ideas. For them momentary release, <u>such as</u> the drugs can give, is highly beneficial. For our friend however the inner self has been overly involved with wandering, and but lightly held within the limits of the intense focus demanded by physical reality. This freedom catered to his weakness, you see. Had he more discipline it could also have released his strength.

He is beginning to come together again. It is necessary now that he see through endeavors, and face the consequences of his own psychological action.

You may take a break and we shall continue.

(9:32 to 9:50.)

The ego structure had been in danger for some time previous. Psychologically there was some considerable distance between his identity and the physical universe as he knew it. He did not quite make contact. It was too easy for him to stray.

Now. From your viewpoint in three-dimensional reality it is safe, most advantageous, to journey into other dimensions only when you have a reliable vehicle in which to travel. You cannot leap out of the craft in midstream, so to speak, nor have the craft develop serious difficulties when you are far from shore. This is what happened.

Great adjustments would have had to occur in any case, and subconsciously he was aware of this. He could not have survived as a contributing psychological unit within your system otherwise. The causes began, generally speaking, about the year 1938, and were heightened in the years 1942 to 1947. At the time the course was set and the personality was developed, that had taken a wrong course, for it.

A relationship with one woman beside the mother here connected. An incident with candy bars as a child, of approximately 6, or in grade six. An inner formlessness. It was easy for him, deceptively easy, to overlook physical reality, to say that it was a mirage, simply because he had never completely enmeshed himself within it. He never met it squarely.

Now, it is indeed a mirage, but it is a mirage with which you must deal. It is not so much, you see, as he thought, that nothing has meaning. Everything has so much meaning that basically no one thing can have more meaning than another, because all reality is implied within each sample of it.

He projected a meaninglessness upon reality, and then fell prey to it. Here the senses themselves can help revive him. *(Long pause.)* He seems now to be choosing between identities, but there is one waiting for him, and it is a probable ego that he did not adopt as a child.

He has been plunged back into a physical universe that he would not accept even as a valid mirage. This time he will be able to find himself within it. *(Long pause.)* In his case he must accept himself as a human being before he can hope to discover the inner self. The ego got no help from him, and it could not carry on alone. There was a definite splitting of personality elements, and a complete abandonment by the inner self of the ego.

The ego takes care of physical matters so that the inner self can go about its other concerns. To shunt it aside is highly dangerous. The inner self is then in a precarious position, for it must also attempt to deal with physical reality.

Now, it can form new ego elements to help it, and this is what is happening now.

(Long pause.) These are impressions. A room on a third floor. The letters S C R E W, having to do with a name or street name. A Washington, I believe, D.C. connection. A dirty washstand. Bernard at a window here.

I am trying to get a word. My-barrow *(my phonetic interpretation)*—only it is one word. I believe a name or place designation. 1521, perhaps a house number, I do not know. He has been at this place or visited here frequently. Usually the shades are down. He still has drugs in his system, and they should be discontinued, all kinds, completely.

Someone who sees him, a <u>male</u>, is not doing him good at this time. It is important to realize that the condition would have erupted in any case. The usual ego would have been much more serviceable however, for a longer period of time, had he not taken the drugs. The whole personality however needed a readjustment, though <u>this</u> is more drastic than was necessary.

You may take your break.

(10:15. Jane's pace was somewhat faster now, and her eyes opened occasionally. Her voice was stronger and she said she was pretty far-out.

(In answer to a question Jane said she wasn't projecting while giving the above data, but "almost thought I was trying to." I said Sarah would undoubtedly like to know how the material obtained tonight could be put to use so as to obtain a practical result re Gene. Resume at 10:38.)

The change will come from an <u>im</u>plosion, rather than an explosion. He will make the required adjustments on his own.

He had retreated into the formlessness that he had himself created. He will come out on the other side. There will be some distortions. *(Pause.)* Within three months time there should be a noticeable improvement. Now by improvement I mean an indication that a central core of personality is once again in charge.

Whether or not this personality will find merit with Bernard's old friends is another matter, but a central core of personality must, and will again, take charge. It may display in the beginning too much rigidity, as a natural protection, but this in time will pass.

This man <u>will not be a stranger</u>, yet he will not be the old Bernard, and Sarah can only help him by letting him know that she is there, and waiting. This is more important than it may appear, for the new ego will need guides to manipulate within physical reality once again.

The whole self contains the ego, and he ignored this. Any investigations into the nature of existence, and any true learning, must take place within all levels of the self. He cut off his ego to save his soul, and nearly lost both in the bargain. The ego indeed is part of the soul. It is one of the voices of the soul. *(Long pause.)*

It is now important that he relearn the objective nature of your reality, the simple sanity of an apple as an apple. After this then perhaps he can begin to wonder at the reality behind the objective universe. Now he must let it nurse him.

I do indeed wish him good fortune. For now it is sufficient that he take comfort in the familiar physical universe.

(The next original manuscript page, number 3955, is missing. Obviously, Seth gave material for John Bradley. Then:)

We will end the session, or take a break as you prefer.

("We'll take a very short break."

(11:02. During break John told us he has no aunt. This puzzled Jane because she said she had such a positive impression of a woman in some such capacity, connected with John's family. John's mother died a few weeks ago in Philadelphia. We have never met any of his family—wife, children, other relatives, etc.

(Resume at 11:15.)

Now, we will shortly end our session. The impression I have is strongly of a woman connected with the family. Possibly in the fifties. A longtime family connection, and a message having to do with plans or a change of plan.

I am receiving the impression from Philip *(John)*, so he will be somehow connected. The woman's build is stocky rather than slim. She is strongly connected with the family. I took it to be a blood relationship. If not, the psychic relationship is close.

Now we will indeed close for this evening... The Wisconsin connection on your part has already occurred, and we shall try to give you more on this at our next session. My heartiest regards to you all, and good evening.

("Good night, Seth."

(11:25. Jane said her impression of the woman in question was of a person

more masculine than usual for a female, but she didn't voice this during the session. John said that while Seth was speaking the name Laura Bittner popped into his mind. He saw this woman, who is stocky and in her fifties or early sixties, at his mother's funeral, for the first time in many years, and now remembered that L.B. had been a close friend of his mother's when he [John] was a child.

(John also told us now that his wife has an Aunt Catherine who fits Seth's description of a stocky woman in her fifties. He didn't know about a message however.)

SESSION 363
SEPTEMBER 12, 1967 8:45 PM TUESDAY

(This session was held for three of Jane's students. Attending were Venice McCullough, Shirley Bickford, and Ruth Klebert.

(It was hoped that in this session Seth would give impressions concerning the Gallagher's vacation.

(A note added later: I met Ruth Klebert in Gerould's drugstore yesterday, October 31, 1986— she looked okay—has had cancer and a heart attack—knew Jane had died—asked about Seth. Lives on Miller Pond now.)

Good evening.

("Good evening, Seth.")

My heartiest wishes to all here present. Now, we will speak for a brief time on some general matters while we make preparations for the Gallagher material.

Now, all of you in this room know but a small portion of your whole inner self. This inner self of yours, however, knows you well and guides your actions whether or not you intellectually realize its presence.

We will at one time or another speak with you each in a more private session. For now I simply greet you. Joseph, give us a moment if you please.

("Yes.")

These are impressions dealing with the Gallaghers. Arcadia. A name of a place that means low valley in English. A native who is dressed in clothes that do not belong to him: he is performing. The clothes are a costume from another culture.

An A here. A boat. The Gallaghers are on a boat. They pass three islands and land on the fourth. There is something spilled on the boat, and a scramble.

A strange fruit they see, it resembles a coconut but it is not one. It has pink pulp.

A party of four on the boat. The initials M B or M D and a child of six. An initial encounter that is not pleasant. Someone screams. Possibly a child involved.

The Jesuit notices a three-legged dog. He wanders far off from the others, the Jesuit.

There is a plane down, or a ship in difficulty in their locality, and result-ing activity in a port at the far tip end of the island furthest down in this par-ticular group of islands. *(Voice slurred and slow.)* Perhaps planes sent out from the port to search. The initials T B are here somewhere connected. The port at this island seems to be the only main town. *(Voice slow, slurred, long pauses.)*

While we are dealing with this, there is unusual activity around Cape Hope and this is connected with what has happened. *(Mouths words first:)* There is a town or island or bay, some area in the vicinity that sounds like Balinda; this is not it, however. Baly-winda... Baly-wanda....

Now, more personally, our friend the Jesuit. There is a large wooden object that he is taken with, like a totem, fatter it seems though, and not so tall as one. He speaks with several male natives and an American man, from Minnesota, who deals in a business that is connected with salt.

(Voice very slow and slurred all through here, and many pauses.)

An engagement between 4 and 5 today. And loud noises that are music. Two flags on one island, and an administration building that is orange or pink. They eat or talk with a man *(voice very faint)* whose name has to do with grip, you see, as bag or valise. Do you see?

("Yes.")

Some point over the spending of nine dollars in particular, a five and four ones, something outrageously priced.

A visit, a settlement of thatched or straw covered huts, nine to twelve of these. Our friend sees a shaman. A particular walk through a jungle area. Our friend the Jesuit is here, and five others have gone this same way earlier and he knows this: It is his reason for going, you see.

He and the cat lover chose one particular way because they are too cagey and shrewd to take another recommended way. Now one place they stay: has water on one side and foliage on the other, with large square openings in the front, and I do not believe here by the large square openings there is any glass. The steps are from the side, three or four. They find this place on their own. Someone has hung clothing on a line though beside the place. They can stand and look out over the ocean and sight two or three other islands, one they have visited. They plan to see three other islands.

Now you may take a break or end the session as you prefer.

("We'll take a short break."

(9:10 break. Jane didn't seem to be aware that her manner had been very detached, dreamy. She "saw" some of the surroundings, but had no real projection.

(9:20 resume.)

Now a rather odd connection with Grumbacher, or painting supplies, for the Gallaghers.

They meet a man in a hutlike place. He is thin, with a white shirt that is not fully buttoned. He does not have a beard but his face is prickly and dark. He smokes and his fingers are long and stained with nicotine. His trousers are somehow strange, and he wears white shoes or not shoes, but his feet appear lighter, you see. There is a light behind him also and he stands at a partially opened door, and our friend the Jesuit speaks to him. There is an identical structure very close by, perhaps attached, you see. There are steps and men sit on them. The stranger lives on the island and he wears a ring. He may also have on other jewelry.

The cat lover stands on the ground, waiting, and this structure is also facing the water. There is an S connected with the stranger, also an A, and the Gallaghers have come from down a road or path that is somewhat hilly, from a settlement there, and they have been riding, perhaps bicycles or wagonlike vehicles: or a wagon driven by animals; pulled by animals.

There is a church that has burned down and the place is known for an uprising that occurred years earlier.

We are not sure here, the name brings to mind the name of Sacramento, though again this is not the precise name.

A strange building there built 1924. It does not really belong there. There are no others like it and it contains records that have an historical connection, and the records come from another place, another country.

Strongly I have the number 5. Some event at 5 today, however, that will stick in their minds when they return.

Now the grass is growing here but it is turning brown. There is a brown high grass in this one area and the bottom of the trees is black and there are large berries. This is a particular area, a waste area, that has been somehow ravaged and perhaps, once burned, you see. It is ringed in by trees and the historical and psychic connections here are not good, having to do with sacrifices. Monchuco *(Rob's interpretation)* the Monchuco.

(My interpretation is that two words may have been meant; more like Mon-chu-chu? Mon-choo-choo?)

The Monchuco were here and worshiped a half bull, half woman deity and the bull was a black one and sacrifices were thrown into the sea. There is this spot where a thatched temple once stood and in a more distant past a connection, strange as it may seem, with an offshoot of the Inca civilization. This spot is on the third island and this island itself will be involved in a disaster within a short time. It will be, to all intents and purposes, wiped out.

A former governor of another country once stayed at this island also and he was removed from office ahead of schedule or otherwise politically ruined, returning to his homeland in disgrace.

Now we are returning here and we shall close this evening's session. My heartiest wishes to you all.

(9:40 PM. This was an odd session. Jane didn't sound like Seth at all a good part of the time, and she realized this to some degree. She felt as if she were projecting through time, rather than through space at the last; re Seth's moment points. Perhaps Jane was speaking more for herself, with Seth's guidance. She started with the Seth voice then gradually used one that was between her normal voice, and Seth's.

(Venice noticed that the tense changed from we to I for awhile also.)

SECOND PART OF SESSION 363
SEPTEMBER 12, 1967 TUESDAY

(This portion is typed up by Jane Butts from notes taken on the spot by Robert Butts. After the end of the Seth session, I suddenly got the impression of a name, Martha. I hesitated, then asked if the name meant anything to anyone in the room; I was sure it did. Venice said that her sister-in-law's name was Martha. Then I asked if Grandview had anything to do with Martha. Venice said that Martha had lived on Grand Island in Buffalo. With the assurance that this was correct, I went into a trance to see what impressions I could get for the students. When I was finished the results were discussed by the students; they told me what impressions were hits, etc. Apparently about 90% of the impressions were correct. The impressions will be given with a note as to their accuracy.)

I have a connection with Martha and water, perhaps because you told me she lived on Grand Island, or perhaps this is an indication of a street name such as Lake Avenue, Water Street, etc.

(?)

A house with pine trees, back kitchen.

(Yes to both; Martha's house.)

Two children.

(Yes, Martha's.)

A girl with curly brown hair.

(Yes.)

Name like Anna or Annette or Anita
(Name is Alice.)
Boy or girl about 6th Grade.
(No.)
The man, business, bottles or coverings, containers.
(?)
An earlier association further West than Buffalo, several states further West than New York State.
(Yes. Leaving room to fill in information here.)
The name Francis, male or female.
(Yes. Venice has a female cousin by that name.)
Scheduled events included service.
(Yes. Martha's husband was in the service.)
Air Force before it was the Air Force.
(No.)
A history major or deep interest in the past, a hobby of the past.
(?)
Originally five in the family.
(No.)
A woman in the background with a connection with Winchester... Rochester? Rochester or Winchester... Fairly elderly. May have been a grandmother, possibly now dead.
(Most interesting. This did not apply to Venice, but to Ruth. Her present employer's wife has white hair, but is young. She lived both in Rochester and Winchester.)
The impression of 4 stars, service? Not sure.
(?)
A collection of paraphernalia in one place connected with business or hobby perhaps, in basement, strong connection with guns.
(Yes. Martha's husband, Venice's brother, lost his life as a result of war wounds. Martha keeps all his possessions together, including his guns and rifles.)
A lease and four years connected with it, and a new location.
(?)
I'm jumping now to an uncle of Shirley's, with a mustache and with an old photo. This means he is now an old man now or is dead. The fashion of his clothes is old. First a black mustache and then it turns white. He wears a uniform of some sort or fancy clothes, a hat that is strange.
(Yes. All of this describes a photograph of Shirley's grandfather not uncle; a photo she had not seen until approximately four days before this session.)

A European connection... Name, Alfred... Last name beginning with an S, and has several F's. Not right. Sinorfis or something like that.

(Yes. Am leaving room for correct information. Schachter—his name.)

Perhaps on mother's side, a relative or great uncle, name Grayfus?

(?)

And another man, younger, light skin, wears light colored trousers, part of uniform? Worn in work? With stripes? At the time he seems to be 34 but he is older now. Two children and one a male. Previous marriage. Shirley's husband past.

(Shirley said this described her husband who has married again. He wore light blue trousers at their marriage. Leaving room to get more information.)

Now. Sandy hair. Connection with someone—Edward. And an A, with a large family and a particular picture of the family, old, three girls with large hair ribbons, two boys, several years older, picture taken on porch steps very early 1900's. Perhaps in a city B or the name begins with B. And a sister, a career woman before this was general practice.

(? Shirley said yes to some of this. Leaving room here.)

Now, Ruth: a rather early illness, of years, I believe.

(Yes. Ruth had tuberculosis and was very ill.)

I get Anna again, mentioned earlier in connection with Venice. Does this belong to Ruth instead?

(?)

A sister.

(?)

Seems a doctor was a close friend or had a strong effect on your life.

(Yes. The doctor who tended her was an old family friend, knew both the father and son, both doctors.)

Two brothers.

(?)

A mother who... Dropped dead at 35, or something happened drastically to change her, no, died at number 35, or had a psychological tragedy. Seems to be Ruth's mother.

(Yes. Ruth's mother died at 35, shortly after giving birth to Ruth.)

Also a home in the country that seems to belong to your family or husbands.

(Yes. Ruth was born in such a home.)

With wicker chairs in the porch and yard.

(?)

Very old woman lived there, a relative, like a great grandmother, or great aunt perhaps.

(Ruth's grandmother lived there and brought Ruth up.

(End of session 10:09.

(Add data on Ruth K. almost "going under" as she watched Jane.)

SESSION 364
SEPTEMBER 13, 1967 9 PM WEDNESDAY

(Recently Jane received a telephone call from John Pitre, of Chatsworth Road in Franklin, LA. John asked Jane, whom he has never met, if Seth could give any data that might help John's wife Peggy, who has multiple sclerosis. Jane said she would be glad to try, although she had no idea of what Seth would say.

(On Monday, September 11, Jane had held a session in an effort to help a man and wife in Raleigh, NC. This is now in the mail and we await word as to any help it might have extended.

(The session tonight was very quiet. Jane began speaking for Seth, in trance, in a quiet voice broken by many long pauses, and with her eyes closed. Verbatim notes taken and typed by her husband, Rob.)

Good evening.

("Good evening, Seth.")

At a later date we will make some comments concerning last evening's session.

(This is a reference to the session held last night for three witnesses. It was a very successful one. It contained, also, much data on the activities of a couple in the Caribbean, and this will be checked upon their return two weeks from now.)

Now however, give us a few moments to address ourselves to the issue at hand. *(Pause.)*

The case is not <u>yet</u> hopeless, though it is deteriorating. *(Pause. Note: not all pauses are noted.)* The <u>inner</u> will to live must be revived. It is this inner will to live that is lacking now. At the heart of the condition, there is a series of psychological shocks that occurred.

Now give us some time here. *(Pause.)*

Some difficulty lies in the <u>inner</u> psychological relationship between the husband and the wife—an inner issue she does not face, and reacts to the issue in physical terms. The issue itself is based partially in her own relationship to both her mother and father. That is, the issue is frightening subconsciously, because of peculiar and individual attitudes caused by her own relationship to her parents. *(Pause.)*

Physically, there must be fresh air and sunlight, as much as possible. Peanut oil to be rubbed on the arms and thighs. Also calves, twice daily. An addition of iron to the diet.

The mental attitude, the deep and <u>true</u> mental attitude, of everyone involved, should be altered if possible to one that is more hopeful. The woman is picking up and reacting to the negative thoughts of those who believe recovery is impossible.

There seems to be a male relative, I believe twice removed, perhaps an uncle, though I am not certain—a visit from him would be beneficial. *(Long pause.)* As an immediate step all effort should be made to remove negative suggestions, as these are building up about her. She has felt psychologically trapped for some time, this bringing about the physical trap into which she has fallen.

She should be assured that she is loved, but basically <u>free</u>. She should be assured then that love is not a bond, to hold her down. She does not feel free to be the person she knows herself to be. She does not trust her ability to stand up and face the world.

An excellent and carefully-chosen hypnotist, well versed in such therapy, offers her now the best chance of recovery. It is most essential that negative suggestions be drained away from her, and replaced by positive suggestions *(long pause)*, and a massive effort to do so is required.

A man like Le Cron *(author of* Self-Hypnotism: The Technique and Its Use in Daily Living, *copyright 1964, published by Prentice-Hall, Inc., Englewood Cliffs, New Jersey)* will recommend a reliable hypnotist. The other suggestions I have made, the addition of iron and the use of peanut oil, should be begun at once. The bed facing the south. A change in the husband's attitude will affect the attitude of the ill woman.

The husband, now, should follow this exercise three times dail: He should imagine the energy and vitality of the universe filling his wife's form with vitality and health. Not a wishful thinking sort of thing, but a definite effort to understand that her form is indeed composed of this energy, and in this way he can help her use it to her advantage.

If possible he should touch her during this exercise, and it should be done morning, noon and evening. One of the shocks mentioned had to do with a death; one with an incident shortly before her marriage; marriage itself was a shock, and the third one.

Basically she was not ready for marriage. Beside this her marriage had a deeply symbolic, frightening connotation that was deeply hidden. She felt that marriage was a trap—the trap again, you see, and that it was a hampering of freedom. At the time this deeply-held subconscious contribution had nothing to do with her husband.

She has been literally wasting away, and she is at the mercy of the suggestions that she receives. This is why I stress strongly that all effort be made to achieve a more positive inner atmosphere.

You may take a break and we shall continue. I believe at one time she worked in a five and dime store, or store of that type. A girl who worked with her was a friend, and visits from her would be helpful.

(Jane came out of trance at 9:40PM, rested, then resumed in trance as Seth at 9:50.)

The disease cannot be reversed physically.

A physical reversal will be the result of a spiritual change. All those surrounding the woman absolutely <u>must</u> refrain from attitudes of hopelessness and negative suggestions, either implied or spoken. This in itself will bring her some relief. This in itself will <u>allow</u> her to improve to some degree.

A mental change therefore of those within her immediate environment is necessary.

(Jane's pace was faster now, and her eyes began to open and close as she remained in trance.)

If possible she should be taken out into the sun, and the peanut oil will be even more beneficial if it is used then. Look for subtle signs of improvement rather than further signs of deterioration.

Now, all of this may sound impractical, and yet it represents your most practical answer. *(Forceful delivery.)* On your part, do not manufacture hollow, false assurances, but honestly and persistently remind yourself that the physical matter of your wife's image is formed from and filled with universal energy. A block has been preventing her from utilizing this energy with anything like normal effectiveness.

You can help make up for this by your own attitude, and the instructions I have given you. This will give her some breathing spell, when the disease will cease its progression. If these instructions are followed completely, then <u>some</u> (underlined) improvement should take place very shortly.

This will give you some time, for her own subconscious attitude must be altered if any real improvement is to be expected. *(Long pause.)* She must realize that there is hope. I believe you have a fairly small sunny parlor. The room has beneficial connotations for her. Let her be moved there.

There are some past-life influences operating. Some of these will serve to explain her inner reactions. Right now however it is not as important for you to know these as it is that you take the steps I am giving to you.

There is something about a metal chain that is hers, but I cannot see more on this right now. If she wears such a chain however, then remove it. There seems to be some metallic effect circling the neck. Some difficulty here, caused by an allergic reaction.

Parsnips should be added to the diet.

People have not seemed to have confidence in the woman, or she does not feel that anyone is confident of her ability to cope with reality. She does not realize that she has the energy to triumph over this illness. The realization that she can is all important.

The situation is indeed drastic. *(Pause.)* Her desire to live must be wooed. Any small pleasures that she has should be used in an effort to involve her with pleasure. As much pleasure as possible must be given her to counteract the concentration upon hopelessness and disaster. I cannot stress any of these points too strongly.

You must begin to expect that she has hope, for she reacts to all suggestions, as each individual does. Although she is unaware of it, she is telepathically conscious of all such powerfully-negative suggestions. You must try to battle these for her until she can do so again for herself. *(Long pause.)*

If these instructions concerning a beneficial change in mental environment are not taken, then indeed no other advice or medicine will be of help. (Pause.) I will address healing energy to her, to the best of my ability. She is being smothered, you see, by the hopelessness that surrounds her, as well as by her own hopelessness. To relieve any of the environmental negative thoughts and suggestions will bring her some immediate relief.

The simple exercise given you will immediately bring more positive aspects into the picture, then relief from secondary harmful suggestions, and harmful emotional climates. We can begin a program designed to change her own inner expectations.

It is here that a reliable hypnotist would be of great benefit, in uncovering many hidden subconscious errors. There is some possibility that I could help here, but the close contact of such a reliable person would be more emotionally satisfying to the patient.

I stress again that all of these instructions contain more potent aids than you may realize, and recommend that you follow them as closely as possible. There is hope. You must both have the strength and courage to grasp it.

This is the end of our session for this evening. My best regards to you both. Again, I will direct what healing energy I can in the patient's direction. And now good evening.

("Good night, Seth."

(Jane came out of trance at 10:24 PM.

(Jane said that while Seth was speaking she herself felt that Seth was convinced that Peggy would be really helped if the instructions were followed. Seth was especially concerned about the positive suggestion ideas being followed.

(Positive suggestion is a powerful weapon, as Jane and I have learned personally, through trial and error. We now use it as a daily adjunct in our lives, but never routinely. We do not think its results can be overestimated, and now we wonder how we lived before we learned of its benefits. RFB.)

SESSION 365
SEPTEMBER 18, 1967 9:10 PM MONDAY

(Just before tonight's session Jane and I had been discussing her excellent results in part two of the 363rd session. Jane achieved these mostly on her own, and wondered whether the Seth personality would gradually fade away as "her own" abilities increased.)

Good evening.

("Good evening, Seth.")

Now *(smile)*, my friend Ruburt does not need to worry. I shall not desert him. Our relationship will be a steady and enduring one. His abilities are being further developed, however, and other facets will also make themselves known. I will usually be <u>behind</u> him in these endeavors, and he will be learning with my guidance. I will continue to speak to you in this manner also, however.

(In recent weeks Jane's abilities have seemed to be developing at an accelerated pace.)

Now. The development of his abilities is now showing in definite terms because the improvement in health is freeing much energy that had been bound up in his dilemma.

The abilities had been developing but he did not have sufficient energy to use his growing proficiency. I did indeed begin as usual in the Gallagher session, and then I retreated more to the background, so that he could become more familiar with the immediacy involved in going after such data.

(See the 363rd session.)

The transition was relatively smooth under the circumstances of a first try. This experience gave him confidence to continue later with his students, you see.

I told him that at the end of the summer he should have 7 students, and so he has.

(See the 348th session for this prediction, given on June 21, as Jane was mak-

ing preparations for her ESP classes.)

The class will grow. I will have more to say concerning the class and the future of such work shortly. I will also take time to reconcile two points with which he is having difficulty, and to answer any questions that either of you might have since we have last held a quiet session.

Now, give us a moment, please.

These are impressions having to do with the Jesuit and the cat lover. *(Bill and Peggy Gallagher, on vacation in the Caribbean.)*

A particular five-mile journey. You will have to work out the spelling on this: Minn-a-sap-a *(my phonetic interpretation)*. This is as close as I can come. Minn-e-<u>sope</u>-a... *(pause)*. A gee *(spelled out)* dash gee; a gee-gee or gru dash gru. *(Pause.)*

A banana with another significance, used as a symbol.

M-I-dash-Shopin *(shopin, my interpretation)*. The dashes indicate either two words used together, or one word separated by a silence in the middle.

A fine torch. This I believe a Jesuit quote. He assumes an attitude that he does not feel, because of a particular situation. He pretends something. This attitude is toward other people. It is a moment of falseness for him.

Nine people on a boat this time. A temple on stilts. A missionary here with a watch, and five people on a platform. This having to do with a particular colony.

Now, A-my-a *(my interpretation)*, an island somehow the same on three sides and different on another side. The landscape, I believe; or makeup of the land. 1631 and a landing from Portugal, and also a man named Scott.

A small battle and a storm. Five approaches to one place here, one central place *(pause)* of interest. Some tar paper, used for huts or buildings, black, I believe. *(Pause.)* A five star designation here.

The Jesuit, digging for something, finds something else.

You may take a break and we shall continue.

(9:35. Jane's pace had been average, her eyes open fairly often; and with some rather long pauses during the Gallagher material.

(9:40 slower.)

Now, this will not be a long session.

There are several matters that I will discuss with you in the near future however. We will almost immediately resume our basic material. Affairs for you are working out as I said that they would, with some changes caused by the probabilities.

I will go into some material concerning Frederick Fell. You remember that I told you that affairs with him would work out well. *(A faint smile. Seth gave us this prediction perhaps two years ago.)* Unfortunate expectations and various projections operated here however, but the intuitive background was enough to wipe these out within an instant of your first meeting. This was no coincidence.

(See the 360th session for August 16, 1967, held in F. Fell's New York City office.

(As Seth says, a remarkable and instant liking sprang up between F. Fell, Jane and me when we first met in his office. Jane and I were surely surprised, and suspect that Fred was also. A couple of weeks after our return from New York City, Fred wrote Jane a glowing letter.)

Unless unforeseen, drastic changes occur, Ruburt will regain excellent and exuberant health, now, without doubt. His energies and abilities will emerge highly strengthened, reinforced, and developed. This would have occurred in any case. Unfortunately, for many reasons, he chose a hard road, rather than an easier one.

He taught himself the hard way, in other words, out of a lack of faith and expectation.

There will be another development, or new word, about a recent development concerning his book, possibly next week. Or if not then about the third week. *(Pause.)*

You stopped worrying about your car, and focusing upon it and upon its age and condition. *(Pause.)* The trouble was caused mentally, and the condition corrected mentally when you released the mechanism from a negative attention.

(Here Seth refers to a remarkable, overnight resurgence in the improvement in the way our Ford runs. Remarkable is not too strong a word for the car's improvement, literally overnight, in operation two weekends ago. All summer it had been limping along; it could not be driven more than 35 to 40 miles per hour without a strong vibration throughout, and any attempts at a higher speed seemed to be outright dangerous. The garage that services it said it was unsafe to be used outside the city limits, for fear of breakdown, etc.

(Last Sunday, on a trip to see my parents, the car ran at 60 MPH during a brief experiment; it did so smoothly and effortlessly, and had plenty of power left. Whereas during the summer it required a distinct effort to keep it going at even 34 MPH, now I have to be careful to not use too much pressure on the accelerator, for the car will now leap ahead almost without warning.)

A small bolt and a ring *(pause)*, with built-up corrosion. This was the difficulty. The corrosion was washed away. It had not yet eaten through the parts. It was washed away by a quicker flow of liquid. The difficulty had caused other difficulties.

(I wanted more data re the car's trouble and cure, but wasn't sure it was a

good idea to ask Jane more specific questions at this time. I knew she probably also preferred a shorter session tonight. After the session I asked Jane to keep in mind that the car could be discussed again.)

Ruburt's own classes will, I believe, increase to 12 students by the winter holidays. *(Long pause.)*

Attention should be directed here, I believe, for now, rather than in outside classes. The more intimate home classes will help him develop his own abilities also.

(Today Jane learned it might be possible for her to teach ESP in the adult education evening program, held in the local schools.)

I told him to be patient here. He will succeed, and do well. Not overnight, but in a relatively brief time. It goes without saying that he must concentrate his energy in that direction in order to achieve the best possible success. He is doing very well. I believe he will have two more students between now and the 10th of October.

They will be steady ones. He is drawing to him students who will work out well.

Do you have any questions, Joseph?

("They can wait, as long as this is going to be a short session.")

We will then close our session, but I will begin to take up the matters discussed this evening at our next session. You have been doing very well. *(Pause.)*

("In what way?")

In several ways. The relationship between you and Ruburt is now <u>beginning</u> (underlined) to approach a highly beneficial state, that will bring out the best in both of your personalities, and develop your artistic and psychic abilities to the fullest.

This will be a continuing process. Your own attitudes are more constructive than they have ever been, and you have taken strides in your work. Their nature you have only begun to perceive.

We will now close our session. My heartiest regards to you both. I am often here.

("Good night, Seth."

(10:05. Jane's delivery as usual. She said she knows nothing about automobiles. She doesn't drive. I spent a little time explaining to her how a car operates, in the hope that this more specific knowledge would help her relay Seth's data re the Ford in a future session.)

Sept. 21, 1967

Dear Jane & Bob,

Wanted to dash off a note saying I had received the session. Can't tell you how grateful I am. I started immediately doing what Seth suggested. Let me say that things look better already. I just hope I've got that faith needed. I'd like to tell you why I feel optimistic but too much too soon. In a week or 10 days I'll send you a report.

Thanks again and you'll be hearing from me shortly.

John

*John M. Pitre
Franklin, La.
70538*

*(Copy of handwritten letter received from John Pitre, Franklin, LA, 70538. Received on September 23, 1967.
(See the 364th session for September 13, 1967)*

SESSION 366
SEPTEMBER 25, 1967 9:45 PM MONDAY

(John Bradley, from Williamsport, PA, was a witness to the session, which was quite short. Jane began to speak for Seth, in trance, after we had discussed the 364th session with J. Bradley, who is a medical salesman for Searle Drug.

(The 364th session was held September 13, 1967 for John Pitre of Franklin, LA, and his wife Peggy, who has multiple sclerosis. See above [this page] for a copy of J. Pitre's letter, of September 21, 1967. We hadn't asked that Seth specifically discuss the following material, but thought it a possibility in the light of the conversation preceding tonight's session.

(Jane's eyes were closed, her pace rather rapid.)
Good evening.
([John Bradley and I:] "Good evening, Seth.")
Now. We have on two evenings visited the home in question, and we have personally done our best in directing the healing energy of the universe to this woman.

There is indeed some improvement. Much more must follow. We intend to make another journey there this evening while Ruburt sleeps. *(Ruburt is the entity name Seth has given Jane.)*

The very fact that the man has been driven into a corner has made him desperate enough so that he is able to concentrate large amounts of energy on her behalf. We will try to get more on this at a later session.

There is an extract from alfalfa that will be of benefit in approximately three weeks time, if progress continues. The tips of the plant may be boiled and drunk as a tea, if otherwise the extract is unavailable. Not yet however. This step is not to be taken as yet.

(Neither Jane or I, or John Bradley, who is well informed in matters medical, knew anything about any such extract. None of us had any conscious memory of reading about it, etc.)

There seems to be a rather shadowy connection with a woman, perhaps an aunt, that does not seem beneficial. I am not certain of the aunt relationship however. A woman approximately 35, with brown hair.

All efforts already made must be continued without letup. An effort should be made to involve the young woman in whatever activity is possible, to focus her attention away from her condition. Again, frequent assurances of love, but also the assurance of freedom.

We shall check upon her condition this evening.

My heartiest regards as always to our friend Philip.

(Philip is the entity name Seth has given to John Bradley.)

A few notes here to Ruburt. As I told him, the classes will work out well. *(Jane's parapsychology classes.)* Thursday evening is a good time. In any case, the classes are in a period of transition. He *(meaning Jane)* will learn much from them, and he shall help others.

If you have no questions I will take my leave of you.

([John B:] "Are things going as you said they would at Searle? Do you see any changes from your predictions?")

I do not foresee any drastic changes occurring that are different from the information that I gave you. However, give us a moment here and shall check further. *(Pause.)*

Now, there is the impression of a new account. I am not certain as to what this refers to, but put it into the record. There will also be an improving of company prestige, and this development hinges, believe it or not, one man who is at present considered relatively innocuous and unimportant. It will be in the nature of a new scientific development. A rise of stock, a <u>good</u> rise for a three year period, a levelling off, and a drop.

A new product that has been hard to come by, and laws have held it back. I believe that a forementioned death will result in a change of policy in one respect, and a change in policy will help quicken the advent of the new product. Otherwise it would have taken longer, you see.

I also have the impression of a competitor. Now I am not sure here. This is a strong competitor without your company, or it is a strong physical competitor of yours within the same company. There seems to be a D here—the name of David comes to mind, and the Star of Israel, which may mean that the competitor is Jewish.

(Smile.) And my dear friend, my time is not your time, and there are many probabilities and hence often a time variance.

(Here Seth referred to a discussion before the session, concerning the time element and his predictions re John Bradley, Searle, etc., in various previous sessions.)

I bid you all now a most fond and affectionate good evening.

([John B. and me:] "Good night, Seth."

(10:06. John said Seth was correct re the impression of a new account. A Planned Parenthood clinic is to be opened soon in Elmira; neither Jane nor I knew this. Searle makes birth control products, and as Searle's representative John said the clinic's business should be his "if I've done my work well." Jane and I did not know of his involvement here.

(John could not offer any data re any new products by Searle. He knew of no competitors. He mentioned a Dave Gleason [not Jewish] in his company. Gleason is an excellent salesman, John said, but he knew of no way they could be competitors. If there was a chance of this it would be a remote one, and unexpected.

(After John B. had left, Jane said she felt that many of Seth's predictions re John & Searle would work out soon, & all at once. A glimmering from Seth?)

(The following sessions, containing personal materials have been deleted from the record:

367 - October 1, 1967
368 - October 2, 1967
369 - October 4, 1967
370 - October 9, 1967
371 - October 11, 1967
372 - October 16, 1967
373 - October 18, 1967
375 - October 26, 1967
377 - November 6, 1967

378 - November 8, 1967
379 - November 13, 1967
380 - November 15, 1967
384 - December 4, 1967
385 - December 6, 1967
387 - December 11, 1967)

SESSION 374
OCTOBER 23, 1967 9:15 PM MONDAY

(Once again John Bradley was a witness to the session. He is a medical sales-man from Williamsport, PA.

(John B. was also a witness to the 366th session, which dealt with the wife of John Pitre to some extent, multiple sclerosis, etc. I have to correct an error on page 134 in that session. John Bradley was misquoted there; he has heard of alfalfa extract, and indeed remembers his mother using it many years ago. Reading over John Pitre's two recent letters, John Bradley said it is perfectly possible to make alfalfa tea from alfalfa pills, or the plant itself. The alfalfa product should be available at health-food stores, he said.

(Jane began speaking for Seth in trance, in a fairly strong voice, rather rapid-ly, and with her eyes opening often.)

Good evening.

([John and Rob:] "Good evening, Seth.")

And welcome as always to our friend, our cocky friend. I am delighted at his visit.

Give us a moment here however. *(Pause.)* Now. First of all: the affair the other evening with the Gallaghers was legitimate. There was contact made with the Jesuit's father. *(Saturday, October 21, 1967, at a table-tipping session.)* I told you that Ruburt's abilities were developing along several new lines, and this is the beginning of one of them.

Your confidence in him is important here, for he still harbors Irish super-stitions having to do with contacting the dead. The experiments with the table are most helpful, and I did indeed help him out on two occasions with the green table. *(Jane pointed to the large heavy green table up by the living room windows.)* He does not need my help with the small one, and the time and circumstances were not good on the other occasion when he requested my aid.

The whole table experiment is important, but as a stepping stone. He need have no fears now over his classes, as the membership will be maintained.

If students do drop out they will be replaced, for his energies are being properly, and you may tell him, most effectively used, in the classes themselves.

He learns from his students. He is sensitive to their needs, and therefore demands more of himself than he would otherwise. Therefore his own abilities grow. I will help him when he asks me in his classes, as long as he does not ask too often. *(Smile, amused voice.)*

Now give me a moment, for the ill woman. *(Peg Pitre.)*

The psychic environment still needs to be improved. The husband has made good efforts. However, stronger ones must be made. Particular care should be taken in the morning and evening, so that there is no atmosphere of negative suggestion. *(Pause.)* Continue the peanut oil and the other recommendations. The alfalfa should definitely be added now.

Do not tell her of our sessions as yet. *(Pause.)* I am not clear here—there is something to do with bread. Give me a moment. *(Pause.)* Raisin bread should be added to the diet, and rye. Honey and nuts. No pecans. *(Long pause.)*

She should be reassured. Suggestions should be permissive rather than commanding: you can improve, I know you can, for example; rather than, you will improve, you must. These last remarks applying to the husband rather than a hypnotist.

The demand for attention is a healthy sign. There may be a flare-up of mental confusion, accompanying any physical improvement or release of symptoms. The illness has been accepted by the personality in place of deeply rooted problems that the personality would not face. As any symptoms subside the problems will be felt by the personality.

A steady, progressive, but paced release from symptoms will allow for a more orderly mental and physical return to health. Otherwise the personality would become swamped by the problems that it has been trying so desperately to avoid. *(Pause.)*

This paced release allows the personality to face these problems slowly so that it is not overly frightened. Yet even then the personality will resent any healing of the body to a marked degree, and will show resentment.

This then is the result of improvement. Work with a hypnotist should help clear such difficulties. *(Pause.)* There still seems to be some chemical reaction to metal *(Jane paused, eyes closed, then shook her head in puzzlement)*, an acid connection here. I will pin it down when I am able.

The husband's activities outside of his home lead him into a nervousness that can be mistaken for exhilaration. A lack of balance here between various drives. An inducement, I believe, for advancement or change is in the offing, or has recently been given. Connected with a move.

Give us a moment, and rest your hand.

(At 9:38 Jane paused briefly, still in trance, her eyes closed.)

The young woman of whom our friend *(John Bradley)* speaks. Impressions: an A. *(Pause.)* Lived in a town by a river. Connection with two males, one older, perhaps 34, a brother or close friend.

S E V; although these could be initials, I believe they are the first letters of a word. *(Long pause.)* An Irish name or background. Connection with a Barbara. A turnabout in choice of career. A very old relative still living. An A V.

Also a connection with a small child, female, perhaps age 6. I do not know, a niece or sister perhaps. A stage name. *(Jane shook her head.)* I do not know the meaning of this impression, unless she has one name and uses another. Brown hair. Sometimes wears glasses. The left hand.

You had better take your break.

(9:48—Jane said she was well dissociated again. She came out of trance slowly, saying she had no time concept and little memory of what she had said.

(The above data refers to a young woman John Bradley talked with in Hazelton, PA, recently. John has met her the one time, he said, plus an instance where he had coffee with her. She is a nurse at the Hazelton hospital.

(Not knowing her at all well, John could verify little of the data; he took a copy with him to check out with the girl next time he sees her. He did know she had been in Hazelton less than a year, returning there from Philadelphia, which is on a river.

(Jane had an image within, as she spoke, of a capital S and a small e v connected to it. John said the girl's first name is Terry, which is an Irish name, but that she is Italian, with black—not brown—hair. Last name is Repanshek; but there is a puzzle here, since the name doesn't seem to be an Italian one. Spelling is John's phonetic interpretation.

(Terry Repanshek was not wearing glasses when John saw her. He said she has exceptionally small hands for a woman grown, but he noticed nothing unusual about her hands. Will check all the data. The girl's odd name and the Italian heritage may tie in with Seth's reference to a stage name.

(After a discussion on table-tipping, by Jane, Seth resumed at 10:30.)

You have my blessing if Ruburt wants to demonstrate the table for our friend.

The material should be sent as soon as possible to the South.

The left hand reference has to do with a finger, I believe. I will give a full explanation of your table episodes shortly, and I shall stay and watch your efforts. A silent partner. *(Smile.)*

There is a Wednesday appointment for our friend here shortly, that either can hold pitfalls or will turn out to be surprising.

(10:35. Jane was again well dissociated, and came out of trance slowly. John Bradley said he had no Wednesday appointments scheduled for the coming week, but would keep Seth's statement in mind.

(A few notes re the table-tipping experiment which followed the session, and lasted until after midnight, to our surprise.

(John and I were somewhat tired but wanted to try the table. We used the small one, and placed it on the rug to muffle its noise at the late hour. It began to move almost at once, and by tapping out the alphabet told me, in somewhat garbled fashion, that an O B, a family relative, was making contact. Jane did not know who this could be, and I did I not tell her.

(I have seen tables move a few times before, including the much heavier green table referred to in the session, but still find the movement of furniture weird when it begins, since none of us were making any obvious, overt attempts to move said table. It is quite easy to touch one's fingertips to the tabletop, and thus verify that no strong physical pressure is being exerted thereon, even subconsciously; especially when the touch is light enough so that the fingertips slide about, as ours did. We constantly checked each other, also watching our feet. This is easy to do with a small table.

(The table became quite active, spelling out several messages which were quite garbled. I noted them down letter by letter. The movements were unmistakable but the messages unclear, except that O B, whom I have not thought of in many years, repeated his presence. The table finally became active enough to tap up to thirty times in succession, often.

(We finally asked the table to do a dance for us, as it had in no uncertain terms the other evening when the Gallaghers were present. That time it gave a version of a requested Irish jig. This time we asked for another jig. The table was moving well now, and promptly began to spell out the following message, taken from my notes: ILL MAKE A(B) DAN(D)CE.

(Thereupon commenced a wild episode. The table began to hop and dance about the room. In order to keep up with it we had to leave our seats and walk about the rug with it. Each time it reached the edge of the rug we pulled it back to keep it off the bare floor, where it would have been very noisy.

(This was not all. At times the table tipped up on two legs, then would poise there, seemingly balanced by itself. To our surprise we discovered that it required an active pressure from us to force the table back down to the floor so that all three legs made contact. The feeling of this force was unmistakable, and new to all of us. There was no doubt about its existence, since the pressure required to level the table off was obvious to all. This of course did the job that gravity would normally be expected to do. Each time we pushed the table down, it rose up again at one edge. The feeling given by this maverick or opposite pressure was quite similar to the feeling one gets

from playing with magnets, when they are so aligned that one repels the other. Whatever force is operating in such cases of repulsion is invisible, but unmistakably there.

(This feeling of repulsion is the reason for these notes, actually. If the beginning of movement in a piece of furniture is weird to start with, a refusal by the table to sit on the floor as one expects is much more so. This period lasted for perhaps ten minutes or more, while the three of us took turns shifting position so we could all test the pressure required to push the table down to the floor. There is no question that any of us were causing this effect; all of our movements were plain to see. During all of this the table was active to a greater or lesser degree, making it impossible to prop up a leg, say, with a shoe, etc. As interested as we were, we did not lose objectivity.

(The session climaxed with a very active dance by the table, as the three of us left our chairs and followed it about the rug. It described circles, balanced on one leg at a time, then two, in a regular rhythm. At times it scooted in a straight line. The hilarity of all this is hard to convey, but the objective realization of what was taking place, and of how hard it would be to explain to a neophyte, finally got to John Bradley. This was his first experience with a table. He ended up laughing until the tears rolled down his cheeks, as the three of us went round and round the room with the table.

(We finally gave up out of sheer weariness at 12:30 AM; and finally the table just sat there, as any good table should.)

SESSION 376
OCTOBER 30, 1967 9:25 PM MONDAY

(This evening before the session Jane tried to move a table by herself, with little success. At 9 PM I sat at the table with her, and we succeeded only in obtaining a couple of small movements.

(Jane's pace was relatively slower than it has been recently.)

Now, good evening.

("Good evening, Seth.")

I will go into the matter of the tables to some degree. *(Long pause.)* Give us a moment. I am simply clearing our lines. Ruburt did overemphasize his critical faculties this evening, yet he was psychically alert.

You are, as I have told you, far more important than a stenographer, and your <u>active</u> energy was indeed not here earlier.

The willing fingers and good intent, yes, but the active focus of your energies was not here. *(Pause.)* Ruburt does rely on you as a partner in these endeavors. It is not a matter necessarily of how much time you spend, for admittedly your hours are well consumed. It is a matter of your active, active (underlined) interest, and the enthusiastic focus of energy, whether or not you are directly involved in a given experiment.

Now. (Pause.) There are survival personalities who help you. They operate in several different ways. The methods vary according to their circumstances and your own. We will describe one method at a time.

Now. There is a flowing of energy, of psychic energy, from the sitters, that does indeed affect and alter that molecular construction of the table. In this method the impetus comes from survival personalities, acting directly through the physical mechanism of the most sensitive person at the table.

There is also a change of molecular vibration in this person when this method is used. Almost a merging (pause), in which there is a freer interplay of molecules between the table and the physical organism. A molecular bridge-field is therefore momentarily constructed. This field may be widened, including all those sitters. The energy of all contributes.

(Pause.) The molecules are unfrozen, so to speak, and become fluid, following this figure of speech. There is a high energy output on the part of the sitters. The strongest sensitive is like a field operator. He or she consumes energy quickly, but that energy is like a receiving center for the energy of the survival personality operating.

The energy of the survival personality works through the nervous system, causing electrical changes, or rather triggering these in the physical brain. These changes throw extra charge into the body, that leaps into the molecular structure of the table, causing a force field between the organism and the table.

(Long pause, eyes closed.) Any mental message is also received, in an electromagnetic code, and directly transferred, bypassing the conscious mind, into movement of the new temporary force field.

On occasion, when circumstances are unusually favorable, an apparition can appear at such times, because of the power and plastic nature of the force field involved. (Pause. Slow.)

The flexibility and yet the focusing ability of the main sensitive is very important with this method. Numbers of sitters are not important as numbers. The amount of contributing energy needed may or may not require many sitters, according to their varying abilities to direct and focus energy.

Now. There are other methods that are also used by surviving personalities. (Pause.) Such objects may be moved without the help of any survival personality however, by the concentrated focus of psychic energy on the part of one or several individuals.

This usually requires more effort, and there will be no messages on these occasions. In this method detailed above, there is cooperation between a survival personality and the person who is the operating sensitive. Some contact between the fingertips and table is necessary here, to set up the proper requirements for this particular kind of force field.

The field itself builds up toward a peak of activity, and then begins to weaken. Levitation of a table with this method is possible only when the entire table is drawn into the force field construction.

You may take a break and we shall continue.

(Break at 9:58. Jane said she was far-out. Peculiarly, she had a mental image which she described now; while speaking for Seth she had seen, in color, blue water as in an ocean, and white sand and two people running toward the beach in bathing suits. She didn't know what the vision meant.

(10:06.)

Now. In some cases survival personalities, with experience, will directly affect matter, both assisting the sensitive and operating independently once the force field has been constructed.

In this way the force field itself acts as a medium, and these are the best conditions for complete levitation of an object. *(Pause.)* In most cases the main sensitive present will be the operator at your end. In a definite projection of energy however, a survival personality may, again, directly act upon the table.

Levitation may also be achieved when the sensitive is in excellent condition, and at the apex of the force field coordinates. The force field has definite space-time coordinates and a dimensional affect that permits the manipulation of molecules from one system to another.

This is truly a space-time warp, permitting free interchanges. Now the stability and intensity of the force field is somewhat dependent upon other circumstances, including atmospheric circumstances at your end. The clearness of the messages is directly affected by this intensity and stability.

It is difficult to receive a clear message for example when the field itself is not stable. *(One minute pause.)*

For Ruburt's class try the following combinations with the large table: Venice, Paul and Sheryl; Shirley, Venice and Sheryl; Ruth, Joan and Paul. Ruburt for this class should keep one definite place at the table for his own. You have three or four small problems here, rather than one large one.

(Concerning Jane's difficulty in getting the ESP class members to succeed in moving the large living room table, in the Tuesday night class. The Thursday afternoon class moves the same table easily.)

Ruburt's energies are being released more and more. The table experiments will yield good results, and some quite unanticipated ones at that.

Now you may end the session, take a break, or ask questions as you prefer.

("We'll take a break."

(10:21—10:31.)

Now. With practice you will be able to sense those times when a force field of this nature is already building up, and take advantage of it.

I have little to say concerning the episode in the old building. My opinion of it has already been made clear. It would be advantageous to check with me before you enter such endeavors.

(Seth refers to our adventure of last Friday, October 27, 1967. Bill Macdonnel asked Jane and me to attend a seance on the deserted third floor of the building in downtown Elmira, where Bill has his studio. Working on the second floor, Bill had several times heard footsteps on the floor above; but checking the deserted floor, unused for many years, had found nothing except doors mysteriously unlocked.

(Jane and I and some people we had not met before, with Bill, tried to table tip in the darkness on the third floor. Bill took infrared pictures. A foot doctor had committed suicide on the third floor several years ago, and October was the month of the deed. Bill thought we might be able to contact the doctor's personality—name of Willamin—through the table.

(We tried several locations without success, finally standing at a table close to the death scene, a doorway. Seth then came through, and in no uncertain terms told us to mind our own business. We were told, in a strong and echoing Seth voice, to let the poor man rest in peace; he would be "here" for a while longer yet, then leave. In the meantime we had no business trying to contact him. He did not want to be reached, but to rest and be left alone.

(Seth spoke for less than a minute, but Jane said later that she was far-out. When she came out of trance she nearly fell in the darkness, feeling a momentary disorientation because of the depth of the trance.)

Now, beside the information given this evening, it <u>is</u> true that some tables will move more easily than others. This has nothing to do with weight or size, but to the psychic connections that have built up about the object. Your wooden table should be a good one. *(Jane pointed toward our kitchen, where we have a small table we haven't tried.)* The small table is particularly good because it was built by its owner, whose own abilities are definite, though untrained. *(Ruth Klebert's table.)*

The old desk in <u>your</u> family, you see *(Jane pointed to me)*, although the spatial relationships there are difficult. The state of your own mind will have something to do with the type of personalities that you contact, the behavior of the tables and the messages that you receive. We will go into this at another session.

Unless you have questions we will close for this evening.

("I guess not.")

Let Ruburt persist. He is onto something. You can also benefit when you find the time.

My heartiest wishes to you both. The training in the use of energy will be good for both of you, and further aid you in your own separate work. You must get the feel of using it, and of opening up as a channel. Good evening.

("Good evening, Seth.")

(10:42.)

SESSION 381
NOVEMBER 24, 1967 APPROXIMATELY 10:45 PM FRIDAY

(This session will actually report two separate events, lumped together for convenience. Both involve table tipping, and include one Seth session.

(Part one: A table tipping session on Wednesday, November 22, 1967, in our living room, with the following: Jane and Rob, and Claire Crittenden and Carl Watkins. Highly successful, the best achieved up to that time, with seemingly a full levitation almost accomplished.

(This session was not particularly planned, but grew out of conversation on the subject. Claire and Carl are young college students, and were home for Thanksgiving vacation. Rather late after meeting we began tipping the table, which started performing almost as soon as we sat around it. The session lasted for several hours, perhaps until 1 AM, and at its end all of us were exhausted.

(The table seemed to have a mind of its own. Jane at once called upon the table's "inhabitant", A A , to help us out, and we received help aplenty. The table, the one usually used and belonging to Ruth Klebert, one of Jane's ESP students, had been repaired less than a week ago by me; it had been damaged to the extent of losing a couple of its three legs by its violent movements in a recent ESP class .

(I repaired the broken legs with nails and glue, to insure a strong job; before, the legs had been merely dowel-fastened. This Wednesday evening the table performed as follows: Irish jigs upon request, vaulting up into the air while in Carl's grip, chasing around our backs as Carl held it while we tried to keep up with it, skittering across the rug, knocking back and forth, and building up a very strong pressure indeed , when we tried to force the leg up in the air back down to the floor, or rug.

(There were of course all manner of in-between motions given by the table also, hard to describe in words. The pressure manifested, of course, held our intense atten-

tion, since this is so diametrically opposed to our usual unthinking acceptance of the gravitational force. Jane requested A A to manifest pressure often, and usually A A, or the table, obligingly did so. Everything seemed to work together in perfect order—table, our moods, etc. If one chose to call a full levitation 100%, then our evening could be called 90% successful.

(Several times during the evening Carl and I had to use considerable pressure to get the raised third leg of the table back down to the floor. The effect appeared so often that all four of us had ample time to feel it—as noted before, to me this force reminds me strongly of two magnets repelling each other—something invisible yet most palpable, and when things are going well, easily demonstrable.

(The table would rock back and forth beneath the touch of our fingertips when the pressure was requested; as it did so it would begin to feel increasingly solid and heavy; the creaks and groans in it would disappear and it seemed to become one indivisible unit. The pressure would rather quickly build up until members grouped around it—usually standing—would have to really bear down to level it out again. Once it finally groaned dangerously and I feared some part of it, possibly the top, was about to break.

(Carl had a brainstorm; we placed our bathroom scale on the tabletop finally when the pressure was "going good," and requested A A to continue building up the pressure so that Carl, who was on the side of the table manifesting the pressure at that time, could measure the force he used to get the table back on the floor solidly. A A obligingly built up the pressure again; pressing down, Carl saw that he used a hand pressure of 70 pounds, as measured by the scale, to get all three legs of the table back on the floor, whereas usually gravity would effortlessly draw the legs back to the floor when our fingertips were removed.

(Carl and Claire, previously, had used what they considered to be an even greater pressure on the table to level it out. With the experience furnished by the scale, they now estimated they used close to 90 pounds pressure to level the table, this being the moment of highest pressure during the evening. Several subsequent pressures were measured by using the scale on the tabletop, ranging from 30 to 50 pounds.

(Needless to say, when Carl or whoever was measuring pressure on the scale, the other three took pains to see that they were not subconsciously exerting a heavy pressure on the other side of the table, thus forcing a stronger response across the tabletop to get the legs back on the floor. Such checking was easy to do; nevertheless conscious deliberate checks were constantly being made to make certain opposing pressures were not unwittingly being exerted. Most of the time our hands touched the table so lightly that it could move quite freely beneath them, seemingly of its own volition. This steady checking has the added advantage that it serves as a protection against any possible hallucination [although this would have to be a mass effect, and

highly unlikely]; the checking in a deliberate manner was a good method to keep one's feet on the floor, so to speak, even if the table was acting contrary to gravity.

(When we asked for a full levitation, it seemed the table did its best to achieve this, getting all legs off the floor except the last tiny point of contact of the third leg; it would then go in circles beneath our hands, or begin to dance about, eventually. I cannot recall whether pressure was apparent at such times. I am tempted to say that it probably was not as strongly present as at other times when we frankly requested pressure in order to experience it. At just about all times one or more of us was talking to the table, exhorting it to go on, to better its performance, in most positive tones.

(The table was active until after 1 AM. One other distinctive movement involved a seeming vault into the air while Carl held the table at arms length. This tipped the top vertically to the floor, and the other three present touched the top lightly. At first the table seemed to move Carl around in circles, continually being ahead of him, in that it ended up by twisting Carl's arm awkwardly behind him; this made it very difficult for Claire, Jane and me to keep contact with the top. At the same time Carl insisted that he was not deliberately twisting the table this way around himself. The twisting was rapid.

(Carl, being big and strong, could hold the table as he did, with but one hand, the arm extended straight out, for some little time. At the same time we requested levitation. Abruptly the table, still in Carl's grasp, vaulted up toward the ceiling of our living room, very rapidly, until it was upside down to the floor and beyond our reach, except for Carl, who still held on. Carl said he had not consciously made the maneuver, and he appeared as surprised as we were. Later he told us he was afraid the table would either crash into the ceiling—since Carl was tall enough—or would hit a nearby wall where several of my paintings hung.

(After hanging upside down for a short but measurable length of time the table again descended. Later, Carl tried to consciously make the table describe the same upside-down movement, and discovered that he could not exert enough force while using the same grip on the table top edge. The best he could do was to get the table up to shoulder height at the most, and I believe this to be a somewhat generous estimate. Also Carl's arm tired quickly, whereas before it had not. Was he dissociated to any degree when the table vaulted up?

(It is of course possible to balance any object, large or small, and this has led Jane and me to experiment a bit with the table in question. It was soon discovered that by balancing it at a certain angle with the fingertips, then exerting a downward pressure, one can have an illusion of a force from beneath holding the table up with one leg off the floor. However, as far as we can tell this is not the force we have experienced when a leg will refuse to return to the floor.

(One must exert the downward pressure in a manner directed away from the

body while experimenting, in order to maintain the balance and center of gravity, and at least when experimenting this necessity to push down and away from oneself is quite noticeable. When the table is performing well it seems that a direct downward pressure, applied to the edge of the tabletop, is required to overcome the force. The direction of this downward push is quite different, we believe at this stage, from the experimental down-and-away thrust. But more study is required here, and with this knowledge in mind, we will try to more accurately assess the table's performance at future sessions.

(Nor of course does the question involving the downward thrust explain other peculiar table motions, such as pirouetting, vaulting into the air, dancing, etc, since with these motions no great hand pressure is maintained. In fact, it is often extremely difficult to maintain fingertip contact with the table, so rapid can its movements be.

(Even so, when all present withdraw their hands from the table, no matter what its antics have been, as soon as all contact is withdrawn the table falls back into normal floor position.

(PART TWO:

(The 381st session took place, unscheduled, after a lengthy and active table-tipping session of the evening of Friday, November 24, 1967. Claire Crittenden, Carl Watkins, Jane and I, along with Pat Norelli, from Boston, were joined by Bill and Peg Gallagher, Doug Hicks, Danny Stimmerman, Curt Kent and Peg's brother Dick and his wife Carol, for an even dozen present, at our apartment.

(Naturally the table was the center of attention, and within a few minutes of Jane and me and a few others sitting at it, it began to perform. Pressure, the newest attraction, was at once called for, and before long began to manifest itself to various degrees; at first however nothing like the pressure of Wednesday showed, but there seemed to be plenty present, enough so that each person present, especially those who had never witnessed such a thing, could take the time to experience it.

(This evening the table did not vault into the air as it had Wednesday, but was nevertheless very active. The pressure soon was so pronounced that it was unmistakable; all agreed that they experienced it. To save time listing a long recital of varied antics: later in the evening I stepped away so someone could take my place at the table. Jane had already done so. Meaning of course that the table performed as well without Jane's hands upon it, as it did when she touched it.

(I stood back in a corner by the bookcase; the table had worked its way toward the bathroom door, which was closed. At the table were Bill Gallagher, with beside him Pat Norelli. Others were also at the table, but Bill and Pat were on the side showing the strong pressure. The pressure finally reached the point where Bill Gallagher could not force the third table leg back to the floor. As I recall, he was using a direct downward pressure, not the down-and-away pressure discussed earlier.

(At the same time the table was performing so well, Jane was standing a few feet away, talking to it in a loud voice very intently, rooting very strongly for the table to resist Bill and Pat's really strong efforts to level it out. The room was filled with noise, all manner of exclamations, shouts, comments, etc. It could be called a real, almost palpable, peak of mental and physical excitement.

(The next moment the tabletop split in two and a leg was torn free of the central pedestal. The table crashed to the floor. Consternation, a second of disbelief. For a moment I couldn't believe it.

(Jane and I do not know the exact sequence of events. Most likely Bill and Pat exerted so much downward thrust that the table was at last overwhelmed. The force with which the third leg hit the floor shattered it; at the same time, did the top split in two? We cannot be sure. No pictures were taken of course, or notes made at the moment. This account is written several days later, after several conversations by Jane and me with some of the people present. A variation in accounts of course resulted, and we will not try to give these here.

(The two obvious points are that the table broke, and that a great force was needed to do this. I personally witnessed Bill Gallagher pushing heavily down upon the resisting table a few seconds before it broke. My estimate is that the third, resisting leg, was perhaps an inch or two off the floor. I recall at the time being especially intrigued that such a small space between table leg and floor was leading, for whatever reason, to so much human effort being expended.

(Jane and I cannot say exactly who was at the table when it broke, although we know that neither of us was, nor was Curt Kent, who sat to one side drinking beer. We believe that five people were at least touching the tabletop, and perhaps more. The breaking of the table left us delighted and appalled—me especially; and it took me several hours on two succeeding days to repair the table. So much force was used to shatter the table leg that a nail two and a quarter inches long, that I had used in my previous repair bout, was bent at an exact right angle. This nail remained embedded in the detached leg. Other smaller nails in the same leg were pulled through the detached leg and remained in the central pedestal.

(The twice-repaired table has been used in subsequent sessions, but very gingerly for it is now much weakened. Pressure has indicated itself to a small degree, but we have used little force to subdue it. We have tried a few pressure experiments, previously described, with it, very cautiously. We mourn the table's withdrawal for obvious reasons. It is a good responder, and its spirit, A A, seemed quite pleased to communicate with us, in a most forceful manner. We want to keep the table to maintain this contact, even if casually, and for further study on pressure angles, etc. Also to use this table as a springboard for work with heavier, four-legged tables, etc.

(The session with Seth began an indeterminate time after the shattering of the

table. Previous to it, Jane told me she felt Seth; since strangers to Seth were present, we thought it best that he not come through. Jane wanted to go to a back room; but the bathroom door was closed. Someone was inside. Confined to the living room with its gathering, Jane finally let Seth come through.

(There was no doubt that Seth wanted to come through. The evening's events had set the stage most thoroughly. I have no idea of the reaction, subjectively, of some of the witnesses to what must have seemed a very strange happening indeed. Personally, I believe that only the Gallaghers, Claire, Pat and myself had witnessed a session. This left as new witnesses Peg's brother Dick and his wife Carol, Danny, Curt, Doug and Carl; though Carl and perhaps one or two others had at least heard mention of Seth.

(The session, as soon as it began, struck me as being very forceful indeed—perhaps too much so. Seth was deadly serious. Peg, fortunately, took notes. I personally did not think we were unappreciative of what had taken place this evening, but Seth proceeded to drive the point home rather unmercifully, I thought at the time. Later the Gallaghers said they did not think the session had been unduly severe, but I do not think I agree.

(At times Jane's voice grew very strong and loud, but I would not say this was its peak performance. I thought the session a strong reaction to the evening and the gathering. At the highest or strongest points, the voice, while powerful, was not as clear and distinct as I have heard it on other occasions—notably during the extraordinary session recorded for Dr. Instream a couple of years ago. I thought too much excitement might be responsible here. Jane's eyes opened after a time. Peg got most of the material down, and we are indebted to her for this, for Seth spoke rapidly.

(Peg's notes are below. After all but Claire, Carl and Pat had left Seth came through again, dealing with reincarnational data on Carl, and I made verbatim notes on this.)

NOTES BY PEGGY GALLAGHER

(November 24, 1967. Spontaneous Seth session, following a period of working with the table, in which pressure built up to the point where the table finally broke, working through A A)

The name Carol is called Arparka now you have seen a physical object behave in a manner in which no physical object has a right to behave. The physical universe is as unpredictable as the behavior of that table. I come to you as a complete stranger. I am a stranger to you but you are not strangers to me, and so you see, I have the advantage, and I always take advantage of my advantages.

If you have questions, I shall answer them but all of this is meant to show you that reality is more than you thought reality to be... I am not here as the host of a party. I am not here for your amusement or pleasure. I am here for your education and training.

I can say to you what you have not said to yourselves in your private moments. For as tables move so indeed do souls fly. Many in this room have abilities...my dear friend, the Jesuit, whose flippancy does not help him in his dark moments *(to Bill)* for you are not facing yourself and your abilities. This is the crux of the problem. It does you no good to smile. It is yourself with whom you must become friendly and yourself you must face.

I do not see until 1978 a marriage for him *(Curt)*. I am not certain here. I believe a 1938 illness for that one *(Dick)*. If anyone has questions I will answer them. I am not usually so severe but all of you in the room are talented and your responsibility is directly in proportion to your talent and therefore you cannot afford self-pity or complacency or regret.

You have seen the table move. Those of you who come will see more. All of these are childish endeavors *(not sure of that word)*. They amuse you. So be it. But look beyond what you have seen and question it in your own minds. But I say this personally and directly concerns each of you, for unless you develop your own abilities, you shall not fulfill yourselves and you shall not be happy. I am an old man. I have been where you are now. I have been a young man, a young girl, a mother, a father, a son. You must question: why did the table move?

You think of the table as an amusing diversion and this is not the point. I am glad that it was amusing, but amusement was not the point.

(A break here.)

Some questions...

("Who is A A?")

A A is a friend of Rupurt's student, Venice. It is Alexander Anare *(the "e" is silent)*, who died in 1906 and was a friend of her family. He was indeed a lawyer, but also was involved involved in psychic studies with a group in Cleveland called the Brothers of the Fourth Order, and he is particularly interested in the manipulation of physical matter. He had a scientific turn of mind and will, I believe, help you in your experiments.

Energy was used to shatter the table. Energy was used to manipulate physical matter. There is such energy in each one of you. But you are not taking advantage of it, and in not taking advantage of it, you are not fulfilling your responsibilities. I see the Jesuit's fond smile. You have been shunting aside the full responsibility of yourself, and ignoring them and you cannot for long ignore these responsibilities. You must face these responsibilities and face them, you shall. Full freedom for you shall not be reached in any other manner.

Tonight we used a very simple and elemental example, in itself childlike. The energy that was used to manipulate and move matter compares with energy that resides within each of you. But you are not using it to its fullest, including my friends Rupert and Joseph. There are abilities here that should be fulfilled.

A crisis will come in three years and our young friend had better be willing to face it. *(Danny.)* We must get out of ourselves and with a new horizon of reality. You are making excuses. We shall deal with you tomorrow. We have good abilities to be used. A severe crisis will develop by 1970, involving a woman with the initials A L, an extremely difficult situation,and one involving someone with the initials F W, having to do with a past association awakened.

All of you have abilities and potentials but you are held in bond by preconceived ideas of reality. I tell you no. Reality is the table that moved, the table that shattered! Reality is the energy you have. You cannot afford complacency. To be alive is to learn and to grow. How can you close yourselves off in rooms of limited reality. You close your eyes and do not look.

(A question from Dick to the effect that he was not born in 1938; he was born in 1939.)

There was a severe difficulty here. You were indeed conceived. There was a difficulty in the lung area. It had to do with a circulatory ailment that manifested later and should be checked. A circulatory trouble involving extremities. There was no awareness of this on the part of your mother, but the difficulty in her own condition partially caused it, a low blood count and circulatory difficulty in her own condition. She did not realize this had any effect on the child...a difficulty, minor enough, in the lumbar region and fourth vertebra. The condition would have recurring tendencies perhaps in February, April and September but would not be pluerisy. Warm salt pads applied to the extremities would be a benefit and also on the fourth vertebra. I will shortly leave you. I extend to you all my best wishes and if I sound severe it is only that I would wake you up to your full potentials and I speak to the part of yourself to which you are not listening.

(Insert: December 2, 1967 Saturday:

(Later talking to Bill Gallagher: He and Pat Norelli stood at one side of the table, exerting strong pressure to force third leg to floor. Never did get it down. Before they did, one of the 2 legs already on the floor, opposite them, gave way. Tabletop didn't break beneath Bill's hands, he said, but, he believes, when table fell over to floor & struck edge of table top against floor, away from Bill and Pat.

(When Claire, Pat, Curt, Danny, Carl, Jane and I were left, Seth returned

briefly after Carl and I had been discussing reincarnation to some extent. I took ver-
batim notes here.)

431... Germany—the Huns sweep down. This is for our Carl. They sweep
down from the North. He is a woman in a village. A descendant of the Romans.
A-c-r-i-l-a *(spelled out)*, a descendant of the Roman tribes, brought to Germany
by the Romans to secure the Empire.

He has five children. His husband then deals with the cutting of stones, a
stone mason.

He protects his children and dies in so doing, and is born again in France
in 1826, Bordeaux, a merchant. He has not discovered his paramount ability as
yet in this life. It will have to do with graphics, and a combination of mathematics and graphics, and if pursued will lead to an affiliation with a company
beginning with a C.

Now, Ruburt is exhausted, and so I shall leave you. However, be not confused, for my own energy *(loud voice)* is far superior to his *(louder)*, and though
I dare not speak he listens at this hour. Nevertheless I leave you knowing that
my energy is not of this time nor of this place *(voice quieting)*; and you also have
energy that you are not using, and abilities that you do not fulfill. Then use
them. If you shall be friends unto yourself then face yourselves—make peace
with yourselves, and I bid you a fond good evening.

("Good night, Seth."

*(11:35 PM. Jane was truly exhausted, and went to bed at once. Briefly her
voice attained a fairly strong volume. Her delivery had been very active all evening,
the voice loud at times, eyes open often—she had used, undoubtedly, great amounts
of energy.)*

SESSION 383
NOVEMBER 29, 1967 9:15 PM WEDNESDAY

*(Yesterday afternoon, November 28, while working in my studio in the back
of our apartment, I had a vision of a painting. I recognized it as mine, or one I will
do, of Bill Gallagher. I have been thinking over ways to do portraits of both Bill
Gallagher and Bill Macdonnel.*

*(The vision was very clear, lasted for a long enough period to observe easily,
and gave me strong thrilling sensations. It showed a life-size, full-face figure of Bill
Gallagher wearing a long dark coat, as he stood against a somewhat stylized outdoor
background of pyramid shapes in bright colors—either tempera or acrylics.*

(His head was bare and his hair blowing in a wind. The portrait was life-size,

from the knees up, very dramatic and bold in concept and detail, and very effective pictorially. I was delighted to see it, and was at once sure I was capable of producing such a work. The Gallaghers visited us Saturday evening, December 2. I did not see them arrive, but witnessed their departure. I had not mentioned the vision to them, and asked Jane to wait before she did so. As Bill Gallagher walked down the hall away from us upon departing, I saw that he wore a long black coat with I believe a hood upon it—a garment quite like that he wore in the vision, and one I possessed no special knowledge of in his wardrobe.

(The vision had one oddity—I stood at my desk working at something else when I became aware of it to my left. It was large, framed, and cocked at an odd angle to the floor, as if propped up by invisible hands. While I stared at it it appeared to be solid, and very nearly animated—note the wind effect mentioned earlier.

(When I became aware I was seeing it, I faced it and tried to prolong its existence. As soon as I realized this conscious effort I relaxed, in hopes that this would encourage its longevity, but the vision faded and did not return. I drew a quick very rough little sketch of it, dated it, then told Jane about it. I hoped Seth would mention it this evening.)

Now, good evening.

("Good evening, Seth.")

We will not keep you long this evening, as you can use some rest.

The vision that you saw was of a future painting that you will do.

(Rewritten November/2000: The vision grew out of Seth's saying in the deleted 382nd session, on November 27/67, that I'd do well-known painting of Bill Gallagher. It will be based upon the conception of my painting of 1954 that I "sold to Sonja." See session 584 in Seth Speaks, *held on May 3/71.)*

You are allowing yourself more inner freedom again, and so you permitted yourself to see this. There were some—<u>some</u> (underlined) distortions, simply because the painting was interpreted in the light of your present knowledge. *(Jane lay flat on her back on the divan.)*

There were also some hints in it that you will use subconsciously, and from which new developments will grow. The sending out of another manuscript is symbolically important to Ruburt, and represents definite progress. *(High, Low and Psycho.)* Both of you need rest this evening. In your sleep you will correlate recent developments so that better use will be made of them. Your activities in the sleep state will actually be rather ambitious, and you will generate considerable energy from them. We more than made up for missed sessions by the recent developments. I will not keep you therefore, although I will answer any questions if you have them.

("Now that I have conscious memory of seeing the vision, I'm wondering just

how much this memory is going to influence my actual production of the work.")

(*Smile.*) You would have been consciously aware of the painting whether or not you were consciously aware of the vision. It is you who think of the painting in terms of time, and who perceive it in this manner. (*Sitting up as she spoke, Jane began to take off her sweater and shoes.*) The painting exists and in one reality you have already completed it. In your <u>present</u> framework however you <u>seem</u> to be waiting for the developments to occur.

The room is too hot for our purposes.

Now. You are already the self who <u>will</u> paint that portrait. The insights that will lead to it already exist. You could refuse, but the lines of probability so far are against this. The book you are reading puts things simply enough to be immediately practical. You will discover a rather powerful impact upon your lives, both of you, as a result of it.

There is much more here that the author does not understand, but he has hit upon excellent methods, and you can take advantage of them. The paintings that you will paint do exist, because you have in one sense the potential to create them. (*Jane again lay down.*) They exist in potential form. It is not true however that anyone else could pick them up, so to speak, from cosmic energy. They are attuned to you, and only your particular individuality is equipped to pick them up. Do you understand here?

(*"Yes."*)

Here I differ you see with the author.

(*"You're talking about* Psycho-Cybernetics.*"*)

I am. In not developing your abilities to the point where you can tune in on these paintings, that belong to your whole self, you impede your progress, and to that extent deny portions of creativity.

The paintings already exist however as definite potential forms, already created by your whole self. Only you can give them physical reality however. You can only fail in not giving them physical form, and you can only fail to give them physical form by refusing to open up your inner channels to the intuitions of the whole self.

There are some significant differences here you see, in my knowledge and Maltz's interpretation as given in his book. To the extent that you fail to materialize your potentials in physical form, you have failed in a given physical existence. The knowledge that the forms and the paintings are there, however, is all-important.

The natural development of your abilities in other words already exists. You must merely be ready, intuitively alive, prepared and assured, and these developments will appear to you. (*Pause.*) Great artists are those who materialize physically the paintings already created by the whole self in potential form.

Now this whole self is completely unique, yet the energy that composes it is a part of the energy that also is the ground of being, for all other consciousnesses. Therefore when you are true to yourself, when you materialize these paintings clearly, there is also *(Jane pointed at me emphatically eyes open wide)* within them a ground of knowledge, intuition and being, that is instantly felt by all other individuals.

This is what makes a painting great, the validity of the inner ground of being within them, interpreted in highly individual ways. The individuality itself, if it is intuitively valid, will lead to a universal inner recognition on the part of all who perceive such a painting.

Do you have other questions?

("Jane wanted to know about Pell and Fell."

(Smile.) We have given him all the information here that we will for now. The book will be published.

(Here Seth refers to Jane's book of poetry, High, Low and Psycho. *In a very recent session Seth told Jane to send the manuscript to a publisher beginning with an L or V. The book had already been rejected by Viking, the only V in her index of publishers. Checking the L's, Jane was surprised to discover the publisher Horace Liveright, a name containing both an L and a V.*

(Looking up the address of this publisher, she was further surprised to learn that it was at 386 Park Avenue South, New York City—the same address as Frederick Fell, the publisher of her ESP book. But for a further surprise, Jane also learned that Liveright's editor is named Pell—very close indeed to Fell.

(When Jane and I visited F. Fell's office in New York City last July, we stood in the foyer of 386 Park Avenue South and scanned the list of tenants. This list of tenants must include the name Liveright; if we saw it, we have no conscious memory of it.

(Jane has mailed the manuscript to Liveright.)

You may take a break or end the session. However I consider it best that you do not let it run too long.

("Okay, we'll end it then.")

I do then give you my best wishes. In your sleeping hours you will learn much this evening. You need the time to correlate the new data. *(Long pause.)*

You have a wealth of painting material, of potential forms to draw upon. They are simply yours for the asking. They are paintings that no one else can materialize in physical form but you. Knowing this gives you a great advantage.

("Good night, Seth."

(9:46. Jane said she was pretty far-out during the session, and that Seth was

"on a kick" about the data concerning painting. He could have continued, but we decided to cut it short.

(Jane said the room was much too stuffy at the start of the session, and that she couldn't have continued without taking her sweater and shoes off.)

SESSION 386
DECEMBER 7, 1967 APPROXIMATELY 9:50 PM THURSDAY

(This was an unscheduled session, held for Jane's Thursday night ESP class, and not planned at all. There were three witnesses present: Audrey Shepherd, Ruth Chatfield, and Venice McCullough. Only Venice had witnessed a session before.

(The unique thing here is that this is Jane's first session at which I was not present. In the light of the material obtained in the two deleted sessions earlier this week, we believe this to be a significant step forward, a mark of Jane's increasing confidence in her psychic ability, and wholehearted acceptance we believe to be necessary.

(Earlier in the day I had heard Jane remark casually, after a little talk between us, that if she felt like it she would let Seth come through during class tonight. When the session began I was at work in my studio at the back of the apartment; yet, through two closed doors, I heard almost at once when the session began. I was working on the index to these sessions at the time, and the place was quiet.

(Since it was Jane's first session without my presence, I thought it would be interesting to record some of it. I opened one of the two doors and made notes; thus, the students and Jane were not disturbed on the other side of the remaining closed door. Seth's voice was easily heard.

(I did not get the first few sentences down, but most of the following is verbatim.)

... Those who survive physical death are individuals, as they have always been. When communication is set up with those within your physical system, then indeed life meets life. You cannot understand nor intellectually grasp pure truth. It therefore must be given in terms that you can understand. In parables.

One part of the self *is* (underlined) pure truth. The other portions of the personality need translation and interpretation. They do not understand what they are.

You exist in more dimensions than you know, and your own reality *(voice quite a bit louder and stronger)* transcends your understanding, and transcends the limitations of your own intellectual knowledge... *(pace faster, still fairly loud)* these truths must be understood intuitively.... In quiet moments of your existence... *(faster here)* you will know your part in creation... uniqueness, and your own individuality *(now slower)*, for through your own individuality what you call God expresses himself and is known.

The energy that moves through the universe moves the muscles of your hand as you write.... This is what you are after. You have it but you do not realize the knowledge that you have. The person that you seek is here, but he is with you, and has never parted from you, and even though he continues his existence in another dimension you are not divided nor separated; and you will gain from <u>his</u> added development, for he will telepathically let you understand matters that you did not understand before.

Now we shall let Ruburt take a break, or end the session...at his discretion...

(About 9:58. The last few lines above refer to Audrey Shepherd's deceased son.)

In any case I greet you most heartily, and I am glad to be here. I have met you but you have not met me. I regret that through the channels of communication my voice does not always sound as genial as I desire—a matter of vocal cords and other mechanisms.

We shall let our friend Ruburt decide whether to end the session.

(10 PM. Seth resumed at about 10:15, briefly, addressing a little reincarnational data to Audrey.)

... A boy. Relatives from Russia. *(Pause.)* Myshurek *(my interpretation)* last name. In...what is now, or what was, Warsaw. A trader, a merchant, four children. A French wife.

Earlier in 1242 a Dutch existence. There was a Spanish life in the 13th century, and one in what is now the state of California in the very early 1800's. You have been twice a woman, three times a man.

You are developing along certain lines, your interest in the outdoors now reflecting your earlier male existences. We will give you more specific details at a later time. With dates and names.

Now I will indeed leave you, for all practical purposes; though I will be here, I will not speak again this evening.

(10:25.)

SESSION 388
DECEMBER 20,1967 8:45 PM WEDNESDAY

(This session was held for John Pitre and his wife Peg of Franklin, LA, following John's telephone call to Jane earlier this evening. The call ended at approximately 8 PM. See also the 364th, 366th sessions, etc.

(John reported that his wife was very ill, had been in the hospital recently for

several weeks, etc., and had not entered into a very deep trance state during sessions with a hypnotherapist; Seth had recommended Peg see such a professional. This evening John asked Jane if Seth could say something about why Peg had followed, or chosen, such a role in this physical life—a role seemingly without reward or hope; she has multiple sclerosis.

(Jane herself began to wonder, she said, about answers to such complicated questions after the call. Jane said she felt Seth getting her ready for the session early. She began speaking in trance in a quiet voice, using many pauses, her eyes opening often as usual.)

Good evening.

("Good evening, Seth.")

Give us a moment, please. *(Pause.)* Now, we have strong electrical brain discharges, in disorganized patterns.

The woman has strongly resisted the hypnosis sessions, and has suffered relapses rather than suffer the intense psychic and psychological <u>re</u>organization that would be necessary for any meaningful recovery.

Emotions are electrical, magnetic realities. Sufficient enough repression here has caused these rampant electric brain discharges that automatically affect the motor systems. *(Pause.)* Deep within, there is no peace upon which stability is based, hence the constant erratic disorders, and the lack of muscular and motor control.

The hypnotic sessions still represent her best chances, if the resistances can be conquered. *(Long pause.)*

Now. The basic idea of karma is not punishment. Karma presents the opportunity for development; to make use of opportunities that were not taken advantage of, to fill in gaps of ignorance, to enlarge understanding through experience, to do what should be done.

Free choice is always involved. The purpose is always knowledge and development, rather than punishment, self-punishment. The woman, in a past life, was once a man *(pause)*, Italian, in a hill village. We will try to fill you in on times and dates and locations later.

He lost his own wife, and was left with a highly neurotic and completely crippled daughter, for whom he cared for many years. The woman's name as a man *(pause)* was Nicolo Vanguardi *(my phonetic interpretation)* and the daughter's name was Rosalina. He resented the girl, and while he cared for her he did not do so kindly.

He wanted to remarry. No one would have him because of his daughter. The girl, when she could, defied him. *(Long pause.)* She was a rather handsome-looking young woman, though not of stable temperament, crippled but not deformed.

When she was 33 she was more youthful appearing than women much younger who were forced to work in the fields. They had a very small farm, and itinerant help. A widowed man with no children, from a nearby village, came here to help on the farm. He fell in love with the daughter, and despite her condition, took her to his home village.

The father was thoroughly embittered. The daughter had left too late; he was too old. No one would have him. He had no one now to talk to, and he hated his daughter the more, and railed that she had forsaken him in <u>his</u> old age, after he had cared for her through the long years.

This father had a later life, and a very successful one also in Italy, in a town badly bombed in the Second World War. Here he was a woman of some artistic ability, the mother of two sons, one who had been connected with him in the past.

Here the personality was born only fifty miles away, in space, from the earlier existence; and as the wife of a wealthy landowner, often drove through the very land where the small house still stood, with its farm.

In this existence however the personality of its own free will chose to understand in a different context, and work out problems faced so poorly in the earlier life. This time the personality is John's wife, <u>being cared for</u>, you see, rather than caring for; being physically dependent. The personality could not and would not, out of fear, try to understand the circumstances and position of the crippled daughter. Not for a moment could he then bear to contemplate the inner reality in personal terms.

This time he plays that part and is completely immersed in it. There are connections. *(Long pause.)* John was the man with whom the daughter left. *(Pause.)* Now. *(Pause.)* John's wife loves him, and has been made subconsciously to see the good points in his personality. In the past he hated the man who took away the daughter.

Through the change of roles, Peg now gains insight on the past failures, and also helps her present husband, indeed, to become more contemplative, and to seek for answers to questions that he would not have asked otherwise. She is adding to his development, and working out very grievous flaws that existed in her own personality in the past.

You may take your break. The name of the original town is something like Ventura, in the South of Italy. An important train wreck occurred in this area just after the 1930s. Southeast, though not sharply East.

(9:30. Jane had been very well dissociated, and was again when she resumed as Seth at 9:37.)

There were many reasons why John and his wife met and began their relationship. While such situations as Peggy's illness are chosen by the entity, the individual is always left to work out its own solution. Complete recovery, illness or early death, for example, are not preordained on the part of the entity. The general situation is set up in response to deep inner involvements.

The problem is a challenge set up by the entity for one of its personalities, but the outcome is left up to the individual. This was the major stumbling block, the last major one for this personality. Other lives had been fulfilling, but the personality had never set for itself *(pause)* <u>any</u> position in the past that was not one of strength.

The illness itself was secondary. One does not choose illness, per se, for a life situation. In order for the personality to see its own past activities clearly, it felt that it had to adopt a position of dependency this time.

It should be mentioned that in such cases the inner self, as divorced from the more accessible subconscious, is aware of the situation, and finds release in very valid terms *(pause)*, through frequent inner communications, whereby past successes are remembered, and to some extent reexperienced. The dream state becomes an extremely vivid time for these activities, and they are not imaginary.

These experiences, deeply subjective, reassure the whole personality of its complete nature. It knows it is more than the self that it has for a time chosen to be. At our next session we will go into these matters more completely, for there is an inner logic that may not be at first apparent.

John remembers subconsciously the old situation. This is partially the cause of <u>some</u> of the negative feelings, but there is no guilt in <u>any</u> (underlined) of this. No one save the individual entity knows in what directions weaknesses lie that need correction, and it sets about forming life dramas in which these can be faced.

His wife chose to solve several problems this time, rather than string them out. This is a characteristic of that entity—an impatience and yet a daring, because the situation represented such a challenge. All of the weak points were intensified, hence the gravity of the physical condition.

The entity preferred this rather than a series of smaller difficulties. In this John acquiesced, to learn patience and forbearing, to take what he considered his medicine in one dose, so to speak.

We will give you some information concerning his past lives at another session. But both of them have set themselves to learn compassion, patience, and forbearing. They chose different ways because of their backgrounds. In one way he has been too precise, and in another too impetuous. They are both learning from each other.

You may take a break or end the session as you prefer.

("We'll take the break.")

(10:00. Jane was once again far-out. Resume at 10:10.)

Such a situation allows John's present wife to telescope the experience needed into one life-situation, to delve deeply, and face at once problems that could otherwise take several existences.

Only a bold personality, and a courageous one, would attempt this. Spiritually, both personalities will benefit. This is the last reincarnation for John's wife because of this decision. The personality will then have experience in other than earthly existences.

The daughter, the original daughter, you see, is now Peg's mother. No one else from that life is known to them, though the original family was a large one. *(Pause.)* There is an historical connection with the village, or close area nearby; and not too far away a fort, a Roman fort, within fifty miles I believe of the town.

If the overall entity feels that the problem has been sufficiently solved, then it will end this life situation. But there is also a connection here with John, and the wife's personality will not leave until John has also sufficiently achieved all benefits from the relationship that <u>his</u> entity hoped for.

There are also other considerations. This is a last reincarnation. The personality could choose, and attempt, a partial recovery. There is no predestination. Until the personality itself has definitely decided whether or not to end a life situation, no one else can know.

When the decision is made, even subconsciously, then we can know. The answer now is uncertain, for no definite decision has been made. There are other personal problems on John's part, which he must work out in any case. He knows what these are.

Now, I will end the session. In this season I give you what blessings are mine to give.

("Good night, Seth.")

(End at 10:22. Jane was again very well dissociated, and remembered little of what she had said in trance.)

(A copy to J.P.)

SESSION 389
JANUARY 3, 1968 9 PM WEDNESDAY

(Today in the mail Jane received a group of file cards, prepared as an index by

Blanche Price for the copies of poetry Jane had sent her over the years for safekeeping. Blanche died last February 2, 1967, and the cards were sent to Jane by Blanche's friend, Anne Healy; Anne wrote a letter, also, that Jane received on January 2.

(Before the session tonight Jane wondered whether Seth could put her in touch with Blanche in some way, perhaps through a table. Jane also wanted some kind of definite sign from Seth as to his presence and identity, that would be convincing to her.

(Jane began speaking in trance at a rather slow pace, eyes open often.)
Good evening.
("Good evening, Seth.")
Now. Our friend Ruburt was bound to come to this point. Regardless of what he believes about himself, his complete belief in me will only be arrived at intuitively and emotionally.

This is the only basis for any belief, regardless of rationalization. Intellectual acceptance of me as a complete survival personality will follow the intuitive knowledge. The intellect will never, alone, convince the emotions of any fact.

It was indeed intuitive and psychic connections that brought me here, and it will be intuitive and psychic connections that finally cause Ruburt to accept me wholeheartedly.

I will bring about the circumstances with his intuitive help.

(A long pause, well over one minute; eyes closed.) His poetry copies were in a room predominantly blue, light blue, and pink. *(Pause.)* The file cabinets were beneath another piece of furniture, or a top board of some kind. *(Pause.)* There was some question as to what would happen to letters from Ruburt, and others. The letters are still in a strongbox, and have not been destroyed, but Anne Healy does not have them. They have been overlooked. *(Long pause.)*

There was a Saturday afternoon on a November or December 2nd, *(pause)* that Blanche Price deeply regrets. Something that bothered Anne Healy. Now either the date, the year, was 1938, or the reason for Blanche's actions on that afternoon date back to 1938.

She said things at that time that wounded Miss Healy, and her message is that she regrets the words deeply, particularly now. *(Pause.)* I believe the incident occurred near the supper hour, and in a dining room or restaurant. A man, indirectly or directly, provoked the argument. Either the man was Blanche's father, or related to her rather than to Anne, regardless of the relationship. He may or may not have been present, but he was the cause of the argument.

(Pause.) It was not in Saratoga. Blanche was angry and revengeful, and also she expressed, literally, repentance. She felt that the incident disturbed Miss

Healy through the years.

Now the incident either occurred in Miss Healy's dining room, the one with which Ruburt is familiar, or in a room very similar, in color and markings and period. No one knew of the argument but the two women, and neither of them told anyone. *(Long pause.)* The remark made by Blanche had to do with death—something to the effect, quote: when I'm dead you'll be sorry. *(Pause.)* The word freedom was said or implied; death giving one or the other, then, freedom from a situation.

You may take your break.

(9:32. Jane was out as usual but remembered most of the material. While giving the data she had an image, not clear, of the dining room in Baltimore where Jane and a companion ate, in 1951 or 1952. Neither Blanche or Anne lived in Baltimore in 1938. Jane was aware of this while giving the data, but made no attempt to block Seth. Jane met Blanche in 1948 in Saratoga Springs, and doesn't know whether Blanche and Anne knew each other in 1938. Blanche never said and Jane did not ask.

(Jane knows nothing about any argument between Blanche and Anne. Nor is she sure how she could check out personal material of this kind. Jane however lived in Baltimore for almost a year and ate quite a few times at Anne's house, in 1951-52. Blanche did not live in Baltimore then but visited fairly often.

(Jane resumed at a faster, more active pace at 9:45.)

Now. Ruburt wants to see me. He wants to sense me, and to believe that I exist in precisely those terms that I have told him.

Before this he did not dare rock the boat, to his way of thinking. He did not believe I was a survival personality strongly enough to request that I even try to convince him.

I am speaking now of the egotistical Ruburt, you understand. Now his desire will bring results. Before, <u>no</u> results would have been accepted by him.

His desire will also serve as a spur. Before we did not have it to work with. The personality is preparing itself, indeed, to enter completely and wholeheartedly into this adventure. It cannot be otherwise.

He had been fighting his own intuitional knowledge. This is one of the main reasons that he did not publish a meaningful book earlier. He had the ability, very strong creative energies, but he did not have the idea or principle to unite him as a personality and focus his energies. This has been given to him, though it has taken work on his part.

The time was bound to come, for wholehearted acceptance. Before he did not wish for it. Now that he does, we will be able to bring it about. I have always gone as far in this direction as Ruburt would allow me to go, for I have had his health and welfare to consider.

Now, to all our benefits, he is willing to allow me to go further. *(Long pause.)*

We have been away from our theoretical material for some time. Therefore, along with various demonstrations we shall give you more of this, and it will follow naturally as I explain to you the continuing developments.

Ruburt has learned considerable control over his physical body, quite without realizing it, as a result of his difficulties. The control will serve us well, and allow the spontaneous self more freedom in sessions.

We hope now that our regular two-session week will be normally resumed. One session may involve whatever Ruburt has in mind. The other will definitely be concerned now with theoretical material. *(Pause.)* I will make what suggestions I think helpful as we go along.

You may take your break.

(10:00—10:10)

The alternate sessions should be held then in that area *(Jane, eyes open, pointed to our table by the windows)* of the room, by the large table. A candle nearby that is protected from draft for the first such session.

There will be time provided for your notes. These are enough instructions to start you off.

Do you have any questions, Joseph?

("Do you want to say something about John Pitre's letter?")

(After sending J. P. a copy of the last session, the 388th, held December 20, we recently received a very pleased letter from him. He reported that his wife seemed better, that he himself understood more now, and that he had some unasked questions for Seth.)

Not this evening. At our next such session I will do so.

I suggest then, that we end, and let our friend quiet down. He has become nervous because of the import of this session, but this will quickly pass. He will be quite as acquainted with me as he wishes, before we are done, and there may be indications before our next session. During the evening hours.

My heartiest wishes, and we shall see each other shortly, under good conditions. In this case Ruburt shall see me also. Then with his <u>full</u> cooperation we can really begin our work.

("Good night, Seth.")

(10:16. Jane agreed that she had abruptly become quite nervous after realizing the import of Seth's agreement to give her definite signs of his presence.)

SESSION 390
JANUARY 8, 1968 9 PM MONDAY

(This session is a summary of proceedings, from notes made immediately after. As Seth mentioned in the last session, Jane decided this evening to try to contact a survival personality as a medium would ordinarily for interested observers or relatives.

(In a dimly lit atmosphere we sat at the living room table by the windows. Jane asked Seth for signs of his presence; Seth had talked about giving such signs, soon, in the last session. The session began at about 9 PM and lasted until the regular time of 10:30. Jane spoke to Seth in a quiet voice for some little time, but no results were obtained; nothing out of the ordinary was noticed by either of us. Jane then suggested that I speak to Seth, since I was used to doing so; her hope being that by going into trance on her own she might contact a survival personality—namely, Blanche Price.

(Blanche died last February, and Jane had many emotional connections with her from years past; in addition Jane had recently received correspondence from Blanche's closest friend, Anne Healy, in Baltimore. Anne's letter lay on the table before us tonight, with a pack of file cards pertaining to Jane's poetry that Blanche had had on file for safekeeping in Baltimore.

(I believe Jane set the stage for the events that followed, as she herself spoke aloud, and that by the time I began to speak things were well under way even if they were not obvious. Jane and I wanted Seth's assistance in contacting Blanche, without Seth himself speaking, for we thought this would make the session too much like the regular sessions. Jane had repeatedly asked Seth for assistance, and I began by doing the same.

(I asked Jane, who said she felt no awareness of Seth about, to try contacting Blanche by feeling, if possible, rather than mere words. By sensing, or experiencing, pertinent emotions rather than by strict ego-oriented forebrain thinking. The suggestions seemed to be good ones. Not long after I began to speak, Jane began to nod her head repeatedly, in a gentle way. Her eyes were closed, and remained so once trance began to show itself. I spoke to Seth, asking for both his help and reassurance, his protection, and that he help Jane reach Blanche.

(Jane began to breathe more deeply. Her head continued to nod back and forth. I felt that my speaking, steadily but not rapidly, gave Jane freedom and reassurance to do more than she might have otherwise, and she later agreed to this. Now Jane's left hand began to move; it lifted and slapped lightly at her right hand, on the table, and did this repeatedly. I thought this meant Jane had established some kind of contact or feeling with Blanche, or the idea of Blanche, and she verified this later. Her breathing was now heavier, and she began to let up on the head nodding.

(Jane's head did not remain still however, but began to tip to one side at times; then she would right it again while seemingly making efforts to speak. She said the left hand movements were weird to her, and felt subjectively "like a dead hand." As though it were necessary almost for Blanche to go through the experience of being ill once again in order to make contact through Jane, and to even approach the death experience itself. At no time, Jane said, did she "see" Blanche, or feel disembodied herself; yet she felt at the same time that contact had been made. If play acting was involved, Jane said later, it was on a completely subconscious level where she would possess no egotistical knowledge that such was transpiring.

(The session, Jane said, verged often on the unpleasant, as if Blanche had to go through her own last memories first in order to make contact, and we wondered whether a survival personality would want to do this very often. As I continued speaking, trying to help Jane get an emotional feeling of making contact without being engulfed by any strong or unpleasant emotion that Blanche might be reexperiencing, Jane began to whimper in a subdued way. I thought this reinforced the fact of contact, yet at the same time reassured Jane, by name, that she could do very well, and that Seth and I were with her as protectors.

(Jane said later that this worked well, and evidently helped her across several rough spots—the feeling or urge to cry passed after a few moments. Jane now seemed to be in a deeper trance, and began to try to speak. Her voice was quite low and I often asked her to repeat herself. She would first whisper or mouth what she wanted to say, then with quite an apparent effort would finally manage to get audible, understandable data through at my urging. "This is Blanche," was one of the first things she said, after I had deliberately called her Jane for reassurance, while thinking she had probably made contact with Blanche, and was somewhat unpleasantly involved in a sickroom episode.

(After the session Jane and I together put down what we thought she said; as we talked Jane recalled more and more. The following words are the gist of it, without necessarily being in the right order. Practically all of this was given after Jane made several attempts to speak clearly enough so I could hear; and much of it with her head inclining to her right, toward her shoulder, as though she was extremely relaxed and in a deep trance:

("This is Blanche I am Blanche... France... De Beauvoir... Thomas Simmons... And Charles. Summer... 1962... Anne's aunt at a party.... Anne had a sister, died at a very young age... a baptism... a rosary...Blanche Adele... Anne wore blue and a note..."

(Jane later said she thought she said more, but actually we do not believe we missed recalling much. We don't know if it can be checked out. Her trance, Jane said, was quite different than the usual Seth trance, and a few times, particularly during

the crying attempt, Jane felt she might be approaching an unpleasant experience, as has happened a few times in the past. Again, Jane felt that in making contact, Blanche had to go through the last, and so unpleasant, stages of her physical life. After the session we wondered what part Jane's knowledge of the circumstances of Blanche's final days might have played here.

(At no time was Jane aware of Seth as a personality, and neither of us saw any signs of him or from him. One of my concerns when Jane asked me to speak to Seth at the beginning of the session, was whether my speaking would bring on a regular Seth session, but this didn't develop; and the method gave us both confidence for like experiments in the future. Jane said my speaking was a great help for her, and did act as a protective device. My own idea was for Jane to make emotional or feeling contact with Blanche, without whatever emotions she encountered becoming too intrusive and so interfering with any data we might get.

(It also appears that the method we used will be a good one to simply put Jane in a trance state; said state to be used for whatever purpose we have in mind at the moment, offering a protective framework, etc.)

SESSION 391
JANUARY 13, 1968 2:55 PM SATURDAY

(Notes on the first session in which Jane tried deliberately to contact a survival personality for someone else. Present at our apartment were Jane and me and Jerry Kramerick, of Elmira.

(Jerry had recently sent some of her elderly father's clothes to be cleaned. This afternoon when the clothes were returned Jerry found a note stapled to a garment, found in a pocket by the cleaners. This puzzled Jerry, since she had thoroughly searched the garments before sending them out. She wondered if Jane could pick up any impressions from the note.

(The note was from Billie, Jerry's stepmother, who had died in 1965. Neither Jerry nor her father had seen the note before, and it had a strong emotional effect on both of them. A further puzzle was due to the fact that for some time before her death Billie could not write, so Jerry was curious as to just when the note had been written.

(Billie was the third wife of Jerry's father, and she herself had been married once before. Jerry added many italic notes after I'd typed the session.

(On the spur of the moment Jane agreed to see what she could get on her own, without Seth. She cautioned Jerry that the effort would be strictly experimental on her part, and that results could be good, bad or indifferent. Jane sat at the living room table with Jerry opposite; I sat nearby taking notes. What follows is not verba-

tim, since Jane spoke quite rapidly at times, but is close to it, and the correct mean-
ing of what Jane said is always given. Many parts of the record are exact, however.

(Jane put herself in a light trance state while sitting at the table. Most of the
time her eyes were closed, if not all. Her manner was active, and more will be said
of this as the notes progress. Roman type is used to show Jane's words in trance.)

I get a short name, ends with A. A city—Ithaca? *(Hilda? Sister took care*
of her at sickness.) I don't think so. A connection with Schenectady. A 1932.
(Jerry didn't know. Consciously checked it with aunt.) Perhaps wedding. *(Married*
1st time.)

Nine. Could be nine children? ...We'll go back to this later, I'm not sure.
I have the feeling that all this is preliminary, that it leads to something else.

(Jane had been resting a hand upon Billie's note. Now she held it up. She told
us later she'd had the urge to wrinkle it up.)

This was written in 1964. *(Possible. Couldn't write approximately 2 months*
before death.) A connection with Billie and apples. I see a parlor, with a table
with an old-fashioned beaded type lamp, with a globe, on the table. With a
deeply colored scarf, with fringes *(collected antiques, house full of old stuff).*

(While giving much of this data, Jane did not speak as smoothly as the notes
might indicate. The Seth voice did not show at all, nor were we aware of his pres-
ence. Jane's manner of delivery was quite usual as far as stopping, pausing, repeat-
ing, etc., was concerned—the usual manner of speaking.

(Most of the time it was Jane herself relaying the data; but on a few occasions
something else occurred, as will be explained.)

Now. This note was in a closet... An inside pocket *(pause)*, a pocket up
high like a breast pocket, rather than down low. I don't know that much about
(male) clothes. Written in the month of November *(that could be)*, shortly before
or after medical examination. *(Was having lots of exams that November.)*

Connection with initials M S, and a long car ride. The father went with
Billie on a long car trip. That is, not terribly long, but perhaps 20 miles.
(Orlando, FL, 20 mile trip approximately, to hospital, often.) He wore the jacket
that day and the note was in the jacket, and she put it there and he didn't know
it was there.

(Spoken rapidly.)

S A C S... I don't know what this means... Initials or anything. *(Pause.)*

I think Billie isn't pleased with certain sleeping arrangements having to do
with the father... Something to do with a second floor back room bedroom. *(He*
is now in 2nd floor back bedroom. She never saw house. Moved in after Billie's
death.) She thinks he should sleep downstairs.

Now. Some connection with a porch here *(I don't know if Jerry has one)*;

ground floor—some room off a porch, or off the driveway she thinks he should sleep in *(tore front porch off this house—enclosed as sun porch. Tore off—made a plain porch. No room. [Living room TV room off this.])*

This room seems to be less closed in than the one planned... and will make him feel less trapped. If he walks in the night and is restless he will have more freedom without bothering others... *(Long pause, eyes closed.)* You will have to give me a moment here.... *(Pause.)*

I feel that Billie is pretty close about. There is something about a... I seem to sense Billie at this time wearing dark-colored dress, not black, that Jerry might remember, of violet or purple color. Some kind of velvet material... A kind of soft material to the touch. It looks like velvet. At one time it had a white collar that could be detached. *(Pause. Jerry doesn't remember. She was dressy. Very.*

(Jane's voice by now had become quite animated, without increasing in volume.)

She says she knew, you see, when she wrote this, but it was no coincidence that it was found now. Also she seems to have a quick... at least now she seems to have a quick, sputtering voice. *(Yes. Exact voice description.)* She says, and this is my impression: that's no lie, as if that was an expression of hers. And that she and Jerry have guts and gumption. Like "that's no lie" are parts of her own speech patterns. *(All phrases of hers—and swearing.)*

I have no idea what this means. Something about 9 o'clock. I don't know if nine o'clock every night, or if it was a habit, so that there was a phrase used, that said something like "nine o'clock is..." I haven't got the word yet... "time".

It could be "tip-up time". Having to do with a drink, and with Jerry's father. *(Pause.*

(Jane used many descriptive gestures while speaking.) She wore a pin on that dress. A gold one. Part of it stuck out <u>like</u> wings, though they weren't wings. Roughly an airplane shape.

There seems to be a Tony with her now. *(Pause. ? Unless lost child was named Tony. Jerry and aunt have heard of a Tony.)* Jerry tried too hard, consciously, making any contact difficult.

The song, "Little Brown Jug, you and me..." *(She liked this.)* 1936 *(bad accident and lost child)*, and it seems to be connected with an appendix operation. *(Did have an appendix out. Long pause eyes closed.)*

Robbie, I'm going to take a break, before I see what else. . . At least, I think I am. Better write down Savino or Salvatore *(?)*... I have no idea...

(3:25. Jane's voice trailed off and she came slowly out of trance. Jerry and I had said nothing while Jane had been speaking. Now Jerry said that most of the material had meaning for her. As soon as she said this, Jane asked her not to say any

more at this time, and I agreed.

(Jane's eyes had remained closed, as far as I could tell. Her pace had been fast at times, pauses about as usual in a regular session. She sat quietly for several moments beginning at 3:30, then resumed in trance.)

I just picked up something about Jerry don't do something, connected with snow. This is my interpretation: Don't shovel snow? I'm just guessing. It takes me a while to get back in this. *(Jerry broke leg, falling in snow. Billie disturbed.)*

The name Polly? *(A long pause, eyes closed.)* She tried to come through in a vision sort of thing to Jerry one night—this isn't Jerry's dream—two months ago. *(Yes. Jerry felt she was there, right behind her.)*

There seems to be another Jerry. *(Yes, Jerry's aunt. Real mother's sister.)*

She seems to be saying something like "tighten up for Christ's sake—"

(Now Jane suddenly pounded her left fist on the table so hard that the cups and saucers and other objects jumped violently. The gesture was so rapid and violent that I too jumped. I was instantly concerned lest Jane physically injure her hand, so hard were the blows, several now in succession. It is here that Jane was someone else, at least briefly; Jerry later said she had the same feeling, and that Jane's gestures and voice and manner, including head shaking and language, were those of Billie.

(Even in trance Jane felt the effects of these blows, for as she continued to talk she rubbed her left hand. I spoke to her rather sharply, and would have interrupted the session had the physical violence continued. This ended, but now Jane had taken off, evidently wrapped up in the role briefly, for she shouted at a fast and furious pace, shaking her head violently, eyes closed. I was not able to get all she said on paper, but got the gist of it and key phrases. There were many swear words, and the fact that Jane halted at most of them, leaving them implied instead of spoken, reassured me that she was trying for control in the situation.)

<u>I see her banging on the table and she's saying goddammit</u>—she's having a fight with the father —she's swearing and kicked out... and there's kids around. She's hurt her foot. They're fighting and they hit each other and she is calling him names. He is a no-good *(swearing evidently omitted)* ...and something about a check and a job and another woman... And she says—I'm trying Robbie to separate myself—and she says <u>by Jesus I won't stand for it</u>.

(The first heat of Jane's outburst is now under a little more control.

(He did play around, Jerry just found out a short time ago—she did discover it; they did have fights.)

I think a name with an M *(Harold Malin—she called him Malin—said it quickly)*, and she's yelling at him, he's a miserable...trick to play, and I'm trying to cut out the swear words.

Now it's later and he's just sort of sitting there and he's drinking and they're in the kitchen and she threw something—and she says now she'd rather he *(pause)* was really full of life again like he was... Rather than like an old man...

(At times there was a hint of crying, of deep feeling, in Jane's voice.)

It would be better if he was really <u>mad</u> rather than sad. There's something about paper flowers. She thinks the world of him but they fought.

(True, Jerry said. Jane was shaking her head here again; she seemed to be trying to explain Billie's attitude. The pace was so fast I didn't get it down verbatim.

(The effect of the data here was that Billie seemed most concerned that we understand her true attitude toward Jerry's father.)

... but this didn't have a goddammed thing to do with it... That she still cared for him. She chased him all over the house one night. And she's still full of life and he should be too.

And she watches him, and she tries to push him like she used to. *(She did push him and rule the roost.)* She wants him to get up and do something instead of just sitting there. She's laughing as if she's got a good joke... *(Jane too was acting out the hilarious dialogue, in a manner that was not ordinarily her own.)* She says <u>I'm</u> dead. What are <u>you</u> yelling about? She says she's <u>here</u>... And she wants him to get up and act like a man.

(Jane's voice rose again in hilarity.) A panic. You're a goddam panic. She's around and she says she's livelier than he is at this point. <u>I</u> have the impression of a great big round object... I don't know what it is, and a favorite song of hers, I think having to do with violets. Roses and violets, I don't know.

She says <u>she's</u> glad not to be sick any more, and that she's changed, but she hasn't changed that much. There's something here that she likes her crops...crops ... I'm not sure.... *(Gardened always—hothouse even.)*

Something about Linda *(Jerry's daughter—Lorinda. 5 now)*, that Linda is a wild one *(yes, she is wild)*. I don't want answers: is Linda 6? The furniture bill. Something about it coming due. Seems to be important... A bill... Either due on Jerry's house, or for Billie's in the past that Jerry's father didn't meet, or something that wasn't paid for. I think on Jerry's house, but I'm not sure. *(He has bills and just took out another loan—Jerry unhappy here.)*

She wants him to be his old self. *(Pause, head down.)* I seem to see a distant connection with Wisconsin *(? Will ask aunt)*, on Billie's part, I think... A wedding anniversary and a string of beads. *(She wore beads a lot.)* She was trying to get through Jerry to get to the father because she wanted him to know that she was with him as much as ever, and then she sort of laughs and says more so, probably more so.

Now I feel, Robbie, I got more but I'm going to break... I think there's something about Vermont. *(Trip to Vermont ten years ago, to funeral of good friend of Billie's—very emotional on Billie's part.*

(3:50. This proved to be the end of the session. Jerry now said that most of the data was correct, except that since she herself was born in 1937 she wasn't sure about the 1936 and 1932 dates, but would try to check. Jerry agreed to go over a copy of this material and to write in wherever she thought Jane's data applied.

(Jerry said that the data echoed Billie's fiery, hot-tempered disposition very well, and that the phrases Jane cited like "guts and gumption", etc., were the exact ones used by Billie. Billie swore often and talked very fast, as noted in the data. Billie was dominant over her father, Jerry said; she was very insistent and wouldn't back down in an argument.

(Jerry said that emotionally Jane acted much like Billie, that there was good contact here, and that in the fight scene she thought that Jane was Billie. Billie died at age 47. Jane rubbed her right hip as she talked, and Jerry said that Billie had a bad hip in the same area, and rubbed it also as Jane had done.

(Jerry said she didn't see how Billie could have written the note when Jane said she did, in November 1964, since Billie died in 1965 [just two months into the year] and had been unable to write for some time before her death. As we talked however now, Jane said Billie was "still there" and that she now insisted this was the correct time re the note-writing.

(Billie was the third wife of Jerry's father, and she had been married once before herself. She caught the father "running around," Jerry said, and raised hell. Jerry remembered that in connection with the Tony data, the name of Billie's first husband was Anthony. Jerry said that as far as she knew Anthony wasn't dead, but that she would check; perhaps death had occurred.

(All the while we talked, Jane said Billie was still with us, and that she could have resumed at any time. Jerry verified other data I did not make notes on, including the Vermont and Wisconsin names. Supper time was approaching, and so the experimental session ended.

(Jane said that previous experience was a great help in guiding her over the rough emotional involvements like the fight scene—that she "got through" these quite well and wasn't alarmed. She went over the session with Jerry on 1/16.)

TUESDAY, JANUARY 16, 1968

OBJECTIVE DATA

(No doubt, of course, that extrasensory information was obtained; telepathy from Jerry in some cases perhaps—from her conscious and subconscious mind. No information given to my knowledge that was <u>unknown</u> to any living person; some given that was not known <u>consciously</u> by Jerry but she could have picked up the knowledge and forgotten it.)

PERSONALITY CHARACTERISTICS

(Jerry was convinced by my actions in the argument sequence that I <u>was</u> Billie or controlled by her at that time. Characteristic phrases used, also gestures, actions, way of tossing head. She was certain it was Billie. This would represent a personal belief or interpretation of the events—not any scientific evidence at all—but personal conviction cannot be ignored—personality can't be scientifically established with <u>living</u> personalities. The display of personal characteristics, gestures, etc., <u>would</u> be highly convincing to a relation—and to them, <u>be</u> evidential. The medium could telepathically receive this information—then subconsciously act it out, of course; this has to be admitted as a <u>possible</u> explanation.)

MY SUBJECTIVE FEELINGS

(During argument sequence: surprised as anyone else at sudden pounding of hand [has been lacking in strength for some time—had no idea it could pound that hard]—did feel myself controlled by someone else; vivid, angry vital woman, engaged in an argument. I then stepped back, still retaining immediacy, <u>reported</u>—and purposefully became less involved. Note here I maintain more awareness than most mediums I believe—therefore necessity of learning how to protect myself, in such involvement. The break after 1st half hour served to encourage me, personally, that data was okay—before I continued. Greater involvement followed. Session in afternoon—café's drawn but seen in through window gaps—
              ---Jane Butts

SESSION 392
JANUARY 22, 1968 APPROXIMATELY 10 PM MONDAY

(John Bradley witnessed the session. The session started late because John arrived shortly before 9 PM, and we talked for a while first.

(Jane began speaking in a voice stronger than usual, her eyes opening occasionally. Pauses as usual.)

Good evening.

([John and I:] "Good evening, Seth.")

Good evening indeed to our friend. Now, give me a moment, please.

First of all, the affair with the woman, Billie, was quite legitimate. I was present, as an overseer, and Ruburt did well. His abilities here will improve as his faith <u>in them</u> improves.

(See the last session.)

Some new developments should also occur in our sessions, as our reluctant medium finally comes to terms with me. *(Smile, eyes open.)* I am, you must admit Joseph, a very patient man.

("Yes.")

I had some pertinent remarks to make this evening, and since Philip *(Seth's entity name for John Bradley)* is indeed a friend, I shall feel free to make them, although they are somewhat of a personal nature, and directed to you and our reluctant medium.

Now. *(Pause.)* Ruburt has only now begun to take those necessary steps that lead to total commitment. His personality is so constructed that he cannot give time, without conflict, to any matter to which he is not totally committed, or to any matter about which he has any serious doubt.

Now surely to our friend Philip, Ruburt has certainly appeared committed enough to our ventures. He has not been totally committed, however, and as you know, wholeheartedly accepted my august presence. *(Smile.)*

Finally however he has been led toward a greater acceptance. His doubts have held back the overall quality of our material, since I was not often allowed to come through completely enough.

This was not always the case, but in too many instances my intellect has been held back by the stubbornness of his ego. His own abilities have not therefore grown at the rate which was possible. As you know, some of this conflict has been expressed with beautiful and frightening simplicity through physical symptoms.

These are in the process of vanishing, but the lingering nature has expressed indeed his lingering doubts. Of late he has to some extent freed himself. He has taken definite steps, and made positive gestures that he would not have made in the past.

Now we shall put this plainly, for his ego has indeed distrusted his intuitional self, and has been jealous of it. There has been a spiritual expansion occurring however that is responsible for these recent gains, and the late difficulty in sleeping has been the result of a flare-up, a last struggle, on the part of the ego; a rather weak offensive.

The seance affair *(last session)* frightened the ego to some extent. As a whole personality now, Ruburt has found himself operating at prime efficiency in several late incidents, when the ego and intuitive self have worked in harmony. This is a promise of what he can expect with growing regularity.

I wanted to give you this information now. You may take a break, and we shall turn to some other material; and I shall not so ignore the presence of our friend.

([John, laughing:] "Sounds like I'm in for some trouble."

("I doubt it.")

I shall never cause you any difficulty. Any difficulty will always be of your own manufacture.

(10:22—10:32.)

Now, give us a moment. *(Pause, voice much quieter.)* This will apply to our friend Philip. These are impressions. *(Long pause.)*

We are dealing now with a more comprehensive period. I will give the impressions as they come. I believe these relate to the past. G A R. 1947—a spectacular event, or an event deeply affecting him. *(Pause.)*

Disconnected from that, two women, one older than the other, I believe related, perhaps though not necessarily sisters. One with brown hair. Connection with Mary, or the initial M. *(Pause.)* I will try to designate by using the word "now" the separation between impressions.

1938, an illness, I believe leading to a hospital stay, either an operation or thoughts of one.

Now. A connection with a young man who played football. Now either there is an Ohio connection with him, or his name began with an O, and was short. Another young woman beside his wife, with a name much like hers, this Mary connection still returning.

Now. A Mississippi connection. A professor, this separate again, who particularly had Philip's respect or notice. On the lean side, glasses. F O B connected with him, and a connection with economics or mathematics. *(Pause.)* Two children.

1961. An event of which Philip has not told you, that involved him, or could have involved him in a change of important consequence. A disruption, a decision made on his part, that was in the overall beneficial. This may have involved a woman.

Also a legal matter, separate, pertaining to a man perhaps—perhaps—a relative. This may have been on the part of the relative, a brother-in-law or some such, in a court action, I believe about the same time.

Now you may take a break and we shall continue.

(*10:47. John said that nothing in the impressions meant anything to him; he could see no connections—so much so, he said, that as Seth gave the impressions John wondered if they were really directed to him. Since the data was remarkably consistent in that none of it applied to John, Jane and I began to wonder if it was not displaced from someone else.*)

(*Jane's voice had been subdued giving the data. When she resumed it was stronger at 10:58.*)

Now. We do apologize.

The information as given applies to the minister Ruburt met last evening—the whole content as given.

(*Last evening Jane had spoken on parapsychology to a group of 18 members of a Methodist church group. Among them had been the minister of the congregation, and he had made an impression upon Jane.*)

The error having to do with the name Philip—the minister at one time in his life was called Phil. The upsetting circumstance mentioned—the decision—representing the basis of conflict that perpetuates many of his physical symptoms. This material was received last evening, and displaced in this evening's session. It could have been delivered last evening, you see. (*Long pause, eyes closed.*)

Now give us a moment, though we shall not keep you much longer. The minister, by the way, was recently from a town—Allison, or Addison. Perhaps this at least you can check for your purposes with Ruburt's student. (*Venice McCullough, at whose home Jane spoke.*)

("*What state?*")

I believe New York. For a three-year tenure period. (*Pause.*)

Within a month, at the most two months, I believe, an offer, now to our Philip, of a new position. The neck difficulty (*John B.'s*) caused by inner conflict, resulting in a slight misalignment of the 4th vertebra. (*Long pause.*)

It is unfortunate that the displacement in material occurred. Perhaps Ruburt can check some of this out, with what her student knows of the man's background. I also believe he has another child from his past. We will now end the session. I believe, in fact, that Ruburt's student will be able to collaborate some of that material.

My heartiest wishes, and I bid you good evening.

([John:] "Good night Seth.")

Your material was displaced, but I hope <u>you</u> are not displaced.

(11:11. Such displacements of material have taken place occasionally. Jane found tonight's event somewhat upsetting, making it difficult for her to continue the session in a relaxed manner. Hence the rather abrupt end to the session.)

SESSION 393
FEBRUARY 14 1968 9 PM WEDNESDAY

(This portion of an unnumbered ESP class session was transcribed from incomplete notes made by a member of Jane's Thursday-night class, beginning at 10:15 PM on December 28, 1967.

(Usually we keep the records of her ESP class in a separate set of three-ring binders, but Jane wanted to insert this one as part of Session 393 in our "regular" sessions: She wanted to show Seth discussing a subject that was emotionally very important to a class member—Audrey Shepherd—whose adopted son had died by drowning last summer.)

[Seth:] In a previous life he was your son by blood. He died in that life in an accident. He came back to tell you there was no death—you would not listen, hear or believe. This time he came back and was a son to you. You knew him again under circumstances highly similar. This time you are listening. He came to tell you there was no death. You have been led here—you are to develop your abilities. This was his last reincarnation. He chose to stay here to tell you. You had too little faith in him. That you thought....

You have been given a privilege and gift. He came back under his own free will to teach you.

Without this knowledge you could not progress in the way you are now. He is teaching you. [Teach you love—he would not die?]

Without this knowledge you could not progress. Consciousness of this boy is indeed alive. Work in this life is completed, reincarnation cycle completed.

Had the boy continued, there would have been complications. Marriage and children for his own nature. Main purpose was with you for you had been Mother. Death was instantaneous. There was some recognition on your part. The boy knew this and understood it.

There was in past life connection with your brother. He was also connected with you and the boy. The brother in this life was the blood father as you were blood mother. Boy's first love and purpose involved you.

He knew only he could teach you this lesson, and no one else whose death would affect you so strongly.

In past he also died by water. Subconsciously you knew this. There was a girl in that past life. He also knew her in this life. There was an afternoon in this life between 4 and 5 years old, and this child visited with her parents. She also will die young or has already died but will not reach adulthood. At the time curly brown hair. She was his wife in the past life, when he died at 32. This involved a shipwreck. No, the manner of death is no coincidence, it is chosen. Some of the boy's friends and acquaintances and neighbors died in this same manner. They were the crew in a ship that sank off coast of Spain. They were not frightened of water. They trusted water. If it led on occasion to death, it also led to adventure. Death by water in those days was an honor, death by land a disgrace. They considered water "Mother of All Earth". He did. He would not want to die by land. He chose to leave when he did when you would miss him most and question most. For the question would lead you to find the answers. He played the harmonica as a sailor. Love of music at first—the result of long days at sea.

I have no particular love for water so I can't explain its meaning for him. To him it meant release and freedom. This time he is truly free for he feels you understand. It is important you understand what lies behind his messages and concern!

ESP CLASS SESSION
FEBRUARY 8, 1968 9:25 PM THURSDAY

(Jane suggested that I sit in on and record this session for the regularly-scheduled ESP class she held on Thursday evening, February 8, 1968. She seldom asked me to do this, since after supper on any Thursday I'd be busy in my studio at the back of the apartment, typing up my crude homemade shorthand notes of the session she'd given the evening before for just the two of us.

(And once again, as she'd done for the session of last December 28, she wanted tonight's material to be presented as part of regular Session 393. I was glad to do it—and note that Jane's class sessions usually are in marked contrast to those we hold for ourselves, for books or whatever in the future. As would be expected of a gathering, class sessions were full of energy and repartee and questions and serious thinking both with and without Seth.

(And they were loud. Often I felt sorry for the other tenants in the big old

apartment house we live in on West Water Street, in Elmira, New York. Our good friend Leonard Yaudes, who lives directly below us on the first floor, would sometimes leave the house on class nights. Yet he never complained.

(At times Jane and I have speculated about eventually publishing the class sessions—with the permission of those involved, of course—but have been so busy we haven't tried to follow through.

(This session witnessed by: Carol Bliss, Sue Newman, Lydia Nesbitt, Jean Kluft and Connie Allison.

(Jane's voice was somewhat stronger and more forceful than usual, and quite serious.)

Now good evening. I wish you all a fond good evening.

("Good evening, Seth.")

I have said this before, and I will indeed say it many times again: Those of you who come here, come here for a reason.

You are at a particular point in your existence, and it is a time for you to learn and to develop. You are at a point where you are ready to look into yourselves, and to take the next steps that must indeed be taken.

You are ready to expand your own consciousness. You are ready to learn about your past lives, and to prepare for your future ones. Do not be frightened of me. On occasion I can be a very humorous and kindly gentleman. This evening however I am concerned with your education, and when I am concerned with your education I am apt to be rather dry.

All of you were meant to come here, and your lives have already been changed. They have been changed in beneficial ways—you have already begun to question your existence. Before you came here you wondered. You are ready now to embark upon the inner roads of your own existence.

All of those now in this room are coming close to their last reincarnations, and when these are done you must know yourselves thoroughly. It has been meant that help be given to you. It is also meant that you use your own abilities. Therefore, for most of you there are two or three existences in the physical plane still left for you. If you do not understand yourselves there will be more.

Subconsciously you all know this, and so you come here, and because you have come here do I speak to you.

(Now Jane speaking as Seth, pointed to Connie.) One I have known vaguely in my own past. However you would not recognize me now, though I do indeed remember you. Now, you would not know yourself, for you were a small boy of three to four years old when I knew you, and I did not know you well. This was in Denmark, and your father was a baker. You had indeed a very short life, dying at nine or ten, of diptheria. You see, you are older than you knew you

were.

(Smile. Many times before Seth has told us he lived a life in Denmark in the sixteenth century.)

For some time you have all been searching, and I hope to show you how to ask the proper questions; for in the questions you will find the answers, and in the answers you shall be yourselves; and knowing yourselves fulfill your purpose, and expand the limitations of your own consciousness until you can search out the past and the present and see yourselves as you are, and know that you are more than you think you are, and fulfill those abilities which you have partially developed in past lives.

Within you there is indeed innate knowledge of all the selves that you have been, and of all the selves that you shall be, and this knowledge sustains you even when you do not know consciously that it exists.

I have been biding my time, seeking for the most auspicious moment in which to speak to you, and to announce my presence—for I am here in these classes, as indeed Ruburt knows that I am.

You may now take a break and we shall continue the session or end it, as always at your convenience. And you may tell Ruburt for me, Joseph *(smile)*, that I thank him...

("For what?")

...that he has welcomed me. Tell him that I shall see to it that he learns what he wants to know.

(9:52. Jane came out of trance. The last lines above referred to a discussion Jane and I had earlier in the day.

(Connie Allison now told us that for many years she has had a fear of diptheria, strange as it seems. At break Lydia commented that she thought Jane's delivery as Seth sounded Germanic. She also said that when speaking as Seth, Jane tended to use the same gestures and facial wrinkles shown in the portrait I have painted of Seth.

(At break reincarnation was naturally discussed, with Lydia voicing some doubts on this score. Session resumed at 10:05. Seth pointed at Lydia.)

Now, we shall shortly end our session.

However, you will reincarnate whether or not you believe that you will. It is much easier if your theories fit reality, but if they do not, then you do not change reality one iota. Give us a moment here.

1832... Near a place now called Bangor, Maine. You spent 41 years there, a slim man. I will give these impressions as they come. Richita *(or Wichita?—my phonetic interpretation.)* An Indian name... a war that is not Indian against white man, but Indian and white man against Indian and white man. Not nationality but trade. This occurring somewhat further west but in the same general area, involving Indians down from Canada, and an 1852 or 1856 resolution of this battle.

He then had two children. One child now the present husband, and one a very distant relative.

("What was his name?")

Son-of-the-Northern Willows. In your language R A K E S *(spelled)*; either Andrus or Andrew as the first name, and a French background here also. Buried however near Lake Champlain, to the northwest in an old burial ground.

(Jane, as Seth, again pointed to Lydia.) His daughter then marrying a man called Lines, a merchant. Difficulties in the left leg from an old wound. Also difficulties with the right ear and teeth. An overreliance upon emotionalism then, and a headstrong attitude, little given to reason. This time an effort being made to right those characteristics.

A half sister at that time. Miranda Charbeau, from a French side of the family, who married into an English branch, into the Franklin Bacon family of Boston.

Now, *(in a quieter voice)* I am here this evening merely to tell you that I am here. I am not here to do wonders. I am here to tell you that I have survived physical death, and that you have survived physical death time and time again. Quite simply, this is my message to you this evening, and I bid you a fond good evening...

And I am aware of many things that you think and do not say. Do not be afraid of old age, you who are so young, for you have been old many times before. And you are young now, and you learned from each lifetime, as indeed you shall learn from this lifetime. *(Smile.*

("Good night, Seth.")

(10:20. As I suspected, the session was not yet over. During break Lydia told us that she had lived in Bangor as a preschool child, and had been very attached to Maine; so much so that when she left there and moved to New York State, she at first refused to say she lived in New York State. Lydia also told us that she had many relatives in Boston, Massachussetts.

(Resume at 10:30.)

The name begins with an O.

(Here Seth refers to a discussion during break concerning some of the previous data; I cannot now pinpoint what was questioned. Jane thinks the O may refer to the name Rakes. One of the witnesses may remember, and space is left below for any notes.)

Now give me moment, Joseph.

(Seth pointed to Jean Kluft.) Here... Mesopotamia, before it was known by

that name. *(Pause.)* And here we do find abilities shown, ignored and misused through a succession of lives. A rather classic example of the progress followed by many psychically-endowed, but in poor control of their personalities and abilities.

China and Egypt, lives in various religious capacities, however, without the necessary sense of responsibility. Unfortunately taking advantage instead of the fortunes made available to those in ruling classes throughout the ages. For this reason the abilities have not as yet come to fruition. Only in this existence is there finally some understanding, and a growing sense of responsibility. The personality in the past used psychic abilities for the wrong purposes. Therefore they did not fully develop and the personality was at a standstill.

There was a death by fire on two occasions. *(Pause.)* There has been dabbling in occult matters, and some chicanery. The personality relying largely upon its own resources. 1525... Ireland...1721, a small town 25 meters from Charterous. *(Pause.)* The nearest approximation here: C H A R... *(spelling unfinished)*, Charteris. *(Pause. My phonetic interpretation.)*

Manupelt. *(Again my phonetic interpretation. Jane as Seth repeated the word.)*

("Can you spell that?)

M A N A U P *(pause)* A U L T the last name. A curia. *(Pause.)* Some connection here with the first historical personality whom we have run across. A very far distant connection to Joan of Arc, on the mystic's father's side, twice removed. And that name, approximately as given, in some records.

("Where would the records be?")

An old cathedral. In...of...the name that I have given you. The family name, the town, and the cathedral name are the same.

Now, my dear friend Joseph, I have Ruburt in a good state. Do you have any questions for me that can be answered here now?

("How is it possible for you to know this information?")

(Smile.) We have had our sessions for how long now...and you ask me this?

("I just wanted you to explain it to the people present.")

Very well. Your idea of time is false. Time as you experience it is an illusion caused by your own physical senses. Your physical senses force you to perceive action in certain terms, but this is not the nature of action.

You must perceive what you do of reality through your physical senses, but your physical senses distort reality. They present reality to you in their own way. The physical senses can only perceive reality a little bit at a time, and so it seems to you that one moment exists, and is gone forever, and the next moment comes, and like the one before it disappears. But everything in the universe exists at one time, simultaneously, and the first words ever spoken still ring throughout the universe; and in your terms the last words ever spoken have been said time and time again, for there is no ending and no beginning. It is only your perception that is limited.

Reality is not limited. There is no past, present and future. These only appear to those who exist within three-dimensional reality. Since I am no longer within it, I can perceive what you do not see. But there is a part of you that is not imprisoned within three-dimensional reality, and that part of you knows that there is no time, that there is only an eternal now; and that part of you that knows is the whole self, the inner personality that knows all of your lives.

When I tell you that you lived for example in 1936, I say this because it makes sense to you now; but you live all of your reincarnations at once. Only you are not aware, and you cannot understand within the framework of three-dimensional reality.

Pretend that you have seven dreams at once, and you the dreamer know that you are dreaming. Within each dream 100 earthly years may pass—but to you the dreamer no time has passed, and there is no time to pass, for you are free of the dimension in which time exists. The time you seem to spend within the dream, within each life, is only an illusion, and to the inner self no moment has passed, and to the inner self there is no time.

("Thanks, Seth." End at 10:55. Jane, as Seth, had delivered the last material, on time, rapidly and in an impassioned manner.

(Jean Kluft now told us that she has always had a fear of fire. Also, Joan of Arc has figured rather prominently in her life; in school for instance she was called Joan of Arc, withch, etc.)

SESSION 394
FEBRUARY 19 1968 9:09 PM MONDAY

(The first part of this session was held for John Pitre, who telephoned Jane about a week ago from Franklin, LA, on behalf of his ill wife, Peggy.

(Jane began speaking in trance at a very slow and deliberate pace, I had the distinct feeling that she wanted to get the information through in as undistorted a manner as possible, as Seth began to discuss the material John had given during his call.)

Now. Concerning the ill woman.

The dream of which the man spoke to Ruburt had some clairvoyant elements in it, but the time of the woman's death is not in the <u>immediate</u> (underlined) future.

She does indeed sense it, and she is not afraid. (*Pause; one of many.*) There seems to be some other important event that will intervene or happen first. (*Eyes closed; Jane gestured as though attempting to understand.*) I believe to someone else beside the man and his wife—the man, or his wife.

We must be very careful here. The event may involve the wife's mother.... (*See page 185. Pause.*) There is no basic contradiction between the man's ideas and those orthodox ones followed by his wife. The difference is only an apparent one. A difference of interpretation. She has clothed a basic idea of reality in certain garments, and he has chosen other garments. Both are necessarily distortive, but beneath both is the same reality.

He has wondered about this. There seems to be some connection with the initials A S for him I believe. This may be in terms of business or a business venture. In any case there seems to be a feeling of permanency with this—something that once undertaken will continue. This could be a partnership of sorts.

I will not give him any date, or approximate date, for his wife's death. The knowledge would not be to his advantage, nor in some ways would it be to her advantage, for his attitude toward her would change.

The other event of which I spoke will occur first, but this does not mean that the wife's death will immediately follow. She is indeed receiving instruction when she is in the dream state, and she has already on several occasions had a preview of things to come.

I am not sure here. It seems that a very young boy, a survival personality, has met her on these occasions. (*Pause.*) A relative from this life, I think. (*Long pause, eyes closed.*)

Now. Someone named Anna seems to be waiting for her also, waiting for Peg, and further back a Helen or Eloise. This I believe a maternal connection, a relative on the mother's side.

There is still determination and vitality on the wife's part however in regard to this life. Still strongly on my part the feeling that she waits for some event, or that some large event will occur, and that she will not die before it happens.

I suggest your break.

(*9:42. Jane said she had been well dissociated while giving the material, but still remembered it to some extent. Her manner had been concerned and careful, with many pauses and searching for the right words.*

(*This material had been on her mind for the past few days, to the extent that some physical symptoms of her [Jane's] own had shown themselves. Questioning on my part, and Jane's use of the pendulum, told us these symptoms, somewhat annoy-*

ing and at first puzzling, were related to the above material. Since we learned their cause they have slackened a good deal, but I asked that Seth discuss them in case there was more to be learned here.

(Resume at 10:00.

(Insert. Material has been cut as specified by Seth and added later. See page 186.)

Now... Within three years there will be entirely new openings for John, and also many changes of attitude. A strange connection in this respect, not at all clear; having to do with bricks or the laying of bricks, and a prior incident leading up to this that happened in 1963. There will be some relationship or venture, first thought of or encountered in 1963, that will find fruition within I believe a three-year period. Break, as we look in another direction.

(10:11. This was very odd, another break so quickly. It was brought on because our cat Willy, decided to jump up in Jane's lap as she spoke in trance. Usually he pays the sessions no attention. Jane now found this somewhat distracting, and gestured to me to remove the cat. However, I believe she also called for a break because she had finished with material for John Pitre this evening.

(During break Jane told me that she had felt a sideways thrust of energy going out of her; she thought this probably an attempt at projection to Louisiana while in trance. She had also been aware of the same feeling as she sat quietly just before the session, she now told me; both attempts had been abortive however.

(Resume with other material at 10:21.)

(A copy of the above material has been sent to John Pitre. However it is not the full data received during the session; some was omitted, for obvious reasons as will be seen. Two groups were left out. The first goes after the word mother on page 184 as marked after the word mother, as follows:)

...mother. Joseph: the following sentence... *(Pause.*

("Yes?")

... may be deleted from the records for your typing convenience. You may then add it at the end of your own copies, but I suggest that you do not add it to the session that is sent, you see.

("Yes.")

Now. I believe that the wife's mother will die first, but I do not want this sent to the son-in-law. If it is not the mother, then the aunt. A woman very close to the wife, I believe, now, will die before her and be waiting for her.

(Pause, one of many here.) This woman has made that decision. The woman is one for whom the wife feels strong emotional attachment. Since I am

not sure which of the two women, the mother or aunt, is involved, this information from my statement to you, should remain private. The earlier data mentioning an event only may be sent.

(The second group of data was deleted beginning after break at 10:00, as follows:)

Now. For your private information, middle or late March... I do not know whether this is the woman's death *(open eyes, pointing at me)*, but it is an event involving death <u>of a woman</u> *(gestures)* <u>close to the wife</u>, you see?

("Yes."

(Pause)... Or a severe and rather sudden illness or accident. This is not Ruburt's overcaution *(as we had speculated at break)*. The picture is not clear. If this is the wife's death, then it is caused by something other than this long lingering illness of hers. A sudden attack of another sort, or accident.

The man may have more on his hands, you see, than he does now. I do not see any point in informing him, because of the suggestions involved. Probabilities do operate, but I do sense this rather strongly, as if many probabilities pointed in this direction. *(Pause.*

(This ends the deleted material. Now we resume the regular session after break ending at 10:21.)

Now. Except for vacations and a few rest periods, sessions should be regular for overall effectiveness. Circumstances will not always be excellent. However in the long run the routine itself will help develop Ruburt's abilities further, and a larger number of excellent sessions will take place.

Spontaneous sessions may be held, but the overall routine should be continued. The channels have been opened, and as a rule, deeper and stronger contact will follow these same patterns. There is even for Ruburt a certain security and comfort in this accustomed routine, that will allow him to hold some truly spectacular sessions.

He allows me greater freedom within this routine, you see.

Now. He enjoys having sessions to some degree for his students, for he responds to their desire and need, but he distrusts himself more when you are not present, you see. *(Long pause.)* This should vanish in time. It is a new experience for him. In such cases, you see, he must trust himself entirely to me, and since he distrusts himself and me to some varying degree, then there is some conflict. This is not of a severe nature.

I mention it because this has at times been responsible for a break in our regular sessions. I am personally interested in returning to our own material, with personal data being given at your request and when I think it necessary.

The envelope experiments may be resumed, Joseph, at any time. Do you have any questions?

("Were we correct about his symptoms for the last couple of days?" Jane's annoying head manifestations, said by her pendulum to be caused by the Pitre session.)

You were. He felt duty bound to hold the session, you see; guilty that he had not held it; and yet highly uneasy, for he realized it would contain information that could bring sorrow. Added to this was his fear of distorting it. Do you have other questions?

("What do you think of my sculp?" See page 189)

It is indeed what you saw, and has for you a deep meaning. The religious connotation from your past life, given a modern interpretation. *(Pause.)* The crucifix always appalled you, but not the bare cross symbol.

In the past the crucifix was to you a symbol of the Roman Catholic church, and distasteful. The bare cross to you had a pure Protestant feeling. You did not have, in the past life, any idea of joy connected with religion, however, the cross being then a symbol of death, leading to a Puritan afterlife.

Indeed, an overhanging weight. Our studies and any true expression of the inner self, should lead to a joyous encounter with reality and the everyday moment, out of which eternity is spun.

Your cross now hangs freely and is not static, you see. It is a symbol of who you were in your last life.

("In Boston?")

Indeed. But it is not meant to be finished, nor cast, for it is a transition and will lead to another sculp, more in keeping symbolically with what you have learned since.

("What year did I die, in Boston?"

(Instead of answering the question at once, Jane pointed to the sculp, hanging above me as I sat on the couch.)

This sculp represents more, literally, than your past life's feeling, since it is, now, a mobile cross. There will be a change of simple relationships within the structure, and of color and texture, to follow. A less balanced but more maneuverable symbol—still based on this structure however.

Now. 1872, I believe.

Close your eyes and look inward.

(We sat quietly for perhaps a minute. This is how I had received the data for the cross sculp. Now after a bit I thought I had a quick inner picture of a group of men gathered about a church pulpit, somewhat in the distance. Another view or two of a church interior followed, and I was aware, briefly, of empty seats. I kept in mind that suggestion could be operating here.)

We will now close our session. My heartiest wishes to you both.

("I thought I glimpsed some figures in a pulpit, but I'm not sure.")
We will do this more often.
("Good night, Seth."

(10:55. Jane said that during our minute of quietude she felt a projection of energy toward me, not strong but definite, and that this seemed to "open up" into a room. It also involved or contained the newer sculp, she thought, but she was not able to describe or draw it.)

This 394th session was held on February 19, 1968. At the end of the private session of December 11, 1967, I described to Jane an internal vision I'd just had, and made notes about it and a quick drawing. In part: "Briefly but rather clearly I saw this hanging sculpture. I knew it was mine. The piece was of cast iron, with a soft mottled black-brown patina, densely conceived and I liked it very much. It was perhaps two and a half feet tall, hanging from a ceiling by a chain.

"Then, before I realized it, I was 'far away'—seemingly miles from my body, briefly, without sensation or location, etc. I did not feel alarm..."

Obviously, even if I could make it an iron cross that size would be incredibly heavy to hang from our ceiling. So I slowly built up a replica from layers of illustration board, and painted it black. The cross now hangs easily and lightly in a corner of our living room.

SESSION 395
FEBRUARY 26, 1968 9 PM MONDAY

(Peggy Gallagher witnessed the session. Jane began speaking in trance in a voice a bit stronger and more forceful then usual; her eyes opened a good deal of the time.)

Now, good evening.

("Good evening, Seth.")

Good evening to our cat lover.

([Peggy:] "Good evening.")

It has been some while and I am delighted to have you here.

There is an issue, Joseph, that I should like to mention.

("Okay.")

It has to do with Ruburt's book idea, and I hope to give you hints that you can follow.

(Today Jane got the idea for her next book, following the dream book, just completed. She is very enthusiastic about the idea, and regards it as a breakthrough re her habits and thinking. It should be noted here that the dream book was rejected last week by the first publisher to see it, Doubleday; but oddly enough Jane feels the idea was at least partly sparked, for the new book, by this rejection.)

You will always find that Ruburt's writings are precise barometers, giving excellent indications as to his inner state of mind; showing also the quality and direction of his beliefs at any given time.

There will be an uneven display, a gyration you see back and forth as you turn your attention to his poetry, and then to his books. In the poetry you have seen for some time now an indication of acceptance and of belief. This has not shown itself however in anything but the poetry.

The intellect therefore dealt with ideas it did not accept, and you can find this in those statements that he has made. *(Earlier today.)* The intellect and the emotions therefore, as you know, have not operated together, and whole efficiency was not maintained. You have seen, as Ruburt himself now realizes, a breakthrough that is apparent in his outline.

The beliefs of his intellect will be found in the general nonfiction. The acceptance, the intuitional developments, will always appear initially in the poetry. Therefore any large and overall hedging, any significant difference in commitment between the poetry and the nonfiction, can be taken as a sign that the whole personality is divided to that extent.

A large breakthrough has occurred. In retrospect then Ruburt can see the importance of the book that was just completed. The breakthrough was a necessity. Had it not occurred general difficulties would have been encountered in other areas. You can use these hints in the future.

Now give us a moment. *(Pause.)*

My material, now being used in classes *(ESP)*, will indeed draw other students. Not because it is mine but because truth can be sensed within it. It will provide a built-in impetus. It will also bind the students together as a group. There will be a group gestalt operating that should result in very definite benefits to them and to Ruburt. It is no coincidence that he waited this long to introduce the material for class study.

(Smile.) We have managed to do fairly well without anything like his full acceptance. We shall indeed do much better now. This simply means that he has taken several giant steps, necessary ones. But these will make future giant steps easier. There has been a change in our sessions. His more relaxed inner attitude has given us more available energy. Which we hope to use in a variety of constructive ways.

(Seth to Peggy.) My apologies. I have not forgotten you.

([Peggy:] "No, I'm interested in the present subject.")

These points however should be made when they most apply. His performance, Joseph, was extremely heartening, since he trusted his own intuitions this time; that he did not pound his head against the wall, as in the past. He was correct in his afternoon insight. The book was his spiritual and intellectual battleground *(the dream book)*, and this was paralleled by the physical symptoms; the physical battlefield. The inner difficulties therefore being worked out in several areas at once. The new book represents a sign of victory.

You may now take your break and we shall continue. One point *(to me:)* You missed me at Ruburt's classes. You would have enjoyed it.

("Yes."

(9:25. Jane took a bit to come out of trance. Seth, she said, was around "pretty good." She resumed in the same active manner at 9:36.)

Now. The new book will be the reconciliation, and it will mark the beginning of Ruburt's real work.

This cleavage has been literally a torture to him. It has caused him to hold back from fully developing his abilities; not only his psychic abilities. It has caused him to hold back in the development of his full writing talents, for these specialized creative abilities, the writing techniques, will come into their own now that the personality is more fully behind our work.

His classes will show the change. His students perfectly sensed his attitudes, and while he led them with his right hand, he cautioned them to hold back with the other. He offered much, but would only deliver a portion. The classes will expand, and with students who will fit in admirably, for now his position is a stronger one.

The intellect has learned from the intuitive portions of the self. It has not been conquered, it has been freed. The force, the basic vitality of the whole personality, has been gathered together, or rather is just being united for the first time in this existence. *(Jane, as Seth, pointed at me for emphasis.)* And for the first time in <u>any</u> existence.

The strong energy that was being diverted was working to his disadvantage, and you have felt it as a burden and a drag. You should now begin to feel almost immediately the addition of this reclaimed energy as it works for you. I told you that the crisis would come in any case, regardless of the field of activity chosen by Ruburt, but in no other field or activity could victory mean so much, or open so many potentials.

Our own sessions should also show a depth that we have not reached before, and I believe that Ruburt will allow me greater freedoms. I am indeed with you rather strongly this evening. *(Pause.)* I am of course fully aware, already, that greater energy is available, and we shall use it well.

You may take a brief break and we shall continue. *(To Peggy:)* You will be a witness to your friend's improved conditions. On several occasions in the past I would have spoken to you, but it would have been against Ruburt's wishes.

([Peggy:] "Why?")

His own conflicts often made it difficult for him.

(9:52. Jane had been in a deep trance. She took a few minutes to come out of it now, and her eyes were dark and heavy. In fact, it was difficult for her to come fully "back" with any rapidity.

(During first break I had mentioned being curious about what Jane's eyes really see, or are aware of, when they are open during a trance. From scatterings of data Seth had given in the past I thought Jane's eyes, even though wide open, did not see others present as they were, as physical entities, but perhaps as electromagnetic personalities.

(I now repeated my question, partly as a means of getting Jane onto another subject and to help her control the depth of the trance. For some reason I felt at the time that she did not want to explore too deep a state this evening; but events proved me mistaken here. Jane resumed in the same manner, but with her eyes closed, at 10:00.)

Now. When Ruburt's eyes are closed, I still have you pinpointed.

I am aware of you in many ways through Ruburt's nervous system. I am aware of you as human forms and physical entities. Through him I am aware of you as material three-dimensional forms. This is almost a secondhanded experience for me, however, and never too clear.

I am aware of you myself as electromagnetic and psychic entities. I see the essence of your personality in all it's past and present existences, and I must pinpoint you in your time.

I can be aware of you in some physical ways, as now when Ruburt's eyes are open. I can see you through Ruburt's eyes in physical terms. This involves a narrowing of focus on my part, and the use of Ruburt's nervous system.

To save our friend the cat lover from undue torment and inner terror, I suggest you put the frightening monster safely behind a closed door.

(While Peggy laughed I deposited Willy in the bathroom.)

Now. My immediacy varies. According to circumstances I can more clearly become present. On some occasions my nearness is a psychic matter, but more than this alone.

There are many ways in which my reality is made known here. There are—

(At about 10:10 the phone rang. Jane appeared undisturbed as Seth, but I asked her to wait. I talked with Claire Crittendon and her friend Bob, in Fredonia, NY, incidentally answering their questions about trances, etc. Jane herself remained in trance for a few minutes but then came out by the time I hung up at 10:20.

(She had put her glasses on after leaving trance, and now left them on when she resumed, as Seth. Now however there was a marked difference in her manner. Instead of the heavier and strong usual Seth voice she began to speak in almost a normal manner. I knew she was in a trance however, but doubted if a casual observer would be so sure. Her eyes were open and very dark; she smiled and spoke in a pleasant, almost lilting, much quieter voice.)

Now, you see, we are trying something new, and you saw it in operation briefly in New York.

(See the 361st session for August 16, 1967. Above, Seth refers to the brief session Jane held in the coffee shop of the Paramount Hotel in New York City, for Raymond Van Over of the Parapsychology Foundation. In this little session she spoke with Seth "just below the surface" in a crowded room, without attracting attention, and delivered for Raymond Van Over some excellent data which he verified on the spot. This was her first experience with this type of session. Her control this time was obviously much better although this was only the second such effort.)

Now. It is a subtle thing. I am now closely allied with Ruburt, and yet in another way, a new way, there is a balance so that his personality can be the surface, dominant one. He can operate as himself and my heavy hand is not so in evidence. He is simply more quiet than usual. This takes some control, since it is his mannerisms that are retained in a large manner.

I am directly beneath, you see. This is a state in which we can do some excellent work as he learns to help me sustain it. His facial expressions are fairly well his own. Does he not look perfectly normal to our cat lover?

([Peggy:] "Perfectly.")

The smile and gestures are his. The trance state nevertheless is a deep one, but in this condition all of my energies can be used for other work, such as the gaining of clairvoyant material, as in the new work episode.

(All this time Jane had held a half-full glass of wine in her right hand. I had been watching it, but she spilled none. Now she set it down.)

This will take some acclimation on his part; for his manners and gestures and behavior is maintained but my consciousness is behind them. Now in this state I am indeed very close, although it will be more difficult for you to sense my presence.

(Jane now took off her glasses. She paused. Her mood perceptibly changed. Her head dropped, chin to her chest, eyes closed. Her breathing became noticeably loud—something quite rare in the sessions. It seemed apparent that another change, or experiment, was to take place.

(The following manner of delivery was a new one in the sessions. Jane continued to speak with her head down; the result was that her voice seemed oddly muffled, much deeper, far from as clear as just above. There seemed to be an actual effort involved in her speaking—something quite foreign to the sessions. Her eyes remained closed. I watched her closely, ready to interrupt if the experimental delivery seemed to be taxing. And of course Peggy hadn't seen this type of delivery before.)

Now, in this state I am also close to you, and yet there is a difference. The nervous system control... As you see there are large changes, and we are using our energy in a different manner and I can come through to you in this way myself in a more recognizable fashion.

(I missed an occasional word in this passage, for even though Jane's delivery seemed muffled and trying, it was actually quite fast.)

When this method is thoroughly learned and Ruburt allows me greater control, then you shall notice a greater sense of immediacy and vitality. But as I come through to you more clearly in this manner then Ruburt and his own gestures and mannerisms will recede to a like degree.

There are many reasons why this state is also an excellent one for various purposes, and each of these states involves us in various methods by which I can make myself known to you. *(Pause.*

(Jane now sat leaning far forward in her rocker; her head was far down, toward her knees, facing the floor. The voice was still deep but not so muffled, eyes still closed. I can say the voice sounded more like an old man's voice, and not much

like either Jane's voice or the usual Seth voice. The voice now had almost a resonant quality.)

In the development of this state we can, and of necessity will probably end up with changes in the physical face because it is the memory, the memory *(head up briefly, up facing toward the ceiling),* of another nervous system that here begins to gain prominence, and it is difficult. The process thus far has never been completed, and in that respect the breakthrough in this area not made.

(I was watching as best I could for any effect of transposition or facial change, but had noted none.)

It would of course involve the transposition of an old nervous system pattern upon Ruburt's, and using this method the transformation when perfected will be quite startling. *(Pause. Head still far down.)* Initially all of our energy would be used however in this manner, to make the transposition before any of my own personal characteristics could show in other than physical terms.

(Pause. Jane now sat more erect in the rocker, and when she began speaking again it was plain that the familiar Seth voice had returned. The voice was good but not too loud; eyes opened again.)

Now. The nervous system connections have been largely returned to him. We do not strain them, and in this, one of our most familiar methods, I can make my personality plain to you, without any attempt made for any more severe change such as would follow in the method given earlier.

(A long pause, perhaps a minute. When Jane spoke again her eyes were wide open, voice very animated.) This is a compromise method, and a good one. You have the best of both worlds. Now these methods, when perfected, will go a long way toward explaining how I see you, and how I can make my reality known to you. I have put Ruburt on a merry-go-round, and so I shall let you take a break, though I am myself in a fine mood, and it is good to see you taking notes so diligently once more.

(10:40. Jane had been in a deep trance throughout the experiments, she now told us. She knew the first different effect was coming after the phone call interruption at 10:10, she said. Since she had done this once before it did not alarm her.

(The second effect did produce a little alarm when it began, but she mentally told Seth to go ahead. She was well aware of the difference in the two effects. In the second effect, Jane said she felt a distinct trembling in her chin as it was lowered against her chest, but Peg and I hadn't observed this. Jane likened it to perhaps the trembling of an old man's chin, and this is in character with the old man's voice we heard. Jane knew the voice was muffled and strained; it was a completely new experience for her.

(When break was over, Jane once again spoke in the first-effect voice, where

Seth hovered just beneath the surface of her own personality. "I could feel him there,"
Jane said later. Once again her voice was light and easy, her eyes open and dark.
    (Resume at 10:52.)

    Now, in this state I can assist you, and no one need know that I am here
if you need information from me and a regular session would not be convenient.

    (Smile.) This is a tricky method, and I can enjoy seeing you in your terms
as material entities, for Ruburt's system is carrying the prominent spot, and I
use it.

    I will continue for a moment in this state, to tell you about yet another
method, the one that is used in Ruburt's projections from a session. In this case
I keep his physical system going while training him to describe what he has seen
in his projections. This present state is challenging to Ruburt, for he can feel the
interplay between us in a way not possible in the other states.

    I will now end our session for your convenience, for I could continue yet
for some time; and our best wishes to the Jesuit, who is about his holy way. *(Bill*
Gallagher, Peggy's husband, is on a business trip to New York City.) I am very
pleased, and I am with you, again, vividly this evening. A mark of Ruburt's
greater leniency.

    ("Good night, Seth.")

    (10:06. Again Jane's trance was a deep one, and it took her a while to fully
leave it.

    (Tonight then, Jane manifested three different voices while in trance: the reg-
ular Seth voice, somewhat strong, very clear and concise, the one we are so used to;
next the light and lilting voice with Jane's own mannerisms overlying Seth who hov-
ers just below; and finally the muffled, masculine old man's voice, so different from
any produced before this.)

                        SESSION 396
            MARCH 4, 1968 9 PM MONDAY

    Now, good evening.
    ("Good evening, Seth.")
    I want to begin a series of sessions dealing in rather practical terms with
those events that follow immediately after physical death.

    Now, I could not have done so earlier, for Ruburt would not have liked it;
and before, <u>you</u> would not have particularly liked it. Part of the discussion will
deal with the ways in which I can communicate with you. And while the discussions will begin with material giving specifics in your terms, this will be sup-

plemented by other material in terms of electromagnetic realities, and also moment points.

I believe that shortly Ruburt will be ready to deal with some particular considerations. He will want perhaps practical experience in communication with others. If you learn to know yourself as you are, and not simply as you seem to be, then you will become quite familiar with the part of yourself that does survive physical death.

You do not suddenly become a spirit. You <u>are</u> one. Your training—for you are also involved, Joseph—your training has only begun. Without Ruburt's acquiescence neither of you could go further. Your acquiescence has been given. His was given only recently. This permits us to use more energy for our purposes in our sessions.

I will give you theoretical material, and I hope that we shall implement it with our own demonstrations. The coming sessions will of necessity involve us thoroughly in the nature of human personality in its psychic electromagnetic properties. Reincarnation will, of course, enter in here, for you cannot separate it. I am more solidly here in our sessions now *(smile, eyes open)* than I was permitted to be in the past. It goes without saying that there is no other place in those terms, into which those who have survived physical death disappear.

There are indeed no physical places. There are the illusions. The psychological reality, the psychic reality, always forms it own environment. The divisions between various environments have nothing to do with space. There are fields of energy set up and channels that open between various such environments, and communications can be made through these.

Upon physical death you simply step out of the intense focus upon one self-constructed plane. You are released into a wider spectrum of activity. The mental and psychic energy which you have expended in the physical system does continue, to some varying degree, to sustain it. A lingering feeling allows those who have left your system to keep in contact with it if they so desire. I do not mean necessarily that in all cases communication will occur, but a psychic return can be made at will.

An individual who has survived physical death can if he wishes recreate any portion of his own past as it was. He can recreate any portion of his own past in any way he wishes, changing his own actions within it if he so chooses, combining and reforming the entire composition. Such a procedure is usually a dead-end enterprise. The others involved are vivid hallucinations, and he may not realize this.

Some personalities are prone to this sort of activity. Until they realize the nature of such actions, two or three personalities may join as partners in such an endeavor, in which case the situation is more difficult to untangle. Here there is simply an arrangement and rearrangement of a time already dealt with.

It is as if an artist finished a painting, and instead of going to a new one he does countless variations of the original, without realizing what he is doing. This is a between-plane existence, and legends refer to it as purgatory.

Such individuals are usually beyond reach from anyone within your system. They are not beginning new reincarnations, nor resting, nor going on to new realities. They will eventually awaken to the nature of their activities, for there will be no counteraction of personalities, you see, and no growth.

Those who struggled and did not achieve fame for example, will sometimes recreate their past, manipulate hallucinatory relationships and events and achieve it within that counterfeit environment. This is simply an example. Some may attempt to gain revenge in this way, finding satisfaction in gaining control over another, finally, but the victim in such a case is only the hallucinated image of the victor.

In a considerable number of ghost or apparition cases this is what is involved. Here the emotional energy is at such a pitch that the individual appears out of context within your physical reality, but has no freedom within it.

He is acting out the past so vividly and with such a frenzy that electro-magnetic patterns are momentarily disrupted. He breaks through into "current," in quotes, physical reality, but he cannot step forth freely into it, but is imprisoned by his own overpowering and blind purposes.

He does not realize his condition. When this momentary breakthrough does occur however, then someone with disciplined and developed abilities can explain the situation to him. He can then release himself. In such cases the break with physical reality was somehow incomplete at physical death. The stubborn spirit, usually impelled by still strong unfulfilled wishes, refuses to break contact.

Physical death alone is not enough then. A misguided individual can still cleave to the physical system, though he cannot operate within it as before.

You may take your break and we shall continue.

(9:44. Jane's delivery had been a little fast, though with pauses; animated and forceful, eyes open much of the time. Resume in the same manner, at 9:57.)

In any case, such a situation could not be maintained indefinitely. The individual involved is indeed a ghost image of the personality.

Even the misguided desires behind their activities diminishes. They are not utilizing energy correctly. Their sense of time is completely different. They do not experience centuries, you see, though they may remain attached to your system for centuries of earth time.

As some of your reading material of late suggests, the more you know of the nature of reality the better equipped you are to deal with the point of transition. Here your inner beliefs are your only contact with reality. Believing for example that death is a complete end can result in a quite unnecessary period of unconsciousness.

Believing in a physical hell can cause quite unnecessary psychological torment, with hallucinatory images. Believing in the stereotyped idea of heaven can cause no <u>harm</u>, but a delay in facing up to new responsibilities. Those who have known you and with whom you have had true rapport, will help you.

More rapport may have existed between you and some forgotten friend, you see, than between you and those bound to you through various other relationships in earthly existence. There may be some who have known you in past lives, to assist you.

(Jane, as Seth, pointed at me, her eyes wide open.) I will greet you, of course, though you did not know me in a <u>physical</u> relationship in this life, you see.

It is far easier to learn and to make contacts now, for this is training that will be invaluable. With the change in Ruburt's whole attitude, I hope that I can make many of my points more clearly, and give you quite practical training. If all goes well you should both be able to see me quite clearly, mentally. This will involve time, but the inner concentration is growing on Ruburt's part.

I told you some time ago that you could resume your envelope tests if you desired, and I repeat this now.

The material, the Seth material, will now serve as a cohesive binder in Ruburt's classes. A very small but definite beginning has been made here. For our material will indeed spread. It will be published, but Ruburt will also work with it in the psychological workshop of the classes.

(Long pause.) One point however. A continuity that Ruburt overlooks, having to do with his continuing interest in religious matters from the time of childhood, echoed in the poetry and in the science fiction. He was even then leaning toward our direction, by nature, ability and inner desire.

The psychic development was hardly as alien to him as he supposed. The workings of the personality led to the science fiction direction, and could have short circuited him, ending far before the inner goal was even glimpsed. Hence the difficulty after *Rebellers*. All elements of the personality were not united.

His writing ability can now begin to develop fully. Before he developed it as far as he could, but he did not use it fully for he had nothing he wanted to say to propel it forward.

You may take your break or end the session. Our sessions will deal with the subject matter I have outlined. There will always be room for any questions at the end of the session, to be used also for personal remarks I feel helpful.

("We'll take a break then.")

(10:22. This actually proved to be the end of the session.)

SESSION 397
MARCH 6, 1968 9:15 PM WEDNESDAY

Good evening.

("Good evening, Seth.")

Now. We will continue from our last session.

In the case of the apparitions and ghosts mentioned in that session, there was one main difficulty behind their situation. Even though the physical image as such had been left behind, the individuals were not able to change their focus of attention away from the physical system.

At times they are able to be perceived as pseudoimages. They are doing subconsciously what came naturally, attempting to form, as always, their own physical construction. However it is impossible for them to create a consistent solid image in your terms, for while they are still focused within your system the inner self knows well that the individual is finished with a given life situation, is out of alignment so to speak, and is therefore denied full use of its own energy.

The focus of attention cannot be as strong as it was in physical life, hence the inability to deal with energy in those terms. The personality insists on behaving as if it were in the physical condition however, and out of habit attempts to construct a physical form. He is not imprisoned within this pseudoimage, since he forms it, but the energy used is misdirected and largely futile.

The image can be perceived at times. Contact can be made by those who are psychically aware. Now. It is obviously beneficial to learn now to change your own direction of attention away from your physical system. When this is accomplished then legitimate firsthand experience can be gained, that is not physical in your terms.

You can glimpse other realities, and this knowledge and confidence will automatically be of benefit to you when the transition takes place. You can indeed then leave your body while still conscious, and arrive so to speak with your senses about you. *(Smile.)*

Otherwise you may have consciousness drugged or in a disintegrating state, because of the body's condition. Under those circumstances the transition is not as easy.

The full personality consciousness indeed places an additional strain upon what you may call the overall body consciousness, and prolongs the sense of pain connected with that body consciousness. Each cell, as I told you, is aware. In a terminal illness, the personality consciousness, the I as you know it, bears down in panic upon the body consciousness when it does not understand the state of affairs.

It is like Ruburt keeping the bird alive, you see. *(Last summer, Jane found an injured bird, and for several days tried to make it live.)* When the personality understands, it can indeed then will itself to leave the body in an aware state, and as it goes bless the body consciousness who has served it so well, release the tiny birdlike awareness within each cell, and go on to its own transition.

There is release also, you see, for the body consciousness, which as you know then changes to other forms. The exercises which Ruburt is barely beginning will be of great help in our work, and in the development of his abilities. They are also however excellent exercises that will result in the training so advantageous at the point of transition.

If you know now that you exist independently of the body, if you have experiences within other realities and messages from them, then you need not fear leaving the body, for you can already begin to make inroads.

I will tell you this *(pause, eyes open)*: Neither of you realize as yet the full extent of Ruburt's inner change of mind, his commitment now to our work, the commitment of his abilities to these matters for his lifetime.

He does not as yet consciously know the extent of his changed attitude. His body knows. You and Ruburt both know subconsciously, and you have begun to sense the implications on a conscious level, but barely. All of this directly affects your own personal and joint—I will have to use the term for you—future, experience; both in this life and later.

This change will also attract more energy *(pause)*, bring it forth from you Joseph *(pointing at me)*.. And for you. Give us a moment with this. *(Pause.)* You will use more energy in helping to sustain Ruburt, but you will because of his new affirmation have more available. Enough in fact to show itself considerably in new impetus in your own work.

Now you may take a break. One point: Ruburt's whole personality did indeed protect itself, for unless it were integrated and fully committed it would not have the energy to sustain the activities with which it will now be involved.

(9:45. Jane's delivery was active and positive, with her eyes open much of the time. Resume at 9:58.)

Now. You read a theory to the effect that cells ejected signals as they died.

Consciousness ejects signals, the consciousness within the cell, not the cell, you see. Now the consciousness is within the cell, all <u>through</u> the cell, not localized within it, and yet it is not the matter of the cell.

Basically speaking of course the matter of the cell does not exist. You were correct in the assumption that upon death the personality sends out signals; but the personality constantly sends out signals, in any condition of existence.

In one of our earliest sessions I told you that trees have consciousness, and that consciousness resided within all things, as the plants within this room to some extent are aware of you, and the happenings here, can sense strangers, and can strongly sense emotional and psychic atmospheres, to which they do indeed react. *(In Volume 1, see sessions 9 of 12/18/63, and 18 of 1/22/64.)*

Ruburt was correct in his assumptions about your cat. All of this has to do with the nature of existence and personality, for your personality directly affects your plants. Personality can have a corrosive or soothing effect upon such unlikely things as the paint upon your walls. So smoothly and yet so constantly do these effects change as personalities come and go that your universe as it seems to you, seems to continue to exist.

I will comment here for all of this fits into our discussion. Existence is not a game in the terms spoken of by our Mr. Watts, though he is often on the right track. We do not have a static god, recreating himself as he is in various guises. Using those terms, we have a god constantly in the process of creation, action acting upon itself, always with new possibilities, each existence bringing forth new varieties. *(Pause.)* Legitimately, each personality is a co-creator, and part of All That Is, but this All That Is constantly develops, and develops in terms of growth fulfillment.

There is a turning inward upon itself, but the inwardness is not a static condition. It is difficult to put this into language. *(Pause.)*

Evil, so termed, is a lack of knowledge, a lack of fulfillment, a lack of growth, measured against that which <u>has</u> felt inward enough to understand more of its nature. Evil is therefore less desirable. The whole process however is toward understanding in which the evil is doubled and erased, but the growth <u>must come from something that is not yet grown</u>, and you cannot call a seed evil because it is not yet the flower.

We will in the future deal with the problem of evil, and hint of some of its implications in our life after death material.

Disease is not evil, for example. The murderer kills no one, yet if his intent is to do so then he must face the consequences of his intent. Crime after death is not punished. There is no crime to be punished, but between those last two statements lies a world of understanding, and knowledge that must be attained. And punishment enters in between those two statements as the individual takes the consequence for the action and the intent.

By the time he realizes the truth of the second statement, neither crime nor punishment affect him.

There is no final judgment, for nothing is final. *(Long pause.)* There is no judgment because all is in transition toward greater knowledge and understanding. Between those two statements again lies worlds that must be deciphered.

The child is not evil because he is not a man, and cannot be judged for his childishness. Value fulfillment is always working, yet there is between those two statements—you realize the ones to which I refer—the idea of judgment as an impetus and spur against the inner self's knowledge of the growth that must come.

You may now take a break or end the session as you prefer. There are several subtle points here; I want to make sure that you have them.

("We'll take a break then."

(10:25. Jane said that her trance was good, that Seth was coming through fine. She had a sense of energy and that the material was beyond her, or coming through her.

(At break, Jane showed me some yoga exercises she has recently resumed. 10:30.)

Now. We will end the session after a few personal remarks.

Ruburt is now, you see, again taking joy in physical motion. This is because the spirit is regaining its joy. The earlier resistance against exercise was quite understandable, for it was a symptom of the inner resistance.

The yoga will indeed benefit him. He is fully ready for the combination of psychic and physical mobility. He is on the move again, and we can all be grateful.

The difference in our sessions will be quite apparent if it is not already so. *(Long pause.)*

We will continue with this material, the main material of the session, at our next session. You may use the last portion for personal questions or comments I feel pertinent. The sessions will have a format again, you see.

Your point earlier is a good one. You have experience in concentration in regard to your paintings, but Ruburt has not been used to concentrating in that manner. The practice in bringing images into clear focus will help him do the same with inner information of a specific nature. Have you any questions?

("I hope I didn't confuse him this morning with our discussion."

(Concerning Jane's writing, and her use as a basis of it of the Seth material, and what she has learned through personal experience as a foundation.)

I had thought of going into that matter this evening. *(Pause.)* Give us a moment.

The main focus in his work will now begin to show itself. There was resistance against it in the past. It will involve this material. United with the unique nature of Ruburt's own writing abilities.

They will be fully developed best, easiest, in dealing with this material and through his poetry. He set himself this main goal at a very young age. He did not know why he had the writing ability, nor what he was to do with it. He will work out the best way of doing this, for it will be a natural development, an alchemy, resulting from the nature of his own writing talents, which are considerable, his own intuitions, and the material. They will form a natural whole. They will combine to a natural art production and career.

The peculiar alchemy involved here will show itself and grow now rather rapidly. He will know the first development, an intuitive one, when it occurs. *(Pause.)* It will represent a change and yet the elements within it will be seen to have existed already. They will simply be combined.

The whole energies of the personality will be behind this work, adding to its effectiveness, and I shall also be behind it and within it. As <u>you</u> suspected, this is an inevitable development, <u>if</u> he did give full commitment, which he has now done.

His personality could not be wholly committed to something that left his writing abilities outside, dangling, you see.

We will end the session, and in gladness and gratitude.

(10:50. Jane said Seth was very affectionate at the end.)

SESSION 398
MARCH 11, 1968 9 PM MONDAY

Good evening.

("Good evening, Seth.")

Now. I have several points to cover, and they tie into our topic directly or indirectly.

(Smile.) Joseph... Ruburt does not have to ask me questions. I automatically answer those questions in which he is most deeply and seriously concerned. It is true that in the past he would often block personal comments, but he had simply not developed enough to overcome his own nervousness, his own emotional state.

(The above in answer to a question of mine, mentioned over the weekend.)

Often I answer his questions without mentioning that they had been in his mind. Now, I will particularly mention that he has been concerned over various problems having to do with your own father, and with your Miss Callahan.

(Miss Callahan, with whom some of the early sessions were concerned, died this past week. In Volume 1, see sessions 28 and 29, February '64.)

He wondered about their mental condition in relation to the overall consciousness. Now. Consciousness can never fully express itself in physical terms, as you know. Through various reincarnations the entity attempts to express itself more and more competently within the framework of physical reality.

In a situation such as your father's or Miss Callahan's, the overall consciousness is not less, but less of it expresses itself in physical terms. It either has less and less control over the organism because it has not solved its problems well enough, because it has already largely decided to leave the system, but does so gradually; or because in some instances there is a psychic block, which prevents full utilization of energy in this important regard.

The personality is less and less apparent within the physical organism. The personality itself has not disintegrated. Its control over the organism, for various reasons, has lessened. In these cases the personality gradually makes inroads into the next reality. It gathers its energy within the next system.

Now there is a comparable situation occurring on some occasions in a completely different direction, and for completely different reasons. At birth the past reincarnated self may in some cases refuse or be unable to let go control over physical matter. When this happens there is awareness on the part of the new personality of the old life, but more, a clinging over, a tenacious holding onto, on the part of the previous self.

The consciousness of the personality has not left <u>too soon</u>, or unusually soon, as in your father's case, but stubbornly persists. It is as if an artist found the last painting showing up over and over in the next one. In such cases there is a lack of understanding. The inner identity does not understand that it is simply taking a different guise, fulfilling different obligations, or using unfulfilled energies.

The ego is so strong that it clings even to the new materialization. There are two faces of the same problem, you see. As I am sure you know, your father is not unhappy. You never knew your father. The man who was to have been your father left. This does not mean that you were an orphan in that respect, nor did he leave out of cruelty to you. Give me a moment here.

(Pause. Jane's pace had slowed considerably with the start of this material, and she began to take many pauses, some of them quite long. Her eyes continued to open and close however.)

He left you and he left your brothers something you hold in high regard. Lingering within the man you call your father there was always the sense of the unfinished. There was a feeling of the searcher. There was the need from which creativity springs. In some measure this became your impetus. You sensed it intuitively.

He left you things to do in your own way. He worked with photography because he could not paint. He could not create himself. He could not see himself in physical surroundings. As the photographer he was often out of the picture. He did not leave you empty-handed.

(Long pause.) He could not materialize. In a sense he was more your passive mother than your father. He could not communicate. His love of machinery was his attempt, his strongest attempt, to make his being physical. The man you call your father is happier now than he has ever been.

The whole personality has for a long time been waiting in another system of reality. There is no law that says that a personality must fully materialize within a given system, though it is usually wiser to do so.

(Long pause.) Are you tired?

("No."

(Long pause.) Your father and two brothers were originally part of the same entity. Your two brothers and Ruth Butts are part of the same entity. Now hear me. This is difficult. *(Pause.)* The main energy of the man you call your father left long ago, as I told you. He *(pause)* gathered his energies together and is waiting, but part of his energies were given to the son of Ruth *(my first cousin).*

This is a voluntary arrangement. The boy needs the additional vitality. I do not believe the boy will live to old age. The father loaned this vitality and helps the boy, knowing beforehand the boy's difficulty. The boy is unable to relate fully to physical reality. When the man called your father dies his energy will return to the self who is waiting. That self <u>will then</u> call back the energy which it has loaned to Ruth's son.

If the boy has learned to relate by then he will call for reinforcement from his entity and receive it. There may be a temporary illness for example while transitions take place. If not he will die or be largely incapacitated.

Your father has therefore helped the boy. He has also served to you as an example, and he knows this; for you did not want to relate fully.

All of this is not as complicated as it sounds. If you have time left over you help others. If a personality is between systems it loans its energy to others.

Your mother is facing realities she would not face in the past, and seeing in physical terms the results of her own inner actions. There was no other way for her to learn. What may seem a disaster to you in your scrutiny of her life, is a well-learned lesson in reality, and a victory.

(Eyes wide and dark, manner once again energetic, Jane stared at me, smil-

ing.)

Now. Do you see how much better I can come through now?

("Yes.")

And can you feel my presence here more satisfactorily?

("Yes.")

Out of regard for you, my auspicious friend, I will *(smile)* let you take a break and rest your quick fingers.

(9:44. I thought Jane had been in a deep trance. Now, she leaned back in her rocker, with her eyes still closed. A minute passed. "Are you here?" I asked, but received no response. Jane sat quite still with her eyes still closed and her hands clasped together gently.

(I walked about a bit while she sat waiting. Finally I sat down at 9:49 and picked up my pen and paper. "Okay," I said. Jane then murmured my name faintly, her eyes still closed. Another minute passed. Then she resumed at 9:50, and as she did so her eyes began to open as usual, and her manner was again somewhat animated.)

There was a particular time when your father said goodbye to you. You were two.

You were playing. You were on your mother's lap, in their bedroom, and he said simply "goodbye", to you both. And you both knew that he meant it. *(Jane sat with her head down.)* It had followed a quarrel with your mother. He went out of the house and when he returned he was not the same man. Yet you understood subconsciously, and he left in you that moment the desire to create.

Personalities are not static things. Entities are eternal. *(Eyes narrowed and dark.)* They are not as nicely nor as neatly packaged out, one to a body, as your psychologists believe. They constantly change. They grow. They make decisions. They use the physical body fully, or they partially depart according to their own inner needs and development.

When psychic gestalts are made and formed they are not static. They make different alliances until they find their place in a whole identity that serves their purposes, or are strong enough to become indestructible. They are always becoming, they are not closed units.

Your father was not simply your father. That identity that is his has grown, developed, changed its circumstances and its physical components many times, searching for the psychic soil that will best develop his own potentials.

This is not simple to explain, yet I would do poorly by you if I left you with a simple explanation. Emotional feelings are vital. Emotional identities are indestructible. Personalities that you have known in past lives will know you after transition. This does not mean that for their own purposes they have not joined in psychic mergers that you cannot presently understand. As I am joined in a psychic merger with you now, and am still myself, and you <u>yourself</u>.

There are spiritual bridges but they are formed by individual personalities. Your father is forming a spiritual bridge. He is one rung of the ladder, yet he is also part of the rung above him, and the rung below. Because you cannot put your finger upon him does not mean that he does not exist, and that he has not helped you fulfill yourself, and that he has not helped teach the woman you know as your mother.

Now I hope that you will understand me intuitively, for what I have said confounds the intellect to some considerable degree. But I speak through Ruburt, and Ruburt is himself and I am myself, yet without your support of Ruburt I could not speak. This in no way minimizes my reality, or Ruburt's. So your father's use of his own energies does not minimize what he is, nor his over-all sense of direction.

He did not leave you with no thought. He left you what he thought was the best he had to give you, a need for creativity that he could not express in physical terms. *(Long pause, eyes closed, head down.)* He left for your young brother a sense *(smile)* of sweetness, an innocent, untouched quality that will always sustain him.

He left for your middle brother *(smile)* a stubborn persistence that will help him if he uses it correctly. He left for your mother the questions she need-ed—what had she done that she should not have done; for that question was important for her development.

Now all of this pertains to our main discussion, for the implications are plain. He, in the old-man body, enjoys the solitude that he always wanted. Your mother was originally the spark that made him relate <u>at all</u> to physical reality, and that is why he resented her, why he fought her, and why she could not respect him. He enjoys the luxury now of not reacting, in his terms. *(Pause.)*

There will be a joyous gathering together of his identity when the body dies. These are like the weaving together of mosaics, the weavings of the personality in and out, and no effect is meaningless nor without benefit. In this life you were meant to create, <u>and</u> teach. All creation is teaching. Your entity is older than your father's. You and Ruburt and I have been connected many times. The gestalt, the conditions, have in the past been beneficial for us all.

You have already traveled the way individuals like your present mother and father have traveled. All is a process of development therefore.

Now, I am here in this room. I am also in another place in another time. Your father is in several dimensions at once. All of this is value fulfillment. It is growth.

We are doing well with Ruburt. We are coming through so clearly in fact that he is now in the process of learning how to disentangle himself from me. I leave willingly, but my energy is so strong that he does not know how to let me go. He is fully relaxed. He is not used to feeling my presence however so strongly.

I suggest you speak his name, his present name, three times, and touch him. This is only a temporary procedure, and a mark of our progress. He will quickly learn the procedure, and then there will be no need.

(*10:20. Once again Jane sat quietly with her eyes closed. I followed Seth's suggestion. As I touched her after speaking her name three times she came easily out of trance. But she had been far under, and looked a little disheveled, for she had been running her hands through her hair as she spoke, at times.*

(*Jane remembered the last part of the material. "But I didn't know what to do at break," she said. "I was still Seth at break, but I could tell when you got up and moved around, across the light, even with my eyes closed... Everything now is fading away as I talk to you. I felt real funny when the session ended."*

(*As we talked Jane said she got something additional from Seth—to the fact that my first cousin, Ruth Butts, was a masculine personality. Jane then said that "days must have passed, as far as time went, for just an hour and a half.")*

SESSION 399
MARCH 13, 1968 9 PM WEDNESDAY.

(*Jane began speaking in a very quiet voice, but quite actively, and with her eyes open at once.*)

Good evening.

("*Good evening, Seth.*")

I am here. Now. Ruburt just now wanted to tell you that he felt somewhat differently now immediately before sessions.

(*Just before 9 PM Jane had been telling me she was more aware of Seth's presence preceding the session.*)

He finally is more aware of my presence. I have a few remarks for you that should be gratifying. Your own lingering symptoms will disappear as Ruburt's lingering symptoms disappear, and he has made great strides, as I think you must now, my dear friend, agree.

You will both feel the difference, for his inner attitude has held you both down. Do not forget however that initially you had some strong effect here. But there will be a very noticeable additional energy available to you both, individually and jointly.

It will help you in all of your projects. It will help you financially also, after the period of six months approximately; but this is a good approximation. Events will have begun that will insure that you will have no more financial worries.

(Smile.) Now the immediate effects of the cold cash will not then be in your pocket, but your pockets will always be filled. There is no distortion here.

I will want to continue along the present lines of our session discussions but you are ready, or Ruburt is, so that any information on reincarnation should come through very well now. It is simply a matter of getting to it, to the subject that is. Any questions concerning your own individual lives or historical information, we will do our best to deliver.

Ruburt's ability to allow me to speak without distortion has grown. There may be errors having to do with verbal interpretation. These occur in <u>any</u> communication of this kind, and we shall attempt to clear them up when I notice them, or you bring them to my attention.

You, Joseph, though I speak softly, should also now be aware that my presence here is stronger.

("Yes.")

Now you can indeed expect help from me when you request it. You can do so mentally and I will help you personally whether or not a session is involved. I will try to introduce into your mind when you request it, any particular information, or answer questions having to do with your development.

Now I have come through in Ruburt's classes rather frequently of late, and this has been to his advantage. The students are helped when I speak to them through him. They in turn set up a supportive psychic atmosphere that adds to Ruburt's well-being.

The book he is writing now is merely a beginning, and an excellent one, the act of faith from which other developments in your own psychic lives will grow. His writing ability has always been based on intuitive leaps. In fiction and poetry he allowed himself this intuitive freedom, but he was afraid to apply it to the real physical universe. This is why his most effective and publishable fiction was in the form of fantasy.

There were two worlds to him instead of one, and he would not apply his intuitions to physical life directly. Nevertheless he helped develop <u>your</u> inner freedom so that you could apply it to your painting. There will be changes to come in your own work, and you are now reaching toward them.

You both have individual and yet joint purposes in this your last reincarnation. You are <u>meant</u> to contribute individually and jointly. This does not mean that you would automatically do so. You had free choice in the matter. If you fulfill your abilities then your contribution will be far greater, individually and jointly, than you realize.

Now, with new energy available and with many problems behind you, this possibility is very strong.

There were many roads you could have taken, in which case you would not have been able to communicate with me, nor I with you; and if this had not happened, that possibility of ideal fulfillment could not have occurred.

The relationship between you was a basis for this communication. Your own existence after your future deaths *(smile)* is of course dependent upon your actions now, but already you can be sure that I will be with you.

Now the degree to which you evolve spiritually depends upon your faith in our work. Yet I have not asked you, and never would, to go on faith alone, for I have given you, and will continue to give you, evidence of abilities that would not exist if you were merely physical creatures.

More "evidence" in quotes, of my independent existence will appear in direct proportion to your belief in it, and Ruburt's. For as you believe in me you allow me to manifest more completely.

You may take a break and we shall continue.

(9:30. Jane said that during break she was in a rather "half and half" world —half in trance, half not. She never used to be aware of such a feeling, she said; and during sessions now she is "just out." She is much farther out than she used to be, she said, and feels now more and more like Seth and less like Jane. Nor does she have as many scruples about allowing the deeper trance state.

(Resume at 9:38 in the same soft-voiced manner; pace good, eyes open often.)

Now because of your particular backgrounds, your overall development would come <u>later</u> rather than in your early years.

There are interchanges of energy within you constantly, as you know. Your personality per se changes in this life. It is never static. The components of Ruburt's personality and of your own, Joseph, have changed since our sessions began. Now, Ruburt's whole personality had to assimilate the knowledge that he was receiving, but this automatically changed the personality from what it was.

He literally could not operate until he assimilated these new experiences or denied them, in the main. Your encouragement was essential, and your support and encouragement is now. You are separate individuals and quite separate personalities, and you will continue to exist as separate identities. Nevertheless you are also part of other identities. And you two, you two form a gestalt, so that working together you have more knowledge, ability and information than you have separately.

This has nothing to do with me, except that working together in our sessions helps me come through more completely. That is, I am not that gestalt formed by your united identities. That additional energy does help me communicate however.

Now there are ways you are not using that will enable you to take advantage of that psychic and psychological gestalt formed by the two of you. Joint psychic endeavors should be very successful and help you both develop your abilities further. Joint creative endeavors will be very successful if you ever attempt them. You do not realize the extent to which your own intuitive abilities have been awakened by your contact with Ruburt. He does, I believe, realize how his have been collected <u>together</u> and directed because of his association with you.

Now that many psychological frictions between you have been eliminated, you will do well in any ventures that combine your talents. Joint attempts at projection, with practice, should be very successful. Ruburt's experience in this would help you, and the knowledge that you were with him would tend to offset his own fears.

This may seem to have little to do with our discussion concerning experience after death, and yet it has; for as you feel yourselves change now and experience the various alterations in your own personalities, you will not be afraid of those changes after death.

The more aspects of yourselves that you are familiar with, the more prepared you will be. You will still learn to give yourself, your intuitions, the upper hand in your work, Joseph, so that the form and the technique, so beautifully plastered, is secondary, and flows automatically from the idea.

<u>Now</u>, underlined, I tell you that from our sessions changes will take place that will affect many. I could not tell you earlier because Ruburt's abilities were being held back. They are <u>still</u> to be developed fully. The energy from our quiet sessions will however transform your lives, and through your works the lives of millions.

Now Ruburt is not speaking egotistically, for himself. This is not a superiority complex. *(Long pause, eyes open.)* The two of you from past development and association, were a fuse. Whether or not the spark was to be lit was up to you. It was lit, though Ruburt fearfully tried to close it down. *(Pause.)*

You will have a more active part to play as a teacher than you now suppose. *(To me.)* You will spend later years lecturing in various cities, and your own artwork will be fulfilled. Ruburt has still, without realizing it consciously, made his decision, and through him signs will be given and words spoken, and a movement begun that will outlive you both.

The movement will be the material. It will make its mark because individual men will recognize its truth. Had I said this earlier Ruburt would not have believed me, and there are long years ahead of you, and developments that must come before perhaps you can see the truth behind these words.

Ruburt sensed that he had a particular destiny since birth. In his own way he has tried to be true to this, but his own critical faculties threatened to disunite him. Now alone he would not have been able to proceed. And alone, Joseph, you would not have been able to proceed in the way your entity intended. *(Pause.)* Are you tired?

("No.")

Now. I have another point to make, and it will seem to you a strange one. *(Jane stood up and hunted for a cigarette while she spoke.)* You live together as man and wife. You are sexually therefore attracted. This attraction is strong and a basis for daily behavior. It exists, is recognized, and a blessing. It is good.

The fact remains that neither of you sexually want children. I have told you what you will leave behind you. The very deep love that you have for each other, my dear friends, is in the overall a bisexual love, for you have known each other many times, and in different sex roles.

Your present personalities need sexual fulfillment, but the main energy of your life is in other directions. This is why you did not marry young, Joseph, and why Ruburt first chose a man in whom he was not sexually interested. Your deep attraction in this life has strong sexual connotations that must and will be satisfied, but it goes beyond this. *(Pause.)*

The psychic connections are indeed sexual ones, but interwound so deeply in your minds that the physical materialization of them is secondary. You are more a part of each other than you realize, and this common background of sexual knowledge is always latent within you both.

Neither of you want physical issue, for the primary purpose now is to leave behind your work, paintings and writings, and my communications. These communications are not important because they are mine, nor because they come through you, but because they are messages from other dimensions, telling man of his own nature.

You may take a break, or if you may, end the session.

("We'll take the break."

(10:16. Jane was once again very well dissociated, and took a few minutes to get her eyes open. During break we discussed the fact that Jane's ESP students had plenty of questions for Seth to discuss. It seemed they always could use a session, and I wondered if Jane had the energy for the extra demands; and to what use the class

sessions would be put.

(Resume at 10:25.)

You need have no fear in that regard, Joseph. The classes however will be a means of Ruburt developing his abilities, and of helping others, for the development of these abilities is meant to help others.

I will let our friend off and close our session. He will learn to operate within this new trance state quickly. His intuitive knowledge however <u>will</u> become a part of his present personality. *(Jane gestured, amused.)* He will <u>not turn into me.</u> This is one of his secret worries, you see. *(Partial laugh.)* He is not going to give up fun, and become a long-faced spiritual fogy. Even I am not that.

(10:28. Jane sat quietly, her eyes closed. When I finally realized the session was over I said good night to Seth. Her eyes remained closed for another minute or two, then opened very slowly. She said she felt very heavy-eyed and sleepy, and once again wasn't sure just how to go about getting out of the session.

(Jane asked me if I noticed any physical changes in her face toward the last, since she was so strongly aware of Seth. I could only say that for the last few paragraphs the set of her mouth and chin had seemed to me to be somehow different, older, not quite like the set I am used to. But I don't believe any transmigration figured here. I think it quite possible that Jane's emotional appreciation of the Seth personality accounted for the changes as she was involved in delivering the material.)

SESSION 400
MARCH 20, 1968 9 PM WEDNESDAY

(At the supper table tonight Jane and I discussed our painting and writing, and said we hoped Seth would discuss several problems that had arisen in these fields. I was particularly interested in the painting information, and spent some little time explaining why to Jane.

(Jane began speaking for Seth in her usual manner; voice on the quiet side, a few pauses, eyes open often, etc.)

Good evening.

("Good evening, Seth.")

Now. A few preliminary remarks are in order, and then I shall do my best to answer your questions.

Ruburt need not spend 24 hours a day thinking about his work. Remember he is to trust the inner self. Now let him keep his regular hours. He must remember to focus within the present. When he is going about household chores for example, let him give his mind a rest. Concentrate upon the chores joyfully.

Not only this, but he needs other interests to refresh him. I have in the past suggested he resume painting. The yoga is good, excellent for him. It should be done joyfully. He need not always be so serious. These points sound obvious, but they should be followed. This gives the inner self freedom. He has been hammering again, though now he hammers with a better purpose. *(Smile.)*

The season will itself offer advantages here. Let him work so many hours and <u>then</u> concentrate elsewhere. He is trying too hard. He sees he has changed his ways, and now wants to do so with a vengeance, you see. *(Humorous emphatic delivery.)* He has dropped the relaxation exercise, and this should be resumed. For him it is most beneficial.

He has felt the need of sleep because he has been overly anxious to set things right. These suggestions, followed, will return him to his proper course. I am able to tell him such things now. Months ago he would not have allowed me to speak until he had a return of symptoms. We are short-circuiting all of that now.

The inner gains have been made. He is on the right track, but now he wants to gallop down it at once, you see *(more humor, eyes wide)* to show us all that he has changed. Now this too-much-too-soon attitude was reflected last evening in his class. Working with the table was sufficient, you see. His own interpretation of the communication attempt is correct, so I shall not waste time discussing it.

(Last night in ESP class, Jane tried to contact a newly dead friend of some class members. She said she felt she had achieved an emotional rapport or contact with the "person," whom she had never met.)

There was a connection. Circumstances were not good at the other end, and also he had done quite enough that evening.

I intend to use the rest of the session to deal with the matters you were discussing earlier. I will give you a brief break. Then, according to the material and Ruburt's condition, I may speak rather continually while some points are covered.

(9:22. Jane came out of trance easily, but said that once again it had been a deep one as has been the rule lately, and that even now at break she could feel Seth's energy.

(When she resumed her voice abruptly became somewhat stronger and more forceful. 9:30.)

One more note. Ruburt should remember to keep other interests also. This lets him take his conscious attention away from psychic matters and allows them freedom. Dancing, gardening, painting. He can afford to play. *(Humor.)*

Now that he is "good," in quotes, he need not make a saint of himself overnight. *(Emphatic.)*

Now give us a moment. *(Pause.)*

For you *(pointing to me)* always there has been a love of land, and the <u>fruits</u> of the land.

(An obvious connection I had never consciously made; since I enjoy using apples, oranges, fruits, eggs, etc., for models.

(Long pause.) You deal with emotion and creativity, and have always done so. Your own ability as a draftsman, if the term is the correct one—your technical ability—was adopted for two reasons.

It was a tool of your art. It was also a part of your talent. It added to the dimension of your work, but to some degree it was also adopted as a protective mechanism, to give you some feeling of separation. Your mother's emotionalism frightened you so that you distrusted strong feeling, even while you must use it, and be vividly aware of it in order to paint.

In this life therefore this high technical ability allowed you <u>to</u> paint, for without it you would have been too frightened of the inner sensibilities necessary. It has always had these two meanings for you, these two faces.

The precise delineation helped create the subject of the painting beautifully, with almost "supernatural" in quotes, precision. Yet the lines also served to protect you from that which you were painting, and from the feeling involved.

It allowed you to feel that you were capturing the subject, and to assure yourself that the subject was not capturing you. You wanted to be sure that you were using your emotions or feelings and not that they were using you.

The realism has several significant meanings for you also. Your mother felt literally trapped by physical life and circumstances. As a youngster you felt that recreating portions of physical reality gave you a mastery and control over them. The more precise and faithful the recreation, the more complete the mastery.

(Pause.) Now, a moment. *(Pause.)*

The emotionalism within the household seemed to be threatening, and in a free form. You never knew when it would erupt, and as a child you felt helpless before it. Through precise renderings you felt that you imprisoned it, and therefore controlled it. In the beginning this had quite magical connotations for you. Basically you have felt this magical commitment to realistic work, for to leave it would be to break the lines of this imprisonment, letting loose the emotions that you feared.

In the beginning you could not have painted if you had not allowed yourself to develop this technique, which allowed you to use emotion and yet contain it. *(Long pause.)* These elements helped form and define your abilities, adding to their particular and peculiar nature.

You are recognizing certain limitations that these developments put upon you. The inner attitudes must be completely changed, though your methods and styles need not necessarily change one iota. It would help you however to attempt larger work. You are afraid of tackling too much feeling at once, and the mere fact of working larger would free you from this to some considerable extent.

At times you have been afraid of putting too much of yourself in your work, as if the painting then could imprison you. In the back of your mind you thought of your mother and father, imprisoned in their house. The house an emotional framework, but quite physical.

The technique can follow beautifully through as a handmaiden of the intuitions. The technique can be channels of line through which feeling may flow. *(Long pause.)* Let the medium and technique follow naturally from the original vision. Allow the vision then to take its own form. But do not <u>impose</u> (underlined) a form upon it. Then this fine technique will be truly used to advantage.

You may take your break and I shall continue.

Imagine the vision on the board, forming itself and evolving outward into physical reality, and let your fine technical abilities simply help the vision flow outward.

(10:03. Jane was far-out again, but once more left trance okay. Resume at 10:13.)

Imagine the inner vision flowing through your mind outward freely onto your board. Then let your flawless technique follow the vision, and on occasion help define it.

This attitude alone will help you greatly. A child develops in his own way. A parent should not try to force, but follow the child's natural bents. So let your technical ability follow the visions natural bents.

Give us a moment. *(Pause.)* Your feeling toward oil—you like it because you consider it basic and powerful; and for the same reason you have also not wanted to use it, resenting its personal connotations to you of raw emotion.

You did not consider it refined, in terms of process, enough. Neither did you find yourself at home however with the acrylics, that you felt were over-refined, and too far away from basics. Your problem being your overall attitude toward the emotion from which your art springs, for your attitude is then projected outward upon your mediums. To some extent the present dilemma was initiated by your parents' condition.

There is a feeling that emotion is formlessness.

Now freedom, a sense of freedom, has been emerging, which has led you toward a desire for larger work. Let the vision in your mind emerge naturally, and it will expand and grow.

Working with subjects that initiate joy within you will also help free you, though you are to some extent frightened even of joy, distrusting it. Still you will experience freedom when you deal with subjects that are evocative to you, of the joy of life or abundance of nature. *(Pause.)*

Inner visions of a psychic nature also give you freedom, since strangely enough your background did not give you any particular fear in that regard. There is no personal tie up with the early distrust of fantasy.

Now in portrait work, looking at a subject easily for example, try to see him as he was in past lives. This will add depth and dimension and vastly increase your own interest. Now form is extremely important, but forms change constantly, and no form is permanent. Therefore let your fine draftsman's ability carry in itself that message: beautiful form but already in transition, with the vision beneath ever ready to adopt new shape. *(Long pause. I consider this to be excellent and perceptive material.)*

Think first in terms of being yourself a medium, through which visions flow. They will each to some degree suggest their own forms which you can faithfully follow. Do not try consciously to settle upon any given medium, oil, et cetera *(pause),* or <u>consciously</u> try to set up a lifetime program, in those terms, now.

The development will come naturally from within, following the general trend followed by these inner visions. Because you are you, you will attract your own unique visions, and if you follow these suggestions each vision will indicate its form and medium, and the general pattern of these will then be seen to be following along certain lines.

These lines—I mean directions—overall, will give you your uniquely original style. You will not be forcing yourself along certain lines, nor trying to mold a pattern upon yourself from without. The original style and so forth, the original slant and direction that you seek, will be the result of your own inner vision freely followed according to the suggestions I have tried to give you. It already exists and is apparent in some of your work.

Now you may take a break.

Some of this is habitual. You have freed yourself to some considerable extent already, but you must remember to give your vision its own freedom, and then follow it.

(10:40. Again Jane was well dissociated. Her eyes opened easily, it seemed, but as she said, "it doesn't mean much." She was even at break still very much aware of

Seth's presence and energy, which seemed to flow through her. When she resumed her voice was quieter at 10:52.)

Now. Again, the vision will imply and even sometimes dictate its own form, but the form should always exist as an attribute of the vision and not be imposed upon it.

Therefore concern yourself with the vision and the other matters will take care of themselves. The vision must always be allowed freedom, for <u>it is greater</u> than its form. That is important. The vision shapes itself. Let your hand follow your intuitions then, and the form will be seen to vibrate, for <u>then</u> the form and the vision are one.

The vision will take another form, but if you have faithfully followed through, then the vision and its adopted form become one moment point. *(Pause.)* Allow the vision to express itself in form; again, do not attempt to impose the form upon the vision. The form should grow out of the vision.

You will, quote, "pick up" visions that no one else can. If you are a channel for these, your development is assured. All of this presupposes of course the kind of technical training and background, and knowledge of the art necessary. This you have. So as Ruburt is to try to be a channel, so think of yourself in those terms.

The vision that comes to you or through you has been automatically processed as it comes through. This automatic processing is highly individual, and is what you do as a creator. The vision comes seemingly from without. As a creator you translate it into physical terms.

Now the change in the colors represented a sort of poltergeist activity on your part.

(Concerning the fading of colors in my temperas.)

A rather random activity in this case. Initiated in part *(pause)* by your parents' situation, and in pure annoyance at the dilemma we have been discussing. *(Pause, eyes closed.)* Give us time.

Your materials must always serve your inner vision or you will be dissatisfied with them. You must be bold in following the inner vision, free enough to follow it. You have been somewhat hampered by your father's overcautiousness and timidity. This can be resolved however.

When you paint the land, do so thinking in terms having to do with its past as well as present and future. Its inner development that has resulted in its present form, the energy behind the form. Remember in your painting the relationship of one object to another, not in terms of space necessarily, the interrelationship of the vitality that forms the objects; the vibrating always changing reality within, say, the skin of the apple or the orange, the quite living consciousness within the molecules that make up what seems to be the solid surface of the fruits' skin.

This is realism. Realism is more than the surface of things. *(A pause longer than one minute, eyes closed.)*

The tempera has been important as a resting place for you in the dilemma. Now, we will take a break or end the session as you prefer.

("We'd better end it, I guess."

(Pause.) Stop thinking in terms of the medium, then, and let each vision suggest its own. I will give you additional material on this subject when you want it.

("Monday, then. Good night Seth, and thank you."

(I thought the material excellent. Jane was well dissociated. Once again, she felt as she used to when the voice was very loud—inside it, so to speak.)

SESSION 401
MARCH 27, 1968 9:05 PM WEDNESDAY

(Note: somewhat brief sessions were held last Friday evening, March 22, with Bill and Peggy Gallagher, and Claire Crittenden and her friend Bob as witnesses; and on Tuesday evening for Jane's regular ESP class, March 26, 1968.

(Jane began speaking in trance this evening with her eyes open at once, her voice a little stronger than usual. She used few pauses and many gestures, and it was evident from the outset that the trance was a deep one.)

Good evening.

("Good evening, Seth.")

Now. Sketching freely outdoors will allow you freedom that will be beneficial.

It is easier then to sense and feel the alive energy within and beneath the physical forms that you see. It is easier to feel yourself as the artist, also a part of the landscape that you paint; to sense the merging of your own energy into the scene before you, and to realize that you are a part of it also. For you paint reality from within.

You cannot step outside it for a better view. *(Humorously.)* It is easier to realize that the vision and the everalive energy is far more permanent than the forms. The permanency and the timeless quality do not belong to the shapes of the mountains and the trees, but to the conscious energy that forms them.

You as artist, symbolically speaking, should not step backward to see the landscape more clearly, but step into it so that you can feel it more clearly. If you sense the peculiar and overall gestalt that is beneath the form at any given time, then creation of the form will follow naturally and truly.

The form is caused by a characteristic condition of the energy at any given time. If you are intuitively aware of that miraculous neatness, if you allow yourself to be enveloped within that particular moment point, then the painting will form itself about you in somewhat the same manner that I am formed about Ruburt's voice. But your painting of course will be more visible.

You should in any case whenever possible sketch outdoors, for you are personally renewed by such an encounter, And the implications are very different. When you are outdoors sketching there is before you a large expanse. It is easier to think in terms of size and expansion. Thoughts of expansion will help your work, so that the energy and vision are not imprisoned by form but are within form, even while in the process of change.

When you are sketching outdoors, as a helpful exercise I suggest the following: attach your focus of attention to one small thing. It may be a flower or a stone. Something however that catches your own eye. Imagine the energy within that object perpetual, but in terms of being endlessly alive and vital.

Pretend that the energy within that object is the center of life, so that the whole rest of the universe derives its energy within that stone or flower. Do this until you can feel that energy pulsate within the form of the object, so that the form itself is ever mobile while it retains the semblance, as in a stone, of immobility.

Think of the energy as radiating outward from the object, giving life to all other things, whether or not many specific objects are to be in any given painting. This will result in paintings in which your chosen point of attention radiates through the form, illuminating all other objects in the painting, and psychically radiating outward from the painting.

It will automatically be evocative of other objects not in the painting, and will automatically remind the viewer of the universe that you did not paint. Expansiveness is built in psychically in this manner.

I believe that some Spanish artists in the past utilized this same sort of idea.

(*I am not an expert on Spanish art, but the above passage reminds me of Velazquez for some reason. Nor does Jane know Spanish art. For instance, she doesn't particularly admire Spanish artists, or talk of any one or group of such artists, etc.*)

Now in other ways it was also utilized by your old masters. The expansiveness then was also of a spiritual nature. Whatever objects were shown in the painting automatically presupposed the existence of spiritual realities, and other universes, though these presuppositions were highly ritualistic.

The meaning behind them was known to all. Each of the great masters' paintings somehow suggest the existence of far greater realities, of which the paintings were a part. They saw the objects within their paintings as portions of a greater whole that was suggested by the painting.

Now the suggestion I have given you is the same sort of thing. There is no dependence upon agreed ritualistic symbol, however. The exercise itself will allow you to make the necessary transformation, where the one becomes all. Now this is the expansion of which I am speaking. It will cause immediate physical evocative reactions. Do you follow me here?

("Yes." I thought the material excellent.)

The timeless quality will be built in, for the painting itself, though flawless in form, will suggest the changing quality of form, and stress the permanent quality that gives it its meaning. If you as artist are also aware that the same energy that fills the form that you paint also forms your own image, then the transformation into something better than excellent art is made.

You may take your break. (Seth paused, then resumed.)

Now the energy can be best suggested by transparents, rather than opaques, for the opaques are too ponderous. The opaques can be used effectively to suggest the form, superimposed lightly over the transparent energy, but never with a heavy hand.

(This is sound painting technique. Jane paints in her own manner, quite different than mine, but the above data is not her way of thinking in painting terms as far as I know. I have never heard her mention this, at least.)

A good use of transparents in oils will make you more pleased with using them. Movement can be best portrayed also with transparents, and even for rocks. While opaques may be used to suggest physical heaviness, transparents should be used also to show that in actuality rocks are as light as air, and to hint at the ever-mobile energy that forms them.

Now again, much of this has to do with your own interest. Opaques are excellent to suggest a heavy or dark mood. In portraits, while the inner skeletal structure must be hinted at, and while the figure should be well done, still there should be the suggestion of the personality going beyond the image, and of the personality's energy radiating outward.

In a portrait, do the same exercise as given earlier. Imagine the individual as the center of all life, so that when the painting is completed it automatically suggests the whole universe of which the individual is part. Nothing exists in isolation, and this is the secret that the old masters knew so well.

In the smallest detail of the smallest still life they managed to suggest the reality of the spiritual universe, <u>of which</u> that detail was a part, and through which the energy of the universe spoke.

To use your talents, and they are considerable, you can do no less. Are you tired?

("No." Even though it was 9:45, Seth obviously wanted to continue. Jane's pace had been good. Pause.)

Give us a moment.

Painting or sketching outdoors for a while will aid you considerably in your ability to sense this inner unity, to see each natural object in its individualistic momentary majesty, and yet to realize that it is in one way a center through which all energy moves.

In itself an object should be then felt as its unique identity, and as a part of the whole universe. A stone or a flower is a very small thing. When you attach your attention say to a flower, it is not only a matter of imagining yourself as the flower, or trying to sense what a flower is. It is also to imagine the power of the energy that causes that flower to grow; and yet in a landscape you will have perhaps many flowers. They must each suggest the reality of the overall pulsating vitality that makes their appearance possible.

Now oils themselves suggest the earth. The medium is a fairly natural one. Let the medium then stand for and represent the physical appearance of permanency in any object, the physical continuity of any given human form in a painting. Let transparents represent the constant renewal of energy that always escapes the form. These lift the medium itself into another realm, and the two together can suit your purposes well.

You may do as you like, break or continue. Ruburt and I are fine.

("You might as well continue for a while." 9:55.)

You had better. It was a good decision.

Now one other small point. (Pause.)

An apple can do more in a painting than stand before the spirit of all apples, though that is an accomplishment. An apple can imply, through use of the exercise I have given you, the whole unseen universe, though not another object is shown in the painting itself.

With oils again the transparents for the mobility and vitality that gives the form meaning, the opaques to suggest the idea of physical time, and to suggest the <u>apparent</u> (underlined) duration of form.

(Jane sat in her rocker facing the living room wall upon which hung my oil portrait of Seth. She pointed to it now.)

Now. One of the attractions for others in that painting of me is that it automatically suggests an unseen audience, to whom I appear to be speaking.

Not indeed a formal audience, but unseen listeners who represent humanity at large. The unseen is there. 'The figure manages to suggest the universe of men and the world that holds them, yet nowhere literally do these appear.

(Now Jane, as Seth, pointed to an acrylic seascape that I had recently hung on the wall opposite Seth's portrait. This I painted last year. After the seascape Seth inspected an oil of a tree that I had painted in 1960; this hung beyond the seascape, toward the front door.)

The seascape automatically suggests the energy that moves the ocean. Now, the tree does not suggest the energy that forms trees. It does not suggest the universe. The tree does not for others suggest more than you have literally put into the painting.

Ruburt cannot deal with form you see, in painting. He does not understand form in those terms, and never has. You can use it beautifully, as the carrier through which energy flows, and at the same time remember that the form itself is also the energy, period.

You may take your break.

(A long pause, eyes closed, at 10:06.)

Energy fills out the sails of form. The energy is psychic and spiritual. It will endure as long as there are people to look at paintings. If you can suggest this, and you <u>can</u>, Joseph, then you will truly fulfill your artistic abilities. To some extent you have been trapped by the object, trying so hard to identify with it that this kind of expansion was not possible.

The skin of the apple must also give the feeling that it is more than an enclosure, for through it energy from the sun also comes. While it seems solid it is open, and connected with the rest of the universe. An apple in a room goes out into that room. Do you see?

("Yes."

(Another long pause. I asked finally: "Why don't you open your eyes?" But Jane did not do so, and gestured to me to wait. Resume at 10:11.)

An apple is not stuck within a tight hole of space, you see, isolated there. It makes itself <u>out of</u> space, transforms space, <u>into</u> an apple, and this you must suggest.

(Humorously:) Ruburt does not want me to hurt your feelings with apples—

("All right.")

—but this is what you have been searching for in that regard.

(Again Jane paused, at 10:13. This time she told me I had better speak her name three times, as Seth had suggested I do in a recent session, when her trance was deep. I did so now, and very slowly Jane opened her eyes, one at a time, on a crack.

But, as she said later, she never really got out of the trance, and resumed at 10:15.)

Now, some of my suggestions for you this evening come from better sources than I. For as you know I am no artist.

This has something to do with Ruburt's difficulty in breaking the trance state. *(Pause.)* From someone else here... Your figures, to get the feeling of depth and breadth, this is not to get the feeling simply of the flesh and bone within the flesh, but to suggest the personal energy and vitality that is in a riot, to be loose within the flesh.

This is from an artist who always used siennas for initial flesh tones, with a suggestion very lightly of violets. Built up then cleverly with *(pause)* transparent ochre which he had, and a particular green, muted. The top complexion tone lay on this lightly, as if a wind could blow it away, and of course he suggests this. *(Long pause.*

("Can you give me his name?")

We are working on it. Van *(pause)* Elder. *(Pause.)* Dane or Norwegian, domestic scenes, 1700's. *(Pause.)* Straggly grass scenes and small mounds of ground, brownish foregrounds. I am not sure, 1781, or 1881...

("Representing what?")

Having to do with him. *(Pause, head down, hair disheveled.)* Now as the clouds' construction constantly changes—tonight you watched them *(and sketched them after supper)* so the forms of objects constantly change. *(Pause, head down, hair disheveled. Eyes closed. Jane constantly rubbed her face and eyes with both hands.)* We had better get Ruburt out of this for now, at least for a break. Touch his shoulder.

(At 10:22 I did so, and spoke to Jane again. Very slowly her eyes opened; they were very heavy and sleepy and the effort involved was apparent. I said it was the end of the session. When she finally began to talk Jane said this was the deepest trance, the "farthest out" she had ever been, bar no other time. Yet she still remembered some of what she had said, in a general way. She felt Seth had come through as specifically as possible for her at this time, and with great clearness. Jane felt the energy involved: "I had a sense of tremendous power going through me."

(My first question about Van Elder shook her up a little, she said. The Van came through clearly. Jane had the impression at the time of Seth conferring with someone else, she said. The next word, she now speculated, could have been either Elder or Older; Jane said now that she didn't realize this until she voiced the idea.

(I asked the question because of the long pause; I wanted to keep Seth on this track, and thought he might begin talking about another subject. Jane said she had visions of brown earth and clumps of grass while she gave the data. A little earlier, she now added, she had seen flashes of other paintings as she spoke about the old mas-

ters, but she didn't know which paintings were involved by name.

(The Van Elder name was not specifically familiar to me, although it could be said to have a familiar sound. I can say that the painting and energy data given tonight is entirely sound and worthy, however, and certainly beneficial for any artist. The method of using siennas, ochre and violet is not one I have used, but appears to be quite sensible; I may try it soon. I do not believe Jane consciously thinks this way.

(Jane said Seth seemed to have a tremendous fount of information to draw upon as she gave the data tonight, as though he had gathered it together just for this session. Jane felt that either she or Seth, or both, were looking at paintings as she talked.

(Jane said she was so passive at the end of the session that she couldn't assert herself as she usually does; she thought that this assertion on her part helped Seth disengage at the end of a session. I thought this an excellent point, and one not previously mentioned in just such a way.)

SESSION 402
APRIL 1, 1968 9:05 PM MONDAY

(John Bradley was a witness to the session, and had some questions about his job with Searle, and events within the company. However John gave Jane no details before the session, merely stating that he would like to know what was happening.)

Good evening.

("Good evening, Seth.")

Now. Give us a moment.

The changes of which you know are initial ones, that will not affect you as directly, or rather as beneficially as you might suppose, but will initiate changes that will affect you beneficially.

The process has begun, in other words. A grab bag has been set up, and the grab bag is good, but you are not to grab for you will be offered what you want as these changes continue to develop. Play a waiting game. It will be to your advantage.

Now. There seem to be four men playing chess, symbolically speaking. One man appears to have the advantage, but another will take it from him, and your best interests will lie with this second man. The first one now has the ascendancy. Three men work together for their own ends.

S A R. The three exert considerable pressure, or pull. The short man is out. But the way things are changing, I believe you will stay in this area of the country, though not necessarily at your particular location, and perhaps in a different capacity, though in a freewheeling basis.

Events as you know of them right now are transient. There will be further changes, and <u>these</u> will be to your advantage, if I understand correctly your idea of advantage. The third party will be out. The scramble was initiated by a turnabout, and another turnabout is coming.

At a later date even the fabulous four will be unseated, but you should weather this. There is a Stan to be contended with. On your part the terms will be bettered. You may be expected to move now, but waiting for the further changes would serve your interests more. A paper is being drawn up, and I would suggest you hold out.

If you hold out your position will be strengthened. The man closest to you in the establishment will no longer restrain you. He is not in a position to, and his own position has changed. He is one of the pawns.

On your part the king is an unknown entity, but he will make a move. You are the bishop in the game. May should see evidence of the further changes. A quality that you think of as stable now is not. In other words I would suggest that you play it cagey for now.

You may ask questions or take a break as you prefer.

([John:] *"Was I invited to dip into this grab bag, the last time my boss was down?"*)

You were indeed.

([John:] *"In his place?"*)

On his behalf.

([John:] *"To somewhat save him?"*)

Give us a moment here. *(Pause.)* He is no longer in a position to hinder you. On the other hand his ability to help you has also dwindled.

([John:] *"What did you mean when you said the quality is not stable?"*)

The situation is not stable now. The elements in your mind that you consider stable are not. The elements will change at this point quickly.

([John:] *"By elements do you mean persons?"*)

The situation itself. It will soon change. A reaction on your part would be wasted, for the situation will soon change. The grab bag will not be taken away however. Its contents will change.

([John:] *"The promotion of this man in California is not indicative of a general change of values?"*)

The situation will change further. You have correctly interpreted the change in values. But there will be further changes in the organization and personnel.

([John:] *"Can you give me more information of these four men?"*)

Different people will hold the grab bag. Give us a moment. *(Pause.)* Your immediate superior is losing a chance. Yet he offered you a chance at the grab bag for his own reasons. He would give you as a gift. He would give you to others as a gift in order to gain advantages for himself, and in order to gain your loyalty and obligation.

([John:] "Let's take a break while I mull over some of this.")

You may tell Ruburt, Joseph, that I will have some comments concerning his book later this evening or at our next session.

("Yes."

(9:28. Jane's trance had again been a good one, her pace fast, voice fairly strong, eyes closed for much of the early part of the delivery.

(John corroborated much of what Seth had given, and added that he felt that only his own lack of specific knowledge prevented him from corroborating much more of the data. Jane was pleased, saying she tried to relax and not block or distort any of the data .

(John went over the points covered so far, and did indeed agree on many of them. We are not listing them individually here, though they are included in my handwritten notes for future reference if necessary. The data given here makes sense to John, and this is our concern at the moment.

(John gave us much interesting background information about his company. He identified the short man who would be out as Jim Brady. John could not identify the S A R reference. John has already refused, he said, to commit himself re a promotion to Rochester. He said it was likely he would remain in this area of the country, that is, the northeast. Freewheeling basis would pertain to John's interpretation, he said, of the changed mode of operation by which the pharmaceutical industry attempts to sell its products and its image.

(John described to us the promotion of Roy Weideman in California, and how John Cressman has been sidetracked from district manager. to a clinical research associate. This fit in with the first part of the data, et cetera.

(The chess references by Seth were interesting. Neither Jane nor I play chess or know the moves. It developed that John had recently given one of his young sons a chess set; the boy knew the game to some extent and wanted to teach John. More on this later.

(Jane resumed at 9:50, again in a deep trance.)

Now. Four men were involved in the promotion of the man to whom you spoke. One of these will be out for all practical purposes. The others will begin to change the philosophy within the enterprise, so that the climate is more to your liking.

There were others who did not want the man promoted, and these men do not want <u>you</u> promoted. This Stan is against your promotion, except in one particular area where it might serve to his own particular advantage. Otherwise he is against it.

(During break John identified Stan as his regional manager.)

The man in California remembers you as you remember him, and he will speak of you. There will be two other men also of a like philosophy, and the four of you will exert considerable force within the company in the future, and will shape its policy eventually.

One of these men is younger by some years. The stakes are high, for you have indeed always wanted to shape the policy, and that is why you should not move yet. Let the man from California speak his peace.

I spoke of two other men who will be in league with you and the man from California. Now when I say a league I do not necessarily mean in conspiracy. Simply that from four corners your philosophies will meet, and each will see advantage for themselves in the promotions of the others.

Besides this there will be a natural meeting of minds. Of the other two men, one is not in the picture as yet. This does not matter. But the third man must arrive in the picture. His advancement must come before your move can be made with any assurance of success. He is another within the company whose ideas match your own to some degree.

On other issues you do not agree. You have spoken with him. He and the man from California will have some say-so, and you will then add your voice to theirs. The fourth man will come later. This Stan is no fool, but he is being outwitted.

When you have your millions, remember me. You may all take a break.

([John, laughing:] "I'd just like to say one thing, Seth. Are you still with us?")

I am indeed.

([John:] "If I make a million I'll set up a foundation for psychic research.")

My dear friend. We shall be part of an association in the future. I shall be incorporated. *(Eyes wide open, voice getting louder and stronger.)* Now I am glad that you have come to visit us, although I am somewhat disappointed in you. I did indeed use the symbol of the chessboard because I knew that you had been involved with one. I was trying, you see, to make you comfortable by dealing with what I thought was a common point of interest.

(There followed a brief, rapid and humorous exchange between John and Seth that I did not have time to record. It ended with John referring to the chess set:

([John:] "I shall go home and study it.")

You are some bishop.

A note, Joseph. I am pleased with our last session, and hope that you take what I told you to heart.

("Yes.")

And now I will let you take a break, though I am myself in fine form. *(Voice strong. Eyes wide, Jane smiled.)* And because it is April Fool's Day, then indeed I give you all a special greeting, and I know that you will not take offense. It is only because of my great esteem for you, and my feeling toward your problems, that I do not allow myself full freedom this evening, for the matter of the voice could indeed be quite unrestrained.

(The Seth voice was indeed powerful to a degree, and gave brief evidences of soaring, but then quieted. The above was humorous.)

As always I bow to your best interests. I shall reserve the right however to wait around a bit and eavesdrop upon your conversation.

(Jane's voice was again becoming loud and powerful.) Ruburt has his wires crossed. He opened the channels wide in order to receive the information for our friend, And indeed he does not know how to close them. This is why the voice comes through with such raucous glee.

("Well, we can have a break now.")

You had better watch out. This is April Fool's Day.

("I know it."

([John:] "This material you gave me tonight wasn't a joke, was it?")

I should not answer that question. However, no, it was not. *(Pause; smile.)* I feel indeed like a merry old gentleman, sitting here with his cronies. Ruburt's trance state has improved indeed, but having opened the door, oftentimes he does not know how to close it. If you do not want me to go booming through him for hours then I suggest that you call his name three times. I however am perfectly content, and he is fine.

("My writing hand's giving out, though.")

You have more problems than I can deal with. And the artist's name was Van Elver. Elver.... He thinks you do fairly well.

(10:10. Jane paused, and I called her name three times. This broke the trance state, and a few minutes later her eyes began to open. By 10:14 she was out of it as John and I talked to her.

(I thought it a good idea that this be the end of the session, however, Seth came through again at 10:30 as the three of us sat talking about various things. A humorous repartee followed, with Seth answering our questions on a variety of subjects. Two serious notes: Alice Butts, who died last week, has already visited my father. And Dr. Instream, who would say "There is no Seth," has not much longer to live. Also— Bill Gallagher will not see certain truths about himself, etc. Alice Butts not helping Ruth Butts' son, etc. See Session 398.)

SESSION 403
MARCH 16, 1968 8:30 PM SATURDAY

(Session for Pat Norelli of Boston. Recorded and typed by Pat.
(Jane was having some difficulty assuming a trance state. She said she was picking up negative and fearful emotions from me. My emotional condition at the was a mixture of embarrassment for I was about to be exposed; guilt that I was imposing on a friend, for I want to give to friends, not take from them; an utter fear that Seth was about to smash my hopes with the truth. It took concentrated effort on Jane's part to break through my emotional barrier and assume a trance state.)

Now, Good evening.

([Rob:]"Good evening, Seth.")

And good evening to our friend. I do have some remarks for you and I hope that they will be helpful. You must remember to hold your head up. You should know better than to cower when you come here. I have no whip; and I would not use one if I had one. You are not sure enough of your own abilities or of your own worth. You cannot drive through physical life in the same way that you drive your car down the highway. You shall indeed, get traffic tickets and of a different kind, only you yourself give yourself tickets. You cannot force reality to give you what you want. You cannot manipulate events for egotistical purposes. You can manipulate events and you can manipulate them for your own egotistical purposes; but when you do so, you give yourself a traffic ticket. You must want what is best for your own development and the development of others rather than specifically determining what you think consciously is better for you and then trying to force or coerce fate to get this for you. If you want what is best for your own development and what is best for the development of others, then you shall attain it. It shall come to you effortlessly. I am leading up to certain issues here. You are not always aware of what is best for you on a conscious level. Often the person that you think you want or need is not the person you want or need on other levels. When you drive your car you often attempt to speed through reality as quickly as you can, and you are pleased with yourself as the driver of the vehicle. You like driving because you feel that it gets you where you want to go and quickly, and you do not mind breaking a few small rules of the road in the process. Now the small rules that you break, are indeed, minute ones. It is not that you break a specific rule; it is the attitude that allows you to break the rule; and this applies to other roads beside the physical highway. You want to get to your destination too quickly. The destination is within you. You do not have to go any place to get that destination; and it is only when you think that that destination lies elsewhere that you allow yourself to go astray. Your identity is within you and do not look for it in others. This is perhaps the strongest point of my message to you this evening, the one I would have you take to heart. When you realize that your own identity is within you will not spend energy seeking to find yourself in others. Others cannot give you a sense of worth; this is your own. Any lack is your own lack. I may perhaps deal with more specific issues this evening. But I will not discuss them until these points have been made.

Now you have indeed been doing well. And I do congratulate you. You are too impatient both with your own development and the development of others. You want your destination now and you want to get to that destination as quickly as possible, 85-95 miles a minute, you see. You have given yourself several traffic tickets. Now, you have learned a good deal, and I know that you have tried. It does no good to understand issues intellectually, however, or even to understand them intuitively unless you understand them so thoroughly that they become a part of your daily life. Much that you know you have made a part of your life, but you still wish to use your knowledge for your own conscious purposes. You are still not willing to say let me develop as I should develop. You are still saying let me develop as I think I should develop. The I being a highly egotistical I. You are still saying, let me develop as I want to develop. You are still saying I want this person or I want that person or that thing. Therefore shall I use this ability and this knowledge to gain it. And that is why you have given yourself a traffic ticket now and then, What you are learning is a technique for self-development. You cannot use it, therefore, to attain those things that do not pertain to your own self-development and the techniques will not help you get something that you were not meant to have nor that you have before decided as an entity that you should not have. I will leave specifics for later. Nevertheless, the facts remain that your own inner self and your own entity have given you challenges that you have accepted. Now you know these challenges; subconsciously you are aware of them. Consciously you do not want to accept them and this is one reason why you have had difficulty with the pendulum. This is not out of the ordinary. This happens to many personalities. It is nothing to blame yourself for. You are certainly in the midst of a certain line of development. You cannot blame yourself for not being further along the line. The very fact that you are here this evening, the very fact that you are trying as hard as you have been shows that you are indeed developing and that you are indeed learning. There must be an open-minded, an openhearted attitude here. You must not try to use what you have learned in a narrow, limiting way. This hampers your own development. It closes your eyes to many possibilities that will be important to you. It is natural, perhaps, to want to use what you have learned, this information, as a technique to achieve what you at any particular time think desirable, a particular person, a particular thing. But what is important is the inner development. If this is taken care of, it will automatically lead you to the person that is best for you and to the circumstances that will help you develop. To insist that a specific individual or a specific goal be attained through these methods is limiting. There must always be the acknowledgement that you do not consciously as yet realize the depths of yourself, the goals you have set and the challenges, and this material should be used to open up your inner horizons and to lead you in those directions toward which your inner self has already set you. If you then egotistically, say—No—this particular situation is what I want, then you may be blocking the inner direction which has been meant for you. I said I would discuss some particular material and so I shall shortly. But the inner attitude is far more important. I suggest, Joseph, that you take a break and I shall continue.

(*Seth's voice was deeper when the session began again.*)

Now, you fear that I am about to leap down your throat and I can assure you I will not do so. Now your feelings toward me before this session have very much to do with other attitudes that are very important to you and very ingrained. Some of these are obvious and have to do with this life only; others have to do with past lives. Now you have been terrified of your father from the time you were an infant. And before the session began, You thought of me as an old, but wise and extremely powerful male adult, as you thought of your father when you were a child.

(*[Pat:]I had been terrified of my father for the first 19 years of my life. Indeed, I never saw my father as a person but rather as a dark shadow with a club. My father had a temper that was aimed at us children and at my mother. [Yet my father is a very loving person. I know that now. We are very close, now. I love my father deeply. He has mellowed in his attitude toward my youngest sister, also.] We got spanked when we misbehaved, which is something I've always been ashamed to admit to others. I didn't want my friends to know my father spanked us. I wanted my family to be a happy one. I was always afraid to bring friends home for fear my mother and father might argue and embarrass me. Also, I didn't think my dad wanted us to bring friends home.*)

(*Yet, my father was very intelligent and had a good job and held many responsible positions in the community. Others looked to him for guidance. I had felt my dad was very intelligent.*)

Now this also overshadows your relationship with the males to whom you have come in contact. For you have been, on the one hand, terrified of them, and on the other hand wanted a normal relationship. Give me a moment here

—on the one hand you desire more from a relationship with a man than you have any right to expect. No human being could ever deliver what you expect a man to deliver in a relationship. This is because you see the male in terms inspired in you when you were a child. You were terrified of the male, your father. On the other hand, you felt that he did contain wisdom, truth, almost godlike qualities. These qualities you attempt to project into the male that you meet. At the same time you are also terrified because of this background. No man can possibly be as godlike as your inner conception. Therefore, each man is bound to disappoint you. At the same time, you hope and pray subconsciously that the man will disappoint you because this male in your mind has godlike qualities that attract you; on the other, you see him as all powerful and as one who gives out punishment and one who is unreasoning and cruel because you felt that your father was cruel. You are afraid, so to speak, to come under a man's thumb for this reason, to come under his domination. For to do so is to place yourself in a humble position and a frightening position underneath the male figure. Your terror as a child gave you an inner idea of reality and family group whereby you saw yourself completely powerless and helpless under the domination of this father figure. He was the source of all and yet he could at the same time take all away. And you felt, at the same time, that he would indeed do so. Because you were a male in past lives, you resented this all the more strongly. Give us a moment.

Now, you have, if you will forgive me, consistently chosen those males within whom you sensed feminine qualities. And this was to protect you. You felt that the feminine qualities within the male forespoke of a gentle nature, that would protect you from the overall male violence of which you were afraid and which you exaggerated, because of early impressions. When you understand this material I have given you this evening, it will help you and you should read it often. Bringing this out in the open will automatically help you to rid yourself of these fears. They will not automatically disappear overnight, but they will begin to diminish. It is your idea to use this toy this evening and not mine, so I am not going to worry about my remarks being recorded for posterity. This is your worry.

You need help and you have asked for it. Therefore, I will give you what information I have. Now, there was an afternoon, I believe when you were nearly three. Your father was home in the afternoon. They were in the bedroom, your mother and your father. You were taking a nap. Your parents were in the act of making love. You awoke. Your mother cried out. This is far from an unusual occurrence; it happens frequently. You interpreted her cry as one of helplessness and frustration and your father had hurt her. You came into the room; your father jumped up and chased you away.

There was some incident when you were four, I believe, with a boy of your own age or approximately your own age. I am not too clear here, but he hurt you, physically, I believe. Now he hit you with a stick or something of that shape. The symbolism here is obvious. There seems to have been a male teacher in your background also.

([Pat:]I had a crush on Mr. Finfrock for three years, grades 7 to 9. All the girls had a crush on him. But the other girls weren't afraid of him. I was. He knew I had a crush on him; he knew that most girls did. He flirted with us. The other girls flirted back. I'd just stand there shy, scared, and in a dream. Sometimes he'd hold our hands; or if we were in the supply room, shut the door so that we'd be alone and then hold my hand and tease me. Now, thinking back on it, he was rather cruel to do that. I never was interested in boys my own age. I just "loved" Mr. Finfrock. And I was too afraid of him to even speak to him.)

You have been afraid that the male would hurt you cruelly—and on purpose, and at the same time, you have endowed him with godlike qualities, and, therefore, demanded more than any man could possibly deliver. I am sure that you realize that when you drive your car, you see yourself in a masculine role, as one of power and strength and one in which you consider yourself invulnerable. Now you are not invulnerable in that car. The reason that you feel invulnerable is that you are subconsciously identifying with this godlike figure and it could lead you into difficulty. Now you have on occasion been cruel to men you have known rather purposely, intending to hurt them before you could be hurt. When you have settled yourself upon a particular man, you see, it becomes a matter of principle with you that you get him. Oh, it does indeed. On the one hand, you want him, on the other hand, as you had to escape from your father, you must also escape from the man and so you are caught in a dilemma. You want him. On the other hand, you must feel that you have independence from him. There was never any communication between you and your father. Therefore, you find it difficult to communicate verbally with a male.

([Pat:] My father and I never spoke in a close communication. I was always afraid to talk to him about anything. I could never open my heart to my father. He wasn't like a person; more like a club.)

You are not able, at this point, you have never been able to look at a man as an individual human being. You have not seen him as he is, for you have endowed him with all these qualities of which I have told you, and with all the fears that go with them. In the overall then, you deny yourself the experience of really knowing an individual male, for you will not see him as he is. The man realizes, of course, that you do not see him as he is, and each one of the men involved has resented it subconsciously. You do not communicate with an individual man; you communicate with your idea of what this man is, this man with the godlike qualities that can bring both joy and punishment.

I suggest you take your break and we shall continue.

Now, you see, you have been robbing yourself of an experience of truly knowing these individual men, for you have not permitted yourself to see them as they are and as they have been. After three lives as a male, you have indeed acclimated yourself very well. You have been somewhat envious. I sense you yelling to yourself when you see a male in strong action or performance, I sense you yelling to yourself—I can do that better than you can for I have done it before—again this is reflected in the way you drive your car.

(I am very, very impatient with clumsy people who can't open jars or push cars or hammer nails. I always end up opening jars, etc... And, of course, there is no doubt in my mind that I can do it. And I do do it. In fact, I can't let others carry heavy suitcases, etc., because I feel that it is too heavy for them—but not for me. I used to get impatient with Freddy, my roommate, because she was lousy at pushing cars. I'd always have to push our cars out of the snow.)

Again this is reflected in the way you drive your car. Now, the difficulties arising from your relationship with your father also gave you other beneficial effects. This feeling is somewhat responsible for your success as a teacher, for example. For you are then in authority, and you would, if you could, drive your students as you drive your car and force them to go 85 miles a minute. You are easier on them than you are on yourself, however, and you make an excellent teacher. In the back of your mind, however, you are always saying—see Daddy, I am doing something well—for this father of yours in your mind is always behind your shoulder watching you and judging you; now this is your attitude that I am describing. You feel that you must be successful or he will punish you, that you must be perfect; therefore you become panic stricken at any sense of failure within you, and you overexaggerate your failings so that you came here tonight to me as if you were two and a half years old. You would not have been at all surprised had Ruburt *(Jane)* jumped up grabbed a ruler and banged your fingers. Now, a step further, therefore, is that you expect rejection on the part of the male for this reason. Now this only applies to men who are older than you. You are perfectly happy and content with younger males. Give me a moment here.

Now I will tell you the material that I have given you will help you and you should listen to it often. It should make one thing clear. Your Mr. Reed is not Mr. Reed's Mr. Reed. You are not seeing the man as he is. You are seeing the image that you have projected upon him, and no one can live up to that image.

I realize that when you discuss him that you say—I know he has failings. This is to assure yourself that, after all, the male is not so all powerful. But you do not see this man's good points or failings clearly. Some of the qualities that you imagine in him as virtues are not and some of the qualities that you imagine to be failings are not failings. You will never have any relationship with the Dick Reed that you have projected upon a living human being. You may have a relationship with that human being, but there is a world of difference between that human being and the imagined image of him to which you react. And it is that image that you see when you look at him and when think of him. That imagined image is real in your mind, it is reality. But you cannot project that image upon another human being and deny him his own reality. You have no chance in a thousand lives of having a relationship with the man you think of as being Dick Reed, because you cannot have a two-way relationship with an image that is one-sided and has no flesh. Now give us a moment. While we are beginning a job, we may as well do a good one.

We have only dealt with one side of this relationship. Now this Mr. Reed has his own part to play. And his purposes and your purposes to this point have fit together beautifully, for neither of you have seen the other. He has seen his image of you. For his own reasons, he has not allowed himself to know an individual woman. And he does not want to know an individual woman physically—he does not want to. Give us a moment.

One point, you see, this artificial image that you have projected upon others has prevented you from knowing them, and in itself has prevented any legitimate relationship which might otherwise have occurred. As long as you allow this image to cover your eyes, you do not see the individual man and do not react to him for the image is between the two of you. Now you have frightened our young man. On the one hand he resents the image that you have placed upon him, and on the other hand it serves his vanity to accept it. He would much rather have you think of him as this image. He is hiding himself and you have very nicely given him an image to hide behind. You speak to each other in symbols and writing and poetry. You are using the symbols to escape normal human give and take. They are not symbols to aid in communication; they are symbols behind which you hide from communicating.

Let our friend Ruburt and that one *(Rob)* take a brief break. I do not need a break.

([Rob:]"All right.")

And I am not beating you. You have used the whip upon yourself, however, for many years.

([Rob to Jane:] "Want your glasses? ... Suppose you lean forward and take

them. Open your eyes. There..."

([Jane:] "Now see, he's coming through much stronger than he used to, and it takes me longer to learn how to manage the transition. And I can't remember hardly anything at all that he said this time, except that he was trying very hard to make his point clear. What did he say about Dick Reed, that's what I want to know. I remember that. I knew that he was telling Pat something but I couldn't eavesdrop."

([Rob:] "I thought what he said about Dick was very perceptive."

([Jane:] "Okay. What did he say about Dick?"

([Rob:] "What did he say about him?"

([Pat:] "I guess that we are using one another. I suppose... that neither one of us sees the other person for what we are. He hides behind the God image that I project upon him ... he's trying to hide, and, of course, that's a perfect image to hide behind."

([Rob:] "Well, don't forget that no human being is going to see another completely, anyhow."

([Pat:] "He said that all the poems were used to avoid communication, which is something I sensed, anyhow, which is something that I kept trying to get around. In an effort to communicate, I was blocking communication. I've never seen Seth in such a good mood. Every time I've seen him, he's always been bawling someone out."

([Rob:] "Well, most of the sessions were like this."

([Jane:] "Some of them are hilarious."

([Rob:] "I think it would be a good idea if you ask questions, also. When certain points are being discussed, ask questions as in a regular conversation. It won't disturb Seth."

([Jane:] "Was that all he said about Dick?"

([Pat:]"He said he didn't want physical relationships with a female."

([Rob:] "That's a statement that will need explanation later."

([Pat:] "That I would like more information on, not so much for me, but for Dick, if I ever have the courage to let Dick hear this."

([Rob:] "Well, it will help you and Dick, both."

([Pat:] "That's right. I'd like him to hear the tape. It might be embarrassing but it could help."

([Rob:] "I don't know whether to tell you to let him hear the tape or not. That's outside our ability to know."

([Pat:] "Right. It might make him worse. A person hearing this information might react in a way to avoid having to accept it."

([Rob:] "Well, a lot of it depends on background knowledge. I don't know what he thinks of Seth. That's why I don't know whether it would be good for him to listen to it or not."

([Pat:] "But he shouldn't take it as something personal. I know I can listen to this, what Seth says about me, and I can take it, and I can take what he says about Dick, too. I think he could accept it too."

([Rob:] "But he needs to understand the nature of Seth and study the concepts involved , or he will reject anything unpleasant."

([Pat:] "I think Dick is interested in the subject. He wanted to have a Seth session."

([Rob:] "Now if either one of you had mentioned that, it would have been a big help at the time." During an earlier visit.

([Pat:] "But I hate to ask for a Seth session. What right have I got to ask for a Seth session."

([Jane:] "But it probably would have helped you both. It would have helped you both now."

([Rob:] "It would have prepared Dick to accept this session."

([Pat:] "Well, he read your book and he's read the articles on Bishop Pike and his son. I know he doesn't reject the ideas."

([Rob:] "Yes, but when it gets personal, anyone would put up protective devices. It's only natural to do so."

([Pat:] "Yes, I know. And around school he plays the 'cool guy' role, the 'love them and leave them' image. Not in what he says but in his appearance. This is the image that others project on him and he allows the image to stay. The students accept this as being Dick. Most of the other women or men like to destroy the image or try to prove it wrong, but they do that out of resentment; they see Dick as a threat. Now showing that image and suddenly having Seth come along and say he doesn't want physical relations with a female; this could be hard to accept. And yet out of all the people, we would be able to accept this and not see anything wrong."

([Rob:] "Yes, a session that is personal is hitting them broadside.")

Now, you overreact in a relationship with a male. You are overanxious. You are afraid of making a wrong step. You watch gestures. You constantly explore a face for a sign that you have made an error. You constantly explore an expression for a sign that you are being rejected and this is directly related to your early relationship with your father. For then a slip met with instant retaliation. There is an emotional charge connected, therefore, with any rejection. And as you tried as a child to think ahead of your father to see what he might be angry at, so you do the same thing now in a relationship with a male to whom you are attracted. I will incidentally give you time later to ask questions. I do not promise to answer them, but I promise you the opportunity to ask them. Now, a moment...

This attitude of yours places the other individual under very strong psychic pressure. You inflict them with this strong anxiety of yours. They are afraid of saying anything wrong because subconsciously they know that you will exaggerate the slightest movement of the smallest muscle. They become very cautious . Now the information that I have given you this evening should help you to begin to see through this image that until now you have projected upon the males. The information will give you several peepholes through which you may squint and see the individual on the other side of this false image. You can make further inroads through that image. The fact that you have reacted in this manner thus far does not mean that you must continue to do so. In other words you are not fated, you see, to always chase this false image or project it outward. It is not eternal, you have formed it. It has not formed you...

This desire to please your father, to attain perfection has also led you to seek knowledge. It has also given you the drive to develop. It has given you an innate, an intuitive feel toward inner reality. Now do not cry or sniffle. I am not your father giving you an arithmetic lesson. We do not have the time tonight to go into your father's background which is highly interesting from several viewpoints and has something to do with his attitude toward his daughters. We do not have time to go into too much background on your Dick literature.

(At this point, Rob smiled but Pat didn't.)

(Then Seth turned to Rob and said:) Now I have put myself out, Joseph and I've joked and for this I get a tear.

([Rob:] "I'm sure it will pass.")

She has spoken about me in this metropolitan city of hers and when she meets me she is in tears. I do not usually have that effect upon people. Now I am ready to ask you if you have any questions.

([Pat:] "Will Dick publish his poetry and can you give us more information about him?")

Now. <u>Will</u> he publish his poetry or <u>can</u> he?

([Pat:] "<u>Can</u> he.")

Give us a moment. Now, he is afraid of physical contact because he fears plunging wholeheartedly into physical existence and this is his way of holding off. He does not want to accept the ordinary responsibilities of adulthood and has not left his father's home.

... He is afraid of any contacts that would ... It seems here that there is a certain thing that he fears will happen to him if he involves himself in any relationship that would result in a family group. There is something here particularly with him... an intense loyalty from a past life having to do with his parents. There was a situation involving the three of them and he abandoned them in a way that he interpreted as a betrayal. The relationship between them then was different than it is now. He will not leave them now for he feels that he aban-

doned them in the past. In this past of which I speak there was a physical difficulty suffered after he abandoned them; and if he leaves them now, he is afraid
that this physical difficulty will return. The main problem in his case stems from
this particular immediate past life. We are trying to focus in on this.

(*Long pause.*) He was a woman. His present mother and father were both
brothers...the American Revolutionary period, the same geographical area as
now. His brothers were involved, it would seem, as spies. Your Mr. Reed as their
sister told where they were and broke under pressure and fear. Concord... a cel-
lar beneath an old inn... stone walls, floor partially dirt. Your Mr. Reed, then the
sister, was hiding with the brothers here. She went outside for provisions. She
was captured and gave the hiding place and could not then return to warn her
brothers. She felt then that she had abandoned them and betrayed them. There
was something done then to her right leg. A relative was responsible for an
injury inflicted on her right leg connected with a horse.

([Rob:] *"May we have a break, Seth." Tape was running out.*)
You may indeed.

([Jane:] *"Remember when she asked Seth that last question?"*)
([Pat:] *"Will Dick publish his poetry? Then I changed it to CAN."*)
([Jane:] *"Yes, but there was something else."*)
([Pat:] *"Can you give us more information on him?"*)
([Jane:] *"That's it. He took off on that because it was of interest. Suddenly we
were off on something that was hard to get to."*
([Pat:] *"I changed it from WILL to CAN because the situation might be
WILL HE, NO: CAN HE, YES. And I wanted to know if there was at least a pos-
sibility."*
([Jane:] *"Well, of course, there is always the possibility."*)
([Pat:] *"No. I mean is it good enough? I think it is."*)
([Jane:] *"Who's he trying to get to publish it?"*)
([Pat:] *"Nobody. He can't even get it typed. A few friends have tried to type it
but something always happens. I'd type it except I know he wouldn't want me to, not
me. He can't be bothered to type it himself."*
([Jane:] *"Now, as a poet, to me that is incomprehensible."*)
([Pat:] *"Yes, I know. If he hasn't got enough psychic energy to type the poems
he hasn't got enough to get them published either."*
([Jane:] *"It's a weak point in him and, therefore, I would say no."*)
([Pat:] *"Yes, he's got to have the drive on his own. This is fascinating for me."*)
([Rob:] *"It gives you an idea how things can operate on a subconscious level.
He feels beholden to his parents. His psychic energy has chosen this way, possibly, of
establishing karma. It's not an idea of punishment, it's an idea of further spiritual*

development. In this life he has chosen to be a son to these people, in a way to be of service to them, to help others."

([Pat:] "Then he is fulfilling his blueprint by doing this."

([Rob:] "So you see, that puts a far different light on a person's behavior than just to say he's afraid to get married or he's afraid of women." Seth entered here.)

Now, ordinary adult responsibilities, you see, would take him away from these two individuals and so he has taken steps to see that he is not involved . Give us a moment. He is more bound to one of these persons than the other for one was a younger brother. He was extremely religious in his past life and the love of music connected with the church is reflected here. His name was strange, I am not too clear on this. The family name in the past: Achman. *(Pat learned that Dick's family has an Ackerman branch in June 1968.)* The first portion like oxtagon.

He did voluntarily choose to be born as a son in this existence. Now he rationalizes on a conscious level his reasons for remaining home. You said earlier that around the school there was the expression he "loves them and leaves them". You see, a very cruel interpretation and a very literal interpretation of his action in a past life, this coming through in an entirely different situation in this life. He is, of course, aware subconsciously of this and acts in such a way for he feels more honest. Through his actions in this life he is trying to make an honest statement about actions in the past. There is, of course, no punishment involved. His secrecy also is a direct result of these past existences, for once he spoke too much and betrayed too much, so now he remains secretive about matters that he considers important. The two brothers never did hold him responsible, however. They understood the situation. They knew that the girl had been terrified and spoke only out of fear and did not mean to betray them. In this life, then, the parents do not mean to hold him. They are not subconsciously trying to chain him; they are not subconsciously trying to bind him. He has chosen to act in this particular manner. He would be much freer if he'd realize that the brothers do not hold him responsible. And the betrayal, while a betrayal, was understandable, and that he spoke out of fear and did not intend to betray. If you will forgive me, I do not think we should use time in the session with your question about your friend's poetry. It is not important in comparison to other information, nor is it important to the man's development, nor to your own. Now I know that you speak of me highly; and if I wore a hat, I would tip it to you. You are helping other people and you will continue to do so. Now that you have some insight into the reasons for certain difficulties, you can begin to do something about them. Your problem is not with your Mr. Reed. Your problem is to rid yourself of the image that you have that you project upon him.

You will not see him thoroughly until you do so; and in carrying this image with you, you see, you do not see the possibilities in many individuals whom you have already met. For you could not see through this image. When you read or listen to tonight's session, you will see that I have given you some insight into your own overreactions. Now these cause the variation in your moods. You may ask me questions.

([Pat:] "Can a worthwhile relationship develop between Dick and me?")

I will not say to you yes or no. No worthwhile relationship can develop while you project this image on him. Nor have you given me your definition of a worthwhile relationship.

([Pat:] "One that would be beneficial to the two of us and in developing those abilities that we should develop.")

Both of you to this point have inner problems that prevent you from entering into marriage. There is a difference between a wholesome love for another person and a compulsive need to have that person. You are still asking these questions with the other image before you. You are trying to peek through, but when you asked the question, you had the image before you. Do you see why? *(Pat nods yes.)* The very fact that you see this shows that you have learned something this evening. And that does me good, for I would not like to speak so long and so hard without feeling that I had managed to get some small point across. Now I will tell you, Joseph, go out into the air and buy your earthly refreshments and return and perhaps I shall join you for a few social moments.

([Rob:] "Have you ever drank beer?")

I have never. Wine, indeed, and of a particular concoction made of barley.

([Rob:] "How about cigars?")

Frank Watts liked his cigars. Now you should be able to see. And you can tell Ruburt how directly you have seen that the difference in his attitude affects our sessions.

[Rob:] "He worries a little bit because he doesn't remember what he says, though."

He worried when he remembered; now shall he worry because he forgets? I am pleased here. *(Meaning Pat.*

([Pat:] "Do I have any ESP abilities to develop?")

This question comes from a young woman who has already read how many books of my material? You know well, you should know, and now I do indeed take you to task. These are not supernatural abilities. They are abilities within the human personality and I presume you fall into that category.

([Rob:] "Good night, Seth.")

([Pat:] "I would avoid situations to meet people. I would always say, "I can't" when someone wanted to go somewhere or when someone invited me over. I can't remember why I never could. I'd just say, "I can't".)

Now, Ruburt wants me to help him with voice control. You are so used to the image that you have projected outward that you are uncomfortable when you try to face a situation nakedly without the image. You project the image on one specific individual so strongly. You also project it in any of your relationships, as a rule, with men who are older than yourself. You do not want to or had not wanted to face even a transient relationship with a man because you did not then have time, you see, to project this image in any dependable manner. There was also a gap when you would have to face the individual as he was. This made you uncomfortable and defiant because it forced you, however briefly, to meet another individual eye to eye. It goes without saying that you could not see whatever good qualities there were in any man you knew casually. You did not have time to project the image upon him, and you were afraid to see clearly without it. Practice in such relationships would allow you to get used to an environment without this image. If not giant steps, baby steps, each such encounter being a small exercise in seeing another male individual without your image glasses on.

([Pat:] "I had thought of that before. I knew that I should have taken advantage of the opportunities to meet people. I knew that I was probably attracting these opportunities to me because subconsciously I knew the exercises would be healthful.")

The exercise is an exercise in understanding and perceiving the reality of other people without misrepresenting them because of your own inner distortions. The exercise is in understanding others.

When I spoke of exercises, I meant exercises; but the purpose of the exercise is to enable you to understand others. This is not an exercise for you specifically, for you to use specifically for your own reasons; it must also wholeheartedly involve other people. You are not to use them as exercises; you are to exercise your own abilities so that you can perceive them clearly; for you do not understand their reality unless you do so.

You must never become so involved within yourself that you ignore the feelings and reality of other human beings, and you must never look at them with the attitude that you are using them for your own development and purposes. And now I am indeed lighting into you, and I am not misinterpreting your inner attitude there.

SESSION 404
APRIL 8, 1968 9 PM MONDAY

(A long session was held by Jane for her ESP class on Tuesday, April 2, 1968. No regularly scheduled session was held the next day.

(Once again Jane began speaking while in a deep trance, eyes open often, animated, good pace, average voice.)

Good evening .

("Good evening, Seth.")

Now Joseph. A few remarks. These may sound simple to you. Ruburt has learned, the hard way, that the physical image is a direct materialization of the inner state of mind.

He knows this now through direct personal experience. If he had believed me in the beginning, and followed the precepts in the material, he would not have had such an experience.

Now. I recommended Maltz because his exercises are based on truths, even though he does not fully understand what lies beneath. Do you want me to tell you how to better your financial circumstances, or do you want to learn the hard way?

("No. Tell me." See Psycho-Cybernetics, *by Maxwell Maltz.)*

You have been told but you have not taken the information seriously because you were not ready, as earlier Ruburt was not ready to. First of all, all negative attitudes must be removed from your consciousness. You are attracting further financial problems in your desperation. You are focusing upon poverty rather than wealth.

It may seem to you highly impractical, unrealistic and downright foolish to ignore the physical circumstances of debts and expenses. To focus upon them, I tell you, is to bring more upon yourself. The rule of expectation applies.

When you receive a bill do not automatically react as you have, instead as if you were contemplating a new painting. Form in your mind the image of a check to that amount. See yourself celebrating as you pay the final amount on your car. See in your mind's eye a surplus of money in your folder when the month's expenses are paid.

Now your financial situation will not change no matter how you push yourself, unless you apply such simple exercises. You do not do this naturally, which is why they are required. You must indeed think consciously in terms of plenty rather than of want. On several occasions Ruburt has followed these and your wants have been fulfilled.

You have been fighting him in this regard, and this has impeded the efforts he has lately been making. Now these exercises will prove themselves out in practical terms, but you must give them the opportunity to prove themselves.

Your subjective life has been somewhat permeated by thoughts of want, and literally poverty, until you have indeed exaggerated your own situation. The exaggerated situation could come to pass however if you persist in projecting those images outward.

They would not help you get a raise but act to the contrary, and they have done so in the past. I am giving you advice in very practical terms. What you do with it is up to you. But you have severely limited yourself in this respect.

In the past Ruburt helped you generate such negative ideas, but he has been making an attempt to combat them. His own experience has proven to him that I was right in other regards. As long as you believe that others are taking advantage of you, they will do so. The origin is in yourself, and this is what you have not so far understood.

(*"I think I have been aware of that."*)

The origin is not in others. For fifteen minutes a day agree to suspend critical judgment, and following the Maltz method imagine yourself vividly in the position you would like to be. The rest of the time consciously make an effort to control your attitude when you find yourself thinking in terms of want or poverty. Then switch your thoughts to ideas of plenty. This need not involve hypocrisy, indeed must not. You must feel that this is legitimate and practical, because the thoughts of plenty will automatically begin to attract plenty. This is sufficient. There should not be an <u>overemphasis</u> (underlined) on material possessions or security however.

Now this program if faithfully followed will bring results. It will initiate intuitive concepts, ideas in your work which will automatically attract others to possess them. It will initiate other actions that will result in financial betterment.

Do you have any questions pertaining to this particular material?

(*"I have a lot of them. It's hard to ask them all at once on short notice though."*)

Part of your attitude is a result of your family situation and of identification with the past.

(*"I know it. And I'm tired of it, too."*)

Still the old feeling, always an excuse, that poverty is pure and more virtuous. Now. An overemphasis on financial matters is indeed detrimental, but if you are worrying about money you are as overly concerned with it as any miser.

(*"I'd like to forget all about it."*)

If you could then this would also be much more effective than your present course.

(*"I keep telling myself to forget it."*)

Now I am telling you to forget it. I have told you that you will never be in severe financial difficulties again, but you do not trust my word enough, so far. You must instead insist upon watching every dollar in the bank, and fearing that it will dwindle away. And then of course it does, and you think that the physical circumstances certainly justify your attitude. But your attitude caused the circumstances.

("My attitude alone?" This I could not believe.)

Your attitude in the main of late.

("How about the dwindling attendance at the ESP classes?")

Ruburt maintained this fairly well. Your own worries have been causing some difficulties here.

("Why can't his positive attitude override my poor one then?")

On occasion it does indeed. Or he would not have any students left. I mean that literally, since in the beginning particularly you did not believe that any would last for any period of time. He does indeed have the ability to attract money, though in the past he was not able to use this ability. He is only now learning to do so, and free enough to do so. Your combined abilities will serve you well here, i̲f you follow my advice.

("I'm not absolving myself, or trying to, but I find it hard to believe that I am the only one involved here.")

I did not say that you were, but only that Ruburt has been making an attempt in the proper direction, and you have not been able so far to make the same attempt.

("For some time I've felt alone in this deal.")

You felt alone because you felt you were worrying alone. Ruburt has for at least two years been actively concerned, very actively. He has attempted however to give the impression of not worrying, and to constructively think in terms of plenty.

Whenever you mentioned a particular bill even in passing, he has immediately imagined it paid and given himself directions so that the needed funds would be obtained. When your rent was first raised within two weeks he had four new students using this method.

("Does he still have them?")

He has two of them.

("Why does he have less students than ever, then?")

Because he does not have less than ever. He has less than he did at the time.

("That's what I mean, I guess.")

This was because of the interaction with your own attitude. Give us a moment. You think in terms of wealth and sensuousness. Wealth as opposed to art or aesthetics. Your father disliked his brother who was wealthy. To have money is therefore a betrayal of your father.

Since your mother pushed your father to make money, then to make money yourself seems an added betrayal toward your father, and seems to ally you with your mother, of whose emotionalism you were always frightened. To you wealth is in some strange way connected with the feeling you have had toward using oil as a medium.

("I'm getting over that." And am grimly determined, too.)

It was not safe, too rich and smothering, like gravy that you also dislike.

("I've become quite mad at my parents in the last year or two.")

Now these connections should help you. The inner resistance to these ideas I am presenting should to some extent vanish as you reread the session. Your own abilities as a creator are extremely strong, your powers of imagery brilliant. Now in the financial realm you have been using them against yourself.

I would have come out more strongly in this regard in the past but Ruburt would not permit it. Now he does. Your combined abilities can directly change your material status. Do you have a question?

("I used to find it quite irritating when Jane passed it off when I mentioned bills.")

He is, as you know, more than usually or normally attentive and sensitive to your remarks. He has always been much more concerned about financial affairs than you realize. There has been what you may call a natural misunderstanding here. But I tell you that in each of these cases he was attempting to offset your negative attitude, and to use his abilities in the way he intuitively realized he could, to help matters.

On his part in the past years this was subconscious. He did not realize consciously what he was doing, but was strongly impelled to take the stand that he did, and outraged subconsciously that you did not understand why he took it.

("Probably because I didn't see any concrete results.")

You did not look for them, and you denied and of course did not see them.

("I mean things like additional money.")

I know exactly what you mean. You negated them.

("Why didn't he negate my attitude?")

Because at the time, in those days, particularly consciously, he would not permit himself to. He was not sure enough. He was working on hunches, to him, and he always followed whatever suggestions you made. He had his own background also, and he was afraid of being successful. These feelings allowed him to follow along with you.

("*That's why I'm harping on this point that I'm not alone in this deal.*")

I am trying to get you out of this deal.

("*I'm willing.*")

The fact remains that you have in the recent past not attempted to project thoughts of plenty, and Ruburt has.

("*I am fully aware of that.*")

Your combined efforts can change your situation.

("*Yes, I believe they can. I haven't felt that we've been using any combined efforts particularly.*")

My dear friend—

("*Yes?*")

—you are defensive, because you realize too well now the effect of your negative thoughts in this direction. The extent of your reaction should tell you this.

("*Yes, I agree.*")

If you have further questions I will answer them.

("*Let's take a break.*"

(*10:00. I was surprised that an hour had passed. Jane had been in a deep trance again, and now sat quite still, eyes closed. I tried to get her out of it. At 10:05 I called her name three times; finally she began to come out of it slowly, I do not believe she succeeded too well, however, for a remark of mine ended break at 10:13.*)

You do not need to banish the thought of money for you have not been concerned with money, but with the lack of money. You have thought of your dwindling bank account, and I tell you that this is why your bank account is dwindling. The material is not distorted. If you must think of your bank account—

("*I'd rather not.*")

—then make all efforts to imagine in your mind those figures you wish were there.

("*I don't have any.*")

Settle on a reasonable amount (underlined). See them in your mind as your balance, and following Maltz you will then feel those emotions suitably connected with the desired amount. This is what you have not accepted.

("*I'd rather think about painting pictures, I guess.*")

Whenever you find yourself thinking of your bank account follow the exercise I have just given you. I am not suggesting that you take the time out. I am suggesting that you devote the same amount of time constructively that you are now spending destructively, and that the new exercises take the place of the old automatically followed negative exercises that you have indeed been faithfully following.

Simply this. Whenever you catch yourself in the old worries, remind yourself of this session, and immediately substitute one of the minute and simple exercises I have provided. You do not have to kneel down before a money god two hours a day.

For all of your objections Ruburt has studiously taken 15 or 20 minutes a day in what he rightly believes to be practical exercises to better your financial condition. He has had enough success spasmodically to know that the exercises work.

When you have done the same, speak to me again on the same matters. I have not been placing any blame on anyone. I thought I was explaining the simple mechanics involved. In other words you protest too loudly.

("I never used to say anything. I thought speaking up was a step in the right direction.")

It is indeed. I will also answer you now, which is a step in the right direction. Joseph, it is simple. You <u>do</u> have control over your thoughts if you will but exert it.

("I agree with that.")

Thoughts of plenty will bring you plenty in material and financial terms, and in other terms. Thoughts of want will produce want. I have not made these rules. When you think in terms of want, and then see physical materializations of want, you are tempted to think that your fears were justified, and therefore those thoughts are reinforced. But the thoughts caused the want, and I am simply trying to help you stop that cycle. Now, if you and Ruburt could agree on the sort of home you would like, and if you dreamed of it and thought about it specifically, you would have it.

Again, this does not involve anything extra. Instead if you find yourself thinking consciously about the limitations of your apartment, you would then substitute an image of this home, you would automatically be bettering your condition rather than maintaining it.

Now I speak, as you well know, for your own benefit. If you have questions ask them.

("No, I guess I just felt I was alone in the deal.")

You were not indeed, far from it. From the time you purchased your car Ruburt has daily done exercises to lead toward its payment. Whenever your rent has been raised he has done the same, and any outstanding bill for the last six months has met the same treatment. Before this he made subconscious efforts that he felt you did not understand.

(*"He didn't say anything about it."*)

He felt that to open the subject was disastrous to him, for he could not explain, and he did not know consciously how to explain. This is one of the reasons why I chose this subject this evening. Do you have questions?

(*"No, I guess not."*)

Your own visual abilities are often used subconsciously. They are stronger than Ruburt's. He must work for his. Therefore your subconscious negative imagery has on many occasions superseded. You must realize if you can that no blame is intended here. You would be even better off if you could forget the whole issue.

(*"I'd like to. I try."*)

Since you are however so strongly concerned with it these exercises will be of great benefit. I will give you a practical example here. Now Ruburt in his exercises has been imagining vividly his dream book sold, selling. While you have been imagining the dwindling accounts and pessimistically thinking that after all the book may not sell, and to be practical you cannot be sure that the outline will sell and your efforts therefore have been knocking each other out.

Your thoughts are the reality. Do you have questions? You may indeed speak up.

(*"No, I guess not. I can't think of anything."*)

You may pile them up for me at your next session.

(*"Is trying to forget about the whole bit the best course?"*)

The point is to let, permit, allow yourself to forget, not force.

(*"That is what I mean."*)

You must allow yourself to think naturally, and thoughts of plenty will follow. You should not ideally have to do any exercises. They are to counter the negative exercises that you are doing.

(*"I know it."*)

What you should do, you see, is simply trust, for this is the most practical point of all.

(*"Yes."*)

I will end the session unless you have further comments.

(*"No."*)

I cannot stress too strongly however the main points I have made tonight. Give me a moment.

Now, from your own experience, when Ruburt and you are in a condition of positive love, you see, do you sense the inner feeling of abundance?

(*"Yes."*)

This is to some extent of the same nature. That feeling of abundance and trust will in itself bring you plenty and abundance. It will attract intuitive ideas on your part, and intuitive actions on the part of others. Indeed Ruburt read an article this afternoon on brain waves, but I tell you that you send out messages of abundance or want.

Now do not short change yourself. This trust is the basis of your existence. You have much that others more financially secure would envy, and do envy. You have projected those thoughts directing to yourself that which means most to you. Do not ignore what you have. The point is that in this one area you have felt insecure for various reasons, afraid to possess money.

Understanding will help you. The exercises I have given you in themselves will begin to negate the causes behind this failure. Do you see?

("Yes.")

We will then end the session.

("Did you hear me earlier, when I said I'd been mad at my parents for some time now?")

I did indeed; and anger will not help you, nor resentment.

("I don't think I could have really escaped some of that, though.")

You could not have. The point is, if you see yourself as financially independent and of abundant means, this will come to pass and regardless of your parents. They will be well cared for. Burdens will drop from your shoulders when you begin to see yourself unburdened.

("Okay.")

Now I have tried to help you this evening, and I hope that I have done so.

(10:50. Long pause, eyes closed.

("Good night, Seth."

(Jane had been speaking vigorously, rubbing her face and hair often in trance, opening and closing her eyes. Her eyes closed for some time at the end of the session. Finally she began to come out of it; again the trance had been a deep one. She remembered none of the last delivery.)

SESSION 405
APRIL 18, 1968 9 PM THURSDAY

(Recently Jane sent her dream book to Prentice-Hall. An editor rejected the book but wrote a very encouraging letter concerning the publication of the Seth material. Since we were somewhat confused as to what course to follow, a session was held this evening.)

(Jane began speaking in a good trance at a somewhat slower pace than usual, and her eyes did not open as much as usual.)

Good evening.

("Good evening, Seth.")

Now, there are several points here.

Ruburt is not fully familiarized with the material. He must be indeed fully committed to the experimentation and work in which we are all involved. He should be clear in his mind as to what I have said about myself, and what I have not said.

The very point of my material is precisely that it goes beyond ideas conventionally held in most, quote, "mediumistic circles." It is a continuing experiment in that the material will become clearer as his abilities in the sessions grow.

He is not, therefore, <u>supposed</u> to think of me, and I have said this often, as some sort of ghostly spirit in those terms. There is no conflict between what I am and what he thinks I am. Any conflict has been a result of his own misinterpretations.

He has the idea at times that he should accept me in conventional terms, from the books that he has <u>read</u>. The interpretation is his own, colored by subconscious prejudice, and largely a matter of vocabulary. This has resulted at times in a lack of conviction.

I am what I have always said that I was, and I said it in as emotionally neutral terms as possible: —an energy essence personality. It is he who adds any other coloration here, and then reacts to those. I <u>have</u> reincarnated, as the material mentions, and so have you both. I have tried to explain personality gestalts and the connections that exist between us.

Now, the personalities that are reached under ordinary seance quote "conditions", are not personalities such as mine. They are personalities recently dead, in your terms, with strong connections to your environment, and not aware as yet generally of their own larger existence. In other words, this is not what I am.

Put it this way if you prefer, for the simplest analogy: Ruburt operates as an excellent wireless, and brings in messages from beyond those usually received. Now to distort these by coloring them with lesser ideas, ideas incidentally that he did not have when we began our sessions, is unfortunate.

I must answer questions in the terms in which they are asked, or the questioner cannot understand what I say. I explain my material on various levels, therefore, when I am questioned. In our own material usually, I can deal with matters <u>more</u> as I would prefer.

Now. Ruburt's students have helped him, strangely enough, because they helped reinforce his faith in me. He saw that I helped them. I have spoken to them in terms that they could understand. His reaction to their needs resulted in added confidence on his part as he sees them helped.

On the other hand he is too suggestible to other peoples needs, in that your point made earlier is correct; for through the material many more can be helped. The students however, and here you were wrong, will accept certain changes now, for I have already laid the groundwork by telling them of the necessity of studying the material itself.

(Before this evening's session I had said that publication of the Seth material could help many more people than Jane [called Ruburt by Seth] could help person-ally in her ESP classes, and that too much energy expended in the classes took away from that available for the theoretical material available to us in our regular twice-weekly sessions. I had also said that now that her ESP students were quite used to Seth speaking during classes, the absence of this would be resented by them.)

Now often in such circumstances you can help others and not help your-self, use your abilities to help others but not yourself, simply because you erect barriers. Whenever distortions appear in the material it is indeed a tip-off of a given area that is particularly touchy to Ruburt personally, or represents an area in which he is not sure; a lack of conviction.

Now. I prefer you see the vocabulary used in our sessions. He is not Cayce nor Montgomery, nor the woman with the crystal ball. There have been seg-ments, not necessarily distorted, but given in different terms than I would have preferred; for at times I try to accommodate the material in order to get it through.

In the past I did indeed avoid using the word God. It has appeared in our sessions of late because it was the term Ruburt thought should be used, and on occasion because it was the word most comfortable for his students. The word itself hardly approximates the true reality it tries to portray however.

I have avoided it in order to steer clear of a stereotyped image. It was when Ruburt began reading other people's material that the word began to appear. This does not mean that a God did not exist. It means that use of the term auto-matically limits the reality of All That Is by its very connotations.

Because Ruburt is at times so literal, he then did become bothered by thoughts of setting himself up, or thoughts of misrepresentation; and all of this because of the interpretation of the word spirit, or spiritual, and highly colored interpretations at that. Then he felt guilty because he was not living up to other people's interpretation of the word.

His intellect is a fine one, and should have no quarrel at all with our ses-sions. It is only when he uses it falsely as a shield to hide behind that he is both-ered, and an objective reading of the Seth material would show him that there is nothing in it of which he need be emotionally or intellectually ashamed. To the contrary, <u>he does not have to see me as a white-gowned spirit</u>. *(Strong and emphatic.)* I am not physical. But the picture of a white-robed spirit, with <u>those</u> connotations, is not one I have given him.

His work with the material can and should weld his emotions and intellect together in a strong powerful force, but not when he attempts to copy others, or on his own uses words that personally annoy him, to express or interpret the material to others.

Give us a moment. Or if you prefer take a rest.

("I think we'd better rest then.")

(9:40—Jane sat quietly without opening her eyes, then said: "He was saying that I don't have to use other people's paraphernalia." She slowly came out of trance, and briefly seemed about to cry. But this passed. Both of us, correctly it developed, attributed the crying feeling to regret at some of our past efforts that were not as successful as we had hoped they would be, regarding using the material to help others, to get it published, etc.

(Jane resumed in the same active manner, but with pauses, at 10:55.)

Now. He supposed he was being "good" in quotes, when he tried to follow the interpretation of others, and their idea of good. He felt inadequate, he felt two-faced <u>only</u> when he tried to squeeze the material into smaller molds that cannot hold it. This is perhaps one of the most important sentences in this evening's session.

One of the main reasons for this was the old rigid childhood concepts, which were rearoused by his reading, not by our sessions. He began to think of himself in terms of a false priest, you see. This could water down the material considerably.

("Which books are you referring to—recent ones that he's been reading?")

Many, or any of the books, Montgomery comes to mind. Any of the leading psychic books of the day that were, again in quotes, "spiritualistically inclined", for the term itself is misleading. It means something to him *(Jane)*—he will know what I mean. "Many lifetimes..." *(by Kelsey and Grant)* does not apply here.

He was outraged by A A, because he persisted in considering him as a "spirit", in quotes, with all the connotations the word arouses in him. A A is no longer a physical personality, and that is all. He is not a personality fully developed in those larger terms of which I speak. He <u>is</u> a personality however, and he is not Ruburt's.

(A A is a recently deceased personality who has helped us obtain some spectacular results during experiments with table-tipping. See Sessions 374 and 381.)

Personalities are composed of action and of psychic components. This is what you are. It is what I am. There are at all times more various kinds of personalities than there are flower seeds—different varieties. Some mature and develop, some are in ways I have not yet explained, transitory. They merge into other gestalts, but what they are is never destroyed. They operate independently while part of other gestalts.

Give us a moment. *(Her eyes open, Jane picked up the letter from Prentice-Hall briefly.)* This is the direction toward which you should move. *(Now Jane touched the carbon copy of the manuscript of her dream book.)* The energy in this book was not wasted. It was not used as wisely as it could have been. What is preserved of it will be in exact proportion to the amount of perception Ruburt had as to the direction in which it should move.

It is a springboard, and he needed the springboard. Unfortunately the subject was too tender. He could not allow undistorted material about it. Nor would it have been helpful had he known about it in advance. It was his problem and he worked it out in his own way. To solve it for him is never possible. Never in the long run possible.

(I believe that here Seth talks about predictions given some time ago that the dream book would sell; but I didn't interrupt the session to check.)

Had I told him, had I been able to, he would have recreated the problem in other terms, and worked it out in other ways. I did tell him, strongly, to finish the book, because until it was finished he did not even perceive the problem. He had to see the book in its completed form in order to perceive the inner condition.

You know that he worked through problems, then, both physically and creatively. Now I have told you this evening, or I have told him, the direction in which to move. I can do no more. Nor at this point could I do less. The material is his guidepost.

In our sessions and in the Seth material I utilize—I must—the best that he as a personality has to offer, and that is considerable. It includes both intuitional and intellectual faculties. He must be familiar enough, open enough, to be able to accept my ideas in sessions, to be a channel for them. But he must use for a standard the Seth material itself. Do you have questions now?

("I can't think of any."

(Again Jane picked up the letter from Prentice-Hall.) The material in the dream book should be utilized here.

("We'd like to get back to the theoretical material.")

You should indeed, and may at once. I suggest that this summer Ruburt become much more familiar with the Seth material. It is his touchstone.

("What do you think of the book he's been working on?")

I suggest that he let it go. He has not properly used the experiences that he has had. These should go into this book *(the letter indicated again)*. He <u>will</u> <u>do</u> the sort of book he had in mind, but at a later date, and it will be a far better book.

He does not have the material for what he plans, for one thing. For another he planned to use my ideas. He was getting the idea, you see, and those ideas can best be presented this way, now. *(The letter again.)* Other portions of the book he planned could have been written by anyone.

Give us a very brief moment. *(Pause, one of many.)*

Frederick Fell has the book he wanted—the first one, and he will play it to the hilt, for <u>him</u>. *(Pause.)* I am trying to give you some undistorted material here. He thinks, Fell thinks, he is interested in the Seth material. He is playing around with it. He is afraid to take the plunge. He is afraid to say no also.

He is privately enthralled, but business-wise overly cautious. This is why his firm is small. The woman *(editor for F.F.)* has no feeling for the material, as you know, but is interested in Ruburt as a property; and as a property has no idea of how to handle him. She is afraid of me.

Fell wonders if at times he was taken as a fool. He is intuitively aware, but very frightened of his own intuitions. He is also afraid of success.

Now, I cannot tell you whether or not this particular *(letter again)* in quotes "deal" will come through. It is too touchy. *(Smile, eyes open.)* But at least now I can tell you that it is too touchy!

I can tell you, as you personally supposed, that this is the direction in which Ruburt should move. It is a direction now in which he <u>wants</u> to move, but he has been afraid that it was not a financially profitable direction, for he received no encouragement from Fell, no real encouragement, concerning the material; and he <u>did not</u> try elsewhere.

He took it for granted that the material would not be financially acceptable to a publisher, <u>because</u> he sensed this was Fell's opinion. Do you have questions?

("Do you think I was sounding off earlier, when I talked about doing some great work painting?")

I do not. I expect that you shall.

("I feel that I can.")

You spoke earlier of tragedies, and I do not understand you. Great work stands alone. It is a triumph of the human spirit, and it always grows out of experience. As an egotistical creature, alone, you would not choose the experience, even though great work resulted from it. *(Smile, and intent delivery.)*

Learning involves your whole being. Great work is a result of great learning. It is not the result of seeing easy answers scribbled magically upon a blackboard. The flowers thrust themselves up through soil, but they hardly consider the soil or thrusting a tragedy, nor resent the time spent in the frozen earth, for they realize the frozen earth is a condition of their blossoming—a challenge that is an aid, not a hindrance. The light does not resent the darkness which it illuminates, you see? Your inner self is aware of this.

You may end the session, take a break, or ask questions as you prefer.

("I guess we'd better end it then.")

My heartiest wishes then to you both.

("It's been very interesting.")

You may choose the point from which you would like me to begin again, and I will do so; or I will initiate a beginning again—it makes no difference. Shake that Ruburt loose from the influence of others in the, quote, "field."

Take your vacation. *(Pause.)* Give him physical activity then. Stay away from his mother until I tell you. He does not have to prove he is all saintly yet. The time will come. *(Our cat Willy jumped up into Jane's lap.)* Psycho-Cybernetics was good for him, for it stopped at least some of his conscious brooding. He must rediscover however his spontaneous self for these distorted and adopted and <u>superficial</u> ideas—underline superficial—of religious rules inhibited him.

He need not fear his spontaneous self. It will not betray him. The arm symptoms still hanging on represent an inhibiting factor. Telepathy does exist, but existence has a far greater vitality than he supposes. People do have a natural defense. He does not need to watch his thoughts <u>that</u> (underlined) closely.

You <u>are</u> responsible for your thoughts. However your spontaneous thoughts are not nearly as destructive as he imagines, and in <u>over</u>inhibiting them, he also inhibits purely spontaneous, joyful thoughts. Psycho-Cybernetics helps him not to brood, not to worry in advance, and set up negative reactions. This is important. But honest reactions within the present are legitimate.

The present simply should not be negatively projected into the future. This is all-important here. He is afraid of hurting others through his thoughts, but the fear is overly inhibiting him. Do you understand this?

("Yes. I'm a little surprised by it, though.")

By which portions?

("To hear that Jane has such fears about her thoughts.")

He is reacting in an exaggerated manner to a truth—and the truth is that thoughts cause reality. He interprets this negatively *(pause)* because he is so afraid of hurting others. He takes it for granted that natural thought, left alone, will be destructive and hurt others.

But <u>natural</u> thought (underline natural) <u>will be</u> more positive than negative. Does this clear the matter?

("Yes.")

He is afraid of striking out or harming others, and to some extent, still afraid of spontaneity. Therefore the arm conditions still persist.

("Why should he be afraid of hurting others?")

I believe I have mentioned this in past sessions. The overconscientiousness, all connected with conditioning. He understands more now, and tonight's material should help him.

I suggest we end the session.

("Yes. Good night, Seth.")

(10:55. Once again Jane's trance had been a good one. She came out of it all right, if slowly, however. Once again she seemed about to cry, but did not. She did not remember what she had said, but had a feeling of sadness. She said she thought tonight's material would be very helpful.)

SESSION 406
APRIL 22 1968 9:15 PM MONDAY

(Shortly before the session I showed Jane copies I had made of material Seth gave very early in 1964—just after the sessions began; the nine Inner Senses, taking up nine typed pages, and the eleven Basic Laws of the Inner Universe, taking up seven typed pages.

(I did this because in the last session Seth said he would resume his discussion of theoretical material at any point we chose. I thought he could pick from this selection. Jane was tired this evening, and said, "If Seth can get anything out of me tonight he'll be doing good." She had been lethargic today, she said.

(She began speaking in trance as usual however; her start was late because of her lethargy; she "hung around" a bit waiting to see if a session would be held. But once begun the trance was good, eyes opening as usual, pauses as usual.)

Good evening.

("Good evening, Seth.")

A few comments. It is the halt that frightens him.

("The halt?")

(Jane nodded, eyes closed.) For many reasons, most of which you have both discussed. He is somewhat in a state of shock, having been brought up short. He will quickly readjust however, for he now has faith in the new direction of

his work. Now give us a moment.

(Pause.) In terms of value fulfillment you see, Ruburt is trying to assimilate information that has already been gathered, the last several days being far more valuable in terms of inner growth. The psychological changes, you see, are far more reaching than the short duration in time would seem to imply.

(Seth calls Jane "Ruburt" during trances, and also "he," referring then to the sum of Jane's reincarnations. The halt, above, refers to Jane's laying aside the book for Doubleday for the moment, and her decision to begin work on a book on the Seth material itself.)

The inner psychological realization is the important event here, rather than, for example, the letter *(from Prentice-Hall)* itself. The true event is the psychological one. Ruburt's readiness to do the kind of book he will now do was signaled by those episodes having to do with me in the dream book.

The signals were picked up though he did not realize either that he had come to the realization that his work would change, nor that he had signaled so. I add to make him feel better *(smile)*, and you also, that he could not have done —I am going slowly here so as not to offend his sensibilities—he could not have done earlier the kind of book he will do now. His understanding, and even his writing abilities, were simply not up to it.

This aside from the fact that he had not come to terms with me nor the material.

Now as far as our own material is concerned, it has taken short shrift for some time. There are loose ends dangling in many areas. We shall try to add some continuity and consistency, therefore. You have still been given but a sketchy outline, in truth, but we have time to fill it in. For that matter, the outline is scarcely completed.

Give us a moment. *(Pause, eyes closed. Jane's trance was now deeper, her delivery more emphatic and a little stronger.)* We will want to deal overall with the nature of reality as it exists within your camouflage system, as it exists in other systems, and with the overall characteristics that pertain to it, regardless of any given manifestation. That is, certain characteristics belong to reality, regardless of the methods by which it brings itself forth.

These methods themselves will vary. The systems vary, the systems being the manifestation of reality as it shows itself in various forms. The methods by which it manifests itself also vary. Certain characteristics however belong to reality regardless of the very methods and the various manifestations.

Some of these I began to hint at in your basic laws. *(Jane briefly picked up the material mentioned before the start of the session.)* Since you are naturally interested in your own physical system, we will deal thoroughly with the methods by which reality turns itself into camouflage. Also, we will deal with other methods to be used by you, that will allow you to perceive more clearly the basic nature of reality *(pause)*, in quotes "showing through" physical camouflage. *(Smile.)*

Some of this material will automatically answer many questions with which you have been concerned, problems with which your scientists are now dealing. Involved in this also will be the interrelationship that exists between systems of reality, including certain points of contact that <u>connect them all</u>. The last should be underlined. For these various apex points can be mathematically arrived at, and will in some distant future of yours serve as contact points; in some cases taking the place of space travel.

I am trying to give you an idea of the direction in which we will be moving. Questions such as those pertaining to life after death, in your terms, will be covered perhaps in a consecutive number of sessions, in which such matters will be covered in a body of material.

This portion will deal with practical considerations, in your terms, and will be a part of a larger portion concerned with the practical utilization of our material. The practical utilization however must follow an understanding of the material.

A large segment will also be concerned with that portion of reality that has time connotations for you. For you must deal with your idea of time, and manipulate within it while you hold it valid. When you realize it is not valid *(smile)*, then instructions will be useless.

We will maintain some sort of sensible consecutive nature here in the material, though the separation is of course arbitrary. Give us a moment. *(Pause.)* We will also be developing the God concept in terms of my choosing *(amused)*, the pyramid-consciousness gestalts of which I have spoken in the past. This will be given along with and as a part of the basic characteristics of reality, as divorced from camouflage materializations.

In larger terms, the word reality and those characteristics that I will give you as attributed to it, will be seen as part and parcel of a unified psychic consciousness, from which all other consciousness emerges. These emerging consciousnesses form new moment points, create new value fulfillment experiences that constantly allow the overall reality to be created even as it creates.

On a limited scale, very limited, this process is hinted at in the material having to do with moment points, action and personality.

Now you may take your break. Your work is cut out for you, and I am the scissors.

("I don't care. I look forward to it.")

(9:57. Jane's eyes stayed closed while she shook her head from side to side.

Slowly her eyes cracked open. "He's still going on," she said. "The next line was to be:
your current scientific and religious ideas of reality are like children's tales." This
receiving of more data as she comes out of trance is a sign, a recent one, that Jane's
trance was deep.

(Jane's voice had begun to strengthen more, her delivery becoming rather sharp
and rapid. She said she had felt the energy, carrying her along, that has begun to
reveal itself regularly. After break I could tell the trance was deeper and stronger yet.
Resume at 10:10.)

Current ideas of reality <u>are</u> like children's fairy tales. If you keep these
channels open and free, then you will get some material that is as undistorted as
possible. Some distortion is necessary, as you know, simply because <u>all</u> words are
a translation.

Ruburt's range is an excellent one however, for the plane that I have my
main existence within is far beyond those to which those in the physical system
have access. You and he must see to it then *(Jane pointed vigorously at me)* that
he does not color his experiences with me through reading material that 'is highly camouflaged and distorted, even though the distortion is well-meaning.

(In the last session Seth named some books and authors that he preferred Jane
avoid, calling them too "spiritualistic.")

That sort of material has its purposes, and it does do some good, and it
does explain reality in terms that many people can understand, for the props and
fantasies are familiar ones. There is no necessity for them here, however.

Now, specifically this applies to the work of what Ruburt and you would
refer to as spiritualistic. The work of mediums, or books about mediums, that
deal exclusively with conventional religious concepts, and that <u>interpret</u> reality
in those limited terms.

Later, when such material does not affect him, this will make no difference. <u>Some</u> of the Cayce *(Edgar)* material (underline some) is included here. We
will make an effort in the future to give you both some Direct-Experience-in-
Concepts—hyphenated and capitalized.

These experiments will run along with and closely follow the vocalized
expression of the concepts involved. The experiences will give you some small
glimmering of unfortunate but necessary loss of meaning that occurs when any
concept must be communicated in physical ways.

(By now Jane's voice was more powerful, her delivery sure and rapid, her eyes
open often; they were very dark. As she said later, it was along in here that she real-
ly began to experience a great surge of energy, sweeping her along.)

This will be a different kind of in-depth learning, a rather unique and
original development that will be as devoid as possible of stereotyped symbols,

which are usually almost automatically superimposed on strong experiences so that they seem—so that the experiences seem—to be made up of stereotypes. Is that clear?

("Yes.")

Now some further remarks as to a point about which you and Ruburt have both wondered.

I am the Seth that I say I am, but I am also more. The Seth personality that is a part of me is the portion that can most clearly communicate with you. At some future time I will indeed discuss this more thoroughly, and on some occasions in the future you may become more aware of other portions of my reality. *(Very forceful delivery.)* Do you follow me? My reality includes the Seth reality.

("Yes.")

There was no point in my mentioning this before. The Seth portion of me has been intimately connected with you both, and so in that respect have I. *(Pause.)* This is all closely related to the definition of a personality energy essence, from which of course all individuals spring.

(Voice louder.) There is a peculiar corner within Ruburt's personality, also deflected into your own, that allows him a rather clear access into information-al channels most difficult to reach from your system. During this particular session, and at this moment, the contact is particularly good. *(Voice loud and staccato, eyes wide and dark.)*

There is also an access to energy far beyond that which is usually experienced. Ruburt sensed this quite well in the past, and feared to open those channels until he felt himself suitably ready and prepared. There exists, in other words, what could almost be compared to a psychological and psychic warp in dimensions, *(pause)* and that corner in Ruburt's personality is an apex point at which communication and contact can be made.

He feels this very strongly this evening. You had better end the session, and follow the procedure given to end the trance.

("Yes.")

A more powerful connection exists, you see, now; and this means you have reached, as you are well aware, somewhat beyond the personality by which I usually make myself known to you. Even if I continue to speak, end the trance.

("All right.")

(10:33. Jane's eyes were open and dark, and I had visions of her continuing to speak in trance while I competed in trying to bring her out of it. Nothing like this developed. As Seth recently suggested, I spoke her name aloud three times. Her eyes closed and her head began to nod. I repeated the procedure and thought I saw signs

that Jane was leaving trance.

(*As Seth also suggested, I touched her leg at the ankle, since she sat across from me at the coffee table with her feet upon it. This too helped. I continued speaking to her and touched her other ankle. This time Jane jumped, very nearly violently, her eyes closed. In a few moments she said the mere touch caused her reaction. By now she was consciously aware that something definitely unusual had been taking place, and the second touch conflicted here.*

(*Jane said, eyes closed, "I don't know what to do now." Her feeling was related, she now said, to the feeling she'd had all day, the lethargy, in a way she couldn't explain. Yet apprehension wasn't a part of it. She now felt chilly. I got her a glass of water.*

(*Jane said she knew that if I hadn't closed her off she'd still be going; she still felt the energy surging within her. "It's wild." She found herself breathing deeply. She had an odd feeling of elephantiasis in her head, she said: "My ears feel like they're out to here" —and she held up her hands a foot away from her ears. This is an effect both of us have noted occasionally before.*

(*Jane still felt the energy at 10:41. She said she felt that when she stood up she would shoot ahead through the wall—shoot straight ahead—she felt a great energy about her, and wondered about her physical control. Actually she moved about normally when she did get up. Yet her feet felt like lead, to her surprise, and she was surprised at the sheer physical movement.*

(*When the additional energy began to manifest itself after break, Jane said it seemed another channel opened up, a great energy. She felt it being transformed into words through her. It was the best feeling of its kind she'd ever had, "as though this energy was coming from a very distant place, or great depths," yet she was aware of words as she spoke them. This appears to be in conflict with accounts we have read, wherein mediums have no awareness or memory of events in trance. Yet Jane's trance was very obviously an excellent one. Now however, all Jane remembered was that the voice said she was reaching beyond the usual Seth personality.*

(*The energy sweeping her along was so strong, Jane said, that she now wondered how she would have ended the session had not the voice suggested this; but I could reassure her that from observation now I could tell when her trance was very deep, and knew enough now to end it when necessary. Jane said that tonight she was as "un-me" as she had ever been. In retrospect it was a bit frightening—there was a terrific sense of power and energy. She hadn't been as "cozily Seth" as usual; less cozily a personality in our terms; but she also didn't know who or what was responsible, aside from the great energy.*

(*Jane said the feeling involved—so* <u>vast</u>*—doesn't show up very well in the transcript, but never before had she so definitely felt the source or impetus of the ener-*

gy involved as being from someplace else, of its being "not me."

(At 11:07 she still felt the energy, but it was slowly diminishing; although still strong. Jane feels the energy went through her yet left a residue, for she now felt much better than before the session. Again in retrospect, she said the episode was "slightly scary," while agreeing that she had given inner permission for it to take place. She asked me to make these detailed notes for later reference.)

SESSION 407
APRIL 24, 1968 9:10 PM WEDNESDAY

(Much of the material in the last sesssion accounts for Jane's improvement in health. She felt she knew the reasons for the improvement—her new commitment, sense of direction, etc., all parts of her "inside and outside," she said. The energy pouring through her last session seemed to clear out her physical system; she felt a "mysterious muscular release."

(Because Monday's session was so unusual, Jane felt a little hesitant about holding a session tonight. We sat quietly at 9 PM, waiting to see what developed. When Jane did begin speaking in trance, her voice was peculiarly gentle in quality—lighter than the usual stronger and heavier Seth voice by a good bit, almost as though she was proceeding somewhat cautiously. But there were other reasons for this different voice, as we learned later.

(Jane used many pauses, some of them long, in delivery; her eyes opened at times.)

Good evening.

("Good evening, Seth.")

Now. The development in the last session was always latent from our first session.

It was a development that could or could not have occurred. Had it not then many important future developments would have been blocked. The points where this voice was loudest and strong—these points often represented openings through which the development could occur. For various reasons however that method was not used.

(Jane's eyes now opened as she spoke, but she sat quite still and continued in the gentle, almost lilting voice.)

The energy in that case would have been diverted from the voice, in which the energy had already been built up, you see. The remarks made before our session by Ruburt were correct or nearly so.

(When Jane talked about her physical well-being, etc.)

Give us a moment. *(Pause.)*

You must understand that in a good measure much of our material is an attempt to put into words concepts and ideas that are far too vast for any such translation.

The laws of the universe, of the inner universe, for example, are not laws in some book. *(Smile.)* Such laws that might be proclaimed in so many words. They are attempts to explain in words the nature of the inner reality that forms All That Is. I must disentangle concepts, unravel them, in order to explain them, and much is necessarily lost in the process.

I do intend to implement this material whenever possible by helping you both achieve subjective experiences that will fill out the words for you. These will vary according to the circumstances and our conditions, but are much more possible now after the sessions' latest development.

Each simple law of the inner universe that I have given you is in actuality a small and inadequate statement in single-dimensional terms. Yet it is more than most are given, and the best approximation that can be made of the basic facts that are beneath any existence, the best statement that can be made under the circumstances under which we work.

Give us a moment. *(Pause over one minute.)*

As words would tell little, or give small hint of the reality of sound or color to someone who did not experience these, so the words used can only give insight into the nature of reality. I hope through the addition of various subjective experiences in the sessions to give you the feel of concepts when this is possible.

The inner senses to some extent will allow you to perceive the reality of inner existence, and Ruburt incidentally in this new development is involved with the use of these inner senses in a more effective manner than before. There are some changes in the way connections are made. This gives Ruburt a feeling of strangeness as he makes inner adjustments.

He is now soaking up energy, so to speak, within his physical system as a sponge soaks up water. *(Smile.)* He is using the new energy where he feels he needs it most, which is quite legitimate.

He has been reading various sections of the material, including portions having to do with the ego, personality and action, and you see attempted to set himself aside from the action in which his whole personality was intimately involved. As impossible [to do] as the ego's general attempt to insist upon some sort of permanent, unchanging, stable identity, since it is composed of action.

One portion of the personality therefore set itself aside and therefore was unable to use the abilities and energies inherent in the personality as a whole, constructively; and erecting barriers in one respect, the barriers were erected in all important regards.

He is warm physically now; again the energy available during the session is being largely utilized by his psychic and physical system. It was not possible in the past. The barriers to the energy have been let down, the action no longer impeded. The energy is rushing into these areas that have been hungering for it, you see. The system filling itself up, so to speak, and replenishing itself.

The task upon which Ruburt will embark will be performed with zest, for the physical system will be replenished and adequately supplied. There is a change in blood count going on, an imbalance corrected, a decrease in white cells, and a bodybuilding process at work.

Again, this is simply a rushing in of energy where it was most needed, once the barriers have been removed. This is a natural reaction. *(Long pause.)* Whenever the ego gains overcontrol, or sets itself up to oppose deep and basic action within the whole personality, then in doing so it also blocks to some considerable extent the passage or use of the whole personality's vital energy.

The physical system suffers. It is impossible for the ego to block off specific connections with the whole personality, therefore any barriers effectively impede whole blocks of active and necessary vitality. In Ruburt's case now, the floodgates to the inner self are opened, so that the vitality rushes into those areas that have been to some extent denied.

Give us a moment. *(Pause, hand to eyes. Jane's voice still persisted in the light, gentle, almost lilting quality, quite different from the usual deeper Seth voice.)* The Seth personality has been an intermediary, and a legitimate one. *(Pause.)* The information already given to you regarding the nature of personality gestalts should make this development seem indeed a fitting one.

(Pause. This information was given perhaps 200 sessions ago.)

Seth is what I am, and yet I am more than Seth is. Seth is however independent *(smile, eyes open)*, and continues to develop as I continue to develop also. *(Smile.)* In the spacious present you see, we both exist.

Some material he can present to you more clearly than I. This was particularly true up to this present point. *(Pause. I wondered: if Seth isn't speaking now, who is?)* He is closer to you in personality makeup and closer to your reality, therefore he could transmit ideas to Ruburt in more understandable terms than I.

There was a point, you see, of interpretation and translation *(pause)* as Seth interpreted material from me in such a way that Ruburt could then receive it. At our last session, with the greater efficiency and the development on Ruburt's part *(pause)*, the material was more direct, and the translation at his end automatic and smoothly performed.

(Briefly, Jane's voice became a little stronger.) While I was the source of the material, Seth as you think of him was at times a silent partner, helping Ruburt make the proper translations while standing aside in a personal manner. There are various mechanics that still must be worked out, that will develop naturally as the sessions continue. Perhaps a brief readjustment period as various methods are tried. *(I interrupted by coughing.)* You may take a break. Seth will always be an element in the sessions as you know him. He is the connective between us, and he has been a part of me that I have sent out to you. He has gone willingly.

(10:02. Jane stopped speaking, then nodded when I asked if she was all right. Her eyes began to open soon afterward. She had thought the session terribly slow, and thus was surprised at the amount of time passed. She had thought of pauses between individual words while she spoke. She didn't recall any of' the material after the part about soaking up energy.

(Jane wasn't worried while speaking, and didn't force anything. Tonight she felt some of the energy of last Monday, but didn't feel she could do anything with it— she just enjoyed soaking it up.

(She now told me that just before tonight's session she felt a cone effect up over her head. This represented energy; Jane felt that it stopped with her, that she soaked up energy from it and the words then came out. She said she had also felt the cone on Monday; and through the terrific energy it contained the words poured out of her.

(Jane now sat with her eyes closed for over a minute before resuming at 10:26. Once again her voice was on the gentle side—not like the usual strong Seth voice.)

All divisions are to some extent arbitrary. The <u>source</u> of this material (underlined) is the same as it has always been.

I, who am the source *(pause)*, sent a portion of myself, an independent portion, to you. Seth as you then thought of him, was far more than a delivery boy however, for it was his peculiar personality, and his particular qualities, which gave the material life for you.

He transmitted it in personal terms, made it understandable through the transmutation of himself.

(Jane now sat leaning forward, quite close to me, eyes open, speaking very carefully, lightly and deliberately before leaning back after a few sentences.)

You have always been then in contact with me, but you were only able to see a portion of me. *(Pause.)* Keep in mind that <u>all</u> names are arbitrary, and we use them merely for your convenience, as we use words. *(Still speaking carefully.)* Basically, Seth's name or mine isn't important. Individuality is important, and continues in ways you barely suspect. *(Long pause; voice light, not like Seth.)*

In one way, in the most important way, and in the only basic way, I am Seth, dispensing with certain *(pause)* characteristics which are mine *(leaning forward)* which I used to contact you.

The Seth personality again, as you understand it, is legitimate and independent, a legitimate and independent personality which is a part of my identity. Seth is also learning and developing, as I am.

Simply, as an analogy, and <u>only</u> (underlined) as an analogy, I am what you would refer to as a future Seth, as Seth in a quote "higher" stage of development. This is not to be taken literally however, since both of us are fully independent, and exist simultaneously. *(Pause.)*

You have already been told that connections exist between you and Seth as you have known him. Therefore it is apparent that connections exist between us also, and that this development is a natural one. The apex point in Ruburt's personality is an extremely fortunate and unusual one, and the reason that such communications can take place.

(After the session Jane told me that in here she began to feel the familiar surge of great energy again—that no matter how fast she spoke she couldn't keep up with the words forming and leaving her. Yet at this time her pace was still but average, with many pauses, and her voice still peculiarly gentle.)

You *(to me)*, are also necessary however, and as I intend to develop a discussion concerning such communications, you will be able to see your own position more clearly.

Regardless of the apex point however, attraction operates, and there are reasons why these <u>particular</u> connections have been made rather than others. There are events that unite us and that have served as turning points in the development of our various personalities. In some strange manner, what I am, now, is linked to what you are. *(Pause. Jane looked at me.)*

(In here, Jane again felt the surge of energy.) There are points of contact having nothing to do with time as you know it, that are extremely significant to all personalities, origins of new energy that are sometimes suddenly brought into existence because of the strong, latent psychic <u>capacities</u> within individual selves.

At these particular points whole conglomerations of new self units come into being, their origin sparked as given in the last sentence. They then disperse and go their own ways, but the mutual origin and the strength of that initial psychic birth remain.

(In here Jane said she had visual inner images, as of stars being born, etc.— attempts, she thought, to put the inner data into recognizable visual terms.)

They may develop in entirely different fashions and in various dimensions, but a strong sympathetic attraction exists between them. There is a point of contact where knowledge can be communicated from these various dimensions; and for too many reasons to give you now, Ruburt is precisely in proper coordinates for such communication to take place.

This communication, while taking place in your time, and in your present, is nevertheless partially responsible in other dimensions for what you would call future developments in your own personalities, which you can now in turn contact. This is partially what I am, far more than you are, or that Seth is as you thought of him.

(Voice still gentle and lilting.) I look back on you as the selves from which I sprang, and yet I am more than the sum of what you will be when you are finished with the other dimensions and times that I have known. For I have sprung entirely away from you, and would be alien in your terms. That you can even contact me *(pause)*, is a most remarkable development. Yet had you not been able to contact me I would not be what I am.

(Jane was now speaking somewhat faster, her voice higher.)

I am far more however than this portion of me that you contact, for it is only one portion of me that experienced that reality. *(Pause.)* It is highly important that the material not be distorted then, for most communications take place on far different levels than this, so closely connected with your own system that even the most undistorted material is highly distorted, because the communicators themselves are so closely involved with camouflages, and do not realize that they create the realities which they then describe.

(Pause.) I have done my best to give you an understanding as a basis for our future sessions. Seth as you knew him will also be Seth as you know him; for whether or not I speak as myself or through him, as you think of him, he is still the intermediary and the connection between us, and he will help transmit energy; but more, he will also appear as himself as you have known him. There are necessary emotional elements that are uniquely his own. *(Pause.)* My personality structure is far different—very rewarding to me *(smile, eyes open)*, but very unfamiliar to you. You will understand him better emotionally, and need, I believe, that strong connection.

("Well, we seem to be doing all right now also.")

I do not want you to feel I have taken away a friend. I am also a friend. In many ways I am the same friend. Still, only a small portion of what I am speaks to you now. *(Pause.)* Other portions of me are concerned elsewhere, for I am aware of my own existence in other dimensions, and keep track of them, and direct my many selves. *(Pause, eyes closed. Then Jane said in a faint voice:)* Call him.

(11:05. I called Jane's name loudly three times, as Seth has suggested doing

before when her trance is deep. She nodded, eyes closed. I said, "I don't know how to say good night here, so I'll just say good night."

(Jane then jumped, her right arm moving almost violently, eyes open briefly. She said she was okay when I inquired. Her eyes began to flicker, then opened. She did not speak, but finally took her glasses from me. "I feel like I'm light as air, you know... Also feel like I've been a long way away."

("According to this, you have," I said.

(11:12. Jane said, "I don't feel I'm all me yet. I'm not projecting, but I feel like I'm half off to the right..." Yet she was aware of sensation within her physical body—a spot on her gum, etc.

(Jane said that before break she had felt the delivery was exceedingly slow. But after break she felt it was exceedingly fast, like a "wink, or a split second." Yet objectively there had been no great extremes, except as noted. Once toward the end of the session I had to ask her to slow down a bit for note-taking. When I did this, Jane said she had an inner feeling of going back and forth. She couldn't describe this any better.

(11:25. Jane said, "I'm confused." Then she had the feeling that this was our channel to cosmic consciousness, or whatever we chose to call it, handed down to us by this personality. Her confusion stemmed from the developments, the seemingly new identity, announcing itself in the session—the lack of our idea of a name, etc.

(Jane had a good point later. First Frank Watts announced himself in the sessions. Then Seth. And now the new development. A progression apparent, then.)

APRIL 24, 1968 WEDNESDAY

[Jane's notes:] Well, something terrific has happened, so I thought I'd write it down at once. The Something is subjective, but its effects have appeared so beautifully and effectively in physical terms, that the physical changes themselves add to the subjective joy, relief, and sense of direction.

Last Thursday a letter from Prentice-Hall, suggesting that the Dream Manuscript *be converted, sort of, into a book dealing with* The Seth Material. *Editor expressing really terrific interest in* The Material. *Just what we wanted; the enthusiastic interest really made me feel great. I was sort of appalled at the lost work in the* Dream *manuscript but realized Rob has been right along; and the editor was right. The Seth Material is my unique source and a literally fabulous one; that I really did not truly appreciate and to which I was not really directed. It is as if clouds of the worst sort have rolled away. In a session that night, Seth emphasized the new direction I should follow.*

Then, re-reading some material I was struck by the massive intellect behind it, the real beauty of the material, and sad that I did not really let myself realize it before; indeed that I had allowed myself to be affected by the lesser writings of others; even to the extent that in some late sessions it affected the material. Told my class last night the whole bit, and said that from now on classes were to be focused about the material; we were going to study it from scratch; this was my life work, my direction, what I was meant to do. Realized yesterday also, going over old notes, that my original 'cosmic consciousness' (borrowed phrases again) experience was with The Physical Universe as Idea Construction *which turned into and developed into the sessions and Seth Material; the natural, intuitive, and logical development; which to a large extent I relegated to the background and sometimes even distrusted. (Largely because I feared setting myself up as some sort of a 'false prophet' or something; or distrusted myself, rather than it, actually.)*

During class, my jaw started to bother me, then badly, so I couldn't get to sleep. Pendulum said, negative suggestion having to do with some old notes I read, plus not wanting to hurt Venice. Hypnotism got me to sleep. Noticed however even during this, a strange and delightful and sudden release, physically with arms, legs, shoulders, neck. This morning, the release much more noticeable. Hands far stronger, left hand definitely has resumed—overnight?—a far more normal appearance, and both much, much stronger; arms much better, neck flexible, shoulders; even think arms have 'let down,' a bit. Spiritual and (psychic) sense of joy, thankfulness, release.

Believe this all has to do with the above, plus with a strange session held the night before last, in which through me the voice said it was sort of 'beyond Seth'; the message coming from a higher portion of that personality; tremendous energy seemed to flow through me and the definite, thank God, certainty, that this came from beyond me, and was automatically translated into words at my end. Subjectively I feel this was as significant a development—almost—as the original Seth session. The sense of contact most ... undeniably there. The feeling I really was in contact with some... all encompassing reality.

SESSION 408
APRIL 29 1968 9 PM MONDAY

(Actually Jane sat with her eyes closed from 9 PM until 9:10, waiting to see if a session would develop. She wasn't particularly in the mood, she said. She had been working hard on her projected book, and was also concerned because she hadn't heard from either F. Fell or Prentice-Hall. The pendulum helped her out here this afternoon.

(Once again Jane began speaking in the light, pleasant, high but not falsetto voice, that we had been told represented the larger personality beyond, and encom-

passing, Seth. This voice is distinctly not the heavy and strong and amused or acerbic Seth voice. It is very well controlled, distinct, almost lilting, with a distant or formal quality.

(Jane seemed to speak for this personality, who is still nameless in our terms, quite easily. She used many pauses however, some of them long. Her eyes soon began to open, though they did not remain open for lengthy periods.)

Good evening.

("Good evening."

(Pause.) The knowledge that we have, myself and others like me, would be incomprehensible to you in its pure form.

Translations are therefore necessary, and in many respects the distortions that will appear of necessity in any such translation *(pause)* are requirements; what might be termed distortion from pure knowledge, you see, is often the result of the translations without which you could not receive nor understand the material.

Beyond this however, some channels are more distortive than others, and we hope to keep this channel as undistorted as possible. As you understand, pure knowledge cannot be put into words, and for that matter it exists beyond your usual concept of thoughts.

What you call thinking is a dim shadow of true comprehension. *(Pause. Jane lit a cigarette. Her voice, with its distant quality, was not faint however.)* This involves being united with knowledge in a way you cannot now appreciate. This kind of comprehension automatically puts you out of self- (hyphen) structures as you think of them, but does not deny identity. Since you are very involved with self-structures as you think of them, then knowledge must be given in such a way that it affects the structure as you know it.

Knowledge in your terms does change your own physical structure, merging with the physical stuff of your image, but your ego remains relatively detached from it, you see. *(Long pause.)* There is a psychic merging with knowledge. To you, knowledge in the abstract means little. There is a merging with concepts, however. This you can understand.

Now you are merged with a concept, now, of what you are. So merged that you cannot see your way clearly out of the concept, nor easily imagine reality from any other viewpoint but the self-structure that you presently imagine yourself to be. *(Pause.)* Another part of your whole identity is quite aware that you are delving into one concept of yourself. To delve into it, you gladly and willingly momentarily forget the greater portions of yourself. You experience the concept fully. Your prime identity is quite aware of other self-concepts that are also being experienced. *(Pause.)*

Self-structures and identities are not the same. Identity requires no structure. Identity knows, and knows that it knows. Self-structures know and do not know that they know. Self-structures are a part of identity. Identities can contain pure knowledge without translation, and use it to seed various existences and to form realities. They do this consciously in your terms. They are far more conscious than you can presently imagine.

You may take your break.

(9:33. Jane paused, eyes closed; then they opened easily, and she was out of trance. This was her easiest transition in some little while. As soon as she left trance she became aware of music playing in the apartment downstairs; before she hadn't heard this.

(Once again Jane had felt the cone effect—not very strongly—mentioned in the last couple of sessions. She said it was like a cone or pyramid suspended above her head, and that as she went into trance she was to "align" herself directly beneath this cone, which is inverted. Jane then feels that pure knowledge is funneled down this cone toward her; that on the way it is changed, distorted out of shape so that finally she can put it into words. We wondered if Seth had been acting as translator.

(Jane now said that she felt the larger personality, speaking freely, might present its data in something like musical notes or tones, rather than words. We viewed this idea and the cone effect as Jane's efforts to construct methods to explain the sessions' data on levels close to consciousness.

(But, definitely, Seth's voice hadn't shown itself. When Jane resumed the same distant and gentle, higher voice returned as before. Pauses also, some long. 9:46.)

You are going beyond Seth, to a part of Seth you do not know.

Seth was all of myself that could come through to you. You are in contact with a larger portion of Seth's reality. You are learning that self-structures are transparent. Any contradictions are merely the result of interpretations. Your first Seth is independent, and I am independent. *(Pause.)* Because he is a part of my reality does not mean that he is less an individual. My reality simply includes more, now, within your particular coordinates; and that last is important.

He is another aspect of me while being himself. *(Pause.)* In your terms, I am a guide he also follows. He is much more aware of our relationship however than you are of your relationship to him. *(Pause; well over one minute long.)* Your time is required... These communications change me as they change you, for they are action on both of our parts. Your egos are being well educated, since they are aware of the sessions, and this will be of great benefit to you when other coordinates come into your perception.

Here knowledge is sifted through self-structures. *(Pause.)* Pure knowledge is not impersonal. To the contrary *(smile; pause),* it is meaningless unless it is *(smile; gesture; pause),* experienced intimately within every part of an identity. But to you it would seem impersonal.

I seem less of a personality to you than the Seth that you knew, because my personality *(pause)* exists in quite different terms. *(Long pause.)* To me, a thought is as real as a day to you. A day that can be experienced in a variety of ways, and that can be viewed from literally endless perspectives. *(Pause, over one minute.)*

In your terms, I am very ancient, and yet what I am is always new. Your early *(smile)* Seth can explain this to you more clearly than I.

You may take a break.

(10:04. Once again Jane's eyes opened after a pause. She appeared to have left trance as she talked, but then said: "If I came out so good, how come I'm still half under?" As before recently, Jane was partially in trance during break, but felt well. She remembered only the last sentence of the material before break.

(When she resumed she used the same higher and gentle voice, with pauses, etc, as before. 10:21.)

In the most simple of terms, we're always helping you.

On the other hand, you are part of what we are. Inspiration always springs from beyond your system, and not within it. It always springs from channels that are available to you, *(pause)* and if it is, again, distorted, without the distortions, you could not use the inspirations.

I will try in your future to explain basic systems of co-ordinates so that you will have some conception of how all creative and inspirational ideas always appear within your system; for only one portion of you appears isolated within it.

You have channels open to those various sources that you have forgotten. *(Pause.)* These provide the motive power that moves your civilizations. These coordinates leave traces within your physical system. There are ways for you to tell when channels are clear. There are ways to open the channels from your end, and we will discuss them. *(Pause, over one minute long.)*

Time, your time, is required again.

Now the pyramid or cone structure Ruburt senses is his symbolic way of feeling, in your terms, the approach of certain coordinates. *(One minute pause; voice unchanged.)* These are projected into your system and opened. Instead of saying, "I will meet you at the corner of Water and Walnut," for example, I meet you within certain precise coordinates. *(Long pause.)*

These are fitted into your physical space structure, though I am not as aware of it as your first Seth. *(Smile.)* I speak from a distance. *(Pause.)* He comes into your room with every reality but the physical.

Now you may end the session. If you feel lonely you may speak with Seth the earlier, if you wish. *(Pause; smile.*

("Yes, by all means. Are you there, Seth?"

(Jane had been sitting relaxed on the couch. Now she leaned forward, eyes closed but with the familiar gestures and mannerisms of Seth.)

Good evening.

("Good evening, Seth."

(The voice was also Seth's, strong, much deeper, and immediate. It was also amused.)

I see you have received some surprise.

("Yes.")

My big brother has come—

("Yes.")

—to get into the act. That is all right *(smile; eyes open),* and certainly I have hinted at this development in past material—opaquely. *(This exchange featured much amusement on Seth's part.*

("Yes. Were you with us earlier this evening?")

Needless to say, I have not missed a session with you. *(Smile.)* It may surprise you that I can remain silent, but it is one of my virtues with which you were not familiar.

("Well, maybe. So now we speak to Seth One and Two, huh?")

(Seth's delivery was emphatic and quite immediate, with many gestures and no pauses. Jane had made the change from the first more distant personality, into Seth, without difficulty—very smoothly in fact. But I thought it a good idea not to continue this exchange too long.)

You are like magicians, indeed, pulling white rabbits out of hats.

("I don't know about that.")

I am speaking with you this evening so that you realize I am hardly deserting you. I have told you I am a teacher, and I have let the principal in the door. *(Amused and forceful.)* But I will hold my own classes.

It is quite true in important respects, however, that the two of us are one. This comes as no surprise to me. There is much regarding the nature of time that I have not given you yet, and it will make this more understandable.

Even so poor a small fish as I, am not bound by your time, and can be quite aware of what would seem to be future branches and developments that will intimately concern my own identity.

("Yes.")

On the one hand, in your terms, I have not reached that point yet. I am not your Seth Two yet. I <u>am</u> aware of him. I will maintain myself as you know me now at the same time, even in your terms, then. *(Emphatic delivery, eyes open.*

("*I see. I think you've mentioned something about this a long time ago.*")

Or I would not be speaking to you <u>now</u>. Our friend, our dear bewildered Ruburt, has had a time of it, and I suggest we end the session. But if you have particular questions, you may ask them.

("*They can wait. I just wanted Jane to hear from you tonight so she can get an idea of what's going on.*)

I am reassuring. *(Smile; pause, eyes closed.)* My heartiest wishes to you both then. If you are on a merry-go-round, you may catch the golden ring. *(Pause.)*

("*Well, good night, Seth. It was good to hear from you.*")

I never desert my friends.

("*I hope not.*")

You are in good hands with either of us.

("*Will we hear from you, usually, each session?*")

There are mechanics to be worked out. *(Pause.)* This is new for me also. As soon as <u>we</u> arrive at the most beneficial conditions, I will tell you. *(Pause.)*

("*Good night, Seth. Thank you.*"

(10:52. After a brief pause with her eyes closed, Jane then came out of trance. She had no aftereffects or fatigue, etc.

(She said she remembered none of the material until "he" asked if we wanted to hear from Seth. Then she was subjectively aware of the Seth voice and the change in personality, without remembering what Seth said.

(Jane said that when "he" asked for a pause, in our time, while giving the data about coordinates, she thought that Seth might be called in to explain this material to us in our terms. She said she felt that "his" abstract idea behind or beyond the term coordinates, was far removed from our earthly experience.)

SESSION 409
MAY 1, 1968 9:25 PM WEDNESDAY

(At 9 PM we sat waiting to see if a session would develop. Jane wasn't aware of anyone being present at first, but at 9:15 she got a slight impression of the cone effect, described in the last two sessions. We talked about the material on coordinates, and at 9:25 Jane got a sentence within concerning them. She didn't think it was from Seth. She also said it disturbed the connection when she talked about what she had received.

(Once again Jane began speaking for Seth's entity, as we have come to call the personality beyond Seth; her voice had the same higher and distant, clearly enunci-

(ating quality as before. There was no greeting to us as Seth usually gives. Jane spoke with eyes opening at times, and with many pauses, some of them long.)

These coordinates are psychic structures, and they form the cornerstones of all realities.

In the beginning of your sessions, Seth spoke about what he called the fifth dimension, and gave you an analogy meant to represent it. His tiny wire analogy can now be considered in this light. These are of course imaginary, but the image will help you understand the concept. *(Pause.)*

The intersections of the various wires forms various coordinates. Some of these are of such immense intensity that they form systems *(long pause, over one minute)* that contain what you would call universes.

(Pause. Our cat jumped up into Jane's lap as she spoke. I didn't know if he would bother her under the new circumstances, so I got up to put him in another room. Jane appeared undisturbed. Later she said she was aware of the interruption.)

Through these openings whole groupings of self-structures experience, and reexperience in different ways, the dimensions within those coordinates. But no boundaries really close a system, and within any set, any given set of coordinates, there will be others. *(Pause.)*

We will take your physical system as an example. There is general and mass focus of all self-structures within that system, binding enough and cohesive enough so that the appearance of a permanent and all-pervading physical reality is maintained. The ego part of the structure concentrates with great intensity, directing itself within those coordinates that form physical reality.

As Seth explained, even this cohesiveness is rather an illusion. You exist at the same time within many other coordinates. A shifting of focus is quite simply the main requirement for perceiving these other coordinates. But to shift focus to them presupposes a knowledge of their reality. Otherwise only a momentary and accidental encounter with them can ever occur, as far as you are concerned egotistically.

The realities are formed by psychic intent, and the true cohesiveness is intuitive. The deep connections that occur, for example in various reincarnations, are not apparent to the ego. The connections between us, now, are far more logical than any simple cause and effect.

The psychic intensity of an experience shatters all concepts of time. In your terms an intense experience can unite and spark developments encountered by one through many reincarnations. All identities do not choose physical existence. All identities do not have to be physical at any quote "time."

Those that choose physical existence, once having done so, must follow through. Some of my own self-structures were never physical. These communications, in your terms, quite simply act as boundaries, though the boundaries as you know do not really exist.

The coordinates are composed of intensities. They are electromagnetic in structure—at least this is the closest I can come in explaining them to you. For while they are electromagnetic, as Seth told you, they are living in that they are something like psychic projections.

The apparent boundaries of your own physical system therefore are composed of psychic intensities and projections that are set out by the entities who have decided to experience physical reality. (Pause.) You agree upon your time concepts—they are like gentlemen's agreements. You have agreed, a large number of you, to ignore the existence of reincarnation. When you decide to accept this, then of course adequate proof for it will be found. (Long pause.)

As far as what you consider the race of man to be, unsuspected value fulfillments and progress will follow after this mass recognition. This will change civilization as you know it.

This will not come however for many reasons, for some time. Value fulfillment would not be achieved in some important directions if man ceased killing because he knew death did not exist. He must cease killing while he believes death does exist. He must solve the problem in the context that it developed.

We will be working to explain coordinates to you. We are barely beginning to hint at their reality and importance. Every reality exists within unique coordinates. There is some overlapping, but the main focus within any system is entirely unique. There is no contradiction, no exception. This applies in the most minute circumstance. (Pause.) No experience is ever like any other, no individual or no self structure.

What your scientists have learned about the physical genes barely scratches the reality of diversity, even physically. The miraculous and pristine originality of every moment, even as you know it, can hardly be vocalized. The diversity of atomic structure is as yet hardly suspected. And all of this is but the physical materialization of the inner reality within one system.

You may take a break.

(9:58. Jane sat with her eyes still closed, but nodded that she was okay to my question. Her eyes opened a minute later. She had used the new distant voice throughout, as before; this time though her pace had usually been better. She said she didn't get the cone or pyramid effect after the one time noted before the session began.

(Jane said she doesn't really know how to begin the sessions lately. She sits and "listens inward." She hears a word and then begins. She was aware of the different voice. With Seth, she always felt he was present, immediate, alive and strong. With *the new source, Seth's entity, Jane said she feels it is way up above her, talking; but once she gets the first word there's no problem.*

(I wondered aloud if we should ask definitely for a name for the new voice, since it might give Jane more of a sense of familiarity with the new voice, and help in writing up the notes; but it was no big deal, we decided.

(Jane resumed with the same new voice and delivery at 10:13.)

Your lifetime, you see, is basically not important in terms of years, but in terms of intensity and value fulfillment.

The coordinates have nothing to do with time as you know it, nor with space as you know it, though in your system they form the reality in which time and space appear. A creative event is far more significant than twenty years of boredom, you see.

I did not say <u>idleness</u>, for this can be creative, in terms of creative enjoyment. You changed your own coordinates to some extent when the Seth sessions began, for you have freedom within the system.

As I told you, Seth as you know him will continue in the sessions. For a while however I am speaking rather exclusively, to get Ruburt acquainted with the operation of various inner channels. *(Long pause.)* This will be a brief session, as inner adjustments are being made, and all information you require will be given to you in your time.

Seth is of course a part of the session whether or not he speaks, as you are accustomed. In one way Ruburt's pyramid image is quite legitimate, for you and he are at the base, with Seth in the middle and myself at the top. This forming simply a structure of coordinates through which information can flow.

I will end the session. *(Pause.)* If you prefer you may take a break, and I believe that you could speak with Seth.

("Well, we can take the break and then see what develops."

(10:25. Jane came out of trance easily. However, she said things weren't just right; she felt there was a disturbance at the other end—it wasn't coming through as strong from "there." She was not bothered by noises in the house, etc., and remembered none of the material until the end.

(I thought the session was over. Jane lay back on the couch as we talked about coordinates. Then I saw her eyes close; her face took on a certain familiar expression, she smiled, and I knew Seth was going to speak. 10:30.)

We have not coordinated our coordinates; I am simply here to reassure you.

(Jane said later she got this line just before Seth began to speak. As usual the Seth personality was immediate, strong, and very humorous. Eyes very dark, open often and looking at me.

("Yes.")

I know you miss my wit, and shaggy dog personality.

("Yes.")

I told my friend that you were ready for this development. Opening the new channel is the important thing. Then you can find out what fish you have hooked through it. Opening the channel requires work on my part also.

("I'll bet the fish is a big one.")

In order to be bigger than me, of course. *(Pause.)* You are working with something else again, however. The strong emotional content is not there, you see, in your terms.

("No, it isn't.")

When the proper conditions are stabilized however, the new development will be more than worth your while, and mine. And you can always get me, you see. *(Amused and emphatic.)*

We will indeed end the session, and you will be given all your information in good time. Do not let it bother you that you do not have a name.

("Okay.")

Look how many years passed before you knew you were Joseph.

("True."

(Pause.) And tell Ruburt he is a rascal. He will know what I mean.

("What __do__ you mean?")

He will know, and tell you.

("Oh... What do you think of the remark Jane made the other day—that the earth represents our subconscious?)

It was a very good one. He used the term unconscious; and it is legitimate. For the basic earth that gives you sustenance is formed from your own vitality. When you look at the state of your world therefore, as a sign of man's condition, then also consider the stability, in your terms, and the bounty, that is also a sign of inner vitality. And this sustains you regardless of your wars.

(Pause. "Good night, Seth."

(10:39. Jane came out of trance easily after a short pause. Seth had been very animated and amusing—funny, with a good voice, eyes open often and looking toward me as Jane lay flat on the couch.

(Jane made the remark about the earth representing our unconscious last weekend while we were driving through the countryside.

(She said the rascal reference concerned data she received from Seth tonight, but did not speak aloud. The data was to the effect that she'd hear from Prentice-Hall within three or four days; but she didn't voice it because she had been distorting predictions recently, and didn't want to do so again now.)

SESSION 410
MAY 8, 1968 9:05 PM WEDNESDAY

(Notes for what they are worth: The 410th session was due Monday, May 6, 1968. On that day Jane received a letter from Prentice-Hall, outlining plans for publishing the Seth material. After supper we discussed this. Jane drank two and a half quick beers, which affected her enough so that no session was held.

(At session time she sat waiting to see if a session would develop. None did, but she received brief notes from Seth: "You don't have to worry about me drinking too much. I'm sick now from drinking what I did. Be comforting and put me to bed.... I can't hold liquor. The problem will never arise. I drank too much and I can't let Seth speak in his own voice, to answer my questions." These Jane recited to me in her own voice.

(I thought excitement from receiving the letter had as much to do with Jane's feelings, as the beer.

(As we waited for the session to begin tonight, Jane said she still wasn't used to the new method, the new voice; she still waits for its beginning, then is okay once started. Now, the very definite Seth voice and personality are missed.

(Just before the session, Jane told me later, she was again aware of the cone affect, which she calls an obvious intellectual attempt to visualize the new as it is postulated in the sessions. As before, Jane felt the presence of the base of the cone at the top of her head; this is where she and I fit in. Just above us is Seth; above both is the new development that we have come to call Seth's entity; this is the peak of the cone. Jane gets her data, she said, from this peak and it seems distant and relatively emotionless.

(Again tonight the voice was clear, somewhat distant, and higher pitched than Jane's usual voice. The voice was not faint however, and if anything was a bit stronger tonight than previously. Many pauses in the beginning, and the pace increased considerably as the session progressed. Eyes closed at start; then opening often later.)

Good evening.

("Good evening.")

(Pause.) These coordinates form all realities. They are unique points through which vitality expresses itself. Camouflages spring up *(pause)* along the coordinates, and moment points offer endless opportunities for further expression and development. The inner fabric of reality is far more complicated than outer camouflage as you know it.

The physical body is but one small aspect of the various inner forms of which you are personally composed. As the various portions of your physical body are connected and interconnected, so the various portions of your other forms are also interconnected, and one to the other. *(Pause.)*

It goes without saying that as you create physical reality you also form the other planes of existence in which you operate. You do operate simultaneously within all levels of reality and if you become familiar with various coordinates, the self that you know could become aware of your own other existences.

Your scientific fields of endeavor may stumble upon the mathematical probabilities involved in such other fields within perhaps a 60-year period, but they will not recognize the significance of the discovery—which will probably be made in an attempt to obtain more data concerning an <u>idea</u> related to Einstein's special field theory.

This related idea will be developed by another scientist, based on the Einsteinean concept.

It is very possible that physics rather than psychology will give the first hint that human personality is multidimensional and that the inner reality of the mind far surpasses the physical universe that it attempts to probe. *(Pause.)*

There are other drugs however, and if these are discovered and utilized, then these developments could occur within the field of psychology itself. The drugs release certain barriers that *(pause)* stand between the physical body and its other forms.

One such plant resembles the cotton plant, yet with very small yellow or yellow white seeds, and grows in certain portions of Africa. Its effects would seem to be highly hallucinatory. The hallucinations however would be quite valid journeys into other realities.

(Apropos of the above, I quote briefly from an article in the New York Times *for May 9, 1968, written by Walter Sullivan and datelined May 8 from Cambridge, Massachusetts. However, Jane and I did not see the article until the <u>day after</u> tonight's session; note that this session is held on the same day the article was published. A friend gives us the* Times *after he is through with it, the day after publication.*

(The article concerns the drug supply available in plants, and the paucity of our knowledge about this vast field. A few quotes:

("Another rapidly growing field of knowledge concerns the alkaloid family of chemicals, which includes a wide variety of hallucinogens, substances that induce hallucination. Some of these, long in use in Latin America, stimulate fantasies of a specific type."

("For example an analysis of an ancient Mexican drug, sinicuichi, has shown it to contain five alkaloids that produce giddiness, an illusion that surrounding objects have become very small, and a feeling of remembering events before one's birth."

(Other drugs are described, including some from Africa that promote forget-

fulness, feelings of smallness and largeness, and other effects. South America is also included in the data. The article is on file.)

New discoveries of the qualities <u>inherent</u> in the molecule will lead to an understanding of molecular consciousness, at least a rudimentary knowledge. The implications here again will not be recognized for some time.

Together, psychology and physics could bring about a new understanding of the nature of man, but the hints and signs will remain dormant and unused.

Physicists however will be forced to recognize that the energy within molecular structures <u>has its origin elsewhere</u>. *(Jane was restless during this delivery, rubbing her face and hair.)* They will be forced to postulate the existence of an unknown force, <u>always existing</u> despite newer current theories. No postulated new force theory will be able to explain reality.

(Pause, well over one minute long. Eyes closed. Emphatic.)

I want to make this clear: no postulated new force theory will answer their questions until it is realized that no system is closed, and that the physical universe is not the origin of, but the result of, the energy that they seek. *(Pause.)*

The physical universe is like a very poor photograph. As the pictures and representations in a photograph are only dim, incomplete symbols for the people and objects they represent, so the physical universe is but a dim image of the reality for which it stands.

You would learn little of what it means subjectively to be a human being by simply studying a picture of one. And you learn little of basic reality by studying the physical universe <u>as if it were more</u> than a symbol of what it represents.

(Jane's delivery was faster and quite emphatic in here, in the new higher voice. Eyes open often. Now she took a long pause.)

True identity is as much divorced from ego reality as the photograph is from the person. There are connections between an individual and his photograph, and there are connections between the physical individual and the inner self, but the person must recognize the image in the photograph, <u>for it will not recognize him.</u>

You may take your break.

(9:36. Jane's eyes opened almost at once, and she easily came out of trance. There was still an element of unsureness in it, she said, but her ease of operation under the new regime was obvious.

(Jane said she saw a photographic "size and shape" while she was speaking, but the visual data weren't clear here. She was aware of traffic noises as she left trance, but felt good; she missed the "good rich" Seth voice and feeling however.

(We wondered why Seth's entity chose to give this data, since it seemed Seth could have done so. We thought that probably it was in preparation for later events.

Jane resumed in the same dispassionate, higher voice as before, at 9:45.)

We are using these channels so that they will be open, and prepared when they are needed.

It is Seth's way of making still more information available. None of this is meant to deny the reality of your own physical system for you. The very nature of our sessions should show you that self-structures are indeed transparent, and communications can flow through them.

We are as vividly experiencing reality in our own dimensions as you are in your own. I will be able to activate certain abilities of Ruburt's *(pause, eyes closed)*, by helping him alter certain coordinates within his own inner system.

These in turn will activate certain areas of the physical brain in a most advantageous manner. These areas have to do with the storage of information that is usually available to unconscious layers of the present personality, and we hope to make them more consciously available.

There is quite simply a higher frequency being used when I speak. *(Long pause.)* My communications are dependent upon Seth's permission as well as Ruburt's. The material should still be called the Seth material, for I am an aspect of Seth that you did not know, and in the past I helped him deliver material though I did not directly attend sessions. *(Long pause.)*

He is a part of the overall entity that did become physical, although now in your terms that portion of his existence is finished. *(Smile.)* This portion was never physically materialized. *(Long pause. This last sentence referred I believe to Seth's entity itself, from inflections given.)* In one way I am a whole that is more than the sum of its parts, while I am also a part of more than I am. *(Long pause.)*

You may take a break.

(10:03. Jane again came out of trance easily. The sudden break surprised us. At the last break and this one, I had felt that Jane's delivery slowed down as break time approached, something like a spring unwinding. Not that energy wasn't available behind the material, but that perhaps something got in the way of the delivery. Perhaps, still, the newness of this latest approach.

(Again, now, Seth came through to close out the session. His appearance was abrupt, although expected, and as usual was forthright, strong in comparison with that of his entity, and very emphatic and humorous. Jane's eyes opened often and she was very animated. 10:14)

Now—

("Good evening, Seth.")

—I give Ruburt my heartiest wishes for his birthday, though he is far older than his tender 39 years. He misses me.

("That's right.")

That is fine. We are experimenting. Some time will be involved. *(Pause.)* He was uneasy when our sessions first began. I knew he would not take this as a lark. *(Leans forward, humorous.)*

I could have delivered this evening's material. I would like him to become familiar with our innovation. *(Smile.)* He participates more when I speak in this manner. In one way I am indeed able to make closer contact, but we must take advantage of all of our sources, and so we shall.

I am present in a different manner. I am not speaking as one who has been physically oriented when the other voice comes. *(Pause.)* Now to some extent this allows me to dispense with certain distortions necessarily a part of any personality who has been physically oriented.

The intimacy and personal characteristics by which you know me to some extent drew you to me. At times they will simply be dispensed with, so that a clearer flow of information can be given. *(Pause. Seth smiled.*

("What's so funny?")

Both of us have always been behind the sessions. I find this amusing for I have often, as you know, hinted of such a development.

("Yes.")

I am also amused because Ruburt feels more comfortable with me now. Identity has many selves, many self-structures, and my identity is always the same. If what I say sounds confusing—

("No.")

—you will understand. I am glad to see that you do.

("Yes.")

I also participate to some degree, personally, in your system during our sessions. There is no need for Ruburt to feel uneasy when I speak in a different guise. That other portion has gone a different way, but we, are aware of our relationship.

Do you have any questions, Joseph?

("You once, a long time ago, said something about a dog fragment." Over three years ago.)

You do have a good memory indeed. The fragment is no longer concerned, however. It has left your system entirely. We do at times visit you, your system, by sending projections of ourselves in such innocent manners.

Again however, the dog consciousness was its own. I did not for example control it, but I was aware of it.

You may take a break or end the session as you prefer.

("I guess we'll end it."

(Pause.) And I <u>did</u> enjoy the flowers.

(Jane's ESP students gave her flowers for her birthday on May 8..

("How old were you when you died in Denmark?")

We are indeed slipping in the sneaky questions this evening.

("No, I didn't intend it that way.")

Between, I believe, 52 and 7. Between 52 and 57.

("I never asked you before.")

Far older than our junior partner here this evening.

("Will it really be possible to describe to us an existence that has never been physical?" As Seth's entity has mentioned doing.)

We will attempt to do so. The time will come.

("Why has my back been bothering me lately—today?"

(I asked the last question at 10:37, after a lengthy pause, to see if the session was over. Jane sat with her eyes closed, smiling. Well over a minute paused. I thought she was still in trance. She went through a variety of facial expressions, mostly smiling or quizzical, and changed her physical position several times. Two, then three minutes passed. Her eyes were still closed. I waited, wondering if something unusual might be taking place; ordinarily I would have ended the session. Now Jane looked puzzled. Four minutes.)

Now, you had better end the session.

("Yes. Okay, Seth. Good night."

(10:41—I called Jane's name three times, and she came out of trance easily. "I'll tell you what happened," she said, "after I..." She rested briefly, then explained. When I asked the question about explaining a nonphysical life, Jane said she felt that Seth tried to switch to the other source or voice, after his own brief answer, so that we could get more data. As noted, a long pause followed here, but Jane subjectively was not aware of this. My next question, about the back, then threw her off, seeming to come instantly after the previous question, and she couldn't make contact with Seth's entity. Although she felt "up high."

(The result here, Jane said, was that she wanted to end the session, but couldn't get her own voice back, and "nobody helped her out." This was when I sat waiting to see what developed. As it happened, I was about to end the session when Seth spoke again and suggested that we do so.

(Jane spoke more about the cone effect described at the start of the session. Jane had a feeling of great distance to the top of the cone as it reached above her head. She felt lines from the base of the cone, across the top of her head, reach up to the cone's peak. At the same time she received from Seth's entity the words "Our existence is Joy."

(Jane also received "an inability to translate anything else." This was difficult for her to explain, she said; as though "they" were trying as best they could to explain what they really meant, and all she ended up with was joy. Also "struggle" was

involved. The cone effect was her attempt to receive this data. Mentally she asked for the data in another way, feeling as though she were in "dimension 8" —in between gears. She wasn't worried but it was a weird state of consciousness. At the end of the session she was aware of a radio playing downstairs.)

SESSION 411
MAY 15 1968 9:11 PM WEDNESDAY

(Notes: No session was held Monday, 5/13. Today Jane called Tam Mossman of Prentice-Hall, to discuss the prospectus for the Seth book suggested by Prentice-Hall.

(We sat ready for a session at 9 PM. Jane was still waiting by 9:10 for the session to begin; while feeling a little unsureness we were still confident that a session would be held. Notes later will explain the mechanisms involved.

(When Jane did begin to speak at 9:11, she used the same high, somewhat distant and quite precise voice as before, the one belonging to what we call, somewhat inaccurately, Seth's entity. The voice is very clear, without much volume and many pauses, most of them short. One of its oddities is that a sentence often ends on an upbeat note, instead of the voice dropping at the end as is usual. This effect still fools me at times, for a sentence will have ended whereas I think Jane has only paused briefly in the midst of one.

(There was no greeting. Eyes open often.)

We have told you that information is meaningless unless it is interpreted so that you can understand it.

In larger terms knowledge cannot simply be given. It must be experienced. Although you do not find me as warmly personal as the Seth with whom *(staring directly at me)* you have been acquainted, I am a personality. The information is not coming to you out of nowhere. Knowledge does not exist in those terms.

(This material re personality follows our talk before the session.)

Without the sort of directed knowledge that you are receiving, you have what appears as inspiration, a hit-or-miss affair, highly distorted as a rule. *(Pause.)* In the case of your sessions, you habitually became accustomed to manipulating certain coordinates, and this manipulation constantly increases your ability to receive information from us, and to achieve consistency of results. The coordinates do affect the physical system or any such communications would be impossible.

A personality is needed or the information would appear highly chaotic, and you would not know how to unscramble it, even if you were able to receive it. This is rather important. We not only give you information and help interpret it or translate it for you, but we also add to it our own experience with it. *(Pause.)* Your Seth would say we unscramble it for you, and then serve it neatly on a supper platter.

(Jane smiled, eyes open often, while giving this data. The voice was also a bit more emphatic and fast; perhaps this passage to date reflects the most individuality shown by this personality.)

The unscrambled information, again, would be meaningless, and even undependable. Ruburt's initial experience represented such an encounter. It is only because of his own abilities that he was able to translate the information for himself to any degree.

(Referred to here is Jane's attempt to write the book, The Physical Universe as Idea Construction, *which she struggled with a few weeks before these sessions began on December 2, 1963.)*

Seth gave him the information in a dream. He was afraid of Seth but not of the information.

Now, changing the coordinates does involve a shifting of inner focus and an extension of the inner senses. One of the reasons for the change in the sessions is to give Ruburt experience along these lines.

He is forced in one way to reach further into inner reality, for I do not come as immediately to you as Seth as you knew him did. Since I am not here that immediately, then Ruburt must go further. Seth is always there between us to help in this procedure.

Now in your last session Ruburt was given a very primary experience. You asked what it was like to be a personality never formed into physical matter, and I helped him attain some awareness, subjectively, of that condition. He could not go far enough into that concept, but he was briefly between physical existences as you know them.

He told his students that he felt as if he were between worlds, and he was. The answer in this case was not given in words, and at first he did not realize that his experience was as much of an answer as he could be given now.

(True. Jane's realization came last evening as she described the event to her ESP students. This was news to me, also, for she had not told me about it. She said that in between such events it is surprisingly easy to forget about them. Often a question or statement of mine, for instance, will remind her to tell me something. Note that in the last session, my notes contain no reference to Jane's feeling that she was, however momentarily, between two worlds.)

But keep the event in mind. Some questions at times may be answered without words, though he will be able to interpret the answers. This was our first attempt only.

The sense of rather strained neutrality Ruburt feels now before sessions is simply caused by the strangeness of changing coordinates from the ones with which he has been accustomed.

You may rest and we will continue.

(*9:30. Jane's eyes stayed closed but she nodded that she was okay to my question, then came out of trance easily enough.*

(*"It's just funny," she said, "going in and going out. It's like coming down out of trance; it wasn't like this before. He waits and I find him up there, where before he [meaning Seth] came all the way down to me."*

(*"You think of a trance as going deeper. In this it's all going higher—the voice, the distance, etc. I didn't get the pyramid tonight. I don't know when I start. I just start." Jane said that when the session began she had a tiny hint of first encountering Seth's personality, and then of going beyond this to the other.*

(*Her pace had been faster this evening with the new voice, especially toward the break. We thought her between-worlds experience a very good sign, in that the new personality was already beginning to fulfill functions, to add new dimensions to the sessions. Before, we had wondered at the reasons for its appearance for it had seemed that Seth could have given the data as easily.*

(*Jane resumed at a slower rate at 9:45.*)

My own characteristics are different, yet they will be apparent to you in time.

The contact is only in its initial stages (*pause*) and the approach not sturdy enough as yet to carry full weight in your terms. (*Smile.*) You have a weak signal, even though it is a better one than you have received in the past. Your explorations are simply carrying you further afield, and there are manipulations to make before your signal is as strong as it can be.

You had signs of its potential strength, but that is all.

(*"In the voice?" The question was poorly put. I meant the occasionally powerful Seth voice of the past.*)

In the session in which Ruburt felt energy so strongly.

(*"Yes." This would be very recently. See the 406th session.*)

(*Pause.*) Your own world, from my perspective, does not exist in the way I am sure it exists for you. Your camouflages are not clear to me, though I understand what they mean to you.

(*Smile, eyes open.*) Short range predictions would be most difficult for me, since I cannot break down time as you think of it to that degree. I perceive instead at one glance seemingly whole segments of your time field. (*Pause.*)

Seth as you knew him perceives your own system more clearly. *(Pause.)* From my viewpoint *(pause)* I do not perceive your physical universe then as you do. I do perceive your psychic values and emotional intensities, and realize that you perceive but very small segments of these. As you break down the spacious present into moments, which you then experience, so also you break down psychic identity, gestalts, into small self-structures.

(Pause. Eyes open, Jane gestured, smiled. Again, a flash here of more emotional involvement, as I observed earlier. Jane later said she too felt a more emotional "entrance," though still much muted.)

I ... This is through your friend—a message... He says that I cannot tell time, and that you will consider this a flighty statement.

(I thought it funny, but not flighty.)

And as you break up then an hour into so many seconds, so you break up identities into so many self-structures, without perceiving their innate unities.

I am not telling you that individuality does not exist, that it is an illusion, and that therefore I do not perceive it. I am telling you that <u>you</u> do not perceive your own individuality as a whole identity.

(Pause.) To me this would be highly disadvantageous. From my viewpoint, you are far more alone than I. *(Long pause.)* From my viewpoint, it is difficult to understand your intense preoccupation with a system that represents such a small portion of your whole experience. *(Pause.)*

I <u>can</u> perceive many other systems similar to your own. I cannot with any ease or facility enter into them in any familiar manner however, to experience camouflage as you do. *(Pause.)* This does not mean of course that I am not aware of you.

(Pause, eyes open, then closed.) I am not always aware of the you that you feel yourself to be, however. *(Pause.)* Seth has told me that in some future, in your terms, he would help me in this regard; bringing me closer, he said, for a good look. If so, you should probably know it.

("In what way?")

It would be apparent, though I would not appear as matter. I do attempt to instruct you, for reasons earlier given, and your instruction is also to my benefit.

You may rest.

(10:08. In a few moments Jane came out of trance and opened her eyes. She said she had been aware of the pyramid or cone effect since last break, and this included during delivery. When aware of this she always feels she is going up, through it, not that it is coming down to her. At least she isn't aware of any coming-down feeling.

(Jane said that when "he" began talking about "my viewpoint," she was really "up there" in the pyramid or cone. When I asked the question referring to the stronger Seth voice Jane felt somewhat bothered. The question, the interruption and the sound of my intruding voice, seemed to bother her and bring her down to another level, she said. Not greatly, but she did notice it. Nor do all questions bother her.

(The material following this break reflects matters we discussed during break. Once again Jane resumed in the new voice, with pauses, at 10:25.)

I am speaking of my natural position. I can alter my viewpoint in which case your system becomes much clearer to me.

I can of course alter coordinates and experience concepts directly, but your system is not one that I have explored with any real attention. *(Long pause.)*

Ruburt is intrigued by the extension of his inner senses at this point. He is actually cutting through several systems, but has no freedom to explore them horizontally. *(Pause.)*

This is enough for this evening's session. *(Pause.)* Now, you can call upon Seth if you prefer to.

("I don't know what Ruburt would like to do.")

We will let him decide then.

(10:31—Jane sat quietly for a minute, then her eyes opened.

("Good night."

(Jane said she didn't know how to reach Seth "from that end," meaning while in trance, although she has done so before. She said she'd have to take a break and get him from "here."

(Any difficulty persisted, she thought, just because of the newness in the sessions. But she did like to hear from Seth each session just to make sure he was still there.

(Jane said that when she speaks for Seth's entity "it's like I'm emptying myself out up there someplace," and that when Seth speaks "he fills me up." But in the first case she doesn't know where she goes.

(Seth then spoke out. I was somewhat surprised, thinking the session had ended. Seth was strong and immediate and vital, eyes open. 10:36.)

I sent you—

("Good evening, Seth.")

—messages this evening. Almost but not quite, you had a dialogue going. Often both of us gave information in some sessions, but I did not believe that you were ready for any deep explanations. This is indeed still the Seth material.

("Yes."

(Humorously:) I am the loudest one—

("I can tell.")

—and I am the one who looks in on you. *(Pause.)* I will not keep you.

Ruburt is doing well however with this development. Do you have any questions for <u>me</u>? I do not mind answering them.

(*Seth here was very funny and loud and emphatic. Eyes open.*)

(*"How are you going to help the 'other' personality experience our physical reality?"*)

(*Same funny manner:*) I will take him by the hand and lead him here, figuratively speaking of course. I have told him it would be good for him to extend himself in this direction; and he is quite correct. You will know it if he does.

(*At this point I had two questions to ask.*)

(*"You say <u>himself</u>?"*)

I have to use a term for you, and "itself" is hardly adequate.

(*"Yes."*)

(*I also wanted to ask Seth just how we would know the presence of his entity, but did not interrupt since Seth seemed to want to keep speaking.*)

Understand again that these divisions are arbitrary. We are part—independent portions—of the same personality, he and I. If you have no further questions I will leave you to your domestic quiet. Anytime you want me to liven your sessions up however I will do so. And I will be here often, as a matter of course, in our regular sessions.

(*"You mean we could ask for you to hold the session on any particular evening?"*)

Indeed. I am not taking the background seat, you see, but we want Ruburt to learn to extend.

(*"Good night, Seth. Nice to hear from you." 10:43. Jane left trance easily, saying Seth left an emotional feeling behind him. The other personality was gone at once. Jane had forgotten Seth's data but remembered it when I mentioned it.*)

SESSION 412
MAY 27 1968 9:38 PM MONDAY

(*Jane began sitting for the session at 9:30 PM, waiting to see what would develop. I thought it very likely she would speak in the new voice. Once again the voice was higher pitched, distant, more or less emotionless, and very clear. Pauses, eyes open at times.*)

Good evening.

(*"Good evening."*)

Now. Knowledge exists as realizations, and realizations presuppose personalities.

Knowledge does not exist, ideally, in abstract terms. It is true it must be interpreted in many cases so that it may seem to you that it exists as some sort of isolated principle, ultimately. This is not the case.

Knowledge automatically changes the personality and the camouflage structure through which it flows. Knowledge, in other words, is action. There is of course such action taking place in these sessions.

(*Looking at me.*) You act as a transmitter, Joseph. This has not always been the case. Now, you strengthen the transmission of these communications. Ruburt and you together provide the necessary channels. He is more directly the receiver, but the communications pass through you also.

In your life as a minister (*in Boston, early last century*) you were a receiver in the terms that Ruburt is now, and your congregation acted as a transmitting agency.

You can ask your (*smile*) fond Seth questions concerning that episode. In that case your own personality structure was altered by the information that flowed through you, and it became a part of your earth life heritage. It was yours when you began this present lifetime.

Because of that experience you are now able to help bring in a strong signal. As one individual you serve now in the place of the congregation that was necessary to help you in the past.

Both you and Ruburt therefore had the possibility of such experience already prepared in your personality structures. It was this innate ability and knowledge, your fond (*smile*) Seth tells me, that prevented you from marrying until you met someone who would be able to help you along these lines.

You and Ruburt had of course been in close relationships in past life existences in the physical system. It was hardly any coincidence that you met. This follows the nature of action beautifully. Patterns in your personalities had already been activated and were ready for use and development.

There is nothing, neither knowledge nor beauty nor truth, that exists independently of consciousness or personality. My personality is such that it is not intimate or understandable to you, now, simply because it is a personality based upon different root assumptions than your own, and has its prime existence in dimensions that are composed of personality structures and gestalts based on alien psychological activities.

I am not giving you some kind of disembodied knowledge, however. Knowledge itself (*pause, smile*) is conscious. It is not a dead thing transmitted, since it has no meaning without personality and realization, and since it changes the personalities through whom it seems to flow. In changing them it of necessity is part of the awareness of the very cells it alters.

It is not like a liquid that flows through a bowl. It becomes a part of that which contains it, and therefore a part of the consciousness, in your case, of the cells and all of your structures. Words on a printed page for example are not dead, nor are they merely inert symbols. They share the consciousness of the material upon which they are printed and the various individual letters themselves, by their position and reality, make each unique piece of paper upon which they are written original from all others.

The newsprint to this degree, you see, has a consciousness, even in this regard. The least information is not inert. All symbols have a meaning therefore in themselves also, and a reality apart from that which they are meant to display. You can see this easily. The painting of a tree, while a symbol for the tree, nevertheless has its own consciousness and reality.

The consciousnesses is composed of the individual consciousnesses that make up the material that is within the painting, and yet there is also a gestalt consciousness that is the result of the artist's overall conception. Anything that an observer learns from looking at the painting is always living knowledge, that alters his own makeup.

Your Seth has helped me out here. You could say that you are merely symbols of your own greater reality, since your own greater reality exists in as many other dimensions as the tree exists from a rendering of it. Yet you are conscious and aware. Therefore behind every actuality in each dimension there are always other actualities and dimensions.

Consciousness so varies in degree that as yet you have little real idea of its basic unity and of its endless diversity.

You may rest.

(10:07. Jane nodded that she was coming out of trance when I asked her. Her eyes then opened. She tapped the top of her head in an inquiring manner. "You just have that funny feeling of extension, you know. You know damned well there's no pyramid up there. But you feel there is."

(Which is to say that Jane once again felt, or was aware of, the cone or pyramid effect, the extension reaching to a point up above her head, and explained in various recent sessions. This effect symbolizes Jane and me at the bottom or base of the pyramid, with Seth in the middle and Seth's entity, represented by the new voice, at the top or peak.

(Jane's pace had been fairly good with the new voice, faster than it has been, and remained so when she resumed at 10:23.)

Your fine friend (meaning Seth) is more at my end this evening, and will relay some messages.

The affair to which you have just referred was quite legitimate and it was an exercise in the use of the inner senses. Ruburt was also learning to receive and focus energy, and this is what occurred in the hand manifestation. In this case the class members were transmitters also, while Ruburt received and focused the combined force.

(*"Seth Two" referred to events in Jane's ESP class of May 21, 1968.*)

If you will give us a moment, your friend would like to speak to you more directly.

(*Pause at 10:25. Jane now sat quietly, eyes closed, for a few moments. Then her expression became animated and her mannerisms changed into those of Seth. Eyes closed, she hitched her chair forward, smiling. The voice was strong and immediate and amused.*)

Now—

(*"Good evening, Seth."*)

—good evening.

I have several remarks for you. (*Eyes open.*) The woman's death was foremost as far as probabilities were concerned, and yet at many points at the time of our session she could have altered those probabilities.

Had she taken the session to heart, the probabilities would have been altered. (*Pause.*) There were past-life circumstances operating. However, the woman chose the time of her death, with the subconscious knowledge of the whole family.

The child who found her knew beforehand that this would occur. (*Long pause.*) The personalities involved in the family relationship have worked out many problems. (*Pause.*

(*Here Seth refers to the suicide of a woman last Wednesday, May 22. A few weeks ago Seth gave a recorded session for the woman at the request of a member of Jane's ESP class. The woman had threatened suicide before. The family was due to leave Elmira because of a new job opportunity. A few days ago Jane learned that the woman for whom the session was intended had never listened to the tape, refusing to do so even though she had requested the session.*)

Give us a moment here. (*Pause.*)

Three of the children will attain some prominence, for which the psychological loss of the mother under the given conditions will be responsible. Subconsciously the mother also knew this. One child will make out very poorly, with health and mental problems, if the probabilities are not changed.

(*Jane did not meet the woman or children; she did meet the husband last year while job hunting.*)

The woman had already decided upon an Ohio birthplace for her next existence, some 30 years from now. (*Pause.*

(Smile.) The new conditions in your sessions unsettled Ruburt to some extent, so that he was the more dependent upon any other small established procedures you had between you. He thinks my friend a cold fish *(humorously)* but then, he was never a fin.

I would suggest a dependable performance for two months, followed by a week's rest, for a while. This will allow your own energies time to regenerate, and in the overall will be more dependable.

Now, when you are weary you do not have sessions in any case, and this sense of dedication can be better maintained with alternate periods of work and rest.

Your own father *(meaning mine)* has been in contact with his relative recently dead *(Alice Butts)*. Suggestion will help you with your dream memories again. Tie these suggestions in with what I have told you—that your father is <u>free</u> now. Do you have any questions for <u>me</u>? *(Humorous.)*

(Pause. "I can't think.")

That is some admission.

("I don't know.")

I enjoy being with you. I will visit with you at your next session, and hope to find you more bouncy.

("It's pleasant to hear from you.")

It is indeed! I am always here in some way during your sessions. Ruburt is not good enough yet to change his channels quickly, but he is learning. *(Pause.)* Since you do appear less bouncy than usual, you may end the session; but I may stay a while now that I am here. I am a cheap houseguest. My heartiest wishes to you both.

("Good night, Seth."

(10:45. Jane left trance easily, saying that she still had a trace of the pyramid effect even while Seth spoke—and at the end of the session. Seth had been his usual energetic self, in marked contrast to the cool and distant voice of his entity, so called.)

SESSION 413
MAY 29, 1968 9:15 PM WEDNESDAY

(Once again Jane began the session speaking in the new voice: higher in pitch, clear, formal and somewhat distant. Again, sentences often ended upon an upbeat.

(Jane said that now she is starting to get "little glimmerings before a session," telling her when it is to begin, with the new voice. When Seth came through regularly she always knew beforehand of his emotional presence, she said, and so had no

doubts or questions about beginning a session.

(Jane gave a rather long and intense session last night for her ESP class, speaking with both voices. The session was recorded, and when obtained a copy will be inserted into this record.

(As usual tonight her eyes opened often; with pauses.)

Good evening.

("Good evening").

There are endless coordinates, like infinities of prisms, fitting within, into, transposed upon, and permeating your own physical system, but your outer senses do not perceive them.

These coordinates are simply points where other fields of reality come into contact. Each exists to some extent where the other is, and yet the camouflage structures make it necessary for those within any given system to recognize the certain characteristics, only, of the one in which focus is to be maintained.

At physical death, in your terms, the personality structure is able to approach certain coordinates, to perceive them, and to change focus from one system to another. When this occurs the primary physical construction, the camouflage material, loses its power. The individual would seem to disappear with no trace remaining.

The personality does indeed turn its focus into another field of reality, and does desert the camouflage image that it maintained. However, some trace of that personality remains in that camouflage reality, quite literally, as what you might call a ghost image.

This phenomena is not meant to explain legitimate instances in which the personality and consciousness itself returns for purposes of communication. This image trace is a lingering manifestation, an imprint within your system, a part of its reality, and is held within it as you might for example retain an idea in your mind long after the idea has been expressed physically. As a painting that is destroyed physically may still be retained in your mind, so in the reality of the physical system a trace remains, an image trace of the camouflage structure that enclosed a given personality.

It is as if the physical elements themselves retain, in your terms, the memory of all the images that they have ever been a part of; and this is a simplified explanation of what indeed does occur. It is a difficult matter to explain to you, for the words that I must use necessarily must be couched in somewhat questionable terms.

For example *(pause, eyes closed; one of a series along in here)*, I was about to explain by telling you that these image traces are not, of course, visible physically, but latent. I believe your word latent suggests something that has not yet shown itself, however, and the particular kind of ghost image to which I am referring has instead already been manifested physically.

It exists after death in a latent form, in that *(quite animated here)* it can be materialized again. The possibility is there, but as a rule this does not occur. This image exists below the threshold of matter. You might call it an earth-memory image. *(Pause.)*

There is a corresponding image, held always within the inner consciousness of those who pass out of your system. *(Long pause. One of several here.)* This is indelible, but not always immediately available for reference. It forms a part of the whole inner self. We would prefer that you not think of any given entire entity in terms of a physical structure, though we have ourselves used the term structure to make explanations simpler, and will probably do so again.

The concept, structure, can be used by you in many ways—as a vehicle to carry many differing ideas. A personality communicating with your system, who was once a part of it, can make use of this trace image. The trace image is not his consciousness however. His consciousness is aware of the trace image, and on occasion can utilize it.

You may rest.

(9:42. Jane came out of trance easily in a few moments. She had experienced the pyramid or cone effect again to some degree, but wasn't sure whether she had done so while delivering the material. She had been aware of the effect during last night's unscheduled session also.

(The new voice had maintained its characteristics this evening while perhaps showing a little more animation than usual; becoming a little stronger as the session progressed. Jane resumed with the same voice, at a slower pace, at 9:57.)

Consciously, you are able to focus within, understand, and gain development in, one field of reality at a time. *(Smile.)*

These points, these coordinates, are all about you and impinge upon your physical form and your universe constantly, but you cannot understand nor perceive them. Consciously you work with what you call a one-reality field psychological structure. Other portions of your entire entity are not so limited.

This is simplified. Consciously you deal with those problems of one given physical life. Consciously you are not aware of what you call reincarnations, though these occur within your own system. Now these are not separate existences at all. They only appear so to you. Your earth identity *(smile)* in singular terms, is one existence. When you sleep at night and awaken, you do not suppose yourself a new personality, or imagine that you have died during the night. This is what you do when you imagine that you have several existences as different people.

Your real existence, even within your system, is too much for you to deal with in conscious terms, therefore the seeming segments. You know you live these seemingly different lives simultaneously, as you gain development, but it is always you gaining development in a variety of roles. I stress therefore that unity. It is only because consciously you do not realize the unity that the various reincarnations seem so diverse and separate.

So while you operate in a one-reality field psychological structure, you do not on a conscious level even perceive its entire reality, nor your place in it. The word progression is a poor one, and again however I must use it. *(Pause; smile.)* Seth's material on action will help you here.

Your consciousness expands and develops according to its own abilities. Previous lives are handled in conscious terms when you are in existence between physical lives. When you are completed in those terms you <u>may</u> operate within a two-reality field psychological pattern, in which you are consciously aware of existing in two systems at once, and able to manipulate with full awareness within each.

A psychological existence presupposes experience, experience in terms of value fulfillment *(pause)* and the emotional manipulation and direct knowledge of subjective states. This involves a capacity and ability to throw yourself whole-heartedly into a reality enveloping situation, and yet to be aware of the self who is then so lost or enveloped. *(Pause; emphatic delivery.)*

I am barely beginning to hint here of the psychological structures and capacities. In some way the inner self becomes the conscious egotistical self in <u>your</u> terms. *(Pause.)* Consciousness handles more and more activity. *(Pause.)* Feeling then is allowed to directly *(long pause; hesitant)* activate. *(Pause.)* We are not getting this concept through as clearly. *(Pause.)* Thought instantly becomes as real as your physical universe is to you.

Ruburt spoke before the session of handling aggression. Consciously you have the emotions of one personality to contend with and to direct constructively. One set of responsibilities and potentials. At other levels you have the problems, potentials and responsibilities of many to contend with in the same manner.

You may rest.

(10:25. Jane sat quietly for a moment, then jumped and came out of trance. Her voice had been the same throughout, and almost fast at times. She said she knew she was having trouble at the one slow passage, above. She was making an effort to get something through by using words that were correctly suggestible. It was very difficult, even though both sides were doing what they were supposed to.

(Jane said she was getting intuitive flashes that were just feelings, or things that

could not be put into words; she couldn't translate them even to herself.

(She said that sometimes "these personalities" seem to be able to look into her mind and see how she is going to deliver a bit of data; if they don't approve, then they can change the way they give it to her to speak, so we'll take it the right way. Jane said she used to distrust this process greatly, but no longer does so. She thinks this may be why she doesn't completely lose consciousness during sessions—so she can aid the personalities as they make use of her verbal discrimination.

(Jane resumed in the usual higher new voice at 10:36.)

These sessions themselves are a very slight evidence. As you have mentioned, Ruburt's egotistical self is now aware of potentialities and problems that did not exist for it earlier. For the reality did not exist consciously then.

In conscious projections you are also learning to deal to some extent with multifield psychological realities. Much that I will tell you concerning my psychological structure will be initially based upon some information you have concerning the inner senses, for these are my conscious senses.

Using them consciously automatically brings about a psychological reality so different from your own as to be alien. In terms of value fulfillment there is such a multitudinous variety of simultaneously held experiences that you could not contain them and hold the realization of your own identity.

I am able to change them as action while retaining the knowledge that I am that which changes, and find my stability in change. You must hold the action back for perceptive purposes. You do not really hold it back, but your one-reality field psychological structure only experiences in tiny segments.

There is enough in this session to give you some evocative insights, but the material will be explained in much more detail. A message I am relaying to Ruburt: the answer is to concentrate upon freedom. Freedom in emotional states keeps the system clear. Only impeding actions block it up. He feared to use emotional freedom.

(The above in reference to a discussion earlier in the day.)

This is enough for this evening's session.

(Jane paused. After a minute, at 10:47, I said good night to each personality, figuring that Seth had been present even if unheard. Jane's eyes opened briefly. Her expression changed, she smiled, and I knew Seth would speak. He came through in a strong and animated voice.

("Good evening, Seth.")

I prodded Ruburt's students. They are learning at a faster rate than they realize. *(Smile.)*

I am here simply to let Ruburt know that he can reach me. The session has been long enough this evening however, but know I am here whether or not you hear—my pun—my melodious voice. I bid you both a fond good evening.

("Good evening, Seth. Nice to hear from you.")

(10:50. Jane left trance easily. She had been tired this evening but the session had been a good one.)

SESSION 414
JUNE 5, 1969 9:05 PM WEDNESDAY

(Two unscheduled sessions were held on May 28 and May 30. Jane also had a long unscheduled session last night. All three of these sessions were for ESP classes.

(Jane felt much better today after hitting something of a low spot recently. Today also saw the shooting of Senator Robert F. Kennedy. John Pitre phoned this evening from Louisiana, with three questions for Jane. These concerned John's uneasy feeling about his wife Peg, last week; the strange loss of feeling in his legs in hot weather; and an effort to learn something from Seth about a pilot who disappeared some four years ago in a light plane near John's hometown, Franklin, LA, which is close to the Gulf of Mexico.

(We did not know which personality would speak this evening, nor what subjects would be covered. We sat for the session as usual at 9 PM. As it developed Seth spoke the entire evening, in a voice about as usual, with pauses, eyes open often.)

Good evening.

("Good evening, Seth.")

Now. You are concerned about some rather earthy matters. Distressing ones.

Nations, like individuals, go through cycles of emotional reactions. An individual may be swept by certain emotional patterns and then thrust them aside, and come under the influence of other emotional patterns, so nations do the same. Nations being made of individuals, overall problems are solved in a series of acts.

The acts are attempts to solve problems. They are often attempts to rid the mass psyche of exploding, misdirected, poorly understood aggressions. As a physical organism tries to thrust out poisons that impede its health, so the mass psyche organism, symbolically speaking, attempts to rid itself of this now-poisonous overdeveloped aggression.

The physical organism forms weak points through which the poison can be ejected. In order to save itself as a functioning unit, it sacrifices a portion of itself. The same thing happens with the mass psyche. Certain individuals are peculiarly suited for this function, because of their own inner background, the aggregate result of strong challenges they have set for themselves.

By naming the poison they attract it. They become, with full inner knowledge, vessels, or rather channels through which the poison can be to some extent ejected. Obviously this does not end the matter. But through them and their apparent destruction the poison is seen and recognized for what it is. Only then, in your system does this inner necessary realization come, because of the exterior circumstances.

These mass killings are your nation's way of pinpointing an extremely dangerous inner trend, that otherwise could have far more severe worldwide consequences. Obviously serious consequences result from these particular recent murders.

The consequences however for the nation and the world would be far more disastrous had these hates and aggressions not found these therapeutic, almost surgical, unfortunately necessary, outlets.

I am not condoning, you understand, the situation. The inner hate and aggression has not been recognized by the nation in the past. A holier-than-thou attitude developed into a spiritual hypocrisy. A portion of this was the result of ideals that could not be lived up to in practical terms—an overidealization. This does not mean that good intentions caused these situations.

The ideals were mouthed but not believed. Individuals only gave them lip service, and yet individual and mass guilt grew because of the difference between ideals and behavior. The country did not face its own inner reality. You have a schizophrenic condition then. Those who stood in the positions of King *(Martin Luther)* and of both Kennedys bring the inner psychic problems to a head. In one way they act as physicians, but they are also the patient who dies.

(Note that here Seth implies that Senator Kennedy, who was alive at the time of this session, would die. In fact the Senator did die the next morning, close to 5 AM, EDT.)

There are close psychological connections in all cases—psychological webworks, and psychic recognitions that bring together the slayer and his victim, and these are known to the inner self. The stature and meaning behind the victim adds to the horrible nature of the act, and of course this is the point.

The point would not be nearly as clearly made, you see, were the victim a man giving himself to crime. He must be in one way or another a symbol of those idealized qualities that the individual and the massed natives of the land give lip service to. These ideals are highly vital and important. The strength of the inner unrecognized hatred and aggression can be disastrous, and yet it works for the service of the ideal.

It operates, this aggression operates, as a constant check. It shows the rate of progress. It is a measure by which you can see failures. Were it not for this you could fool yourself, as your nation fooled itself for some years, not realizing its inner psychic condition. The ideals then are mouthed, but they are not taken seriously. Without these recent deaths, your country could have initiated a disastrous war.

Initiated. Without the struggle for these ideals a complacent vacuum develops. Now the real struggle for these ideals results in strength. The struggle results in strength. *(Long pause.)* If there is an honest struggle, an honest effort toward peace and brotherhood, then even if war erupts on a practical level then the psychic development is healthier than if no effort toward peace is made, or if ideals are merely mouthed.

If ideals are merely mouthed, and the idea of peace not seriously strived for, then this is an inferior state, <u>even if there is no war</u>. These men are showing the nation the difference between ideals and actions. Their deaths point the way and will give the impetus that was sorely needed.

They provide crisis points. Your nation, <u>because of its greatness and ideals</u>, must judge itself accordingly against those ideals. It therefore cannot afford to judge itself against others, find itself superior, and rest. Such murders would have been taken for granted in some other nations. Those who point the finger now however know, in one respect, that they have the right to do so since you are the ones who have set forth the ideals of peace and brotherhood. It is against these, then, that you must judge yourself.

Strength does not come in national terms, real strength, by bullying aggressive stance. But it does come when the people within a nation are making an honest effort to bring about in physical reality the materialization of their individual and mass ideals. The best that is in them, whatever their point of development. The unity and strength is psychically recognized.

I will let you rest. *(Humorously.)*

(9:50. Jane said that just before the session began, she had a "flash" to the effect that another Kennedy was to be involved in a tragedy, or that the present situation involving Senator Kennedy would evolve into another tragedy.

(Before the session Jane did not sense the pyramid or cone effect, as she usually does when Seth's entity is to speak. Then Seth came through.

(During break I wondered aloud if Seth had to communicate with his entity before getting permission to speak. I did not really mean to use the word permission, meaning instead whether there had to be any sort of understanding or agreement between the two personalities as to who would hold the session, or at least begin it. The funny consequences are apparent when Jane resumes as Seth at 10:00.)

<u>I do not need permission to speak.</u> *(Loud and energetic.*

("Okay. I chose a poor word.")

I do not need a permission slip. *(Leaning forward, eyes wide.)* Say you as a personality can write and paint. Do you need the permission of your writing self in order to paint?

("No.")

Do you have any other questions that I can put down in such quick manner?

("No.")

Without these murders the nation would not know what was wrong with itself. The murders are symptoms, but without symptoms the patient will not realize that anything is wrong with the inner self.

Give us a moment. *(Hand up, eyes closed, one minute pause.)*

Ruburt's earlier thought was correct, granting probabilities at this time.

("Which thought?")

Another tragedy due, either closely connected with the present situation, with those involved in this present situation, or with another member of the Kennedy family.

Now Johnson *(the President)* could also be in for some difficulty, in terms of health, and his heart. *(Pause, eyes closed, gesture.)* Do not ask questions while we thicken Ruburt's fog... There is something we are trying to get through about Humphrey... I believe his will be the nomination.

I believe Percy will have some part to play, either at the convention or perhaps in the lineup of a new government. When the first brother, or rather President Kennedy died, then it was known that this present situation would occur, and Bob Kennedy knew this very nearly at a conscious level.

He courted or adopted his dead brother's characteristics and gestures not because, as it was thought, he wanted to bank upon his prestige, but because he had an inner compulsion to do so, knowing the events that would occur.

On the other hand, he fought against this tendency. With this incident one full cycle has come to an end, beginning with the former president's death and ending with the present incident.

("Do you think Senator Kennedy will live?")

I asked for no direct questions.

I understand your concern, but obviously had a reason for my request. I am trying to give you what information I think you want, in the least distorted manner. Ruburt is doing much better in this respect, but not so well yet that a voice with a question is enough to change the level of the trance when the question is a highly significant one. So give us another moment.

(Pause, eyes closed. There followed a three-minute pause as Jane sat quietly in

the rocker with one hand raised to her eyes.)

The eldest brother in the Kennedy family initially intended to take President Kennedy's role. The two were closely bound, but the elder refused the role.

He himself changed the probabilities purposely, and his father realized this. But the probabilities thus changed, the two other brothers of which we have spoken this evening came into different positions of action.

The third is frightened. He will remain in a passive capacity relatively. *(Note: Summer 1975. Kennedy [Ted] said he wouldn't run for presidency. JRB.)* Take your break, and take care of your beloved monster.

(10:34. Our cat had become caught behind a venetian blind, and was making a racket trying to get free. I freed him then deposited him behind a closed door while Jane sat waiting, eyes closed .)

Now. I believe Garrison will come into the news again shortly... As a cousin of the Kennedys... *(Long pause.)* I do not myself know medical terms clearly enough to transmit them so that Ruburt can translate them.

Occlusion *(Jane looked at me questioningly concerning this word and I nodded)* for Kennedy. Pressure on a frontal lobe. Perhaps a hole, or another hole drilled to relieve pressure. With all of this and his knowledge and acceptance of his role, and his <u>choice</u> of the role, there is still a tremendous <u>will</u> on other levels to survive within your system. And a chance for rally.

His effectiveness and his role are completed, however. I believe he will succumb. This is his moment however, and his inner choice. The next moment is never predetermined. Never, regardless of what you may hear. The individual can change the probabilities. They point now to his death. *(Pause.*

(This session was held on June 5, the evening of the same day that Senator Kennedy was shot. Damage to the rear portion of the brain, the cerebellum, had been announced after the operation attempting to save Senator Kennedy's life.

(By June 7th, articles were carried in the newspapers explaining how there had been damage to the cerebrum also—the forebrain which is the seat of thought processes. Jane did not know this at the time of this session, for it had not been publicized.)

If he can adapt in this life to another vital but different role, then he could live; but to some extent, basically, with a different alignment, in <u>your</u> terms only, taking on the problems of the next reincarnation without changing physical forms. Now this is often done. I do not believe he has the strength for it. *(Long pause.)*

Tuesday. And separately, the 15th. Just include these.

He is discussing affairs with his brother now. In the background of this incident, and connected with the slayer, a woman, a sister or like a sister to him.

A small grocery store.

(At this writing, much of this material has not been checked by events. Some has, however. Immediately after this session, upon turning on TV, we tuned into an interview with the proprietor and wife of a small grocery or food store where the Kennedy assassin, Sirhan Sirhan, had been employed.)

A meeting either in a bar or in a place that somehow has to do with flowers. For the connection here is the word dahlia.

(There is a bar in Elmira, The Dahlia. Jane wondered after the session if this was used as an associative link.)

You had better write this, though it is not clear: a <u>mine establishment</u>, which may be something underground, you see.

(Again, learned via TV after the session: The assassin evidently belonged to a pro-Arab, anti-Israel organization of an inflammatory nature. Jane knew of his Arab identity before the session.)

George—this may be separate, or connected with the Garrison data. *(Long pause.)*

Indeed, the Arab connection and foreign language and a meeting of three joined first in a conspiracy, not definite. Then made definite after the debate. Two other men in particular. One whose name has strong A sounds. And a money connection with him.

(Again, seen on TV after the session—the two brothers of Sirhan, in Pasadena, CA. One is named Adele. Jane did not know this before.)

The other with a name that comes through to Ruburt like Farouk, though this is not at all precise. Now, either there is a connection with a boy of 17, or the meeting took place on a 17th street or with 17 in the address.

C A C H E *(spelled out)* and more money to come; but it was known in advance it would not be delivered. N I. *(Spelled.)* The woman in the background mentioned earlier. The three at the meeting strongly connected with another group of seven men. *(Pause.)* An inner portion of an organization. And unclear here: the organization is not a front organization, yet it is not what it seems to be either.

The Arab-Jew conflict <u>more</u> involved than it appears. Possibly some knowledge on the part of the Jews, not specific maybe, but suspected, that this would happen, and a political realization of its consequences—beneficial to the Jews, that prevented warnings. Is that clear?

("Yes."

(During subsequent days there was some talk about this sort of possibility; especially was the Arab-Jewish conflict brought into the picture, at least by implication. Time will reveal whether there is more specific application of this data,, and that

immediately following.)

I do not know whether the <u>specific</u> instance was known, but its likelihood is suspected *(pause),* and in some way some Jewish money may have been involved though not necessarily the money paid to the prisoner.

Another arrest or arraignment. Perhaps of a man 36 or thereabouts.

(After this session we learned that the suspect's brother, Adele, was questioned by police. Adele is 35 and was arrested a few months ago. A connection?)

Now, we will end the session, and you may turn on your monster screen, and watch for developments. There were several other issues I would have touched upon, and there is information concerning the entire family that you would find interesting.

(As noted, we turned on TV immediately after the session, and saw some of Seth's data seemingly begin to bear itself out. Probably many weeks. however, will have to pass before we learn the full story behind the Kennedy assassination; then this data can be more accurately evaluated.)

As Ruburt suspected, there is also a connection with his own emotional cycle and the two events. He knows what I mean.

(Here Seth refers to several clairvoyant dreams Jane had, referring to two recent deaths in our circle of acquaintances.)

You may, actually, take a break and continue if you choose, or end if you prefer.

("I guess we'd better end it.")

(Humorously:) Big brother and I say good evening to you then.

("Nice to hear from you, Seth.")

I thought I would brighten up your living room, even though the evening's occasion was not pleasant.

(Seth paused, rather than withdrawing, so I asked a question.

("Have you got anything to say about the faces I've been painting lately?")

(Seth paused, smiling faintly, eyes closed.)

All right. A postscript then, to the session. *(Pause, at 11:08.)*

A strong coming-into or focusing of inner reality into the objective form of the painting. You are allowing now the inner form to come out fully, and, to bring its own reality and environment with it. *(Pause.)*

The man Ruburt thinks of with the funny eyes is a fairly good portrait of the artist I told you of. He always wore a cap, however. *(Long pause; slower pace, eyes closed.)* It is as he was in a Belgium life.

(Here Seth refers to a portrait I am working on without a model, of a bald man with rather young features. He is fully bald, and as I painted it I wondered why he was bald. See the 401st and 402nd sessions. Seth then gave the artist's name as

Van Elver, saying he was from Norway or Denmark and that he was giving Seth painting data to be passed along to me.)

This time, 1317-1351. *(Long pause.)* Beside him a table and a golden goblet. A red velvetlike chair, with ornate wood. *(Eyes closed, Jane made gestures.)* Draperies behind a self-portrait he did of himself. *(Pause; pace slow.)*

Your technique vastly improving, flowing out from your intuitive understanding. *(Long pause.)*

You had better end, and speak... to Ruburt ...

(11:20. Jane appeared to be on the verge of falling asleep.

("Okay. Good night Seth, and thank you."

(I called Jane's name three times. She acknowledged faintly, without moving, but in five minutes her eyes were open. I had not touched her while calling her name, forgetting that this was the full procedure suggested by Seth in such instances. Jane wanted me to touch her, she now said, but was unable to tell me to.

(After Seth withdrew, she said, the energy was still around her and she didn't know how to get out of it. She needed the touch for physical reassurance. The state, she said, was like being lost in work, but much deeper than this.

(Jane said that she saw the scene with Van Elver, as she described it to me; including his self-portrait. Very colorful and strong.)

SESSION 415
JUNE 10, 1968 9:05 PM MONDAY

(On June 5, 1968 John Pitre telephoned Jane from Franklin, LA, seeking answers to three questions: the reasons for John's uneasiness concerning his wife Peg last week; the reasons for the loss of leg feeling John experiences in hot weather; and data on a pilot, Albert Blevins, who vanished on a flight in a small plane near the Gulf Coast about four years ago, presumably near Franklin.

(It was perhaps our hottest and muggiest night to date here this summer, and Jane was not at her best. A short session did develop however, after we sat for one at the usual 9 PM time. Seth gave data on Albert Blevins; perhaps John can check some of it. Seth promised the rest of the data John requested in the next session.

(Jane began speaking in trance in a somewhat subdued voice. We had to have windows open, and traffic was a problem, as is usual here in the summer. I had no trouble hearing her, however. She used many pauses, some of them quite long, in delivering this material.)

Good evening.

("Good evening, Seth.")

I can drown out any noise, if necessary. Now give us a moment. *(Pause.)*

These are impressions. *(Long pause, eyes closed, then open.)* A death by drowning, rather than fire. A number, one three. Something seen but not reported, by a man owning or working in a small store that sells tackle; and either rents out boats, or did. *(Pause.)* He did not realize the implications, the immediacy, of an object pulled up as he pushed. This was in the gulf. The 13 mentioned earlier may possibly refer to highway numbers *(pause)* of a road running past the tackle shop.

(Slower pace.) Fuel difficulties; not a lack of fuel, but the fuel was not getting where it should get. A stalling *(long pause)*, in the air. *(Long pause.)* The pilot bailed out. *(Long pause.)* The chute landed on top of him, never fully opened. *(Pause.)* A connection with an April day. Night was when the accident occurred.

He decided to head in another direction from the one first planned, to visit a friend. A male. All I have here are the letters *(spelled out)* D E L. Someone connected with him has a sister in Spokane. *(Pause.)* There was no explosion. *(Long pause.)* Where the plane fell was not as far out from land as it would seem.

There is a current underground, underwater, that captured the wreckage. *(Long pause.)* The body of the pilot was not so captured however. The gulf here is more narrow, or there is an island here. The plane did not fall in the middle of a huge expanse—perhaps between the mainland and another shore. Is that clear?

("Yes.")

(Pause.) The pilot intended to try and bail out over the land. Very shortly here the gulf is wide again. A town perhaps beginning with a B or P, that sound. Take your break.

(9:30 to 9:42.)

Letters Q U A still a connection here. A town of approximately 2,000 people nearby. *(Long pause.)* Now give us a moment.

In our next session I will give some material pertaining to the woman. Conditions are not of the best this evening. This having to do with Ruburt's characteristic chemical patterns in the first warm weather. His system makes overall adjustments, having to do with utilization of his own energy, and the way he individually utilizes it. We will end the session unless you have questions, Joseph.

("No, I guess not.")

My heartiest wishes to you both.

("Good night, Seth." 10:45.)

SESSION 416
JUNE 12, 1968 9:15 PM WEDNESDAY

Good evening.

("Good evening, Seth.")

I did indeed, only now, tell Ruburt that if your Roosevelt held his fireside chats, I could hold mine, even without the benefit of a fireside.

("Yes."

(Seth's humorous comment above refers to an insight Jane received from him just before the session began.)

In some respects this is meant to be a cozy, confidential session. Now. At long last our friend has really embarked upon our book. Now beside everything else, Joseph, there were stresses and strains put upon Ruburt's personality. They were not caused by me, and yet the experience itself, as any new experience, any worthwhile endeavor, any breakthrough, was bound to challenge the abilities of the personality.

My personality itself has been a stabilizing influence, and I have given Ruburt counsel even when he was not aware of my doing so. His personality, like your own, has benefited in ways you cannot measure. As you have always known, his attitude toward our book represented, of course, his attitude toward our sessions. Intuitive freedoms should now be realized on his part. He had been blocking many of these. I will say little of the symptoms. They will vanish as he continues to come to terms with himself.

Do you have any questions for me?

("No. Why don't you just continue as usual?")

I will indeed. There is some material I have to give for your correspondent, and for this give us a moment, please. *(Pause.)*

The situation with the woman is as I have given it.

Now as you know, I am a teacher, and interested in instruction. I am not a doctor. This means that my approach to a given problem will be vastly different than the approach of another personality, even on my plane, who has different interests. Therefore I am concerned with, and I emphasize, the importance of inner knowledge, and see physical symptoms for what they are—a reflection of an inner reality.

The reality may be a problem. A doctor will try to the best of his ability to relieve the symptoms, and most of them, regardless of their plane of endeavor, are content with this. To heal a disease by any method is not to remove the inner cause, unless other precise steps are taken.

These steps, ultimately, can only be taken by the personality involved. If all illness has been adopted by a personality for a particular reason in this life, then it has been adopted so that the personality involved will understand the illness as a materialized symbol for a challenge or problem that the personality has set. The personality therefore, if he or she solves the problem, will conquer the illness.

In some cases the personality deliberately places himself in such a position that the illness itself, the bearing of it, brings about certain needed spiritual characteristics. In such cases the illness serves a purpose. Illness is not thrust upon anyone however. We have given information concerning the woman's past lives, that have led to the adoption of this illness.

Now I understand that to one closely and daily involved with the woman, it is difficult to see purpose or reason in the condition. Since the egotistical knowledge of the woman does not include this data, there are of course difficulties here also. But the inner self of the woman knows that in facing such a condition and finding nevertheless some moments of joy, even some compassion for others, that the personality has satisfied many of those feelings of inadequacy from the past existence. *(One minute pause, eyes closed.)*

Now. No (underlined) physical condition is irreversible, with the exception of loss of limbs and definite organs. The personality is always free to choose, in your terms, its future. But the choice is with the inner self, which is the real identity. There are of course other elements entering into any such situation. Telepathically received suggestions from others, and so forth. *(Pause.)*

The man's deep concern in itself has done much to enlarge his own psychic and spiritual understanding. A physical doctor would be of no help. The source is not in the body.

You may take your break and we shall continue.

(9:47 to 10:00.)

Obviously the cause behind illness is not always the same. In a reincarnational sense, the personality for a while takes the role of a sick person, as an actor would, and is completely immersed in it. Obviously again, more dimensions are involved here than in an actor's role. The actor would merely try to imagine how it would be like to be in such a position. The person in the reincarnational role is as immersed in it as possible. He decides to take the role for various reasons of his own, and the inner self knows that the role was chosen.

The inner self does not feel threatened, therefore, only the part of the personality that is momentarily unaware of the true situation. Others also respond, and are in this drama for their own reasons. *(Long pause.)* The drama has a theme, and through working out the problems therein presented the theme becomes clear. In some psychological circles there are therapeutic groups that operate by setting up such dramas. Remember, the purpose is therapeutic, though it may not appear so. And none of this should be taken to mean that the sufferings are not quite real to those involved.

Now give us a moment. *(Pause at 10:10.)*

Knowing all this, it is still necessary for the husband to continue his efforts, for his own benefit.

Earlier I recommended a good hypnotist, hoping that the woman might find her way if positive suggestions were given; for even if the inner self had solved its problems, it would need help, psychological help, in reversing the physical trend. I hoped such a hypnotist could act therefore as a guide, if the personality was ready to begin a journey to health. The inner personality was not ready.

Give us further time with this.

(Jane's pace was now rather slow, and was to get much slower, with many long pauses. Most of these will not be indicated here.)

I understand the husband's deep concern. The doctor and the medium mentioned by Ruburt are quite legitimate. I am aware of his work. No doctor in your plane or mine, can relieve an individual of symptoms if the symptoms are serving a valid purpose to the inner self; or, in relieving particular symptoms, others will arise.

However, the doctor of whom I am speaking also has an excellent bedside manner, so to speak *(humorous and slow)* and he usually communicates with other levels of the personality that are unknown to the ego. *(Long pause.)* There would be no harm then, and perhaps some good done, by making such a contact.

I have given you my own views as closely as I can. I have looked in on the situation several times. *(Long pause.)* I have made contact with the woman on one occasion. *(Long pause.)*

My ideas are so different from those with which she has been accustomed that it was difficult for us to communicate. I am trying to put this in simple terms. *(Pause.)* We are all individuals regardless of our plane of existence. The woman could not relate to me well. The doctor of whom I have spoken has a more fundamental approach, you see. Do you follow me here?

("Yes.")

I am used to lecturing. He is used to speaking quietly with patients at their level of understanding.

Now you may end the session or take a break as you prefer.

("We'll take the break, I guess."

(10:30. Jane smiled and came out of trance easily. She was quite surprised

when I told her that it had been a slow one, indeed with quite a few long pauses interspersed. She had not been aware of any such delays while in trance.

(She said she knew from Seth that Seth had frightened Peg somewhat; that is, his approach had been one she was unaccustomed to, and it would have been better had he talked with Peg about Jesus, His love and healing power, etc.

(The doctor referred to by Seth is George Chapman, an Englishman. His abilities are detailed in the book, Healing Hands, *by J. Bernard Hutton, published 1966 by David McKay Co., Inc., New York, NY, at $3.95.*

(Resume at 10:40.)

Now. You had better end the session. I will however give you a few notes. First of all, within your system, relatively speaking, there can be and usually is, some lapse between my own thought and Ruburt's verbalization. The control over the physical system is not as complete as when Ruburt is in control of it. When I am deeply considering a matter therefore, there is a pause on my part added to the natural lapse mentioned earlier. We will discuss this more fully for it will lead us into some other matters in which you will be interested. I do not operate Ruburt's controls as automatically as he does, you see.

Other elements at times will also cause pauses. Various adjustments also enter into this.

My heartiest wishes to you both, and to your correspondent and to the woman involved.

Now, I am in fine form, but I understand the circumstances under which you operate. Therefore I will not keep you. I have such tender regard for the state of your fingers.

("They're okay." Pause. "Good night, Seth."

(10:47. The session ended on a humorous note.)

SESSION 417
JUNE 17, 1968 9:10 PM MONDAY

(Earlier today Jane and I had been discussing how best to go about writing her projected book on the Seth material. At the moment Prentice-Hall is considering a prospectus for this book. We decided we would like Seth's help with this problem, and so expected to hear him speak this evening.

(We sat for the session as usual at 9 PM.)

Now, good evening.

("Good evening, Seth."

(Long pause, eyes closed.) Within certain obvious limits, you will receive the

same basic material whether or not you attempt to limit or specify the subject matter of sessions or not.

The personal matters, questions, affairs of daily concern, that may be mentioned because Ruburt's emotional image triggers their inclusion—these will always be used as examples to give you material that you would receive in any case.

With this method, the examples come from your own life. There will be an inner unity here, though you may not always perceive it. It makes no difference then which course you follow in that regard. Oftentimes however you do receive information that you may not have received ordinarily until a later date, simply because Ruburt's emotional interest acts as a trigger.

You do direct the focus of the material in that, again, your emotional interests are important. They automatically reach out in certain directions. I respond to you as any personality responds and do not consider you simply as scribes, ready to write down my words of wisdom, regardless of your own interest.

The emotional basis does not limit the quality or extent of the. material, but adds to it. The information is carried along in the emotional stream. If there are small side-streams now and then, they always return to the larger one. If a few bits of debris go sailing merrily down the stream *(humorously)*, the answer is not to cut off the stream but to recognize the difference between what the stream carries.

The debris, in any case, is only such by comparison. Small bits perhaps disconnected from larger patterns. They will fall into place—a bend in the stream *(smile)* and disconnected patterns will meet again. The stream has its own reality then, and the ego sees only the surface.

Your personalities, in a symbol now, form the two sides, the two banks, of the stream through which the material flows. The bottom represents the underground connections of your own past lives. The interworkings of your personalities form the various currents within the stream. The material is that which flows through the stream. I am the source of it, for your practical purposes. *(Smile.)* I am the land from which the two banks are formed.

(Humorous.) The stream flows down from high inaccessible mountains, but it will all pass by if you are patient.

Now it makes no difference, basically, how you present the material, as long as it is presented; whether you let the stream flow on consecutively, one wave at a time, or whether you present it a bucket at a time, scooped up from various places. Pure, sparkling *(smile)* water is pure sparkling water, and a taste will lead to more when the populace is in a period of drought.

Some must be carried in buckets to irrigate inner lands. The material is a source. It will be given to various people in various ways. It is not up to you to decide which way is best, nor even to me. It will be presented therefore in many ways through the years. The consecutive method, from the early sessions through, will appeal to those who have little knowledge of such affairs, and will serve to let them *(smile)* get their feet wet, bringing them this time into the stream little by little.

To some extent this should be done for those people. This does not mean, necessarily, a consecutive presentation that includes each session. There are those however who are ready for headier stuff. For these the above approach is not necessary. One approach at one time does not negate the use of another approach at another time.

To think in such a way could be to limit the good the material can do, and the numbers and kinds of people it can reach. Like action, the material moves out in all directions. It can be presented at various times in various ways, each complementary. There <u>will</u> be, at some time, those interested in a study in depth of the material; and as Ruburt's students have seen to it that their need is satisfied, so will these people see to it. This will involve a session by session study.

Ruburt can do the book he now has in mind, of the outline given. It will serve as an introduction, and from it various complimentary books will flow.

This allows you to take full advantage of knowledge you did not have when the sessions began. Let him, whenever possible, include along with the material on any given topic, my personal comments. It should be obvious in the book that the material is not disembodied but sifted through the personality that is mine. <u>For this is part of the message</u>.

It is not to be simply the presentation of ideas, though these are, of course, a main part of the whole. It is also to be the fact that a highly alive individual, such as myself, gives the material. For if you will forgive me, the material is much more significant because it is backed up *(deeper voice)* by someone who is no longer within your system.

The personality characteristics therefore will in themselves be adequate proof to all but nincompoops, that a fully independent and highly articulate personality is behind it. If I may say so myself my personality does much *(amused)* to lift any pseudospiritualistic elements from this affair.

In other words, the inclusion of my personality characteristics with the material will take away any long-white-gowned spiritualistic connotations, and put the survival personality thesis in a more proper light. As any good writer should know, tell Ruburt he need not explain my characteristics; simply include excerpts that show them.

If he does this to the best of his ability, he will consider his excerpts from two standpoints—what to say, and how I say it, so that the personality and the material are clearly shown together. It will make it lively. *(Long pause.)* The personality is action, and as I have shown myself to you in sessions, this has added to the action of the sessions.

It does not matter that I am a part of more. What I am as you have known me is legitimate. I go beyond the apparent boundaries of that self by which you have known me, but it is that self that could communicate with you before you could know anymore about my reality or understand that I might be more. *(Pause.)*

My personality is what makes the material unique, for it is information sifted through an individual that is unique from all others. Ruburt therefore should not attempt to disentangle the material from my personal characteristics. It is perfectly proper, beneficial and legitimate for him to make any intellectual investigations he chooses, concerning differences in perception in our sessions, and when he is psychically involved on his own, and all other, intuitive or intellectual studies of this sort he has in mind. But he should not present my ideas as if they come from thin air, for this is to rob the material.

I say this out of no misguided egotism, but because the essence of personality is the only meaningful basis behind idea. Any other approach would rob the material of rich dimensions, for I am the proof in my own pudding, you see. This is not the Cayce material, with information seemingly coming from some vast storehouse of knowledge. In those terms no such storehouse exists.

Knowledge does not exist independently of the one who knows. Someone gave Cayce the material. It did not come out of thin air. It came from an excellent source, a pyramid gestalt personality, with definite characteristics, but the alien nature of the personality was too startling to Cayce, and he could not perceive it. *(Pause.)* I am giving you the material through a personality that you can understand; one that is mine, one of my favorite selves. *(Smile.)* In this way the point is made so that it is clear.

Now you may take your break or end the session as you prefer.

("We'll take the break."

(10:10. Jane snapped out of trance easily. Certainly this had been one of her longer deliveries during the sessions' four years. She resumed in the usual Seth manner at 10:30.)

Now. There are creative strains in your own personalities that show themselves in all your endeavors. You do not always see these in perspective.

(To me:) Because you are so drawn to Ruburt, there is the struggle to actualize your emotions toward him in daily life. This of course superimposed on

your early fear of emotionalism in this life. Part of your artistic impetus does come from this inhibited emotion, but fresh impetus is received when the emotion is allowed to go outward toward Ruburt; and through Ruburt, acting as a symbol to you, to the world at large.

In other words the repressed emotionalism will only carry you so far before you need to be refreshed in Ruburt's reality; and through approaching his reality you also gain, in a different manner than you usually know it, refreshment from the natural world.

Now in many ways this applies to Ruburt also. The two of you seek refreshment together, then plunge into your inner realities. He is more emotionally attuned than you, in that it is easier for him, when coming out of his private world, to rush toward you with spontaneity. You are both equally dependent however, basically, on this necessary emotional refreshment. You both drink it in, and it sustains you for some period. It is used in your work, and in your joint work. It forms an inner framework of which you are sometimes aware. *(Smile.)* Without your feeling toward Ruburt and the resulting urge to emotionally actualize yourself to another personality, your background could have prevented even artistic development. *(Pause.)* Rather than serve as a springboard for creativity.

On the other hand your relationship teaches Ruburt to direct and mold his strong emotional feelings into meaningful, productive work. The creative strain therefore benefits you both. You should be alert however to the fact that emotional actualization in daily life is necessary, even though at times it will be much stronger than others, for the reasons given.

Because of your natures you will seek this, be refreshed, plunge into your work, and again seek refreshment. While this pattern shows rather contrasting elements you will find a natural pattern; and some emotional actualization must also be evident in daily life.

Ruburt's emotional demands are a spur to your own development. Your resistance is a spur to his development. His need of you on the other hand also keeps him from plunging, as he did in his past life, too deeply and emotionally into other realities without the brakes that the intellect usually applies. *(Amused.)*

If the emotional actualization and refreshment is withdrawn for too long, he obviously will show the first signs of difficulty. You will also feel them, but he will be instantly aware of them, and show them.

He will feel rejected, as you know *(pause),* and this can lead to resentment. If your periods are not synchronized, these periods of which I have spoken, and you are not ready for this emotional actualization, and he is, then there can be also resentment of your part. *(Pause.)* The periods eventually synchronize and you should both attempt to realize the feelings of the other at such times.

Your individual work, and our work, are involved here also.

Now, I have given you what you wanted, and some information that I thought you needed, and I will end the session: like Old King Cole, a merry old soul was he. *(Smile, emphatic.)*

My heartiest wishes to you both.

("It's been very helpful.")

I always try to be helpful. *(Amused.*

("And usually succeed."

(Smile. One minute pause, eyes closed.)

One other point. *(To me:)* Now, you sought solitude. You wanted to be alone, amid your family. *(Still in trance, Jane got up and walked into the kitchen, looking for a cigarette. Long pause.)* The family had its severe disadvantages, but you were certain of its framework, which was to some extent at least, supportive.

Ruburt in this life also was alone, without that supportive framework. *(Pause.)* The framework about him as a child was not supportive, but threatening. Therefore he is very aware of your partnership with him.

In the beginning he was terrified lest it be taken away.

In times of stress he looks to it for support. *(One minute pause.)*

We have covered now what I had in mind, and I will leave you. *(Pause.*

("Good night, Seth, and thank you."

(11:02. Again Jane came out of trance easily. She said that at the end of the session, just before she left trance, she got a message that she would hear from the publisher Prentice-Hall, within three days concerning the prospectus they have for the book on the Seth material.

(But Jane did not receive, or did not retain, any data about the content of any message from Prentice-Hall.)

SESSION 418
JUNE 24, 1968 9 PM MONDAY

(We expected Seth to speak tonight, and to deal with material Jane and I had been discussing just before session time. This was the case. Seth plunged in, in a most animated way, without preliminary greeting. Voice loud, eyes wide open, very active and intimate, pace fast and very humorous.)

I am the one who should do the psychological study from inside—

("*Yes, Seth.*")

—what it is like to speak through Ruburt. Now, <u>that</u> has never been done.

("*Okay, why don't you do it?*")

There are psychological adventures in my system also.

("*It would make a great chapter.*")

(*Aggrieved but smiling:*) I had much more than a mere chapter in mind. I had a <u>complete book</u> in mind, though not of <u>great</u> length. It would involve the various mechanics necessary for such communications on my part; the necessary preliminaries in order to make Ruburt aware of my presence initially—

("*Sounds great.*")

—the problems involved in educating what your friends refer to as the Buttses, and the various interchanges between you, Ruburt and myself. It would include the ways in which perceptive mechanisms operate, the manners by which I must activate Ruburt's associative patterns in the case of clairvoyant information, and what your life looks like to me who observes it from such a unique perspective.

Such a book would be written during our sessions however, dictated by me, for our friend Ruburt would not let me inside his own writing hours.

("*That sounds like a fine idea.*")

I thought you would be interested. (*Dryly.*)

("*So would Ruburt.*")

There would be unity, of course, and this would take care of the organization of our material. Do you see?

("*Yes.*")

It would all be done however from my viewpoint.

("*Fascinating.*")

I thought I would come to your assistance, for such a book would solve many problems. It would take care of the sessions' organization, for one thing.

("*Yes. It would also be unique.*")

(*And as we said at break, one of those ideas that seems so simple, once heard; so obvious that we wondered why we hadn't thought of it long ago ourselves.*)

It would indeed. It has not been done before, in such a way, to my knowledge.

("*I don't believe so.*")

We would enjoy such an inside-out arrangement. (*Pause.*) Give us a moment.

It is obvious that such an arrangement could not have been made before, since Ruburt would not have been ready—nor, I believe, even agreeable. There is no reason why other such books could not follow. (*Humorously:*) I have the time.

("With this book: you would see to it that you introduced yourself to the unini-tiated reader, giving the necessary background and introductory material from the very start.")

The first book would of course introduce me, and it would involve a study of mediumship; not from the viewpoint of the medium, but from the viewpoint of the personality for which she speaks.

It would involve a look and an examination of your system of reality as it appears to me. It would include my statements as to how these communications take place, and what manipulations are necessary from my side.

Such a book would do much to explain how the medium is led, wherever possible, to make those correct statements that add up to almost what your parapsychologists like to call a hit—for she is almost literally hit with them.

(Smile.) I would of course provide the reader with a statement of my own background, and to some extent compare my attitudes toward your system of reality, for when I lived within it my opinions were far different than they are now.

I would make clear the nature and conditions in which I now have my existence, and explain some of the reasons for the various, often contradictory, statements made concerning life after death. Statements received by various mediums, in which quite different pictures of afterlife reality are received.

Such a book would also include, of course, my methods of entry into your system, and the sort of psychological bridge personality that results. For what you have during sessions is not really my complete identity. *(Pause.)* Your reality cannot include all that I am. There must be some sort of psychological structure present for me to use during my communications, generally speaking.

At times however my identity comes through, and my reality, so clearly, that <u>comparatively speaking</u> (underlined), I can exist independently as myself without Ruburt's usual assistance.

All of this of course would be explained in detail. *(Pause. Jane's pace had slowed considerably by now.)* Ruburt could if he chose, add his own notes and comments, for his experience in our sessions is vastly different from mine. *(Pause.)* Such a book would have nothing whatsoever to do with Ruburt's writing, which should progress at its own rate.

(Pause at 9:30. Jane, as Seth, leaned forward, intent and amused.)

This book would bear my name. But I would dedicate it—

("That's nice.")

—to the both of you. And any profits would be yours. I have little need of them.

("Well, I'm sure Jane would like to know what she would be writing while you're giving us this book.")

Give us a moment here. *(Pause.)*

The man at Prentice-Hall *(Tam Mossman, an assistant editor)*, simply over-stepped, as you both suspect. There seems to be another man involved also, who is cautious. Beside the woman referred to in the phone call. *(Long pause.)*

J A B. These letters simply come to me. I do not know if they refer to the man.

I believe there is an Alice connected with your Mr. Mossman.

("Alice?" I didn't quite catch Seth's pronunciation.)

Alice. *(Pause.)* The name Grossman also comes to mind, but I do not know the connection. *(Cecile Grossman was an editor at Prentice-Hall then.)* Mossman has an uncle, I believe, of whom he is fond, or was fond. The name Albert comes to mind. A 1962 engagement or marriage.

A fragment from the past, pertaining to a child. An initial encounter with the business world that was unpleasant. *(Pause; one of many in here.)* Mr. Mossman has a tendency to go overboard. A grandmother and a connection with a star. I do not know the connection—perhaps her name was Bright.

Two brothers and something wrong with one leg. *(Long pause.)* A dis-agreeable, I believe, family situation in 1953 for him. *(Long pause.)* A mild astonishment or surprise for him, having to do with something French or for-eign. *(Long pause.)*

Miss Carr, *(referring to Tam's immediate boss)* a spectacular enough achieve-ment early in life, I believe. Two daughters or two women close to her. The name Fred. *(Pause.)* 34. A telling advancement. An unknown quantity three years ago. Connection with a W. *(Long pause.)*

Brown chair and orchids. Something about the lower right-hand desk drawer; we do not have clearly. Someone who visits her office seems to smoke cigars, and place them in an ashtray on her desk.

Connection with racing cars. You had better take your break. The battle of the bulge. She must worry about weight.

(9:49—Jane came out of trance easily, although it had been a deep one. Her pace had been slow toward the end of the delivery. [Note: On a 12/7/68 visit, Tam verified 8 of the above impressions.] Resume at 10:11.)

The introductory book is still an excellent idea, and a challenge to Ruburt's own ability.

(This refers to the book on the Seth material that Jane has now begun.)

He needs the challenge, and I am sure that he will meet it. It is far stranger than fiction, and if he will but see, such a book carries its own built-in suspense.

Now my book will necessarily have some things in it that will not be new to you, but it will have much information of which you have little or no knowledge now. It will be quite an original document.

It may have the air of a series of lectures, but I shall see to it that they are interesting ones. I will add whatever is needed in the nature of demonstrations as we go. *(Long pause.)*

There is no reason why Ruburt cannot work on his own book simultaneously, and from his viewpoint. He should return to his poetry however, and his painting as a hobby. These are his strong points, and the painting represents more than he realizes, for he has a talent for it from previous experience.

(To me, with a smile and earnest manner.)

Now I have an experiment for you. You may not think much of it. *(Pause.)* But try it.

When you are bothered by noise and tumult, by traffic and the sound of neighbors' voices, by lawn mowers and other irritating sounds, try this: do not fight them. Purposely plunge into them; go along with them as action, and they can refresh you.

("I was thinking about that today." After doing a lot of griping last night.)

Do it as an act of will, and your intuitions, oddly enough, will be refreshed. They need not serve automatically as inhibiting factors unless you allow them to. But it is not enough in your case to ignore them and despise them. Let them work for you.

If done in the correct spirit, this will help free your intuitive nature, and to a large extent help wash away automatic blocks that have been inhibiting.

("Okay.")

You do not have to be afraid of going along with what these sounds represent. You will not lose your sense of isolation nor your individuality. This is basically behind your reaction, having to do with your early life. You felt your mother's liveliness and vitality threatening, for it was not disciplined in any manner, but erratic.

This was added to by the sensed power of your father's inhibited vitality. You felt the combination could sweep you aside, and literally destroy you. Undirected vitality and undisciplined vitality has frightened you, and noise to you represents the tumultuous undisciplined emotions that you feared.

The exercise will do much to override this, for you are strong enough and you need inner freedom. There is behind such seemingly undirected, abstract tumult and energy, direction that cannot be intellectually perceived, but can be intuitively sensed. And this is the force that is behind your own art and all creativity. *(Pause.)*

It can even serve as a framework for creativity, for from these raw materials you can forge and direct energy for your own purposes. You can take that tumult and use it, but not if you set yourself up against it. Then, it is threatening to you.

Various sounds rush at you. From one inharmonious high-pitched yell for example, if you listen, you as an artist can sense the self that was forced to make that sound, perhaps emerge with a prize, an excellent portrait, or simply an unique and individual mouth. Or a landscape that screams out as the voice did.

From the sound, the assaulting onrushing sound of traffic, if you listen you can emerge with the prize—perhaps an abstract, with the pulsating sounds transferred to rhythm and color; or perhaps again a portrait, here, of a compulsive personality, driven, and yet behind it all the purpose which is not easily seen, and the reason.

I have given you a few examples simply to clarify my remarks. But these evidences of action, apparently chaotic and undisciplined, are parts of inner frameworks that do have both purpose and reason.

As you know, even your physical system reacts when you brace yourself against these things as irritations. But properly used they can lead you to exaltations, and you would use such exaltations then in a disciplined, directed manner.

("Is that why my left ear bothers me?")

The struggle; now you must not struggle, Joseph, to close out those stimuli that annoy you. Your mother has done this. Use them for your benefit. Those things that annoy you precisely represent the greatest challenges to your personality and abilities.

Used, they can help you fulfill yourself to the utmost. There is no coincidence that it is the left ear involved. You have used the symbolism of right and wrong. The right ear, the wrong ear, bothers you for you do not want to hear what you consider the bad sounds. The left ear and the left portion of the body generally also are connected with the unconscious. And the sounds are somewhat connected with your feeling toward oil paints. Do you see the connection?

("Yes. I've been doing a lot better with oils.")

You have indeed, for you see now how they can be used, and you will see how the sounds can be used. The sounds can be used in your paintings like colors. A freedom will result from this exercise, though you may be uneasy at trying it.

("I'll try it.")

Crystallization follows crystallized experience. Art comes from raw emotion, within your system at least, that is then crystallized and disciplined. The seemingly chaotic is recognized, felt, and then put into patterns. What is not generally understood however, is that the seemingly chaotic experiences <u>do</u> have purpose. The state of your inner physical organism, viewed from another perspective, is a chaotic one, but it works to find purpose.

Do you have any questions?

("I think it's been extremely interesting and helpful. I'll try these things and we'll soon know.")

Very good. It will help also at times if, when hearing various voices that have annoyed you in the past, you try to think of them in terms of images and colors. At other times simply go along with them, without such ideas, and your intuitions will deliver their own product.

("Yes.")

Now voice, by its definition, is aggressive, and it presupposes barriers, for you hear only within certain ranges. Now imagine what these sounds would sound like from the other end. There you cannot hear them. And imagine the impact made within space, and the infinite dance of atoms that result.

Realize also, and I am sure that you do *(smile),* that the sounds penetrate the matter of your body. Imagine their realities in other than auditory ways.

You may take your break or end the session as you prefer.

("Well, I guess we'll have to end it, though I hate to. It's been very good."

(10:52. Jane did not respond, sitting quietly, so after a short pause I said good night to Seth on the assumption that the session was over. But she then resumed as Seth.)

One note: Within your system sounds do form structures, that your eyes do not perceive. It would help you to think of painting these structures, for in some other systems voice is perceived in this manner.

(Pause.) Now a musician translates visual data as though it was an auditory pattern; recreating say, and interpreting a bowl of grapes as a particular medley of musical notes.

(A bowl of grapes sat on the coffee table before Jane; she held up a bunch as she made the analogy.)

You can do this in the opposite manner, building up from sounds visual frameworks that are completely original portraits, created from the sound of voices. Even landscapes, elemental but fragile, built up from the ebb and flowing voice of traffic as it passes by your door. As an artist use everything.

Now I will say good evening, and give you both my best wishes. You can consider this session as your birthday present.

(This session was held on June 24. My birthday is June 20.

("Do you have birthdays?")

Very many. I could hardly keep track of them all. *(Smile.)* I do not have birthdays now, but I have had many. I had many death days, but I do not have those now either.

("Good night, Seth.

(11 PM. Jane took a bit to come out of trance. It had been a deep and effective one.)

SESSION 419
JUNE 26, 1968 9:15 PM WEDNESDAY

(Pat Norelli of Boston witnessed the session. She recorded the last half of it.

(The three of us sat for the session as usual at 9 PM. Jane didn't know whether Seth, or his entity, would speak. Shortly before she went into trance at 9:15, she whispered to me "The other one," meaning that Seth's entity would speak. She also experienced the pyramid effect at this time but didn't tell us until break.

(See the 407th to 413th sessions for many notes concerning the new personality, the pyramid effect, etc. Jane began speaking now while leaning back in her rocker, eyes closed, her voice again high, very clear but distant, very distinct but rather emotionless, ending sentences often again on the upbeat. Pauses occasionally, but pace varied considerably, from quite fast to very slow. Eyes open at times after session underway.

(No greeting.)

I have told you who we are.

Do not be concerned over the contents of the letter.

(A few days ago Jane received a long letter from a Boston reader of her ESP book.)

We are Seth, and whenever we have spoken we have been known as Seth. The entity had its beginning before the emergence of your time.

It was instrumental, with many other entities, in the early formation of energy into physical form. We are not alone in this endeavor, for through your centuries other entities like us have also appeared and spoken.

Our entity is composed of multitudinous selves with their own identities, many of whom have worked in this behalf. Their material and messages will always be basically the same, though the circumstances and times and places of their communications may be colored accordingly.

You need not be concerned. *(Eyes open, slitted.)* You have your own situation and your own conditions to deal with. We taught man to speak before the tongue knew syllables. We adopt whatever personality characteristics seem pertinent, for in our own reality we have a bank of complete inner selves, and we are all Seth.

Again, there are many others like us. We attempt to translate realities into terms that you can comprehend. We change our face and form but we are always the one. We are therefore always a part of the one entity which is the Seth entity. *(Long pause at 9:30.)*

Many of us have not been born in flesh, as I have not been, but other portions of the personality have appeared in flesh; and some portion of us will always be born in flesh, because what one portion of us knows the other portions of us realize to some extent.

Seth as you know him will not be reincarnated, but other portions of our entity will be born in flesh, for we have a part in all worlds and all realities. We are among the most ancient of entities in your terms.

In one way we have seeded ourselves through endless universes. Physically you would find me a mass smaller than a brown nut, for my energy is so highly concentrated. It exists in intensified mass entangled and intertwined with moment points, perhaps like one infinite cell, existing however in endless dimensions at once *(pause)*, and reaching out through interconnections even from my own reality through others to your room.

Yet in such a small mass these intensities contain memories and experiences, electromagnetically coiled one within the other, through which I can travel, even as I can travel through other selves which I have known and which are a portion of my identity—and even as you, so large and bulky in your size, are still a portion of those memories that exist within my identity, and yet so beautifully unpredetermined. For you do not exist as finished or completed personalities within my memory, but you grow within my memory.

(These last few remarkable paragraphs were delivered at so rapid a pace that my shorthand method barely kept pace.)

You grow through my memory as a tree grows up through space, and my memory changes as you change. My memory of you includes your probable selves, and all these coordinates exist simultaneously in a point that takes up no space.

My reality includes all of this, and yet that reality which is my self constantly changes as the coordinates themselves fulfill their values. I speak to you through multitudinous prisms, and these prisms themselves are coordinates which change even as I speak.

(9:40. Jane sat for a long time motionless in her rocker, eyes closed, as I waited to see whether she was taking a pause or a break. Finally she whispered my name. I then called her name and touched her, and she finally began to come out of trance.

(It took a while. After fifteen minutes I had to get her a cigarette, talk to her to keep her awake, etc. However, she said she was not and hadn't been, sleepy. Instead she had been "lost" again; she had a feeling of suspension among Seth, his entity, and herself, her own voice. She was not frightened, and knew I would help her.

(Jane was fairly well out of it by 10 PM, although she still felt some effects. I suggested that the session be considered ended, but she demurred. She resumed short-ly. Once again the voice was high and formal, but I thought not so distinct, not so distant. There was more of Jane's regular voice in it, a touch of sleepiness.)

I told you that in many ways Ruburt's personality acts like a warp. In certain coordinates it exists at certain points that are entry points, and certain coordinates here merge informational channels that are opened.

Personality is itself an energy source. Now this is rather important. The personality operates and has always operated in this manner. Of itself it is like a peephole or a transparent area through which other areas can be glimpsed, and through which information from other dimensions can flow.

Now, the strong ego structure has been adopted as a necessary guard and protection to hold the abilities in check until the present personality learned to develop its abilities to a sufficient level. For the energy behind the personality could have swept the temporary psychological *(word missed here)* ... apart until sufficient preparation had been carried on. So do not berate that ego.

The personality ego structure had to be strong, for the whole personality is in many respects a transparent one through which we can speak and through which other realities can be seen. In most basic respects this statement is meant literally and not symbolically. The personality in itself is formed from components existing in many realities...

(Here Jane was sitting very relaxed in her rocker, leaning back with eyes closed, quite limp, voice slowing after a very fast delivery, above. I thought she might go to sleep, or so it appeared.)

...and is an apex point. The personality without realizing it also operates as a transmitter, sending messages to other portions of reality. The abilities must be used, the creative urges therefore fully utilized in all areas—the psychic, the spiritual *(pause)*, the more earthy writing and painting, for this energy sweeps through the personality and cannot be dammed up. *(Pause.)*

The window cannot see through itself, but you can see through the window. So this personality does not always know what it is about, and yet the results can be seen. The personality is transparent also with your nature, and learning to use those abilities which are natural to it, can indeed then rather easily learn to merge consciousness with natural phenomena.

(Jane sat still limp, eyes closed. Her voice had dropped somewhat in key and

sounded oddly muffled. I almost ended the session here.)

These Seths, this entity, was once a part of old earth gods, as Ruburt wrote about them years ago.

(10:12. I called Jane's name several times as soon as she paused. My concern must have been obvious.)

...There is no severe difficulty. We will sever...

(Jane's voice trailed off. I called her again. She moved several times, coughed, started as though making a quick return from trance. I touched her foot. Her eyes opened and she came out of it more rapidly than she did at break. Once again she had the pyramid effect, she later told us, as she did so.)

AN EXPERIMENT
JUNE 29, 1968

(On Friday, June 21, 1968, Jane sent the manuscript of her dream book to Parker Publishing Company Inc., Village Square Building, West Nyack, N.Y. On Saturday, June 28, a card arrived from Parker with this message:

June 27, 1968
Dear Miss Roberts:
This will acknowledge receipt of your manuscript for Dreams, Astral Projection and ESP. *Our Associate Editor, Mr. Charles Chintala, will be in touch with you soon regarding this material.*
Sincerely,
(Signed) (Miss) Helen Gorman
Secretary to Mr. Chintala

(Jane was sunning herself in the backyard when the mail arrived at about 2:40 PM, and from her position could not see the mailman come or go. She of course knows that our mail usually arrives around 3 PM. She was in the company of two young women, one of whom lives in the apartment beneath us.

(I was painting in my studio, took a break, and went down to our front mailbox and picked up the mail. Upon reading the card I felt it out of the ordinary, more than a mere acknowledgment. I went back to work. From my studio I could look down at Jane and the others, but I did not tell her the mail had arrived. I did not do so because I remembered a dream Jane had had recently, in which I had picked up the mail, then teased her about an optimistic letter from a publisher, concerning the dream book. The thought had crossed my mind that by deliberately waving the card at her from my second-floor studio window, I could almost make that part of

that dream come true.

(Within a couple of minutes however Jane came upstairs; the two others had gone inside. Jane walked into our living room and picked up the card from Parker, after I asked her if she had seen the mail yet. A moment after reading the card she smiled and said, "There's something different about this, isn't there?"

(I agreed. On the spur of the moment I suggested Jane put a finger on the card and see what impressions she could get.

(At once Jane sat at our living room table, which is her work table, and put her right hand on the message side of the card. It was 2:50 PM. I got pen and paper. Jane closed her eyes, concentrated, and gave the following material which is very nearly verbatim:

(They're interested. They're also interested in the Seth material. They might very well take the book. There are three people involved. They are very definitely interested in the book, and they think it's a potential for other books, too. They might want me to cut the first three chapters—not cut them out, but condense them.

(Her pace was normal. Jane said that when she had to stop to wonder, aloud, how far to carry the experiment, she halted it.

(It wasn't until I was typing up these notes at 9 PM on the same day, that Jane realized she could have been in at least a light trance while giving the material; at first she thought she had not been, but then realized she retained only a hazy idea of the material's content—just that it was optimistic. But she did not remember specifics: that the first three chapters might be cut, etc.

(We estimate Parker had the book script in hand on Monday, June 23. Their card was written and mailed on June 27, Thursday, giving someone there three days to read the script, perhaps make some sort of evaluation, etc. Note that their response gave both of us the feeling that something unusual was involved. A little later, handling the card perhaps half an hour after giving the impressions, Jane said she got nothing unusual from it; it seemed like ordinary mail, that is.

(We think such psychometrizing of emotionally-charged mail a good idea, and Jane has decided to keep experimenting in this fashion. We would like to ask Seth to comment on this experiment at the next session at which he speaks.)

SESSION 420
JULY 1, 1968 9:09 PM MONDAY

(The evening was very hot and humid; it was quite uncomfortable even through it had just rained, and Jane wasn't sure we would have a session. She didn't feel that conditions were very good.

(On June 27 Jane had received a letter from Tam Mossman at Prentice-Hall, requesting information on Dr. Instream, Dr. Bernard, both psychologists; and on Ray Van Over. We had talked over the best way to answer the letter, and had made some notes to that end today. But these were unsatisfactory; so much could be said that, once again, answers to what seemed like simple questions could expand with a life of their own.

(Before the session tonight Jane and I discovered during our conversation that each of us had toyed with the idea of asking Seth to answer the letter. This has never been done before by us. Still, we didn't make any formal request that Seth write such a letter. We sat for the session as usual at 9 PM, waiting to see what developed.

(Jane began speaking in trance for Seth in a rather quiet voice; eyes open often, average pauses, etc.)

Good evening.

("Good evening, Seth.")

Now give us a moment. *(Pause.)*

I do not mean to demean you. However I would appreciate it if you would this evening act as a stenographer on my behalf, in a business matter.

("I'll be glad to.")

Would you then take the following letter addressed to Mr. Mossman and Miss Carr, jointly? I will leave it to you to provide the business address.

Now, the letter:

May this letter serve to introduce us. I am Seth. Since matters pertaining to me are at issue here, then I feel I would like to make a few comments of my own, and take it upon myself to answer your last letter, sent to Jane Roberts.

Now. Dr. George Instream is an upstanding and upright man, and a very cautious one. He is so cautious that he allowed Dr. J.B. Rhine to make advances in the field of parapsychology that he could have produced himself, had he been more daring. He holds this against Rhine to this day.

Our results with him were good as far as the tests were concerned, though there was considerable distortion simply because Ruburt's *(Jane's)* abilities had not been sufficiently developed. There were direct hits, in other words, but these results could not be mathematically appraised in terms of the odds against them; and this is was what Dr. Instream was looking for.

(This is the first time Seth has mentioned Dr. Instream to us, since we halted the tests with Dr. Instream. The series of tests, held twice weekly, ran for one year.)

Robert and Jane operated in a vacuum, since he did not tell them anything regarding the tests, negative or favorable. No academic psychologist, including Dr. Instream, will give you a statement to the effect that I am a survival personality. Dr. Instream will give a statement I believe, as to Robert and

Jane's character, the quality of the Seth material itself, and the fact that no fraud of any kind is involved.

Ray Van Over has scarcely met me. I did not speak to him directly. The impressions which were given by me through Ruburt, in Ruburt's *(Jane's)* own voice, were correct, however, and I believe he will attest to this.

We were all complete strangers at the time.

Dr. Gene Bernard has received some excellent material from me, both in the realm of psychological interpretation, and clairvoyant impressions. I had a session for him at his wife's request when he was ill, and in Ruburt's files his answering letter attests to the correctness of my interpretations and impressions.

A few of the early factual statements made were unknown, I believe, even to his wife. However, while you may see these files, I will not have any part of showing my own legitimacy by pointing up the weaknesses of a man's condition. It was not generally known that he was ill, or the circumstances of his illness.

He did not know his wife requested the session, and I do not want it known. He will give you a statement to my benefit, but not the kind of a statement you may want to use. He did attend a session here himself, and you may request a statement on that session.

(Pause.) Ruburt can give you whatever business statements you require concerning the sale of his books. *(Long pause, eyes closed.)*

I have been a teacher primarily. Business letters are not my line. *(Amused.* *("You're doing all right")*

However, I did want to contact you myself on my friend's behalf. *(Meaning Jane.)* I do suggest, now, a meeting in Elmira, at which time any questions you have can be answered without the necessity for long and complicated letters.

Give us a moment. You may delete that phrase from the letter. *(Leaning forward; confidential and amused, eyes open.)*

My material will be published. *(Pause.)* Probabilities always operate, and free will is always involved. However, I believe that you will be my publishers. I send you my best wishes *(long pause)*, and invite either or both of you here.

You may sign the letter Seth, and initial it yourself. *(Humorously.* *("Okay.")*

Now you may take your break.

(9:40. Jane retained slight memory of what she had delivered as Seth. Resume at 9:50.)

Now. The book on the Seth material is not yet an actuality, but the Seth material is, and it is upon the Seth material that the book will be based. Such a visit therefore will allow an examination of the material, if a brief one. This is all that is needed.

You may or may not append that to the letter, as you prefer. *(To me:)* This will be an exceedingly brief session. Do you have any questions, Joseph?

(For reasons that he has explained to some extent, Seth calls Jane as Ruburt, and me, Joseph.

("No, I guess not." I had some, but thought Jane would want to keep the session short.)

I do not intend to take up our sessions with such material, however. I will then end the session. My heartiest wishes to you both.

("Can I ask a question?")

You may.

("How does our weather today bear upon communicating with you?"

(Pause; smile, eyes closed.) The unstable elements are not helpful. The electromagnetic components of the atmosphere and of the personality both are in a state of unbalance, that changes very rapidly. On some such occasions these circumstances can work toward excellent communication. As a rule however the conditions are poor.

(Pace speeding up.) Certain chemical and electromagnetic changes occur within Ruburt's physical system during sessions, and the manipulations are more difficult when there is much instability of environmental elements and physical components.

As a rule body temperature, after certain <u>preliminary</u> stages, is lowered during Ruburt's trance state. The heat therefore can mitigate against us at times. All communications depend upon inner electromagnetic manipulations in any case, even for example mental images, and body temperature is also related here.

(For the benefit of T. Mossman and Miss Carr: Had I interrupted this data to ask questions, Seth could have explained in detail any of the above general statements. Material of this nature is often gone into deeply in succeeding sessions.)

There is a heat conversion. If the physical temperature is too high however, then there are breaks that occur, particularly in the case of ordinary mental images, and in for example reception of clairvoyant impressions.

The relative stability of the physical system in sleep is one of the reasons why extrasensory perceptions so often make themselves known then. Dreams themselves activate physical temperature however, and all bodily processes. Except in periods of extreme physical heat however, the temperature changes and the resulting electromagnetic alterations, are easily converted into legitimate impressions of a clairvoyant nature, precognitive information, and so forth.

In out-of-body experiences from the dream state however, there is a lowering rather than a heightening of body temperature, even though dream elements are involved.

Have I answered your question?

("Yes, and very interestingly, too.")

Little scientific investigative work has been done in these areas. The recent dream experiments are highly superficial in this regard. Until the legitimacy of out-of-body experiences is recognized, no investigative experiments will be carried on, of course.

You may end the session.

("Okay. Good night, Seth."

(End at 10:05. Jane retained a little memory, as before, of the material's content. Sessions usually run until 10:30 to 11 PM these days, so the early end this evening shows that conditions were not of the best. Jane is personally quite sensitive to heat.

(Seth's last words, above, really mean that in his opinion Jane had been in trance long enough at this time. He would have continued answering questions had I asked them, but Jane would have found it tiring. As often as not, Seth will suggest we continue with a session when conditions for communication are excellent.

(It is July 2 as I type this. Today Jane wrote to Gene Bernard and to Ray Van Over re statements. Today also she received a card from Gene Bernard's wife Sarah, who is visiting her brother in Ecuador, South America, for several weeks.)

SESSION 421
JULY 8,1968 9:50 PM MONDAY

(Jane had been having trouble writing her book on the Seth material with her old spontaneity, and both of us were concerned. This evening we worked with the pendulum and began to appreciate the reasons involved.

(It was late by the time we sat for the session. Jane began speaking for Seth in an average voice, with pauses, eyes open often, etc. At times here pace was quite slow.)

Good evening.

("Good evening, Seth.")

Now. Ruburt must indeed prime the pump, as they say.

He should begin to write. He should not read and reread endlessly notes that he has made, for as he begins to work he will find himself writing.

He works out many problems through his work. This is natural for the personality. If he insists upon four to five hours a day of definite work, many of his problems will be solved at an intuitive level by him. The determination and energy necessary to do this will be an indication of improvement. It automatically provides the inner focus and concentration necessary. As you know, his presence in this chair *(eyes open, Jane pointed to the Kennedy rocker in which she sat)* at regular session time provides the same sort of concentration and focus in another direction.

Now, he is not afraid of me. He is afraid of the unknown. He is afraid of giving fully his abilities and commitment to what he does not thoroughly comprehend. There is an old religious hangover here from the Catholic background. Give us a moment.

(A one minute pause.) We have mentioned this earlier. In his mind religion was connected with self-mortification. On the one hand it set itself against spontaneity. The organized church feared it. On the other hand Ruburt was spontaneously religious.

Even the nuns to whom he read poetry distrusted his fervency, and took him to task. They distrusted the dramatic quality. The spontaneous elements of his nature, as you know, frightened him, since others gave him dire warnings as to possible consequences.

He tried to slow down. The pent-up spontaneity helped make our sessions possible, and in one way or another will always erupt. Then, as you know, the opposite tendency began to show.

The daily working methods allow for the natural and periodic use and release of both aspects of the personality. The overcensuring, when it appears, shows itself, of course, in all spontaneous areas of his life—physical, psychic, creative and spiritual.

(Pause. Slow delivery here.) If he will maintain a daily work schedule—his need not be rigorous, but habitual—and if you will try to provide a warmly supportive role, as you have, then the situation can be largely remedied.

He looks to you to look out for him in psychic matters. He allows his spontaneity freedom in sessions because he knows that you will carry on for him those usual sensory characteristics that he temporarily dispenses with.

This is hardly unusual in such situations. Give us a moment. *(Pause.)* He distrusts the spontaneous which is so a part of his nature. As he worries occasionally about going too far when he is dancing, so he worries the same about the sessions—how far is spontaneity to be trusted, you see. Yet he must trust it, and when he does not do so the difficulties build.

Now in the past he felt that you also did not trust his spontaneity. The spontaneity has its own strength that will sustain him if he lets it. Your early (underlined) concern over spontaneous sessions frightened him.

He tried to be spontaneous and not spontaneous at the same time. Spontaneity itself has its own rhythm, with needed periods of rest that follow naturally. These natural rhythms are disrupted when such tampering occurs.

The Prentice letter caused him to react with a burst of spontaneous pleasure. It was highly therapeutic in that regard, and swept before the spontaneity were symptoms and problems. The system cleansed itself. The personality appeared briefly as it should be. A day or so following, the clamps were again applied however, and the old situation returned.

It was, then, the burst of spontaneity caused by the letter that also freed him for the next natural development in our sessions. You can do much by using very simple words to reassure him. The words are these: "You are safe, and I am here. I am looking out for you." It is the fear for safety behind this. (Pause.)

The pent-up spontaneity, too long restrained, then latches upon normal low periods when the personality is tired, and comes out as strong discouragement, feelings of desolation, aggravating normal low periods. It can turn a minor annoyance into anger for example; a rainy day into a creative disaster.

(Pause.) Now, the fear is for safety. The assurances, the words that I have given you, will help here. The fear is exaggerated and needless. It is partially the result of experiences in this life, and of experiences in the last life. (Long pause.)

It was to some extent aggravated by books telling of the experience of various mediums, and by what he has read concerning the attitude of parapsychologists toward them. He projected these feelings then. They were adopted, for no one has treated him in that fashion.

Unfortunately the situation also involved your intimate lives. The intimate relationship added to Ruburt's sense of safety. The regular writing recommendations given here will help also in that connection.

This is not the evening to begin my book. (Humorously.)

Give us a moment. (Pause.) The shortage of sessions is a symptom of the fear of spontaneity. The fear of the unknown, mentioned earlier, is not a fear of psychic phenomena, nor of psychic endeavor. It is a mask, for a fear of his own spontaneity.

Now he was told under emotionally charged conditions, as you know, by his mother, that he could or would lose his mind. He tied this in with any strong spontaneous actions on his part, regardless of their nature. An example: once he found it thrilling to ride in an automobile at fast speeds. Now they frighten him. But to him any spontaneity carried the same danger that, say, speeding definitely does.

When he found himself so spontaneously involved he slowed down, literally. He is solving these problems at his own rate. That is the only way they will be solved.

Earlier the symptoms themselves masked the lack of spontaneity in writing. Now the symptoms are not so pronounced and the other problem, which was there, shows. His mother, for all her emotionalism, stressed intellectual control, contrasting it with the father's lack of control. Ruburt is at the tail end of these inner problems that have been there in this life since childhood.

This session should throw considerable light upon them. I would never suggest continuing with the sessions at the expense of Ruburt's mental or physical health.

Are your hands tired?

("No." It was 10:45.)

His problem is precisely this: the need and ability to throw himself whole-heartedly and spontaneously into a creative endeavor, and the fear of doing so.

You may take a break or end the session as you prefer. You may also ask me any questions.

("We'll take the break."

(10:45. Jane came out of trance easily, though it had been a fairly good one, she said. Break time found me very discouraged. I was angry and disappointed; I was fearful that Jane and I would never be able to rise above our problems and fulfill our potentialities, which I knew to be excellent. I was especially concerned that Jane wouldn't be able to surmount the problems, so explicitly delineated by Seth, above, and so eliminate the symptoms. I couldn't see how she would be able to really give her great creative spontaneity full reign, to accomplish the things I felt she had in her.

(I spoke my piece, filling Jane in to some extent on what Seth had said. My poor attitude alarmed her. Resume at 10:55.)

Now. My dear Joseph and Ruburt...

The stresses and strains also create the unbalances that initiate creative endeavor. On Ruburt's part the early religious experiences also initiated the deep quest for inner knowledge that is behind all creative endeavor, and that served as an impetus.

The particular problems were set by the inner self as challenges and learning guides. The personality solves the problems, not necessarily in the simplest way, objectively speaking, but in the way that will best benefit the personality as a whole.

The quality of the challenges is often an indication of the heights that are possible. In the early background of each individual, in each life, you will find the material for development. The development to be based upon problems overcome and challenges accepted and conquered.

You do not give complicated problems to an idiot to solve. You give him simple ones.

Personalities bent upon great endeavors often set themselves great problems. The problems are not meaningless. They are like examinations. *(Long pause.)* In Ruburt's situation in the present, he is in your terms, freeing himself. He has just been through one of the most difficult problems that he set for himself.

The next one will be to use the abilities that he will then be free to use, correctly. Without the past challenge, or one like it, the various elements of the personality would not be sufficiently united, strong enough, to <u>carry</u> the abilities that have been latent within it.

This also applies to yourself. It often applies to those whose abilities, in your terms, come to fruition later rather than earlier in life. *(Pause.)* It is not a point of how much better it would be had the abilities matured earlier. The abilities, of whatever power or strength, are a part of you; they are not something objective that you possess. Nor can you compare them to the abilities of others.

A young man can misuse and misunderstand his own abilities if they are stronger than the other personality frameworks that compose his identity. Many of your own experiences have strengthened your abilities. Your experiences did not prevent you from using them—the abilities—any more than they helped you form them.

You could have chosen not to develop these latent abilities at all. You could have developed other latent abilities in their stead. You settled upon your particular life situation with certain problems and challenges in mind. In helping Ruburt free and use his own strong spontaneous nature, you also free your own spontaneous self. That particular problem then is also a challenge and a way of development for you both.

The situation when it is settled will result in perhaps the best possible one for both of you, from all standpoints, and such would not be possible had you taken a simpler way. The opportunity to use your abilities therefore is greater. The problems that you have encountered lead to inner recognition and understandings that add to the quality of your work, and actually improve the nature of the abilities themselves.

Now, you may take your break or end the session, or ask questions if you prefer.

("What do you think of Jane's series of dreams, involving her dream book?"

(Since February Jane has had a series of dreams and psy-time experiences involving her dream book, which is now at Parker. All of the experiences have been correct to date. She showed me a three-page typewritten account of them today. The latest, on July 5, revealed the dream book as published.

(Jane, as Seth, smiled, eyes closed.) Now. The personality stresses and strains. The personal problems here have led to an increase of spontaneity in the dream

state, and to added evidence of clairvoyance. The spontaneous portions of the self have come to the aid of other portions. The nervous reactions have actually resulted in more specific and detailed use of clairvoyance.

A need was met. In the past Ruburt would not have permitted this. My answer tells you of course that the last dream was also precognitive.

I had one note: his jumpy-roping is good for him, and he should continue. He should seek motion. Do you have further questions?

("No, it's getting late, I guess.")

I believe I have cleared up several points this evening, and I have given you specific advice, both of you. I should be followed.

My heartiest wishes to you both, and good evening. <u>My book will come</u>. *(Emphatic and humorous, slapping the chair arm.*

("Good. I'm glad to hear it. Good night, Seth.")

(11:26. Jane again left trance easily. This time, she said, the trance had been even deeper.)

THE SETH AUDIO COLLECTION

RARE RECORDINGS OF SETH SPEAKING through Jane Roberts are now available on audiocassette and CD. These Seth sessions were recorded by Jane's student, Rick Stack, during Jane's classes in Elmira, New York, in the 1970's. The majority of these selections have never been published in any form. Volume I, described below, is a collection of some of the best of Seth's comments gleaned from over 120 Seth Sessions. Additional selections from The Seth Audio Collection are also available. For information ask for our free catalogue.

Volume I of The Seth Audio Collection consists of six (1-hour) cassettes plus a 34- page booklet of Seth transcripts. Topics covered in Volume I include:

- Creating your own reality – How to free yourself from limiting beliefs and create the life you want.
- Dreams and out-of-body experiences.
- Reincarnation and Simultaneous Time.
- Connecting with your inner self.
- Spontaneity–Letting yourself go with the flow of your being.
- Creating abundance in every area of your life.
- Parallel (probable) universes and exploring other dimensions of reality.
- Spiritual healing, how to handle emotions, overcoming depression and much more.

FOR A FREE CATALOGUE of Seth related products including a detailed description of The Seth Audio Collection, please send your request to the address below.

ORDER INFORMATION:
If you would like to order a copy of The Seth Audio Collection Volume I, please send your name and address, with a check or money order payable to New Awareness Network, Inc. for $60 (Tapes), or $70 (CD's) plus shipping charges. United States residents in NY, NJ, PA & CT must add sales tax.

Shipping charges: U.S. - $6.00, Canada - $7, Europe - $17, Australia & Asia - $19 Rates are UPS for U.S. & Airmail for International - Allow 2 weeks for delivery Alternate Shipping - Surface - $9.00 to anywhere in the world - Allow 5-8 weeks

Mail to: **NEW AWARENESS NETWORK INC.**
P.O. BOX 192,
Manhasset, New York 11030
(516) 869-9108 between 9:00-5:00 p.m. Monday-Saturday EST

Visit us on the Internet - http://www.sethcenter.com
Books by Jane Roberts from Amber-Allen

Books by Jane Roberts from Amber-Allen Publishing

Seth Speaks: The Eternal Validity of the Soul. This essential guide to conscious living clearly and powerfully articulates the furthest reaches of human potential, and the concept that each of us creates our own reality.

The Nature of Personal Reality: Specific, Practical Techniques for Solving Everyday Problems and Enriching the Life You Know.. In this perennial bestseller, Seth challenges our assumptions about the nature of reality and stresses the individual's capacity for conscious action.

The Individual and the Nature of Mass Events. Seth explores the connection between personal beliefs and world events, how our realities merge and combine "to form mass reactions such as the overthrow of governments, the birth of a new religion, wars, epidemics, earthquakes, and new periods of art, architecture, and technology."

The Magical Approach: Seth Speaks About the Art of Creative Living. Seth reveals the true, magical nature of our deepest levels of being, and explains how to live our lives spontaneously, creatively, and according to our own natural rhythms.

The Oversoul Seven Trilogy (The Education of Oversoul Seven, The Further Education of Oversoul Seven, Oversoul Seven and the Museum of Time). Inspired by Jane's own experiences with the Seth Material, the adventures of Oversoul Seven are an intriguing fantasy, a mind-altering exploration of our inner being, and a vibrant celebration of life.

The Nature of the Psyche. Seth reveals a startling new concept of self, answering questions about the inner reality that exists apart from time, the origins and powers of dreams, human sexuality, and how we choose our physical death.

The "Unknown" Reality, Volumes One and Two. Seth reveals the multidimensional nature of the human soul, the dazzling labyrinths of unseen probabilities involved in any decision, and how probable realities combine to create the waking life we know.

Dreams, "Evolution," and Value Fulfillment, Volumes One and Two. Seth discusses the material world as an ongoing self-creation—the product of a conscious, self-aware and thoroughly animate universe, where virtually every possibility not only exists, but is constantly encouraged to achieve its highest potential.

The Way Toward Health. Woven through the poignant story of Jane Roberts' final days are Seth's teachings about self-healing and the mind's effect upon physical health.

Available in bookstores everywhere.

Printed in the United States
65781LVS00003B/79-120

9 780965 285582